COMPARATIVE METHODS IN PSYCHOLOGY

COMPARATIVE METHODS IN PSYCHOLOGY

Edited by
MARC H. BORNSTEIN
PRINCETON UNIVERSITY

LEA LAWRENCE ERLBAUM ASSOCIATES, PUBLISHERS
1980   Hillsdale, New Jersey

Lawrence Erlbaum Associates, Inc., Publishers
365 Broadway Suite 112
Hillsdale, New Jersey 07642

Library of Congress Cataloging in Publication Data

Main entry under title:

Comparative methods in psychology.

  (Crosscurrents in contemporary psychology)
  Includes bibliographical references and indexes.
  1. Psychology, Comparative. 2. Ethnopsychology.
3. Psychology—Methodology. I. Bornstein, Marc H.
II. Series. [DNLM: 1. Psychology, Comparative—
Methods. BF671 C737]
BF671.C58   155   79-27558
ISBN 0-89859-037-X

Printed in the United States of America

For Helen,
nonpareille

Series Prologue

CROSSCURRENTS IN CONTEMPORARY PSYCHOLOGY

Psychology is today increasingly diversified, sophisticated, pluralistic, and specialized, and psychologists venture beyond the confines of their narrow subdiscipline only rarely. Yet psychologists with different specialties encounter similar problems, ask similar questions, and share similar concerns. Unfortunately, there are far too few forums for the expression or exploration of what is common in psychology. The series, *Crosscurrents in Contemporary Psychology,* is intended to serve as such a forum.

The principal aim of this series is to provide integrated perspectives on supradisciplinary themes in psychology. The first volume in the series was devoted to a study of *Psychological Development from Infancy;* the second volume explores *Comparative Methods in Psychology;* volumes three and four, in preparation, will examine relations between psychology and allied disciplines and issues in the segmentation of behavior. Each volume in the series thus treats a different issue and is self-contained, yet the series as a whole endeavors to interrelate psychological subdisciplines bringing new or shared perspectives to bear on a wide variety of issues in psychological thought and research. As a consequence of this structure and the flexibility and scope it affords, volumes in the *Crosscurrents in Contemporary Psychology* series will appeal, individually or as a group, to psychologists with diverse interests. Reflecting the nature and intent of this series, contributing authors are drawn from the broad spectrum of the social sciences—anthropology to zoology—but representational emphasis is placed on active contributing authorities to the contemporary psychological literature.

Crosscurrents in Contemporary Psychology is a series whose stated intent is to explore a broad range of supradisciplinary issues in psychology. In its concern with larger problems, the series is devoted to a growth of interest in the interconnectedness of research, method, and theory in psychological study.

MARC. H. BORNSTEIN
Editor

Contributors to This Volume

Thomas M. Achenbach, *Laboratory of Developmental Psychology, National Institute of Mental Health, Bethesda, Maryland 20205*

Alfred L. Baldwin, *Department of Psychology, College of Arts and Sciences, University of Rochester, Rochester, New York 14627*

Colin G. Beer, *Institute of Animal Behaior, Newark College of Arts and Sciences, Rutgers University, Newark, New Jersey 07102*

Marc H. Bornstein, *Department of Psychology, Princeton University, Princeton, New Jersey 08544*

Robert J. Dooling, *Field Research Center, Rockefeller University, Millbrook, New York 12545*

Gustav Jahoda, *Department of Psychology, University of Strathclyde, Glasgow G1 1RD, Scotland*

Peter R. Marler, *Field Research Center, Rockefeller University, Millbrook, New York 12545*

Victoria Seitz, *Department of Psychology, Yale University, New Haven, Connecticut 06520*

Steven Zoloth, *Department of Public Health, University of California, Berkeley, California 94720*

Contents

PART II: DERIVATIVE COMPARISONS

Preface

Psychological inquiry proceeds in large degree by comparison. Since the inception of psychology, several far-reaching types of comparison have accrued to the psychologist's basic experimental armamentarium. Principal among these are animal, developmental, cross-cultural, and statistical comparisons. Together they furnish data and theory describing and explaining behavior from points of view requisite to a comprehensive psychology. Historically, however, the value and critical relevance of comparisons like these to the conduct of psychological research and to the nature of psychological theory have been underemphasized.

The purpose of *Comparative Methods in Psychology* is to make available to the psychological community thoughtful essays that examine the history, philosophy, theory, methodology, and experimentation representative of major comparative methods. The chapters in this collection are intended to introduce students of psychology to specialized modes of comparison from the perspectives of prominent contributors and to promote mutual discussion among comparativists of issues and concerns common to all types of comparison. In this respect it is fortunate for this collection that a group of outstanding comparativists could be enlisted to summarize, examine, interpret, and evaluate these century-old comparative methods.

The chapters in *Comparative Methods in Psychology* are organized into two sections. Following brief introductory observations, *principal comparisons* are treated in Part I; included are perspectives from animal behavior, development, cross-cultural studies, and statistics. Part II, on *derivative comparisons,* captures the tendency among comparativists to invoke one or another's domain either formally or metaphorically; included are perspectives on animal behavior and development and cross-cultural developmental psychology. As a whole, this collection fits the theme of its parent series, *Crosscurrents in Contemporary Psychology,* in that it is devoted to examination of an issue that crosses traditionally separate psychological sub-disciplines.

Several individuals aided in the preparation of this volume. Among them, I would like especially to thank H. G. Bornstein, N. Brenna, K. Ferdinandsen, A. Kronewitter, A. Lizza, M. A. Opperman, and A. Rakower.

Marc H. Bornstein

COMPARATIVE METHODS
IN PSYCHOLOGY

1 On Comparison in Psychology

Marc H. Bornstein
Princeton University

INTRODUCTION

Charles Robert Darwin opened *The Origin of Species* (1859/1958, p. 1), "When we compare...." Comparison is at the heart of scientific inquiry, and it is central to psychology. The wide variety of methods and designs employed by experimental psychologists is intended to compare individuals and groups or treatments and conditions in order to describe behavior or test hypotheses. The minimum laboratory study in psychology assesses an experimental effect by comparing a condition where a treatment has been applied with one where it has not. Statistical analysis has developed to verify comparisons, hence the psychologist's umbilical connection to it. The overarching significance of comparison to psychology is second nature to investigator and theoretician alike.

During its first century, psychology's methods, strategies, and fields of inquiry have proliferated. Yet in this proliferation two clear, albeit diverging, directions of investigation have emerged. On the one hand, laboratory investigators seem evermore drawn to narrower and more limited questions and by experimental designs that more exactly satisfy the requirements of the psychological scientist's experimental conscience. Here, as with other sciences, psychology has typically advanced by attaining more definite answers to more circumscribed questions. On the other hand, psychologists are increasingly lured by meaningfulness, relevance, and the potential for a more general validity in their work. Insofar as sectors of the psychological community have wished to reconcile these otherwise conflicting tendencies— to address more general issues without sacrificing experimental rigor—they have found certain comparative methods increasingly attractive. Principal among these methods are phylogenetic, ontogenetic, and cross-cultural comparisons. Such comparisons allow more naturalistic perspectives on behavior and greater generality of empirical findings. They serve to augment the power and utility of psychological investigation as well as to enlarge the scope of the discipline. In fact, they may be deemed necessary to a full understanding of psychology.

PRINCIPAL AND DERIVATIVE COMPARISONS

Psychology is concerned, broadly, with describing, explaining, and predicting mental processes and behavior in humans and other animals in a wide variety of environmental contexts. Man is the reference point in this psychological nexus. Phylogenetic, ontogenetic, and cultural comparisons are principal in psychology because together they encompass the scope of substantive thinking and empirical study of man's mental processes and behavior in the widest variety of contexts. A phylogenetic perspective is necessary in psychology to assess species capabilities, to evaluate similarities and differences among species, and to ascertain the nature of psychological adaptations. An ontogenetic perspective is necessary to ascertain how man's psychology changes or maintains over the life cycle. A cultural perspective is necessary to ascertain how adaptable and plastic or inflexible and fixed human psychology is. (Additionally, experimental design and statistics underpin valid comparisons, allow for their verification, and circumscribe their interpretation.) Thus, each comparative perspective contributes invaluable description to the corpus of psychology, and each contributes uniquely to the overall analytical goals of psychology, viz. explanation and prediction.

These principal comparisons do not always stand alone. In practice, animal behavior and cross-cultural comparativists frequently invoke or employ a developmental perspective. Animal-behavior developmental and cross-cultural developmental perspectives derive from the principal comparative methods but are not secondary to them. Indeed, vis-à-vis the goals of psychology, these derivative comparisons may play a more significant role than do the principal comparisons; for in combining phylogenetic or cultural perspectives with developmental ones, the scope of these comparisons and their implications for psychology are inevitably enlarged and rendered more complete.

EMERGING PRINCIPLES OF COMPARISON
IN PSYCHOLOGY

Psychological comparisons among species, ages, or peoples, although different in substance and subject populations, nevertheless share certain assumptions, philosophies, methodological issues, and goals. As a consequence, insights may accrue to psychology from a joint consideration, first, of differences among them and, second, of their similarities.

Comparing comparisons reveals underlying tensions. Levels of analysis among them differ; so, too, do the units of study, the purposes behind specialized experimental designs, and the origins or antecedents of behavior each presumes. For example, in assessing what motivates behavior, cultural studies have focused on social aggregates (as exemplified in Durkheim, 1895/1938, 1897/1951), psychological studies have focused on individuals (as exemplified in Freud, 1900/1966, 1924/1952), and animal studies have focused on biological mechanisms (as exemplified in Darwin, 1859/1958, 1871/1913). Likewise cultural studies have traditionally been occupied with description and content, and psychological studies with process or hypothesis testing. (This is not to imply that these research traditions never cross; cultural studies have often historically invoked the individual "psyche" to explain cultural phenomena, whereas paradoxically psychological studies have frequently invoked "culture.") Explanations of psychological phenomena that have been traditionally proffered by different comparative approaches also differ. Many animal comparativists tend to see psychological explanation in reductionism or positivism; developmentalists tend toward interactionism; and cross-culturalists toward either universalism or relativism. The goal conceptions of comparativists are not necessarily at odds, only of different relative value or concern vis-à-vis method.

Notwithstanding these differences, the principal comparisons in psychology share a significant number of philosophical and theoretical assumptions, orient themselves similarly to empirical inquiry, confront similar methodological problems, and are invested in reaching parallel kinds of conclusions. The disciplines are therefore, in a host of metatheoretical ways, mutually relevant and interrelated, and it is rewarding to examine some formal similarities among them.

First, they share antecedent assumptions and philosophies. All comparisons in psychology are motivated by the common aims of description, explanation, and prediction of behavior. In this regard, decisions about the level of detail or analysis investigators ought to strike in examining behavior commonly cross comparisons. Further, comparative studies share the twin purposes of assessing the universality of behavioral phenomena or their variance (across species, ages, or cultures) and of discovering and defining new or idiosyncratic phenomena. Thus, nomothetic and idiographic concerns are chief among comparativists of all stripes. Concomitantly, issues of nature and nurture doubtless occupy the thoughts and influence the expectations of all comparativists.

Comparative practitioners share several other philosophies in approaching psychological phenomena. One: comparativists demonstrate that description per se occupies an especially valuable place in psychology. Two: comparativists typically perceive psychological phenomena as integrated into a larger setting, sometimes ecological, sometimes chronological, and sometimes social. (In several interesting ways, as we see later in this volume, the origins of each major mode of comparison are found in writings of the naturalist Darwin. Perhaps because of these common historical roots, animal, developmental, and cultural comparativists tend to view principles of adaptation and specialization as prominent in behavioral analysis.) Three: comparativists frequently converge on the same substantive or topical areas of psychology; language and communication, for example, is a prominent recurring theme in animal, developmental, and cultural research. Four: comparativists are known to seize on common, advantageous methodological tactics to advance unique experimental solutions. Sometimes they select particular "preparations" by species, age, or culture to study general problems. This has been a successful strategy across comparative methods. Hodgkin's (1964) and Huxley's (1964) selection of the squid (*Loligo*) giant axon to illustrate and study nerve conduction and Mead's (1935) selection of the Arapesh, Mundugumor, and Tchambuli of New Guinea to evidence the power of socialization processes more than adequately represent the spectrum of this common comparative strategy. Other times, an animal or culture is sought because a particular manipulation is not ethically or practically feasible otherwise. In short, in several ways, animal, developmental, and cross-cultural comparisons share assumptions and philosophies related to interest, intent, and action that forerun research.

Comparative methods hold additional methodological considerations in common. It ought not to be surprising that methods that attempt to compare behaviors across species or across ages or across cultures should confront similar problems and issues of praxis and consequently have arrived at similar experimental styles and solutions. All investigators who cross groupings must grapple with questions such as the following: Are stimuli, stimulus levels, and perceptions functionally similar for different subjects? Are the same responses or response styles similarly equivalent? Is subject motivation controlled? Is experimenter-subject communication adequate? Two simple illustrations will help to amplify this kind of methodological issue.

Comparative experiments of all types can show only what some being (of a given phylum or age or culture) can do; they can tell us little about what these beings cannot do. Thus, Lashley's (1949) caveat, viz. to adapt questions to optimal modes and levels of the organism's capacity in order to obtain comparable results in animal studies, can be heard echoed very frequently in the writings of cultural and developmental comparativists. Likewise, problems associated with response bias undercut comparative investigations of all kinds; the use of the signal-detection technique has successfully obviated this difficulty in psychological experiments that test different species of animals, individuals of different ages, and members of different cultures. Common problems frequently meet with common solutions.

All comparative investigators are faced with problems of delimiting subgroups by species, stage, or society, of selecting subjects for study among diverse animal phyla or developmental levels or human groups, and of deciding on the number and composition of subject samples appropriate for the comparison of interest. Sample selection in animal, developmental, and cross-cultural study is frequently arbitrary, though it is sometimes dictated by hypothesis. In either case, the representativeness of sampling is of common concern. Are the species, stages, or societies selected for study appropriate representatives for the study in question or of the animal kingdom, human ontogeny, or human culture generally? How is representativeness in the general or the particular case established? It is also necessary in comparison to ask whether the animals, ages, or societies under study are legitimately comparable. On how many different dimensions do they vary?

In critical comparisons, things other than the value or behavior of interest ought to be equal. The canons of formal experimentation commonly dictate the counterbalance, the control, or the measure and statistical account of extraneous variables; comparativists of all kinds frequently find these prerequisites impossible to meet in full. For example, subject populations in comparative studies are infrequently sampled randomly. As a consequence, comparative investigations are often not true experiments, but "natural" ones wherein experimental control over the independent variable is problematic and the assurance of initial equivalence among contrasting groups remains in doubt. Investigators in every line of comparison have, at one time or another, criticized pairwise contrasts, natural experiments, and simple ad hoc sampling that have pervaded past paradigms common in comparison (e.g., Campbell & Stanley, 1963). Solutions to these problems apparently arrived at independently by comparativists working in different areas have included, first, adopting multimethod strategies of research and multivariate procedures of analysis and, second, looking at patterns of relationships among measures rather than at degrees of equivalence among single measures.

Although the goals of everyday psychological research are clear, it is commonplace criticism that the degree of realism ("external validity") psychologists would like to attain is often, unfortunately, sacrificed or compromised in the laboratory. However, comparative investigators, by virtue of the settings, behaviors, and experimental conditions they select, often attain high degrees of naturalism in their work. In this connection, each of the three principal comparative methods has had coincidentally to face and to resolve issues and criticisms related to a distinction between laboratory and field; in the theoretical writings of many comparativists, the need is expressed for greater cross-communication and collaboration between research efforts in these two settings. Consensus suggests that parallel studies in and outside the laboratory will enhance methodological acumen as well as ecological validity.

Last, comparative methods share their impact, effects, and conclusions. Given increasingly sophisticated expectations and methods, contemporary practitioners have brought comparative methods in psychology a considerable distance from their heritage of informal reports and anecdotes circulated by hunters, parental biographers, and travellers and missionaries; they served as the wellsprings of animal, developmental, and cross-cultural perspectives and once fueled psychology's interest in comparison. Today, comparisons play a pervasive role in psychological research. They influence the selection of research problems, govern research investigators' expectations about outcomes, fix the organization and interpretation of results, define normative processes, and act heuristically, alerting investigators to further possibilities.

Most importantly, comparison continues to project toward both specificity and generality in psychology. Comparativists sometimes focus on idiographic, sometimes on nomothetic phenomena, questioning whether their findings are specific to individual organisms of a certain developmental status with particular social experience, or whether they are universal to some degree crossing species, ages, and cultures. The success of a comprehensive comparative psychology seems to reside in answering these questions. The purpose of science to those with nomothetic ideals is to tend toward evermore abstract and comprehensive levels of explanation. The route to such an end is through broad comparison and analysis at more global levels of behavior. In this connection interspecies, interage, or interculture comparisons have all from time to time engendered some philosophical indignation. In the context of animal research, Harlow articulated the critique this way, "Basically, the problems of generalization of behavioral data between species are simple—one cannot generalize but one must." In the same vein, it is not uncommon for investigators interested in universals (or in minimally generalizable results) to buttress their analyses, interpretations, and conclusions by referring to pertinent animal, developmental, and/or cross-cultural observations. The mutual relevance among different comparisons is further linked to progress in deriving broad principles of psychological functioning. Psychological laws, like generalization (Hull, 1950) and differentiation (Lewin, 1935; Werner, 1948), easily cross comparisons. So, too, do philosophical points of view, such as reductionism, relativism, etc. In closing, Harlow argued that, "If the competent do not wish to generalize, the incompetent will fill the field [Harlow, Gluck, & Suomi, 1972, p. 716]."

A drive toward universalism pervaded the writings of early comparativists, who regardless of subfield often tended not to appreciate the high degree of psychological variability we know today is warranted in looking across species, stage, or society. Investigators with more idiographic outlooks therefore find that the proper reasons for comparison reside in close examination of unique behavioral attributes and of distinctions within or among phyla, ages, or cultures. In this vein, qualitative (different) considerations have preempted quantitative (deficient) ones in debates comparing groups across phyla, across ages, and across cultures.

In the pages that follow, prominent comparativists discuss the historical roots, philosophical underpinnings, theoretical concerns, methodological issues, experimental contributions, and future directions of animal, developmental, cultural, and statistical perspectives in psychology. Not only do general principles of psychological comparison emerge in these chapters, but mutual interrelations among the subspecialties and between each subspecialty and psychology in general come into clearer focus. This collection of essays on comparison is intended to promote widespread interest in comparison and in interrelations among comparative methods. There is growing recognition of disutility in the separateness and artificial distinctions constructed among psychological subdisciplines concerned with comparison. The state of the art is such that comparisons in psychology are sufficiently well developed to formulate valid, appropriate, and meaningful questions on the basis of which psychology is destined to make still more valid, appropriate, and meaningful comparisons.

REFERENCES

Campbell, D. T., & Stanley, J. C. *Experimental and quasi-experimental designs for research.* Chicago: Rand McNally, 1963.

Darwin, C. R. *The descent of man, and selection in relation to sex.* London: John Murray, 1913. (Originally published, 1871.)

Darwin, C. R. *The origin of species by means of natural selection, or the preservation of favoured races in the struggle for life.* New York: New American Library of World Literature, 1958. (Originally published, 1859.)

Durkheim, E. [*Suicide*] (J. A. Spaulding & G. Simpson, trans.). New York: Free Press, 1951. (Originally published, 1897.)

Durkheim, E. [*Rules of the sociological method*] (S. A. Solovay & J. H. Mueller, trans.). Chicago: University of Chicago Press, 1938. (Originally published, 1895.)

Freud, S. [*A general introduction to psychoanalysis*] (J. Riviere, trans.). New York: Washington Square Press, 1952. (Originally published, 1924.)

Freud, S. [*The interpretation of dreams*] (J. Strachey, Ed. and trans.). New York: Avon, 1966. (Originally published, 1900.)

Harlow, H. F., Gluck, J. P., & Suomi, S. J. Generalization of behavioral data between nonhuman and human animals. *American Psychologist,* 1972, *27,* 709–716.

Hodgkin, A. L. The ionic basis of nervous conduction. *Science,* 1964, *145,* 1148–1154.

Hull, C. L. A primary social science law. *Scientific Monthly,* 1950, *71,* 221–228.

Huxley, A. F. Excitation and conduction in nerve: Quantitative analysis. *Science,* 1964, *145,* 1154–1159.

Lashley, K. S. Persistent problems in the evolution of mind. *Quarterly Review of Biology,* 1949, *24,* 28–42.

Lewin, K. A. *A dynamic theory of personality.* New York: McGraw-Hill, 1935.

Mead, M. *Sex and temperament in three primitive societies.* New York: Morrow, 1935.

Werner, H. *Comparative psychology of mental development.* New York: Follett, 1948.

PRINCIPAL COMPARISONS

Securing scientific evidence involves making at least one comparison.

—D. T. Campbell and
J. C. Stanley (1963, p. 6)

Phylogenetic, ontogenetic, cultural, and statistical comparisons are principal in psychology because together they add uniquely to substance and method in the discipline and because these perspectives contribute to verifiable description, explanation, and prediction of behavior. The four are treated in Part I of this book. Part II treats two derivatives of these principal comparisons.

Animal Behavior Comparisons

Aristotle (see Ross, 1913) believed that all animals were connected in a graded scale of perfection (*scala naturae*) with man at the top. Later Darwin (1871/1913) restated "continuity" theory emphasizing that man was neither physically nor intellectually unique among the species, behavior at large being a product of universal, adaptive forces. The phylogenetic perspective and its implications have gained prominence in psychology ever since Darwin: Infrahuman animals serve as subjects of psychological investigation for their own sake, as behavior models, and in comparison with humans. Some of the major questions to which animal comparisons have been directed include: Which behaviors are species-specific, and which are species-general? What are legitimate or appropriate comparisons of animal and human behavior? In chapter 2, Colin Beer touches on these and other issues central to animal behavior comparisons. The design for this chapter is a discussion, comparison, and contrast of comparative psychology and comparative ethology, whose orientations toward the study of animal behavior differ in several ways.

The modern history of comparative psychology, defined as the psychological study of animal behavior, began with Romanes (1882) and Morgan (1894). Down to Watson (1924) and Skinner (1938, 1971), behaviorists have traditionally assumed consistent positions on several critical issues: Individuals and animal species are mutually deficient as opposed to different; universal laws underwrite learning; and positivism constitutes valid explanation of behavior. Beer's treatment of comparative psychology goes considerably beyond simple dissection of mechanisms of learning or schedules of reinforcement into premises, laws, and the underlying coherence of behaviorism.

A form of animal comparison heretofore neglected by a majority of psychologists is comparative ethology, defined as the zoological study of animal behavior. Ethologists concern themselves with interrelations of structure and function, the role of instincts and internal constructs, and adaptation and other phylogenetic perspectives on behavior. Many of these perspectives are foreign to behavioral psychologists at present.

Though both these traditions in fact derive from Darwin, they have diverged historically over foci and philosophy, and they are today as distinct in style as in substance. Not only does the one's focus on mechanisms of learning contrast with the other's naturalism, but questions of the relative importance of laboratory versus field and nomothetic versus idiographic analysis differentiate the two. Further, as Beer suggests, humanities act as a vehicle of explanation in ethology but have no parallel in psychology. The modern schism between Skinner's associationism and Lorenz's naturalism represents a culmination of historical divergence between these two perspectives, which in current times calls for reconciliation. Today, the value of an ethological perspective on interspecies comparisons is increasingly recognized by psychologists. For these reasons, the balanced presentation afforded in Beer's chapter is particularly relevant to contemporary and future comparisons in animal behavior.

Interspecies comparisons check the possibility of anthropocentrism in human psychology. Further, they help to extend the study of psychology and thereby to elucidate a greater variety of phenomena than would otherwise be known. A plethora of widely applied psychological concepts derive from them, although increasing knowledge of animal behavior per se has helped equally to ward off *in*appropriate comparisons and inferences among the species.

Developmental Comparisons

The phylogenetic perspective constitutes one major basis of comparison in psychology. A second principal mode of comparison has concentrated on ontogenesis, comparison of behavior over the life cycle.

In response to a note published in *Mind*, Darwin (1877) was moved "to look over a diary which [he] kept thirty-seven years [before] with respect to one of [his] own infants [p. 286]." The origins of an ontogenetic perspective on behavior therefore are similar to phylogenetic ones (and, as we see later, to cultural ones as well). Other early developmentalists, like Freud (1905/1962, 1923/1960) in central Europe, Hall (1883) in America, and Binet (Binet & Simon, 1908/1916) in France, descended intellectually from Darwin. Though these men took divergent approaches to the study of development, the issues with which each became explicitly or implicitly identified share several features. They and many developmental psychologists since have expressed continuing interest in describing and comparing behavior at different points in the life cycle and in explaining the antecedents of behavior and the mechanisms of behavior change in terms of heredity, experience, or their interaction.

Not unexpectedly, some of the persistent questions to which ontogenetic comparisons are addressed parallel those posed by other principal comparisons. For example, which behaviors are age-specific, and which are stable and independent of age? Other questions are unique to developmental comparison, however. How do organism and environment transact over time? A treatment of developmental comparisons in chapter 3 is divided between Alfred Baldwin, who defines development and recapitulates history and the major theoretical perspectives on ontogenesis, and Thomas Achenbach, who reviews methodology and research considerations made in developmental comparisons.

In Baldwin's view, development is synonymous with individual change, and he analyzes historically and theoretically prominent causes of change. Axiomatically, there may be two sources of variance in behavior of the individual over time: one arising within (heredity) and the other outside (experience) the individual. (Notice that these views are conceptually akin to those of comparative ethology and comparative psychology, respectively.) Baldwin introduces the reader to both and to other central concepts of developmental comparison—state and process, disposition and situation, etc.—through simple case studies of physical growth and semantic acquisition.

Doubtless, however, *interaction* of nature and nurture are recognized as patently more important to the construction of developmental theory. Though nature and nurture have heretofore determined the course of theory and research in developmental psychology to an undeniably large degree, neither alone can explain ontogenesis; and various kinds of research phenomena, including twin studies, the critical period, and the several functions of experience, have been invoked to illustrate some of the ways the two interact. However, taken individually or in interaction, nativist and empiricist positions carry corollary constraints and implications. Thus, matching subjects by age or by experience indicates underlying theoretical bias.

Although nature-nurture views represent theoretical parsimony, they do not necessarily represent truth. A contemporary, more sophisticated—though substantially encumbered—alternative view of development posits that organisms actively structure their interactions with the environment in ways that reflect the level of their physiological, cognitive, and social development, and over time they are in turn altered by those interactions. The components of this developmental view—stage theory, dialectics, and transaction between organism and environment—are not at all new. However, their modern synthesis is argued by many to mirror nature more realistically and, by recapturing active processes, to advance developmental theorizing considerably over traditional interpretations of development based on simple static interactionism.

The central concerns of the companion and complementary section by Achenbach are research and methodology in developmental comparison. Here is a survey of the most common strategies, methods, and designs as practiced with their potential advantages and pitfalls weighed and assayed. An overview of experimental methodology makes explicit the weakness in a central assumption of cross-age research, viz. that it is possible to vary age "other things being equal." Other things are almost never equal in developmental comparisons (or interspecies or cross-cultural comparisons, for that matter), and Achenbach codifies practical solutions to this problem.

Developmental comparisons engender special considerations; the relative status of description and explanation is one example, and the interplay between theory and research another. In developmental study, description stands independent of explanation but is also prerequisite to it; Achenbach reviews a variety of strategies that developmental description has adduced to explain both behavior origins and behavior change. The connections among history, theory, and research in developmental psychology are direct, and Achenbach shows how, historically, theoretical issues, topical questions, and social policy concerns have motivated developmental research in nearly equal degrees.

Developmental comparisons guard against adultocentrism in psychology. Among the major comparisons practiced today, developmental ones are perhaps the most common. Their principal functions within psychology are twofold. More than one comparativist has observed that no behavioral phenomenon or process can be fully understood without reference to its origins, nor can any phenomenon or process be assessed in the first place without a description of its ontogeny over the life cycle. In the absence of life-span description, examination of origins, or assessments of change, psychology is less well informed and substantially more limited in scope.

Cross-Cultural Comparisons

The centrifugal impact of Darwinism during the growth of the British Empire opened the study of psychology to a cultural perspective. Darwin himself persistently invoked comparisons among human societies in his discussions of *The Descent of Man* (1871/1913) and *The Expression of the Emotions in Man and Animals* (1872/1915). The origins of cultural comparison, like those of animal and developmental comparisons, are thus to be found in Darwin, though Hume (1826) and especially Mill (1879) were central to formulation of the role of philosophy in cultural comparison. Moreover, more than other disciplines, anthropology influenced the development of cross-cultural psychology. Many early anthropologists of the British school, like Nadel (1951), were originally trained psychologists; likewise, many turn-of-the-century psychologists, like Rivers (1901), engaged in field experimentation throughout their careers. Indeed, the first proponents of cross-cultural psychology, among whom were Wundt (1916) and Galton (1869/1914), acknowledged debts to contemporary anthropologists, including Tylor (1871) and Lévy-Bruhl (1923/1966). In general, the anthropological point of view increasingly sensitized psychologists to similarities and differences among humans, and, as a result, cultural comparisons have enjoyed increasing prominence in psychology.

Some principal psychological questions about culture and behavior that have persisted include the following: Which behaviors are culture-specific, and which are universal? What is the full range of human experience? What is the full diversity of behavioral expression? Gustav Jahoda's comprehensive chapter 4 on cross-cultural comparison addresses these questions and psychological issues related to them.

Like Beer, Jahoda compares psychological comparison with a nonpsychological one (anthropology) to the mutual enlightenment of the two. In doing so, for example, he contrasts definitions of culture from the points of view of anthropology, i.e., culture as unitary structure, and psychology, i.e., culture as grouped variables. The implications that flow from these variant definitions are crucial to understanding the role of cultural comparison in psychology versus anthropology; for example, the emic-etic distinction is significant from the structural approach but not from the multivariate one.

Cross-cultural comparison has been motivated by many reasons. Not all of them nor the designs used to execute cultural comparative research are equally compelling, and the enterprise has been criticized for its structural inability to answer important theoretical questions. Gustav Jahoda addresses both these important issues in his chapter. First, he provides a critical but helpful appraisal of the major approaches in cross-cultural comparison; one of the most worthy in Jahoda's view is the assessment of variation and invariance in human behavior broadly conceived. Second, Jahoda elects to foil the modern critique of cross-cultural psychology by showing how the enterprise renders meaningful comparisons and critical tests of psychological theory. In several ways, therefore, his chapter functions as an informative guide to cross-cultural psychology, past, present, and future.

A cross-cultural perspective checks ethnocentric tendencies among practitioners of the study of human mind and behavior. It exposes the richness of psychology and the diversity of its antecedents, thereby enlarging the scope of psychological description. Cross-cultural comparisons help further to test and to refine psychological theory and explanation. Finally, cultural comparisons help to expose influences on behavior that may remain hidden in monocultural investigation.

Statistical Comparisons

Comparison provokes (and merits) qualitative commentary. However, many comparisons in psychology necessitate formal quantitative assessment and verification in advance of qualitative comment. In such cases, statistical analysis of individuals or groups and conditions or treatments has evolved as the common procedure of verification. In the first half of her chapter 5 on statistical comparison, Victoria Seitz discusses how and why mathematical comparisons are performed; that is, what assumptions underlie them and which procedures ought to be applied when. This chapter overviews major issues in statistical comparison of typical psychological data related to the linear model, homogeneity of variance, sampling, and robustness, and it provides the reader with an intuitive understanding of the statistical approach, with tips and rules of thumb useful in everyday statistical evaluation, and with a plethora of resources for further reference.

The second half of Seitz's chapter addresses statistical issues specifically relevant to forms of comparison that cross species, ages, or cultures. Some discussions particularly germane to ontogenetic comparisons include correlation, the measurement of change, and interaction. Others specific to animal and cultural comparisons include unavoidable violations of statistical assumptions by natural groupings (such as cultures or animal populations) and the statistical versus experimental control of variables. In both cases, Seitz suggests multivariate and scaling procedures, and she advances solutions to otherwise knotty issues in complex comparison. A knowledge of statistical treatment is essential in psychology; this chapter conveys the hows and whys.

The four chapters included in Part I cover major comparative approaches that supplement standard laboratory methods in human experimental psychology. Here are introductions to the history, philosophy, theory, methodology, and experimental contributions of each type of comparison. These chapters demonstrate that the analysis and understanding of behavior across diverse species or among human beings over the life span or across cultures are a part of the mainstream of substantive psychology and are integral to a comprehensive conduct of psychology.

REFERENCES

Binet, A., & Simon, T. [The development of intelligence in the child.] In H. H. Goddard (Ed.), *The development of intelligence in children* (E. S. Kiffe, trans.). Baltimore: Williams & Wilkins, 1916. (Originally published, 1908.)

Campbell, D. T., & Stanley, J. C. *Experimental and quasi-experimental designs for research.* Chicago: Rand McNally, 1963.

Darwin, C. R. A biographical sketch of an infant. *Mind,* 1877, *2,* 286–294.

Darwin, C. R. *The descent of man, and selection in relation to sex.* London: John Murray, 1913. (Originally published, 1871.)

Darwin, C. R. *The expression of the emotions in man and animals.* New York: Appleton, 1915. (Originally published, 1872.)

Freud, S. [*The ego and the id*] (J. Riviere, trans.). New York: Norton, 1960. (Originally published, 1923.)

Freud, S. [*Three essays on the theory of sexuality*] (J. Strachey, Ed. and trans.). New York: Avon, 1962. (Originally published, 1905.)

Galton, F. *Hereditary genius.* London: Macmillan, 1914. (Originally published, 1869.)

Hall, G. S. The contents of children's minds. *Princeton Review,* 1883, *11,* 249–272.

Hume, D. *Philosophical works* (Vol. 3). Edinburgh: Black & Tait, 1826.

Lévy-Bruhl, L. [*Primitive mentality*] (L. Clare, trans.). London: Allen & Unwin, 1966. (Originally published, 1923.)

Mill, J. S. *A system of logic* (Vol. 2). London: Longmans, Green, 1879.

Morgan, C. L. *An introduction to comparative psychology.* London: Scott, 1894.

Nadel, S. F. *The foundations of social anthropology.* London: Cohen & West, 1951.

Rivers, W. H. R. Introduction. In A. C. Haddon (Ed.), *Reports on the Cambridge anthropological expedition to the Torres Straits.* Cambridge: Cambridge University Press, 1901.

Romanes, G. *Animal intelligence.* London: Kegan Paul, 1882.

Ross, W. D. (Ed.). *The works of Aristotle.* Oxford: Clarendon Press, 1913.

Skinner, B. F. *The behavior of organisms.* New York: Appleton-Century-Crofts, 1938.

Skinner, B. F. *Beyond freedom and dignity.* New York: Knopf, 1971.

Tylor, E. B. *Primitive culture.* London: Murray, 1871.

Watson, J. B. *Behaviorism.* Chicago: University of Chicago Press, 1924.

Wundt, W. *Elements of folk psychology.* London: Allen & Unwin, 1916.

2 Perspectives on Animal Behavior Comparisons

Colin G. Beer
Rutgers University

> *We all of us, grave or light, get our thoughts entangled in metaphors, and act fatally on the strength of them.*
> —George Eliot (1965, p. 111)

> *The notion of a scientific or philosophical verbal structure free of rhetorical elements is an illusion.*
> —Northrope Frye (1971, p. 350)

INTRODUCTION

A book devoted to the comparative method in psychology is liable to suggest that we are dealing with something like the Stanislavsky method in acting or the soft-ground method in etching: one among a variety of alternative techniques or ways of going about the business in question. It is true that there are psychologists who are called comparative to distinguish them from their colleagues who practice psychology called cognitive, clinical, social, and so forth. Yet there is a sense in which comparison is common to all kinds of psychology—indeed to all kinds of cognition. In the use of language, for instance, we depend on the fact that names have been given to objects, qualities, and relations, which fix certain similarities and differences in the flow of experience as boundaries containing it, dividing it, directing it. Whenever we describe, we class things or properties or events together or apart on the basis of the similarities and differences marked by the words we choose. Consequently, to the extent that science begins with description, it begins with comparison.

But no two things, no two qualities, no two events are alike in all respects, or alike in none. Any description singles out some similarities and differences to the exclusion of others, which could be the basis of alternative descriptions. Consequently, a demand for a complete description of anything amounts to a contradiction in terms. A demand for a pure description would be equally incoherent, for, of necessity, the similarities and differences that we pick out when we describe anything will depend on what we intend the description for, our expectations about the matter in question, considerations of relevance to some focus of interest, and other prior assumptions. Comparison necessarily assumes perspective.

Perspectives differ among sciences, among schools within a science, and among scientists within a school. Consequently, the history of science is no less littered with controversy and confusion than the history of philosophy, art, or politics. The conception that we have of something is often so deeply and firmly embedded in our minds that we cannot even entertain the possibility of an alternative. Such a conception governs our very perceiving of the thing; we cannot see it any other way and "know" that that is the way it really is. Anyone who claims otherwise we regard as purblind, or perverse, or just plain crazy. The closed-mindedness that can result from this sort of conviction is one of the sources of what my teacher, Niko Tinbergen, used to call "nothing-but-ism": behavior is nothing but reflexes; morality is nothing but self-interest; everything is nothing but matter in motion.

One of the consequences of nothing-but-ism is a parochial attitude within and between sciences that fails to see any value in any but its own kind of work and interest. Many physiologists despise those biologists and psychologists who settle for levels of analysis less molecular than that at which they are convinced the only worthwhile understanding of nature is to be found ("all the rest is merely stamp-collecting"). I have heard people who study the behavior of wild animals in the field ridicule their colleagues who study captive animals in the laboratory for believing that they could discover anything of value about real, natural animal behavior in such impoverished, contrived, and artificial conditions. And the recent fashion for sociobiology has promoted itself with similar disparaging assertions about those to whose territory it lays claim. The arrogance to which such attitudes lead is, all too often, a consequence and cause of ignorance of what the other person is really up to. The subject matter of animal behavior comprises so much variety and heterogeneity, both of phenomena and problem, that no one conception, no one approach, no one perspective can, at least at present, cover everything. Each conception, each approach, each perspective gives only a partial view of the whole. Consequently, recognition of one's limits can broaden one's horizons.

In his now classic book *The Study of Instinct*, Tinbergen (1951) divided the study of animal behavior among four questions: immediate causation, ontogenetic development, adaptive significance, and evolution. In a later publication (Tinbergen, 1963), he defined ethology in terms of these four questions and went on to say: "It is useful to distinguish between them and to insist that a comprehensive coherent science of Ethology has to give equal attention to each of them and to their integration [p. 411]." Tinbergen has always opposed the sort of parochialism that I have just discussed. But there is more than that standing in the way of the integration of which he wrote. Each of the kinds of questions he distinguished, and others that can be distinguished within them and in addition to them, has its own methods, the results of which seldom bear directly on the other kinds of question; in some cases the language and concepts in terms of which a question is framed have no translation or parallels in the language and concepts of other questions. For example, the understanding that has been achieved in the study of social systems and social communication is embodied in its own terms, which at present defy reduction to physiological terms. It is therefore more than just "useful" to distinguish among different questions: It is necessary if confusion and misunderstanding are to be avoided.

Confusion and misunderstanding have been chronic conditions in the study of animal behavior. They helped to sustain the "anti-instinct revolt" in which Watson (see Watson & McDougall, 1929), Dunlap (1919), and other behaviorists attacked the nativist doctrines of McDougall (1912), just after World War I. And they were involved in the revival of the issue, which joined American comparative psychology and European comparative ethology in just as bitter a controversy, shortly after World War II. Comparison of the behavior of different kinds of animal, and of different kinds of behavior, was common to the rival camps in this controversy; but how it was used, what it was used for, and what it presupposed were matters that divided them, without their being fully aware of how much. In this chapter, I attempt to show these differences by sketching some of the history of comparative psychology and comparative ethology.

Gray (1973) described comparative psychology and ethology as "twins reared apart." If historical parentage is judged by lineal descent or historical continuity—ancestry rather than anticipation—then I should argue that their relationship is no closer than that of half-siblings. Their shared parent is Darwinism, which got comparative psychology out of associationistic psychology and ethology out of comparative anatomy. At least that is the story that I tell.[1] I argue that in both cases the connection to behavior was effected by the kind of comparison we call analogy. At least for that part of comparative psychology that stems from behaviorism—which is very much the larger part—the core conception consisted of the principles of

---

[1]It is not the only story. Neither comparative psychology nor ethology is a sharply defined school of behavior study, but it can be objected that I take too broad a view of the former and too narrow a view of the latter. For instance some comparative psychologists would insist that their discipline be distinguished from the animal psychology of behavioristic learning theory, and in another context I should comply. That it suits my purpose here to emphasize continuity and shared tradition instead, exemplifies my theme that what one picks out for mention depends upon one's choice of perspective.

associationism, sometimes combined with those of hedonism, with stimulus and response put in the places of sensation and idea (cf. Broadbent, 1961). For comparative ethology the principles of comparative anatomy were applied to behavior by putting behavior patterns in the places of morphological structures. These analogies are so firmly embedded in their respective traditions that they are seldom recognized as such. They exemplify the way in which some similes graduate to metaphors that end up being taken for identities. But when a metaphor dies its ghost may stay around to haunt its context with a hidden assumption. An implicit analogy can have a more insidious influence than an explicit one. Nevertheless, analogical comparison should not be condemned. It is true, as every schoolboy knows, that argument by analogy is a species of fallacy. It is also true that such argument has been, again and again in the history of science, the means of important discoveries. Indeed, according to such philosphers as Black (1962) and Toulmin (1953), argument by analogy, or at least imagining in metaphor, is of the essence of productive thinking in science.

It can be argued, then, that scientists share with poets a "motive for metaphor." I argue that in the case of ethology there has been an even closer merging of scientific and aesthetic values. Such a merging harmonizes with the choice of "perspectives" for this and other chapters of this book. Comparison and analogy can be put to many uses. I use them to try to show that there is both more diversity and more unity in the study of animal behavior than has usually been supposed.

COMPARATIVE PSYCHOLOGY

The Darwinian theory of evolution gave new and mundane expression to an old and metaphysical idea: There is an ontological continuity running through and linking up all the forms of nature in a natural order—the Great Chain of Being, *echelle des êtres, scala naturae:*

> Vast chain of being, which from God began,
> Natures æthereal, human, angel, man,
> Beast, bird, fish, insect! what no eye can see,
> No glass can reach! from Infinite to thee,
> From thee to nothing! [Pope, 1733/1969, pp. 128-129]

Darwin took the factual bases for this idea, especially the evidence of shared patterns of structural organization, and correspondences among features of different anatomical forms, presented by comparative morphology, comparative embryology, and the fossil record, and made a compelling case for their being no more than one would expect if organisms were related to one another through descent,with modification, from common ancestors. The modification, being so often a beautiful fit between form and function, had been marvelled at and expounded as evidence of the rationality and ingenuity of God by such devines as Paley (1802) and the writers of the *Bridgewater Treatises*; but again Darwin brought things down to earth by arguing that all could be interpreted as adaptation consequent on natural selection.

The idea of evolutionary continuity provided a two-way street. As applied to the relationship of man to the other creatures, it invited both a thinking of other creatures in human terms and a thinking of the human in terms of other creatures. As R. S. Peters expressed it (1962, p. 694), one had the options of humanizing the brutes or brutalizing humans. In regard to psychological matters, Darwin's followers began by taking the first course; they argued in a manner now disparagingly called anthropomorphism. The best-known representative of this way of arguing from man to animal was Romanes, who is also credited with being the first to use the term "comparative psychology." Here is how Romanes (1882) summed up his reasons for taking the approach that he did:

> The mental states of an insect may be widely different from those of a man, and yet most probably the nearest conception that we can form of their true nature is that which we form by assimilating them to the pattern of the only mental states with which we are actually acquainted. And this consideration, it is needless to point out, has a special validity to the evolutionist, inasmuch as upon his theory there must be a psychological, no less than a physiological, continuity extending throughout the length and breadth of the animal kingdom [p. 10].

Because psychology had previously been virtually restricted to study of the human mind, it was natural that comparative psychology should initially have been conceived as the study of the varieties or degrees of mind in the animal kingdom (even extending to the plants and microbes). Romanes assumed the categories and concepts of associationism—the mainstream of psychological thought in nineteenth-century Britain—and attempted to arrive at criteria for their application to minds other than the human—the similarities between human and animal action that license analogical inference from behavior to the mental acts and subjective qualities underlying it. He appealed to common sense to back up his judgments. Common sense probably still finds most of his kinds of judgment irresistible most of the time, in spite of what science has had to say.

Probably Romanes's least defensible position was on the question of how he collected his evidence. His method was to go through the literature of natural history, travellers' tales, missionaries' journals, and the like and cull reports of animals behaving in ways that would place them on the scale of psychological capacities. The accuracy and reliability of such reports, it stands to reason and experience, will vary with the acuteness and credulity of the reporter; and because the unusual tends to catch the attention whereas the commonplace goes unremarked, even the most conscientious of diarists is likely to record a selection of unrepresentative instances. As Thorndike (1898) commented later, "Dogs get lost hundreds of times and no one notices it or sends a scientific account of it to a magazine. But let one find its way from Brooklyn to Yonkers and the fact immediately becomes a circulating anecdote [p. 4]."

Anecdotalism was thus added to anthropomorphism in the charges leveled against Romanes by those who came after him. One of the first of these was Morgan. Morgan (1894) is most famous for Lloyd Morgan's Canon, which, in his own words, is this: "In no case may we interpret an action as the outcome of the exercise of a higher psychical faculty, if it can be interpreted as the outcome of the exercise of one which stands lower in the psychological scale [p. 53]." Even though this principle did not carry any guarantee of the truth of the premise it assumed—namely that, as far as animal psychology is concerned, this is the simplest of all possible worlds—it became received doctrine for later generations of comparative psychologists and helped to turn comparative psychology round to face in the reductionist direction. Despite this, the old-fashioned language places it in a time and context remote from present-day conceptions of how animal behavior is to be thought about. The reference to higher and lower faculties and "the psycholgical scale" echo the pre-Darwinian notion of the Great Chain of Being and its related notions of continuity in the varieties of mental life. This latter idea had been developed and elaborated on in the widely-read writings of Spencer (1855, 1904).

The aim of Spencer's ambition was nothing less than a synthesis of the whole of human knowledge. In working out this "synthetic philosophy," Spencer made continuity and progressive change, which for him meant evolution, the universals that draw everything into relation and hence into ultimate unity. Applied to psychology his view was that reflexes, habits, instincts, and reason differ only in degree, not in kind; the more complex functions having been derived gradually from the less complex as consequences of "the continuous adjustment of internal relations to external relations [1855, p. 374]," both in the life of the individual and in the history of the species. The inevitable direction of this "continuous adjustment," Spencer argued, has been and continues to be toward greater and greater heterogeneity, complexity, and subtlety in psychological processes, as the "mental" approximates closer and closer to the heterogeneity of the phsyical world with which organisms have to contend. Thus the most sophisticated forms of human thought are simply at one end point of a continuum, at the other end of which are the simplest forms of irritability such as can be found in a plant. As part of the explanation of how this comes about in the history of a species, Spencer (1904) offered "evolutionary associationism":

The familiar doctrine of association here undergoes a great extension; for it is held that not only in the individual do ideas become connected when in experience the things producing them have repeatedly occurred together, but such results of repeated occurrences accumulate in successions of individuals: the effects of associations are supposed to be transmitted as modifications of the nervous system [p. 470].

This, of course, is Lamarckism, and perhaps one of the reasons why Spencer goes unread today, apart from the fact that modern tastes find him unreadable, is that Lamarckism has been discredited. Yet Darwin ended up converted to belief in the inheritance of acquired characteristics, partly, it appears, through Spencer's influence, at least as far as the application of the idea to psychology was concerned. And it was Spencer, rather than Darwin, who brought the evolutionary perspective to psychology and so directed it along biological lines, especially in Britain and the United States. Darwin dealt with psychological matters selectively and unsystematically. Spencer worked out what appeared to be a comprehensive and integrated system of psychological doctrine and expounded it in a book, *The Principles of Psychology* (1855), which, especially after *The Origin of Species* (Darwin, 1859) had created an atmosphere of thought receptive to evolutionary ideas, became a leading authority and standard textbook on its subject for many years. When William James began teaching psychology at Harvard in 1875 he used Spencer's *Principles* as his textbook. In James's own *The Principles of Psychology* (1890) there are twenty-five index entries for Spencer, only six for Darwin. James expressed exasperation with Spencer's vagueness and verbosity, but he gave high praise to Spencer's "having been the first to see in evolution an absolutely universal principle [James, 1924, p. 124]," and his "insisting that, since mind in its environment have evolved together, they must be studied together [pp. 139-140]."

James was apparently not very deeply interested in the comparative study of animal behavior; in his *Principles* the chapter most concerned with it is one of the least satisfactory in the book. In other respects, however, he set an example of what a comparative approach should be: He was curious about all varieties of psychological phenomena, the kinds of problems they raise and the relationships between them; he was undogmatic, even inconsistent, letting each view have its turn and then arguing its pros and cons.

James was too eclectic to have been the founder of a school or system of psychology. Nevertheless, he had enormous influence on the psychologists of his own and succeeding generations in America. Among those he taught were Edward L. Thorndike and G. Stanley Hall. They were very different from one another, but in their own ways they both belong in the company of those who are called comparative psychologists.

With Thorndike we briefly return to Morgan, for it was Morgan who decided Thorndike to work on animals for his graduate research. Thorndike attended lectures that Morgan gave at Harvard, in which, among other things, there was discussion of the use of experiments in the study of the workings of animal minds. Thorndike took his cue from this. First at Harvard and then at Columbia, he devised tests of the problem-solving abilities of domestic chicks, cats, and monkeys, the outcome of which was, in the words of Tolman, "*the* theory relative to which the rest of us here in America have oriented ourselves [in Bitterman, 1969, p. 452]." The book in which Thorndike's theory appeared was entitled *Animal Intelligence: An Experimental Study of the Associative Processes in Animals* (1898). The associative processes in animals! As original and revolutionary as Thorndike's theory was, his inheritance of the predominant preoccupation of psychology's long past (and even its short history) was reflected in the title of his book.

The predominant preoccupation of psychology, up until the end of the nineteenth century, was epistemology: the question, how do we come to know what we know? The answer that won the widest following was that all knowledge comes from experience, especially the experience of seeing what goes with what—in a word: associationism. Intelligence was thus conceived of as the use of past experience in the solving of present problems. Thorndike designed his experiments to see to what extent his animals could use experience of what had led to the solution of a problem to solve the problem when they encountered it again. His results led him to three conclusions that were especially important in the history of experimental and comparative psychology. The one for which he is most famous was that contiguity by itself is insufficient to effect an association; the experience must also include attainment of a state of affairs that the animal is striving to bring about, such as removal of distress or assuaging of appetite. This is the Law of Effect. Or, rather, it is the Law of Effect in words that Thorndike would not have let stand, for implicit in his statement of it was the second of the conclusions that I am emphasizing, namely, that what are associated are stimuli and responses, not sensations or ideas.

Thorndike thus used Lloyd Morgan's Canon more devastatingly than its inventor. Whereas Morgan still found it necessary to continue with the traditional mentalistic language of sensation, memories, ideas, and so forth, Thorndike pointed out that everything that can be seen to occur when an animal learns something can be stated in terms of the situation in which the animal was placed (the stimuli), the behavior it performed there (the response), and the outcome of the performance in terms of reward or punishment. Thorndike even made a case for talking of connection rather than association, so as to avoid the mentalistic associations of associationism. The third conclusion was that animals of different sorts differ in degree but not in kind as far as intelligence is concerned. Monkeys can learn to solve more complicated problems than can cats, and cats are similarly superior to rats; but they all do no more, nor less, than connect stimuli to responses through experience of reward. Thus Thorndike continued the career of the idea of continuity that Darwin and Spencer had done so much to promote. Inclusion of the human case in this continuity implied that the principles of learning discovered in animal behavior applied to people as well. Thorndike went from his study of animal intelligence to work out the lessons it taught about the education of children.

Hall also made education and child psychology the focus of his mature work. However, in other respects, he was a very different psychologist from Thorndike, being much less tough-minded and positivistic, much more eclectic. Hall's concern with animal behavior was a matter of theory, not practice; and the theory was that of evolution. The theory of evolution informed most of his thinking on psychological matters and the interpretations that he put on his psychological observations—so much so that he was once described as the "Darwin of the mind." An example of his application of evolutionary ideas is the account he gave of the stages through which a child passes in the process of psychological development (Hall, 1904). According to Hall, the child repeats as an individual the course that the mind has followed in its evolution as a specialized adaptation of the human species, going from reflex to habit to instinct to progressively refined forms of intellect. This was Haeckel's (1866) biogenetic law—ontogeny recapitulates phylogeny—read into psychology. It implied that education must be tailored to the psychological stage, and that understanding of the earlier or lower stages may most conveniently and usefully be sought in study of the behavior of animals, especially species whose mature behavior is representative of lower levels of the scale. Again continuity of mind was assumed, both in ontogeny and phylogeny, even though unqualified belief in it was hardly consistent with full appreciation of what evolutionary adaptation entails.

The process of evolutionary adaptation, through natural selection, has caused divergent specialization between different lines of descent, as well as historical change within such lines. As Gruber and Barrett (1974) and others have pointed out, Darwin's image for the course of evolution was not a chain or a ladder but a many-branched tree or bush. As this image conveys, there is historical continuity in the vertical dimension representing time; but at any horizontal level beyond the first branchings from the stem there are spaces representing divergence associated with adaptive specialization which can be of quite different sorts in different branches. In the comparative study of behavior, we are limited to evidence from just one of these horizontal levels, namely the present, in which the gaps may well represent discontinuities of kind resulting from adaptation to different environments. This did not bother Hall, in spite of the problem it entailed for the idea of continuity. On the contrary, Hall argued enthusiastically for the view that mind and mental capacities such as reason and learning can be properly understood only as adaptive specializations evolved to meet the demands of environment in the struggle for survival.

This view of mind as adaptive function gave the perspective and identity to the school of psychologists of which James and Hall were the forerunners. Dewey (e.g., 1896) and Angell (e.g., 1904, 1907) made it a first principle of the psychology they taught at Chicago, in opposition to the narrow German psychology devoted to the experimental dissection of sensory content, which Titchener had transplanted to Cornell. Titchener (1899) obliged them by calling them Functionalists, a name they were only too happy to accept, for it aptly described their position and put it in contrast to the Structuralism of Titchener and his school. To arrive at an understanding of mind in terms of evolutionary adaptation, the Functionalists explored the ways in which mind is put to use in dealing with the problems of life in the world and in society, especially in adjusting action to circumstance—which, of course, is adaptation in the sense applying to individual existence and a short time scale. Learning from experience is the type of such adaptation for the psychologist; learning was the main topic of research for the Functionalists. They thus deepened what was already American psychology's mainstream. Rising in epistemology and fed by evolutionary theory and experimental methodology, the study of learning directed most of the psychological laboratories in this country, particularly those devoted to research on animal psychology.

Animal psychology, in spite of Thorndike's work, continued to be preoccupied with the varieties, or rather degrees, of animal consciousness, until well after the turn of the century. The mode of inference was the "ejective" technique used by Romanes: You presented your animal with a problem and from the way it went about dealing with the situation you reasoned, from your own experience of acting in that way, what the animal must be perceiving, feeling, and thinking. Small, (1899, 1901) discovered the convenience of the white rat and the maze for this sort of research, and so turned most of American animal psychology into rat psychology. At Chicago, the Functionalists attempted to work out how the rat uses its consciousness in learning to master a maze. One of the graduate students engaged in this program was J. B. Watson. His doctoral dissertation, which was supervised by Angell and published in 1903, was entitled *Animal Education: The Psychical Development of the White Rat.* In 1907 he was still holding to a conventional Functionalist line when he reviewed for the *Psychological Bulletin* a book called *Behavior of the Lower Organisms* by H. S. Jennings (1906), Professor of Zoology at Johns Hopkins. Watson (1907a) reproached Jennings for saying that "we have no other criterion than that of behavior for assuming our neighbor is conscious [p. 291]." Yet in a short while Watson turned about-face and went even further in this direction than Jennings. Indeed, in the same year that he wrote his review he also published a paper in which he raised the question of whether references to a rat's consciousness or subjective awareness add anything really useful to a description of what the rat is doing (Watson, 1907b). By 1913 his conversion was complete. In his famous paper entitled "Psychology as the Behaviorist Views It" (1913), he preached that psychology is the science of behavior, not the science of mental life, which meant that all mentalistic terms, all terms with subjective connotations such as feeling, willing, and consciousness, were to be barred from psychological discourse and replaced by objective description of what can be observed publicly: overt behavior and the circumstances of its occurrence.

Bearing on Watson's change of mind was probably the contact he had with Loeb, a German biologist and physiologist who was a colleague at Chicago. Loeb (e. g., 1899) taught a mechanistic philosophy of life, part of which was a theory of behavioral control according to which behavior is imposed on the animal by the stimulus gradients and their configurations to which the animal is exposed and the organization of the response mechanisms on which the stimuli act. This "tropism" theory was particularly concerned with oriented movement, but Loeb developed it into a general conception of behavior as consequent on the play of environmental forces. Indeed there was an unfortunate degree of nothing-but-ism in the deployment and defense of this theory, which cost him some credibility. Nevertheless, Watson echoed something of the spirit of Loeb's mechanistic teaching, and, in his own way, adopted the bias toward the environment.

One of those who argued against putting all the responsibility for behavioral control on the environment was Jennings (1906), whose book Watson had reviewed. In animals as low down in the scale as *Paramoecium*, Jennings had found evidence of spontaneity and endogenous determinants in the control of behavior that he chose to describe as "trial-and-error." He, like Loeb, overgeneralized his point. The first study that covered something like the full range and variety of ways in which animal behavior is directed in relation to the environment was Kühn's *Die Orientierung der Tiere im Raum* (1919). However, in the meantime, Jennings played his part in Watson's career. Watson joined the psychology faculty at Johns Hopkins in 1908 and so became a close colleague of Jennings and the other members of a group of people interested in animal behavior from perspectives different from those that had focused the views at Chicago. Here indeed was the setting that might have produced a truly comparative psychology, for a wide range of animal types was studied, much of it taken up with invertebrates. Watson himself, in collaboration with Lashley, conducted a field study of the nesting behavior of terns (Watson, 1908; Watson & Lashley, 1929), which, at a later date, would have qualified him to be regarded as an ethologist.

However, if the variety and richness in the kinds of behavior to be found in the animal kingdom, and in the problems they raise for study, impressed Watson at all, they did not do so sufficiently to override his psychological heritage. Since the time of Bacon and Descartes, the major preoccupation of psychology had been with the question: How is the mind of a person furnished with knowledge? For Watson this question was translated into the question: How does the organism acquire its ways of behaving? For both questions the traditional empiricism and associationism of the lineage from which Watson's preoccupation descended supplied the same answer: through experience. What Watson came to offer as positive psychological doctrine, as opposed to methodological and conceptual reform, was old-fashioned associationism with stimulus and response taking the places of sensation and idea, the rules being presumed to be the same irrespective of the kind of animal or the kind of behavior. According to this doctrine, all behavior, except the simplest reflexes, is learned, and the learning is effected by experience of conjunction. It remained only for Pavlov (e.g., 1928) to introduce the concept of the conditioned reflex and tie it to what seemed both a simple and plausible physiological mechanism, and Watson was satisfied that the essentials of the whole story had been told. It was a good story, and he was such a good storyteller that many, especially readers of accounts in the popular press, were persuaded that Watson would rank with Copernicus, Newton, and Darwin in the history of humanity's conception of itself.

But the story was too good to be true. Or, rather, it was too simple and crude to be true. It took little time for people to start complaining that experience of concurrence cannot be sufficient to explain learning, for some things can be experienced together countless times without their becoming associated—for many of us sunshine has invariably accompanied our going for a swim, yet going out of doors in the daytime does not always lead to our jumping in the river—and there are other things for which one experience is enough to make a permanent connection—it is rare for a child to touch a red-hot stove element more than once. Then there was the question of what was to count as behavior. McDougall (1912) had anticipated Watson in redefining psychology as "the science of behavior," but for McDougall behavior meant action—what an animal does to achieve a goal—whereas for Watson it meant movement—patterns of muscle contraction (cf. Peters, 1958; Taylor, 1964).

To the first of these questions Thorndike had, of course, already given an answer with his Law of Effect. All that was required to make this behavioristically acceptable was reformulation to get rid of the remnant of subjective reference that Thorndike had retained in the notion of satisfaction; thus the Principle of Reinforcement—reinforcement being whatever has to be added to contiguity to effect learning. But this too failed to bring unanimity to learning theory. Hull (e.g., 1935, 1943) argued that reinforcement must be linked to the meeting of biological needs; from this and a few other first principles he attempted to derive by deduction a rigorously defined and logically secure theoretical system that would be all-inclusive as far as the facts and phenomena of behavior were concerned. The white rat and the maze served to test the implications of the theory. Hull and his colleagues struggled with it through the 1930s and 1940s, but it eventually collapsed as the weight of so much inference hanging from so few premises strained the consistency of the logic, which ad hoc patching only weakened still further. In the meantime other psychologists, such as Hebb (e.g., 1949, 1955), turned to physiology to try to find a deeper account of what learning and reinforcement consist in; and still others, led by Skinner (e.g., 1938, 1950), eschewed the appeals of theory and the demands for explanation in the interest of developing the manipulation of reinforcement into a technology of behavioral control. E. C. Tolman (e.g., 1938) was perhaps the most deviant. He denied that reinforcement is necessary to learning, arguing instead that simply perceiving what goes with what, or the lie of the land, can supply information that can be drawn on and put to use should the context later become one in which there is a problem to be solved or the way found to a goal. His psychology was very like that of McDougall's in some respects, especially in his choice of descriptive categories—he dealt with the "molar behavior" of action, as opposed to the "molecular behavior" of movement—and in his emphasis on the purposiveness that he found inherent in behavior as he perceived and described it. He claimed however, and in contrast to McDougall, that all his descriptive categories and theoretical concepts were rigorously grounded in observation and operational definition, as the precepts of behaviorism demanded and as his calling his system "Purposive Behaviorism" implied. Nevertheless, it was said by one of his critics that whereas Skinner's was a psychology of the empty animal, Tolman's was a psychology that left the animal buried in thought. There were yet other versions of behaviorism and learning theory. Watson's behaviorist manifesto failed in its promise to make psychology into a unified science.

Although these various versions of behaviorism differed from and contended with one another, they were borne along by the same underlying current of tacit assumption and interest, which, looking back, we can see as a mainstream carrying the bulk of animal and comparative psychology for at least the first half of this century. One of the assumptions was that there are universal laws of learning, just as there are universal laws of optics and acoustics and mechanics. This implied that different kinds of animals might differ from one another quantitatively, as far as learning is concerned, but not qualitatively. Hence choice of subject for research to establish the laws of learning will be governed by considerations of convenience or practicality more than anything else: Hence the restriction of the research to kinds of animals preadapted to the laboratory, such as white rats and pigeons, and to simple problem situations, such as the maze and the Skinner box. So Skinner (1938) could write a book called *The Behavior of Organisms* in which the experimental evidence presented comes only from rats and pigeons performing in mazes and Skinner boxes; and Tolman (1938) could make his well-known statement, "I believe that everything important in psychology (except perhaps such matters as the building up of a superego, that is everything save such matters as involve society and words) can be investigated in essence through the continued experimental and theoretical analysis of the determinants of rat behavior at a choice point in a maze [p. 41]." Interest, continuing in the fashion fixed by Functionalism, focused narrowly on learning. Therefore, little attention was paid to such matters as social communication, migration, maternal behavior, comparative study of sensory or motor mechanisms; or to such animals as reptiles, amphibia, and the invertebrates, the learning capacities of which were supposed not to be very advanced. Lorenz (1950) could therefore complain that the *Journal of Comparative and Physiological Psychology* was misnamed:

> I must confess that I strongly resent it not only from the terminological viewpoint, but also in the interests of the very hard-working and honest craft of really comparative investigators, when an American journal masquerades under the title of "comparative" psychology, although, to the best of my knowledge, no really comparative paper ever has been published in it [p. 239].

However, there were eddies in the stream and some tributaries feeding into it from less entrenched regions. Watson himself expressed second thoughts about continuity: "animal studies have taught us that it is not safe to generalize from data we gather on one species to what will be true in another species [1925, p. 306]." Probably the most broadly comparative animal psychologist working in America during this period was Schneirla. Instead of concentrating on rats running in mazes or pigeons pecking keys in Skinner boxes, Schneirla conducted most of his research on the behavior of ants, and learning was only one of a variety of matters that engaged his interest. His perspective took in the whole animal kingdom, and he was more concerned with discontinuities and differences than with continuities and similarities in the variety of behavior he perceived. He elaborated the view that there is a series of "levels" of behavioral organization, the manifestations of which are qualitatively, not just quantitatively, distinct from one another (Schneirla, 1949). For example, comparison of the social behavior of insects and mammals shows the insects to be governed totally by "biological factors"—stimulus-response reactivity modulated by tissue needs—whereas the mammals are also affected by "psychological factors" such as individual attachments and emotional arousal. Accordingly, he described the insect level of social organization as "biogenic" and the mammalian as "psychogenic." A difference of kind rather than degree was revealed as well in comparisons of the learning of insects and mammals. Schneirla (1959a) found that an ant and a rat require about the same number of trials to master mazes of comparable complexity, but that having learned one maze the ant will take longer to learn another, in contrast to the rat, which usually learns the second maze more quickly than the first. Close observation of what the animals were doing in the maze as their learning progressed showed the ant to be building up the correct sequence of turns a bit at a time, ending with a rigidly followed routine; whereas the rat went about the business in a less slavish fashion that apparently informed the animal of the overall layout of the situation and what to expect in similar situations. In Schneirla's view the differences are so much more profound than the similarities (in the maze running of these two kinds of animal) that to describe them both as learning is misleading if the word is taken to refer to a process rather than to just an accomplishment.

These differences between the ways in which ants and rats master mazes reflect differences in the nervous systems of insects and mammals. For instance, the ant's tiny brain has much less capacity for information storage than has the considerably larger brain of the rat, and there are many other differences that go along with this difference in size (see Vowles, 1961). In general, the differences between levels of behavioral organization can be related to differences in sensory, neural, and motor equipment. An amoeba which lacks any structures specialized for the behavioral functions has only protoplasmic irritability to effect its behavior, which is consequently slow, unoriented, imprecise, and rudimentary, by the standards of other kinds of creature. The nerve net, such as one finds in coelenterates, provides diffuse conduction and graded response to external stimulation, which, in some cases, such as the food capture sequences of sea anemones, are sufficient to effect quite complex patterns of ordered movement. But the more advanced levels of behavioral precision, flexibility, and autonomy, such as we find in progressively more sophisticated forms going from worms to arthropods to vertebrates, depend on localization of control in central nervous systems, brains, and ganglia and specialization of function between and within them. Parallel and associated advances obtain in sensory and motor equipment. For instance, refinements in visual receptors add form perception to what, at lower levels, is restricted to the registering of differences of light intensity; and with this come new modes of orientation and social communication. On the motor side, the evolution of muscle bundles and jointed appendages opened up dimensions of precision and complexity in the field of action quite out of reach of the muscle-field systems of the limbless levels lower down. This conception of how the behavior of animals should be viewed and compared was presented by Maier and Schneirla (1935) in their textbook *Principles of Comparative Psychology*. Of this it could not be said that the title belied the content.

Schneirla also applied his concept of levels to individual behavioral development. An important part of this was his theory of "approach/withdrawal" or "biphasic processes." According to this the organism starts out limited to forced responses, mild stimulation inducing approach and strong stimulation inducing withdrawal. Transitions to higher levels of behavioral organization come about through association of the effective stimuli with neutral stimuli, which sets up the conditions for emancipation and elaboration of control, from which the still higher levels of cognitive function emerge (Schneirla, 1959b, 1965). In his enthusiasm for this theory, Schneirla may have attempted to apply it too broadly. As a consequence, he sometimes appeared to slip into circular argument, as when his only grounds for considering a stimulus to be of low or high intensity were whether the stimulus induced approach or withdrawal. Apologists argue that this does not really matter, because Schneirla was not proposing an explanatory theory but an approach to the comparative and developmental study of animal behavior. Whether regarded as theory or approach, Schneirla's perspective has received less attention than it probably merits. Part of the reason is that it was so far to the side of mainstream views.

However, Schneirla was not so far from the mainstream as to be completely independent of the influences that flowed in it. The roles he assigned to experience and association were in the tradition; so much so that Lorenz's polemics against behaviorism included Schneirla with those who were scathingly criticized for being so uninformed about animal behavior as to believe that everything an animal does is learned. Schneirla's concept of levels also has echoes of the old *Scala naturae* idea, even though he emphasized qualitative differences and was ranking behavioral capacities, not kinds of animals. Being a single series of levels, his conception made it difficult to accommodate all forms of behavioral organization neatly, the echinoderms being especially awkward because they were at a relatively low level according to some respects (e.g., lack of anterior-posterior polarity and cephalization) and at a higher level according to others (e.g., discrete muscles instead of a muscle-field system). The levels ordering was not intended to picture phyletic ordering, but in some ways it was at variance with the phyletic perspective, according to which evolution is viewed as a radiating or diverging pattern, within which each kind of organism has its own unique path which may have led it to its own unique kind of behavioral organization. Given his alertness to qualitative differences, this side of the Darwinian view should have, and no doubt did, appeal to Schneirla.

Another who brought comparative perspective to comparative psychology is Beach. In his research, Beach concentrated on reproductive behavior in mammals, comparing different species with regard to the roles of sensory stimulation, experience, hormonal control, and other factors. He has, for example, drawn attention to the extent to which, as one goes from rat to cat to monkey to human, the control of sexual behavior becomes less under the control of physiological factors and more under the control of psychological factors. But he has also warned against the too simple view of seeing these differences as constituting a smooth series, by pointing out anomalies consequent on the fact that each species is adapted to its ecological niche, not the human penchant for linear order (Beach, 1971). With this we have regained contact with the biological perspective that Darwinism gave to functional psychology but which faded from view during the years when behaviorism dominated animal psychology in America.

However, Beach's biological perspective on animal psychology was turned predominantly in the reductionist direction of physiology. Physiological psychology did not begin with Beach. Indeed it was the convergence of physiology with associationistic psychology that carried psychology from the end of its "long past" to the beginning of its "short history" in the middle of the nineteenth century. And, since Lashley, there had been many psychologists with behaviorist affiliations who had sought in brain tissue for the physical substrates of learning and memory. Beach helped to broaden the physiological perspective by treating the causal control of reproductive behavior as something to be investigated aside from any relevance it might have for learning theory, and also by including a range of species sufficiently various to reveal differences demanding a comparative approach. Without going any further into the many developments that have taken place, we can now say that the field covered by the title "physiological and comparative psychology" has at last earned its name.

Even so, the priorities of the parent traditions can still be discerned in the preoccupations of the present. Research on mammals far outstrips research on other kinds of animals in the work of physiological psychology, even on matters other than the physical basis of learning and memory. Moreover, when other kinds of animals have been the subject of study, it has predominately been in research on learning and memory. For example, some people have turned to invertebrates with relatively simple nervous systems in the hope that in such animals the locus of learning can be more easily pinned down and the memory mechanism more easily understood than in vertebrates. Passive avoidance has been taught to isolated thoracic segments of cockroaches (e.g., Eisenstein & Cohen, 1965), and habituation has been investigated in *Aplysia* (e.g., Kandel, 1974). In the case of the latter, the ganglia involved in the change in response contain only a small number of neurones, which have been fully mapped. Isolation of the ganglia and intracellular recording from the neurones have revealed synaptic changes coincident with and presumably productive of the behavioral changes. It seems to have been at least tacitly assumed that whatever is found to be the case in these studies of simpler neural systems will apply to more complex systems, the differences being in degree of complexity rather than in kind (see Fentress, 1976). Again, the doctrine of continuity may have led to the begging of questions.

However, subjecting different kinds of animals to the same kinds of test of learning capacity has produced some results that at least qualify the assumption of continuity. Bitterman has followed this course. He has found, for example, that fishes and rats differ when tested with habit reversal, and also when tested with a probability problem in which one alternative stimulus is reinforced in, say, 70% of the trials, and the other stimulus is reinforced in the remaining 30%. In Bitterman's experiments, a fish never mastered the habit-reversal problem, whereas a rat gets the solution after only a few trials; in probability learning, the fish showed "random matching"—they selected the stimuli in the proportions that matched the reinforcement ratio—whereas the rats "maximized" by settling down to always choosing the more frequently reinforced stimulus (Bitterman, 1965). Bitterman went on to test other kinds of animals and add variety to the test problems; the pattern that emerged was one showing qualitative differences between phyletic levels, with the modes of learning at the "higher" levels (mammals and birds) being "a considerable functional advance" over those at the lower levels (fish and invertebrates). However, Bitterman (1965) noted that ordering the animals according to these behavioral criteria did not reproduce the phyletic relationships between the species selected for study: "Nonlinearities are perhaps to be expected as the behavioral categories are refined and as the range of tests is broadened [p. 409]."

Nonlinearities are also to be expected for the reason that evolutionary adaptation has led different kinds of animals in different directions. Lehrman liked to tell how he once raised with an expert in operant conditioning the possibility of shaping a bird so that it would perform the courtship display of a different species, or court at times, or places, or in ways different from the usual and so serve as a means of analyzing species-specific social behavior. He was told that the plan would probably not work because operant-conditioning techniques do not work at all well with the kinds of behavior he was talking about (Lehrman, 1971). The point had already been made by Breland and Breland (1961), two behavioral psychologists who used the techniques of the operant laboratory in the training of performing animals for circuses, television shows, and the like. They reported that although such applied uses of the techniques usually have considerable success, from time to time there are failures to achieve the intended result. They concluded that ways of behaving are not all equal as far as flexibility to molding by conditioning is concerned. Bolles (1970) arrived at a similar conclusion with regard to avoidance behavior, arguing that there are "species-specific defense reactions" that associate more easily than any other kinds of behavior to aversive situations. Finally, Garcia and his associates (e.g., Garcia, McGowan, & Green, 1972) brought attention to the fact that there are exceptions to the rule that reinforcement must be immediate for either classical or operant conditioning; in the case of acquisition of a taste aversion, the negative reinforcement produced by nausea or sickness can be delayed for an hour or more, at least if the subject is a rat. The survival value of this for the rat is not hard to imagine: The bad effects of eating something poisonous may well not be experienced for some time, and, if the animal survives, its chances of continuing to do so will be favored by its rejecting whatever occasioned the experience. A personal experience of this sort with Béarnaise sauce helped to lead Seligman to question the "equipotentiality premise" according to which any stimulus can be linked to any response with more or less equal ease. He arrived at the conclusion that associability is a variable, the value of which may be a reflection of evolutionary adaptation, as in the case of a rat's (and a man's) predisposition to associate experience of being poisoned with the taste of the food eaten. For the degree of associability obtaining between any US/CS pair, or any stimulus/response pair, Seligman proposed the term "preparedness" (Seligman, 1970; Seligman & Hager, 1972).

The work I have just been discussing is in the mainstream tradition of comparative psychology as I have represented it, at least in that it is concerned with laws of learning and in its predilection for mammals. But with notions like species-specific defense reactions and preparedness surfacing in the flow, we are returned to something like the perspective in Darwinian biology from which we started. And in this return there is convergence with that other stream that flows from Darwin, the European tradition of comparative ethology, which is our next subject.

But first, a short recapitulation. Rising in Darwinism and converging with associationism, comparative psychology began as anthropomorphism and gravitated to behaviorism. A major premise of most of the reasoning was the conception of biological and psychological continuity between man and beast. United with its major interest in learning, this defined for comparative psychology its major goal: elucidation of the universal laws of learning. Only recently have comparative psychologists come seriously to question the assumption that there are such laws. At the same time interest in matters other than learning has increased, and appreciation of the full diversity of behavior in the animal kingdom has come into competition with the traditional partiality for the few types that had been judged most convenient for an experiment bearing on the human case. Even so, there is still some truth to the observation that comparative psychologists are psychologists who study the behavior of animals rather than that of people. In contrast, ethologists are zoologists who study the behavior of animals rather than other aspects of their biology (cf. Lehrman, 1964).

COMPARATIVE ETHOLOGY

The Origin of Species contained two arguments: one for the thesis that evolution has occurred; the other for the thesis that the cause of evolution is natural selection. Evolutionary study has been divided between the two corresponding questions or perspectives ever since: history and process, phylogeny and adaptation. Comparative study provided the clues in both cases. Indeed, it began doing so long before the theory of evolution came into its inheritance.

Ever since the time of Aristotle, comparison of the forms of organisms had revealed that types could be grouped as variations on a theme. Hence came the idea of the *Great Chain of Being* and zoological and botanical classifications. Shared patterns of structural organization, such as we recognize in vertebrates or arthropods, were abstracted and defined as "archetypes" by the anatomists of the eighteenth and early nineteenth centuries. They argued vehemently about how many such archetypes had to be postulated to accommodate all the varieties of form (Russell, 1916); but in the pursuit of evidence to support their cases they enriched and refined the comparative study of morphology. Central to the business was identification of the same feature in different structures. According to St. Hilaire: "the sole general principle one can apply is given by the position, the relations, and the dependencies of the parts, that is to say, by what I name and include under the term *connections* [in Russell, 1916, p. 53]." The concept so defined is that of homology: correspondence between a part of one structure and a part of another with respect to the pattern of organization to which the two structures conform.

Beside this emphasis on purely structural considerations in the interpretation of similarities and differences of form, there was a competing emphasis on function, according to which forms—and hence the similarities and differences among them—could be interpreted in terms of the uses to which they are put, their utility as means of coping with the demands and hazards of an organism's environment and way of life. Thus the differences among the forelimbs of horses, bats, and gibbons reflect their different uses: running, flying, swinging from branch to branch. It was this perspective that appealed to the natural theologians, for it provided what was taken as evidence of rational design in nature and so implied the existence of God as designer.

The question of whether structure or function should be regarded as primary in morphological comparison was another matter about which opinions were divided and hotly debated, especially in France, during this period. Much of this was without useful issue, but the discussion made an important distinction explicit: the distinction between structural homologies and structural analogies. The eminent English anatomist Owen (1848) made a clear statement of the matter. Homology holds between two structures when they occupy corresponding positions in a structural design common to whatever forms carry them, irrespective of the function they serve. Analogy, in this technical sense, holds between two structures when they possess at least superficially similar form in accordance with a function common to them

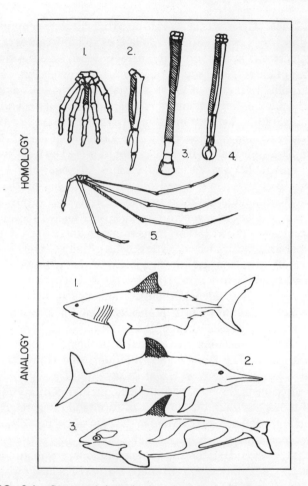

FIG. 2.1. Structural homology and analogy. Homology: the third
metacarpal bones (cross-hatched) of (1) human; (2) bird; (3) horse; (4)
antelope; (5) bat. Analogy: the dorsal fins (cross-hatched) of (1) shark; (2)
ichthyosaur; (3) whale.

both, irrespective of whether structural correspondence exists as well (Figure
2.1). To take the customary examples: The forelimbs of a horse and the wings
of a bird are homologous but not analogous; the wings of a bird and the wings
of a mosquito are analogous but not homologous; the wings of a bird and the
wings of a bat are both homologous and analogous.

This distinction between homology and analogy roughly parallels the
distinction between phylogeny and adaptation. But phylogeny and
adaptation (in this context) are evolutionary concepts; homology and
analogy came before the theory of evolution gave them historical

explanation. Indeed, Owen was never converted to belief in evolution and was one of its most caustic critics. But the similarities and differences of form on which judgments of homology and analogy were based provided an important part of the evidence supporting the thesis of evolution. Taxonomy illustrates the point. In the classification of organisms structure was assumed, generally, to be more basic than function. Shared patterns of structure, on the one hand, and variation between instances of a shared pattern, on the other, defined at least the higher categories in the hierarchical classifications of essentially modern style that we find, for example, in the work of Cuvier (e.g., 1828). Even though he was perhaps the major advocate of the case for function, his classification was based on affinities judged on the basis of similarities and differences of "deep structure." But these formal affinities would obtain if, as Darwin argued, organisms were related to one another through descent, with modification, from common ancestors—if, that is to say, the formal affinities reflected phylogenetic affinities. Thus similarities and differences of form, and classification based on them, provided evidence for, and received explanation from, Darwin's thesis that evolution has taken place. Homology became evidence of common ancestry, then it came to imply common ancestry, and nowadays it means common ancestry, at least according to the definitions in most of the textbooks (e.g., Wilson, 1975, p. 586). This change of meaning has created a problem which we shall be concerned with later. The Darwinian revolution stood many concepts on their heads.

However, after the initial furor had subsided, biology continued in the old traditions of judging affinity on the basis of form and interpreting form in terms of function, but both were viewed in the light of the new dispensation. Comparative morphology acquired a new lease of life as the means of working out phylogenetic relationships and evolutionary sequences; concern with evolutionary adaptation was, in effect, Natural Theology with natural selection in the place of God. In spite of severe harassment from Mendelian genetics, these two traditions persisted in having dominating influence in biology well into this century. However, by the end of World War II comparative morphology was in decline, and it now has only a peripheral place in most biology departments. The study of evolutionary adaptation maintains a central place, but it has had to transform itself to do so. At the turn of the century it was largely a matter of imaginative speculation for armchair biologists, which sometimes gave the impression of playing on a "tumbling ground for whimsies"—as in the case of the assertion that flamingos are pink because it makes them hard for predators to see against the sunset (Thayer, 1909). In 1980, it is largely a matter of experiments and mathematical models deployed in refined ways by ecologists and population geneticists. Among the newer movements in biology, ethology, it can be argued, has been the most conservative—that it remained truer to the spirit of these two traditions and persisted in them longer. That is my view, and in what follows I discuss each of the traditions as they are represented in ethology.

Behavior and Phylogeny

Most of the zoologists who founded ethology were trained in departments in which comparative morphology was still a dominant discipline. Its study required painstaking scrutiny of such things as the appendages of a crab, the bones of a fish's skull, the blood supply to a salamander's respiratory system, or the cranial nerves of a sea leopard, and then seeing how they conform to the arthropod or vertebrate patterns, as variations on the themes of segmental organization. Such work took in both fossil and fresh material, both embryonic and mature forms. The conclusions about what was homologous to what were often far from obvious, and consequently to arrive at the point of perceiving how they followed from the evidence was sometimes to experience intellectual delight of a rare quality, not easily distinguished from the experience we call aesthetic. Take, for example, the demonstration of homology between the malleus and incus (middle ear bones) of mammals and the quadrate and articular (jaw hinge) of other vertebrates. However, training in comparative morphology is tedious, the learning of endless and apparently pointless details in a discipline with apparently no future, compared to the exciting prospects opening up elsewhere in biology. As comparative morphology was shouldered from the center to the periphery of the curriculum it became something of a lost art.

A lost *art*? The play on the word is serious. I believe that an aesthetic ingredient is part of the perception that goes into the pursuit of comparative morphology, as well as into the experience of it. Most of the great anatomists of the past were accomplished draftsmen. In the days before photography they had to depict what they saw. But in composition, style, and finish their drawings often went beyond the requirements of accurate and precise representation.

Bell's (e.g., 1802) drawings of the human body and Huxley's (1936) drawings of the medusae he collected on the *Rattlesnake* voyage are examples of work showing such assurance of line and delicacy of detail that they are now regarded as works of art. Even for the less accomplished draftsmen, competence in morphology demanded the precise eye for details of form and the kind of feeling for spatial relationships that we find in painters and sculptors. Even today, an ability to draw accurately and to visualize complex relationships in three-dimensional space continues to be as useful to the anatomist as his scalpel and microscope. Consider, for example, their application in the reading and rendering of serial sections.

I believe it to be no mere coincidence that the ethologists who have been concerned with description and comparison of what might be called the surface structure of behavior—the outward forms of behavior patterns as opposed to the physiological mechanisms underlying them—have typically been able draftsmen, in some cases even gifted artists. Both Lorenz and Tinbergen have illustrated their writings with distinctive drawings; Morris, Moynihan, and Manley have achievements as artists that compare to their successes as scientists. One could extend the list, and add to it the superb camera work of many field ethologists, of which Tinbergen's is among the most impressive. In general, comparative ethology, like comparative morphology, gives the impression of being sensitive to aesthetic as well as to scientific values, combining portrayal of beauty with the recording of truth. The highly refined sensitivity to form and formal correspondences that the artist's eye brings to the perception of comparative morphologist and comparative ethologist alike gives the seeing of the kind of essential sameness that is homology.

Application of the notion of homology to the study of behavior brought comparative ethology into being. At least that is the story according to Lorenz. In his Nobel Prize acceptance lecture he said:

> I had the benefit of a very thorough instruction in the methological [sic] procedure of distinguishing similarities caused by common descent from those due to parallel adaptation. This procedure led me to the discovery which I personally consider to be my own most important contribution to science. Knowing animal behavior as I did, and being instructed in the methods of phylogenetic comparison as I was, I could not fail to discover that the very same methods of comparison, the same concepts of analogy and homology, are as applicable to characters of behavior as they are to those of morphology [1974, p. 231].

He acknowledged that there had been anticipations of his discovery, just as there had been of Darwin's, but, like Darwin, he could claim to be the first to realize the full significance of what he had found. Darwin himself drew the parallel between anatomical and behavioral comparison. In his chapter on instinct in *The Origin of Species* he stated what became one of the working principles of comparative ethology: "As in the case of corporeal structures, we ought to find in nature, not the actual transitional gradations by which each complex instinct has been acquired—for these could be found only in the lineal ancestors of each species—but we ought to find in the collateral lines of descent some evidence of such graduations [p. 185]." Darwin put this principle to work in later writings, especially in *The Expression of the Emotions in Man and Animals* (1872), where he argued that behavior expressive of emotional state, and hence socially communicative, has derived from behavior having quite other functions. The snarl of rage or the grimace of fear, for example, can be interpreted as derived from baring of the teeth in preparation for biting in attack or defense. The idea that display behavior is an evolutionary derivative of other kinds of behavior was developed further in the interpretations that ornithologists began making in behavioral studies of birds. In Britain, Selous worked with the idea, first implicitly and later explicitly. For example, in an account of the breeding behavior of the Red-throated Diver (or Loon, *Gavia stellata*), he described certain "antics" as constituting a "pageant" or "ceremonial" (Selous, 1914, p. 209); and later he wrote of "formalization" as the evolution of such display patterns from behavior of other sorts (Selous, 1933). Huxley (1923), also writing of the Red-throated Diver, used the word "ritual," hence "ritualization"—"adaptive evolutionary change in the direction of increased efficiency as a signal [Tinbergen, 1959, p. 44]." In America, Whitman took a similar but broader evolutionary view of behavior. In his studies of pigeons and doves, Whitman (1919) found that the way in which these birds drink defines them more consistently and exclusively as a taxonomic group than any morphological characteristic. From such observations, he came to the conclusion that "instincts and organs are to be studied from the common viewpoint of phyletic descent [Whitman, 1899, p. 287]." In Germany, Heinroth (1911) took the same view in his comparative treatment of the behavior of ducks and geese.

Lorenz became a pupil of Heinroth and carried further the work on duck behavior. He studied many other kinds of animals as well, but it is perhaps in his duck work that his approach is most fully revealed in operation (Lorenz, 1941). Like Whitman and Heinroth, Lorenz concentrated on the particularly stereotyped patterns of behavior, for, he claimed, it is among these that one finds the movements that animals " 'have got', exactly in the same manner as they 'have got' claws or teeth of a definite morphological structure [1950, p. 238]" and which can be treated comparatively in the manner that uncovers homology. He came to regard such species-typical stereotyped movements as quite different in kind from all other kinds of behavior. He called them "instinctive activities" (Instinkthandlungen) and argued that they were the only patterns of behavior to which this term could be rightly applied. Against the views of Morgan and Spencer, Lorenz (1935, in Schiller, 1957) maintained that there is no continuity between instinct on the one hand and intelligence or reason on the other, either in a phylogenetic sense or in an ontogenetic sense: "Innate behavior on the one side, and acquired and insightful behavior on the other, are not successive stages, either ontogenetically or phylogenetically, but represent two divergent lines of development [p. 99]."

Here we must pause to consider a problem that was already present in Darwin's writings: the multiple meanings of the words "instinct" and "instinctive." In his chapter on instinct in *The Origin of Species,* Darwin started by sidestepping the question of definition. "I will not attempt any definition of instinct," he said; "It would be easy to show that several distinct mental actions are commonly embraced by this term; but everyone understands what is meant, when it is said that instinct impels the cuckoo to migrate and to lay her eggs in other birds' nests [p. 184]." Having thus introduced the idea of impulsion, he went on to add performance prior to experience of its consequences, performance in the same way by many individuals of the species in question and performance without knowledge of its purpose, all as characteristics of actions that are "usually said to be instinctive [p. 184]." Elsewhere in the book he applied the term to dispositions such as courage and obstinancy in dogs, to feelings such as sympathy in people, and to sequential combinations of a few stereotyped acts ordered to the production of ends as adaptively sophisticated as the honeycomb of a beehive and the nest of a weaverbird.

Although he recognized that "none of these characters are universal" in what is "usually said to be instinctive," Darwin apparently saw no problem associated with the consequent ambiguity of the word. He often used "instinct" as a single concept that combined many different meanings, and hence licensed him to assume that evidence for one of the meanings was evidence for others. For example, he sometimes inferred from evidence for the genetic inheritance of a way of behaving that the behavior is independent of experience in ontogeny. Many others since Aquinas have done likewise; thus Lorenz vested the concept that was implicit in Darwin explicitly in his singular category of "instinctive activity."

But saying something is so does not necessarily make it so. Many of Lorenz's own examples do not conform in all respects to his conception of instinctive activity. For instance, the locomotory movements of songbirds, the feeding techniques of gulls, and most of the display movements of ducks, which Lorenz used to illustrate the kinds of behavior that animals "have got," all show orientation to the situation in which they occur. Yet instinctive activities were supposed to be controlled solely from within the animal: "The turn that orients the animal in space cannot, by definition, be an innate action [Lorenz, 1937, in Schiller, 1957, p. 140]." In some cases, such as the egg rolling of the Greylag goose (Lorenz & Tinbergen, 1938), it was found possible to distinguish an oriented component from a fixed component in the action. For many other actions it is so hard to see how this might be done, or seems so forced when it is done, that the only reason for trying would seem to be to save the phenomenon. Here the distinction is necessitated by the conception of instinct rather than by how the behavior strikes the uncommitted eye. Another problem is that, more often than not, what needs to be proved is simply assumed. Critics such as Lehrman (1953) and Beach (1955) pointed out that an understanding of ontogenetic development requires developmental study, it is not to be had from evidence of evolutionary descent, adaptive significance, or even genetic inheritance. Instinctive activities were supposed to be innate in the sense of genetically inherited, and also in the sense of ontogenetically independent of experience. For Lorenz, the former entailed the latter, but this was to put the logic of a conception in the place of inference from pertinent facts. He conspired in the mischief of ambiguity that the words "innate" and "instinctive" have so often worked, and his doing so reveals the ground of assumption on which much of his theory of instinct was based. This is an irony, for in criticizing the work of others, Lorenz (1950) said: "It means striking at the very roots of the teachings of a scientific school if one accuses it of insufficient knowledge of facts, of insufficient basis of induction.... It is an inviolable law of inductive natural science that it has to *begin* with pure observation, totally devoid of any preconceived theory and even working hypothesis [p. 232]."

But pure observation is a myth, and no scientist could get started without preconceived ideas (see Popper, 1959, 1963). The important thing is not where the scientist starts from, but where he ends up, at least as far as the advancement of his science is concerned. In fact, Lorenz did not stick consistently to his conception of instinctive activity in his deployment of the comparative morphological approach in behavior studies. Had he done so he would have deprived himself of a large number of the cases that have been found to be of value for phylogenetic interests. Behavior patterns need to be no more than stereotyped in form and characteristic of the species to be amenable to the comparative approach and its application of the notion of homology.

Before we can make headway from this point, we have again to grapple with the problem of what homology is supposed to be. I have mentioned how the evolutionary explanation preempted the meaning of the term in anatomy; instead of correspondence of position in structures having the same design, the definition now usually given for homology is similarity due to common evolutionary origin. Even so, anatomists still draw conclusions about evolutionary origins from evidence of homology based on morphological comparison (e.g., Karten, 1969). Clearly there has to be a way of judging homology independently of evolutionary considerations for this to be valid. Such judgment is arrived at in the way in which it always was: by tracing the patterns of connections between parts of structures and comparing them with structures believed to share the same archetype. The menace of circularity that invests arguments using the notion of homology can be avoided by distinguishing what might be called the conceptual meaning of the term from the criteria for its application, or, more shortly, the sense or connotation of the term from its reference or denotation. The sense was transformed by Darwin, but the reference remains much what it was for Owen (Beer, 1977).

The ethological notion of homology has the same sense as the anatomical notion: "similarities caused by common descent [Lorenz, 1974, p. 231]." The reference is different in that it is to behavior in the one case and to structure in the other; but Lorenz and others seem to imply that there is a deeper identity—that the criteria of application are essentially the same for behavioral and structural homology (see Baerends, 1958; Eibl-Eibesfeldt, 1967; Wickler, 1961, 1967). If this is so, if what is really an analogy between behavior and morphology is at all close, then there should be a behavioral equivalent of St. Hilaire's Principle of Connections on the basis of which behavioral homology can be judged. Three possibilities suggest themselves: position in sequences, role in functional contexts, and membership in shared repertoires. Each can be found in use as argument for judgment of homology in such comparative ethological studies as Lorenz's (1941) monograph on duck behavior. None by itself is sufficient to define behavioral homology for all occasions.

The position of a movement in the sequences of movements in which it occurs is often very constant within a species, especially in the kinds of display behavior on which Lorenz focused much of his attention; but it can differ markedly between even closely related species. In such cases identification of the "same" movement in the different species must depend on criteria other than sequential position.

Movements judged to be homologous often occur in the same functional context—courtship interactions, agonistic encounters, parent-young communication, and so forth—and serve the same roles within these contexts—greeting, threat, appeasement, begging, luring, and so forth—but this is by no means universal. As the notion of ritualization implies, evolution can change the function of homologous movements. In any case, if the parallel with structure applies, functional considerations are irrelevent to judgments of homology. They reveal analogy only, which at least since the days of Owen we have been taught to distinguish rigorously from homology. In evolutionary terms the contrast is between characteristics related to one another through descent from the same ancestral character and characteristics similar to one another through adaptation to the same functional requirements.

The idea that behavioral repertoires of different species can be compared to one another as sets with corresponding categories of membership has led ethologists to seek and find in one species the representative of a movement they first observed in another. For example, Tinbergen's description of the display behavior of herring gulls *(Larus argentatus)* in *The Herring Gull's World* (1953) did not include "head-flagging"; he did not look for and find this display in herring gulls until after he had become familiar with the more prominent and obvious version of it in the repertoire of black-headed gulls *(Larus ridibundus)*. But correspondence between the repertoire of one species and the repertoire of another is usually less than complete. In his comparisons of the behavior of ducks, Lorenz found that sharing of a display repertoire between duck species is a matter of degree. Some display types are represented in most species; others are restricted to only a few. This enabled Lorenz to use behavioral evidence to argue degrees of taxonomic relatedness between the species. Here the extent of repertoire held in common was judged on the basis of judgment about homology, so the criteria of homology must have been independent of a sharing of the repertoire.

Failing a consistent analogy to the Principle of Connections, the search for criteria of behavioral homology has to turn to similarity. This is what most of the definitions give as the outward sign of homology (including, currently, even structural homology), but it is vague and begs the question. In the first place, things can be similar in any number of respects; the question is: In what respects must things be similar to be homologous? Second, things may resemble one another only in degree, and it is an open question what degree justifies a judgment of homology. Third, and perhaps most crucial, similarities can arise through evolutionary convergence as well as through evolutionary descent, and the problem, for comparative ethologists and comparative morphologists alike, is to distinguish the two—analogy from homology. In the absence of other criteria, therefore, evidence of common evolutionary origin will be necessary to distinguish those similarities that signify homology from those that do not. For example, the gull display called "head-flagging," mentioned above, looks very much like a duck display called "hind-head"—in both cases the displaying bird turns its head so as to face away from the bird displayed to. Head-flagging and hind-head are not regarded as homologous because gulls and ducks are not closely related phylogenetically. But the head-flagging displays of the different species of gulls are regarded as homologous, as are the hind-head displays of the different species of ducks, because of the evidence of phylogenetic affinity that defines these groups (Figure 2.2).

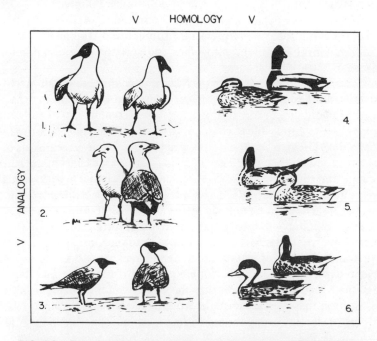

FIG. 2.2.   Behavioral homology and analogy. Head-flagging displays of (1) black-headed gull; (2) herring gull; (3) laughing gull (all drawn from photographs). Hind-head displays of (4) mallard duck; (5) pintail duck; (6) bahama duck (all after Lorenz, 1941).

If judgments of behavioral homology are based on evidence of descent, can we legitimately draw conclusions about descent from judgments of behavioral homology? The use to which behavioral characteristics have been put in systematics, as in Lorenz's (1941) work on ducks, implies that we can. But for the inference from behavior to phylogenetic relationship to be free of circularity we need a definition of behavioral homology that does not include reference to phylogenetic relationship, and this we have failed to find.

Given this situation it is small wonder that some people, including some ethologists, have dismissed behavioral homology, and the whole attempt to use comparison to arrive at phylogenetic interpretation of behavior, as too loose and muddled to be worth a scientist's attention. Thus Blest (1961, p. 103) says, "any statement about specific evolutionary events in a given group needs cautious handling, for it is never likely to be more than an inspired guess." Atz (1970) concurs: "The essentially morphological concept of homology cannot at present be applied to behavior in any meaningful (nontrite) way because of its lack of structural correlates [p. 69]." Hodos (1970) has argued that the only way in which the concept of homology might legitimately be applied to behavior is via the dependence of behavior on structure: Behavior patterns might be called homologous if they were known to have structurally homologous neural substrates. Klopfer (1973, 1976) would likewise make behavior subservient to structure in the marshaling of evidence for evolutionary interpretation. Klopfer and Hailman (1976) find talk of behavioral homology altogether too soft for their tough-minded standards of scientific discourse.

Yet Lorenz accepted his share of the Nobel Prize with the reflection that his "most important contribution to science" has been his discovery "that the very same methods of comparison, the same concepts of analogy and homology, are as applicable to characteristics of behavior as they are to those of morphology [1974, p. 231]." He may well be right. Deep as the thrusts of his critics have been on this issue, they may have missed the heart of the matter. Homology and the comparison that assumes and reveals it are perceptual in nature. The critics have judged the attempts to define homology in the abstract or in general to be failures by the standards of a rigorous scientific logic. But homology in theory may be distinguished from homology in practice. Concrete instances of perceived correspondences in form, both of structure and of behavior, can be compellingly real to anyone who takes the trouble to experience them. The trouble required is not inconsiderable. It is no less than that needed to develop the expertise for spotting significant details of form that, at least since the work of Morelli (see Wollheim, 1973), has become necessary to anyone pretending to connoisseurship in the study of art.

I make the comparison between ethology and art again in all seriousness. The kind of sensitivity to the precise way in which hands, ears, drapery, and so forth are drawn, the motor habits revealed in brush strokes and the movement of line, by means of which an art connoisseur judges a painting to be a Watteau, say, and can place it in the development of that master's oeuvre, is essentially similar to that which enables an anatomist to recognize a bone as from a primitive parrot's palate and an ethologist to see the courtship movement of a duck as a highly ritualized form of preening. Art connoisseurs have, of course, made incorrect attributions from time to time. The anatomist's and the ethologist's perceptions are fallible also. Science aims at being infallible, but precautions against the risk of being wrong can be carried too far. To get at questions of the form "from what did such and such a behavior pattern evolve?" or "do behavior pattern X and behavior Y have the same or different ancestral origins?" we have to be able to put behavior patterns in homological correspondence with one another. If the detection of such correspondence is basically a perceptual matter, then we shall just have to make do with that and take what precautions we can against the fallibility of perceptual judgment. The alternative is to rule, as some have, that such questions about the evolution of behavior are so beyond the possibility of final answers that they should not be allowed to take up a scientist's time.

If such a rule were consistently applied, however, it would carry away with it more than might have been bargained for. Even Darwin's case for the thesis that evolution has occurred would not be safe, for it is a best-fit kind of argument which persuades by its plausibility, not by the kind of deductive proof that justifies "Q.E.D." The arguments of comparative morphology and comparative ethology are also best-fit kinds of argument. They win consent by the order they bring to accumulated fact, their economy compared to alternative possibilities, the alliances they coherently form with other such arguments. Order, economy, coherence—why should it be assumed that the world has these attributes? There is no logically necessary principle that says it must be so. But there is the human preference for simplicity, reasonableness, and stability that would have it so. Again aesthetic values intrude into the cold court of scientific judgment and temper objectivity with taste.

This argument for behavioral homology will appear weak and seem to beg the question for anyone unfamiliar with comparative ethological analysis; and many ethologists will no doubt object to what they will view as a retreat into subjectivity in the suggestion that behavioral homology is basically a matter of how things look to an ethologist's practiced eye. As in the case of judgments about works of art, all that one can finally do to try to make one's point is stand the spectator in front of the works and ask him to look. Examples of what Kaplan (1964) called the "logic in use" of a concept may be the only means of conveying what it means. The logic in use of the notion of behavioral homology is best exemplified by the accounts of ritualization, such as can be found in Daanje (1950), Lorenz (1941, 1958), and Tinbergen (1952, 1959). The interested reader is referred to them.

These accounts of ritualization frequently appeal to evidence from graded series: Highly stereotyped display patterns in some species are linked to relatively unstereotyped "utilitarian" behavior in some other species via intermediate forms exhibited by their close relatives. The argument is that in some species the behavior in question has remained more or less unchanged from the ancestral form it has in common with the ritualized derivatives, which also show differing degrees of departure from this ancestral form. This is essentially the Darwinian argument about "transitional gradations." It is illustrated by the evolutionary interpretation given to the threat display of the Manchurian crane *(Grus japonensis)*, which appeared quite singular until comparison showed that it is continuous with a graded series of patterns in other species of crane (Lorenz, 1935). But this is only one of a variety of types of argument deployed in discussions of ritualization. As we have seen, the judgments of homology are not all founded on one criterion, but on particular overlappings and continuities in the forms of the behavior, the functions and contexts of occurrence of the behavior, what might be believed about the ontogenetic origins of the behavior, and the phylogenetic affinities of the species concerned.

The function for which social displays are specialized (by ritualization) is the eliciting of social reactions in conspecifics. For reasons that have to do with his instinct theory, Lorenz described such displays as "releasers." He likened the connection between a releaser and the reaction it releases to the connection between a word and what it means: both are matters of historically based "convention." Just as common historical origin is the only plausible explanation for the similarity of form of the words for, say, female parent in the languages of Europe—mother, Mutter, mater, madre, moeder, moder, mère, and so forth—so it is for similarity of form between displays that release the same kind of social reaction in closely related species. "Since its specific form, like the signs of a signal code or Morse alphabet, is determined purely historically, the identity of two releasing actions almost *always spells homology* [Lorenz, 1937, in Schiller, 1957, p. 148]."

However, the connection between a display or releaser and what it conveys or elicits may not be as arbitrary as is, in most cases, the connection between the form of a word and its meaning. Displays are often iconic in ways that words rarely are. This iconicity reflects the historical origin of a display, or so it is believed, and thus supplies the comparative ethologist with clues to that origin. According to the observations of Daanje (1950), many of the displays of birds can be interpreted as ritualized derivatives of movements initiating locomotion. The crouch precedent to takeoff, the imminence of which is signaled by the display, is an example. Similarly, the "Upright" threat posture of gulls has been interpreted by Tinbergen (1953, 1959) to consist of a combination of the beginning motions of attacking and fleeing, the actions between which a bird performing the display will be vacillating. These initial parts of actions are known to the comparative ethologist as "intention movements." According to comparative ethological analysis, ritualization of intention movements has been one of the main derivations of displays. It draws on the behavior the tendency towards which the display expresses. Thus the display represents iconically what it signifies, at least in the earlier stages of its evolution.

The accounts of behavioral evolution in terms of ritualization come from several different kinds of analyses. Those distinguished by Tinbergen (1959) are form analysis, situation analysis, and sequence analysis. In form analysis one looks closely at the shapes of the components of a display movement or posture and compares them to the shapes of components of other behavior, both in the same species and in closely related species that might be possible candidates as unritualized or less extremely ritualized homologues. Thus, for example, Tinbergen saw the Upright of the herring gull as a combination of "frozen" components of attack and escape. Situation analysis attends closely to the details of the circumstances in which a display occurs and compares these to the circumstances in which what might be homologous behavior occurs. The herring gull adopts the Upright at the boundary of its territory and other situations where there is reason to believe that the bird is caught between an urge to attack and an urge to flee, the two kinds of action from which the components of the display are believed to be derived. Sequence analysis looks at what a displaying animal typically does before and after performance of the display in question to see whether some sequential relationship to behavior suspected of being homologous to the display might be perceived. The actions most often preceding and following performance of an Upright by a herring gull are attacking and fleeing; this is consistent with the evidence from form and situation analysis that the Upright in this and other species of gull has its evolutionary origin in attack and escape movements. As in comparative morphology, a further source of evidence which is sometimes used could be called ontogenetic analysis. By studying the ontogenetic precursors of display behavior, one can sometimes find support for ideas about the evolutionary precursors. Moynihan (1959) made some use of this approach in his comparative studies of gulls, observing that some of their displays emerge gradually as progressively more distinct and rigid patterns from initially variable and rather formless congeries of behavior, in a manner which he described as "ontogenetic ritualization." The comparisons and the arguments drawn out of them or woven around them have a close family resemblance to those of comparative morphology.

These modes of analysis in comparative ethology have little of the precision that goes with techniques called by the same name in the physical sciences, such as volumetric analysis or spectral analysis in chemistry. For one thing, the ethological analyses and comparisons can rarely be expressed in quantitative terms. Lord Kelvin's (1891-1894) opinion, that unless a statement can be expressed in numbers it is not scientific, is probably shared by few today. Even so, until a discipline has reached the age of quantification it is still regarded as scientifically immature. Ethological comparative analysis has more in common with psychoanalysis than with analysis in the physical sciences, and contemporary opinion has been hard on the claim that psychoanalysis is a science. To return to the comparison that has preoccupied me, comparative ethology perhaps has its closest parallel in art appreciation.

When people look at a picture they often have trouble reaching agreement about what to make of it. The same is true of ethologists when they look at animal behavior comparatively. An action may look like a preening movement to one observer but like a nest-building movement to another. The difference is a difference of viewpoint in a very literal sense; it is a matter of how the behavior looks and how this way of looking draws all the other facts that seem to be relevant into a coherent pattern. Seeing is believing, and it is hard to believe that the other person does not see what we do. Comparative ethology thus has something of the weakness of the introspective method that proved to be the Achilles heel of Wundtian psychology. It is no doubt for this reason that the tougher minds in ethology have been mostly taken up with physiological aspects of behavior and tend to have little respect for the comparative approaches. But only a mind toughened to the point of inelasticity would deny that questions about the evolutionary antecedents and genealogies of behavior patterns are real questions. The different kinds of questions raised by animal behavior require different methods of investigation, which is one of the reasons, as Tinbergen (1963) said, we should distinguish between them. For questions about the phylogeny of behavior, the methods are those of comparative ethology, within which the notions of behavioral homology and ritualization are embedded. In spite of the degree to which their application is an art, the integration they have succeeded in bringing to some of the facts about how behavior patterns resemble and differ from one another is at least comparable to that of a science.

The most recent development in the comparative ethology of behavioral phylogeny has been a return to Darwin's (1872) perspective in *The Expression of the Emotions in Man and Animals*. Human facial expression and bodily gesture show similarities and differences across cultures and can be compared to those of other primates. Ethologists have attempted to make precise descriptions of them and account for them in terms of evolutionary origin. A representative sample can be found in Hinde (1972). For example, Eibl-Eibesfeldt presented evidence that some of our expressive movements, such as the "eyebrow flash," are universal to human beings, and so must be assumed to be "phylogenetically acquired." This view was challenged, in its details, by Leach, an anthropologist. Van Hoof and Blurton-Jones argued opposing positions on the varieties of smiling and laughter and their primate precursors. Point of view—perspective—continues to affect what one sees and how one sees it. Indeed, when our own species is the subject of comparative study, ethologists can find themselves so close to their work that it is most difficult to separate fact from predilection.

It is evident from the number of ethologists who end up working on the human case (or at least on primates) that in spite of the claim that ethology deals with behavior for its own sake, the ethologist, like everyone else, finds that the understanding of our own behavior can take precedence over everything else. Tinbergen (1976) has been quite explicit on the matter, arguing that ethology is ready to deal with the problems of human behavior and that these problems, such as population control and international aggression, are so urgent that they must be given priority. Application of ethological ideas to people stimulated public interest in ethology; ethology responded to this interest by creating a popular genre, exemplified by such books as Lorenz's (1963) *On Aggression* and Morris's (1967) *The Naked Ape*. However, there has been too little heed paid to the obvious necessity for caution in the use of the comparative approach. As Tinbergen (1963) said, study of the phylogeny of behavior patterns can be "pursued mainly through comparison of groups of closely related species":

> This limitation to closely allied forms is necessary because it is only here that conclusions about homology (i.e., common descent) can be drawn with any degree of probability. It is due to this restriction that what evidence we have applies to microevolution, particularly to adaptive radiation of relatively recent origin [p. 42].

The confidence that can be placed in judgments of behavioral homology and evolutionary derivations of behavior patterns decreases with an increase in the taxonomic distance between the kinds of animals compared. Rarely can the approach extend beyond species in the same family with any pretense to precision. When Lorenz, for example, draws inferences about people from observations of coral reef fishes or Greylag geese, it is not on the basis of firmly established behavioral homologies or phylogenies. Instead, the argument has to be by functional analogy, and so it is tied up with the question of adaptive significance, the other kind of evolutionary question. To it we now turn.

Behavior and Adaptation

Ethology derived its theoretical framework from academic zoology, but its subject matter came from amateur natural history. For centuries the contemplation of nature has been a favorite occupation of people with the leisure to give to it. Close observation and careful description of nature were not only experienced as activities having their own rewards, they were also regarded as a practice of piety in that they were believed to reveal the intricacy and cohesion in creation's plan, and hence the ingenuity and rationality of the mind of God. According to Willey (1940), nature had greater theological authority than the Bible during the eighteenth century. With Wordsworth and the Romantic Movement, nature itself was deified. The concern with evidence of planning and design in the created world of Natural Theology led to concern with evidence of function and adaptation in the evolved world of Darwinian biology. The behavior of animals was a source of such evidence, and so we can trace ethology's roots back to such works as *The 7th Bridgewater Treatise: On the Power, Wisdom and Goodness of God as Manifested in the Creation of Animals, and in their History, Habits and Instincts* by William Kirby (1835).

Aesthetic considerations and sheer curiosity also influenced the pursuit of natural history. The beautiful and the strange attracted more attention than the plain and commonplace. Again ethology followed in the tradition. Birds, fish, and insects, and the more aesthetically attractive kinds of these, have (at least until recently) been the favorite subjects of ethological study. And the greater proportion of such study has been directed toward the more dramatic and at the same time enigmatic kinds of behavior, such as the postures and movements of display rituals. Lorenz (1950) has made the point:

> I confidently assert that no man, even if he were endowed with a superhuman patience, could physically bring himself to stare at fishes, birds or mammals as persistently as is necessary in order to take stock of the behavior patterns of a species, unless his eyes were bound to the object of his observation in that spellbound gaze which is not motivated by any conscious effort to gain knowledge, but by that mysterious charm that the beauty of living creatures works on some of us! [p. 235]

The charm of beauty and the fascination of riddles to be found in natural history conspired in the production of one of the minor treasures of English literature: White's (1789) *The Natural History of Selbourne*. It contains letters about a wide range of observations, questions, and speculations that occurred to the Reverend White as he went about his parish. In a letter dated February 8, 1772, he wrote: "Such a jealously prevails between the male birds that they can hardly bear to be together in the same hedge or field. Most of the singing and elation of spirits of that time seem to me to be the effect of rivalry and emulation: and it is to this spirit of jealously that I chiefly attribute the equal dispersion of birds in the spring over the face of the country."

In this humble way, White introduced two of the ideas that were to become as important as any in the history of ethological interpretation of the functional significance of behavior: territoriality and the suggestion that bird song is used for its advertisement and defense. Over a hundred years later

Howard (1920), another amateur in natural history, took up the idea of territoriality and made it the subject of a whole book, *Territory in Bird Life*. Convinced that birds secure and defend territories, Howard was faced with two questions: Why do they do it? and, How do they do it? His answer to the first was that the main reason for territorial behavior is that it spaces out the breeding pairs sufficiently to ensure that each will have private access to enough food for the sustenance of the pair and its offspring. This was to explain the behavior in terms of its adaptive significance or survival value, and hence to locate its ultimate or evolutionary cause in the natural selection pressure consequent on limitations of food supply. Subsequent work has shown that this is not always the whole story and may be less the case for some species than for others. But the question and the answer were essentially of the kinds that are pursued today. On the question of how birds secure and defend territory, Howard's answer was that it is mainly by the display of threat, of which the song of songbirds is among the most elaborate examples. This opinion has been substantiated by observation and experiment so conclusively that investigation now takes it as a premise on which to base more detailed deciphering of the "meanings" of the threat signals that a species might display. Such deciphering also tells what the behavior "is for," but in terms of its immediate consequences rather than in terms of its ultimate consequences. It tells, for example, that singing repels intruders, but not why repelling intruders is worth doing. Both kinds of question deal with the functional significance of behavior and so are parts of the general evolutionary question of behavior and adaptation.

Unlike the purely historical questions about behavior evolution, questions of functional significance can often be asked experimentally. Playing recordings of songs, deafening, or devocalization are techniques available for testing how song functions as communication; this is study of immediate consequences. Essentially, the same approach can be used for investigation of the ultimate consequences. You contrive situations such that what you suspect is the benefit of behaving in the way in question is excluded in one and not in another, and compare survival or reproductive success in the two situations. In this way Tinbergen and his associates (Tinbergen et al., 1962) obtained evidence for the possibility that the reason why gulls carry eggshells away from the nest when the chicks hatch is that eggshells in a nest can attract the attention of a predator, i.e., eggshell carrying is an antipredator adaptation—it has the survival value of keeping low the probability of predation.

However, more often than not, the option of doing an experiment is not open for questions of survival value, because the necessary manipulations or the time that would be needed to obtain results are beyond the range of what is practically feasible. In such cases the only resort is to the less direct evidence of "adaptive correlations" (Beer, 1974), which is another use of comparison.

By adaptive correlation I mean both an approach and its objective: You compare species to see what goes with what in the hope that a pattern will emerge that will make adaptive sense of the similarities and differences. The best example of this approach is Cullen's (1957) comparison of Kittiwakes *(Rissa tridactyla)* with other gulls. Kittiwakes are atypical gulls in that they nest on narrow ledges on high cliffs. Most other species nest on the flat of beaches, marshes, or river beds. An adaptive advantage of cliff-nesting is that it virtually excludes predator pressure of the sorts suffered by the ground-nesting gulls. Kittiwakes lack most of what appear to be antipredator adaptations in the other gulls, such as defecation flights and eggshell carrying, which contribute to keeping the nest from becoming conspicuous. On the other hand, cliff-nesting means little latitude for movement on the flat, much risk of falling from a height. Accordingly, Kittiwakes differ from ground-nesting species in having a more elaborate nest-building technique, by means of which they construct a nest with the base reinforced with dried mud, walls that are relatively high, and young which do not leave the nest until they can fly.

The comparative approach of adaptive correlation is now being deployed widely in a movement that has brought ethology into close alliance with ecology. The structure and dynamics of social systems are being viewed as reflections of the ecological factors that have shaped their evolution. Whether food supply is stable or fluctuating, evenly or unevenly distributed, high or low in nutritive concentration may be reflected in whether there is territoriality or free-ranging groups, monogamy or polygamy, parental care or mass propogation. Looking from this perspective, McKinney (1975, 1978) has found that ducks (e.g., *Anas clypeata*) that breed in stable ponds providing a steady supply of rich food are extremely territorial and monogamous; in contrast other ducks (e.g., *Anas acuta*) that breed in areas of transient ponds with a relatively poor and widely dispersed food supply show few signs of territoriality and much promiscuity. McKinney's continuing comparative study of the *Anas* ducks is adding species and detail to this pattern of adaptive correlation.

Adaptive correlation is not just a matter of what goes with what; it also seeks reasons for why the associations are as they are. In the case of his ducks, for instance, McKinney suggests that the reason has to do with what is likely to bring the most return for effort as far as reproductive productivity is concerned. For the *clypeata* the permanence and abundance of the food supply leave enough of a mated male's time and energy after foraging for defense of the territory against encroachment and for defense of the female against the attentions of other males. He thus ensures that his family will have access to adequate food for its needs and that he is truly the father of the brood. For the male *acuta* on the other hand, the ecological situation is such that defense of a territory is usually not feasible because the far ranging and transient nature of the food supply entails more time and energy for defense than a male has to spare. Such time and energy as he has available are more profitably spent, apparently, in trying to inseminate as many females as possible so as to maximize his chances of fathering young that will be lucky enough to be provided with sufficient food to bring them through to maturity.

Considerations such as these have gone a long way in recent years towards making sense of much that was puzzling about the social behavior of different sorts of animals. It has been suggested, for example, that courtship feeding may serve as a test by means of which a female can assess a male's competence in providing for a family (Mills, 1973). A similar interpretation has been suggested for the "incitement" behavior that females show during courtship in many species of ducks: By manipulating a male into a fight with another, a female can assess his quality in competition with other males and so judge whether he would be a good choice as a father of her young. The prolonged courtship common in species having a monogamous mating arrangement may function, at least in part, to assure each partner that the other is committed to the bond and not involved elsewhere (Trivers, 1972).

As these examples illustrate, the functional interpretations or hypotheses that have been suggested by or applied to the data and comparisons from adaptive correlation studies have frequently been couched in figures of speech drawn from the sphere of human affairs. Just as Darwin drew on the economics of his day for many of his key terms and images, so the ecoethologists and sociobiologists of our day readily talk of investment, cost-benefit assessment, commitment, self-interest, ergonomics, payoff, and so forth in regard to the adaptive strategies of animals. The very notion of strategy in this context is only metaphorically related to its primary use in contexts of human doings, where it implies intention, planning, and deliberate choice among alternatives. Similarly, when we read of selfish genes (Dawkins, 1976), the handicap principle (Zahavi, 1975), the Beau Geste effect (Krebs, 1977), and other such terms that involve discussing the animal as though it were a human case, we are not intended to take the terms literally.

Just how much of the literal sense is to be discounted in such metaphorical or analogical use of human terms to describe animal cases is not always clear. Some of the analogies have been drawn so closely and in such a formal way that instead of metaphorical impressionism we have something that seems more like literal realism. Maynard Smith's (1972, 1974, 1976; Maynard Smith & Price, 1973) application of games theory to the evolution of threat display, for example, presents us with a theoretical model that assumes that the same principles applying in games in which decisions are based on weighing the odds apply also to the evolution of behavior adapted to situations involving chancy outcomes.

Such argument from general principles of theoretical biology, especially the theorems of population genetics, to interpretations of and generalizations about the social behavior and social systems of animals, has been canvassed as the preferred strategy in the study of animal behavior. Edward O. Wilson

(1975) contrasts the systematic rigor of this "postulational-deductive" approach to the looseness and arbitrariness of the more common "advocacy" approach, which amounts to fitting facts into a plausible pattern and arguing that the fit proves the pattern. Only by employing "strong inference" in our reasoning, he argues, can we hope to build "a unified science of sociobiology"—sociobiology being defined as "the systematic study of the biological basis of all social behavior [p. 4]." Wilson recognizes that the systematic testing of hypotheses that his program entails will require enormous expenditure of time in observation and analysis to get the relevant information about social structures and dynamics. His book is heavy with such information, yet it has barely enough to indicate the nature of what needs to be sought on most questions. In the meantime, such questions can be worked at only with the equivalent of what in the physical sciences is known as a thought experiment. Much of the model building and theory construction of current sociobiology is at such a level of abstraction from concrete cases as to seem more in keeping with the refined society of numbers than the rude society of animals.

Such argument in the abstract, together with ambition to develop a general theory, can cause impatience with or disregard for the complexity and heterogeneity in the subject matter in question. Indeed, Wilson (1975) has admitted that "it is out of such deliberate over-simplification that the beginnings of a general theory are made [p. 5]." Of course he is right; but it must be remembered that what the oversimplification excludes may be left outside the theory's explanatory jurisdiction. Sociobiology's starting point is the proposition that the social behavior of animals is a product of evolution, an understanding of which is to be had through study of the demography and genetic structure of populations. An ethologist has no quarrel with this, because ethology has taken the same position all along. But an ethologist can and should take issue with the view that the truth of this proposition entails that the sociobiological approach to the evolutionary question encompasses all the other and different kinds of questions about the social behavior of animals, with the exception of those that have to be left to physiology and cellular biology. This is nothing-but-ism, and it fosters errors of the sort that Lorenz made about instinct. From the fact that ballet is movement of the body it does not follow that everything that can be said about ballet is contained in Newton's laws of motion. From a sociobiological understanding of the evolution of the social structure and dynamics of a species we could not deduce a full account of social communication or social development.

Social communication and social development require their own study, which means methods, concepts, and categories for which there are no equivalents either in population genetics or neurophysiology. In both cases the methods, concepts, and categories are still in a state of flux, for research has yet to settle down to ground where there can be clarity and agreement about the ways to go. For instance, it is still an open question what is to count as a display in communication behavior (Beer, 1977; Smith, 1977), and it has become apparent that past conceptions of animal social behavior gave too simple a view of what developmental study has to account for, at least in some species (Beer, 1971, 1973, 1976). It can be argued that the study of social communication and the study of social development stand alongside "the formulation of a theory of sociobiology" as "great manageable problems . . . for the next twenty or thirty years [Wilson, 1975, p. 5]." The view that the latter includes the former is a confusion, the effects of which have already become apparent in the recurrence of the old nature-nurture controversy in connection with our own species, which has given Wilson's book and sociobiology their widest publicity.

To summarize, I have singled out two kinds of questions, and hence two kinds of comparison, in ethology's dealings with the evolution of animal behavior: questions of phylogenetic origins, which have been tackled by analogical extension of the approach of comparative morphology, and questions of survival value, for which the comparative approach has been that of adaptive correlation. I have argued that in applying the idea of homology to behavior there is a problem of definition that can be partly resolved by distinguishing a theoretical sense from the ostensive use of the term and conceding that the latter is largely a matter of perceptual judgment. In its pursuit of adaptive correlation, ethology has converged with ecology and population genetics to achieve considerable advance in the interpretation of varieties of social behavior and social systems in terms of natural selection. But not all questions about behavior, including questions about social behavior, are questions about evolution. The secession of the sociobiologists should not be allowed to condemn us to repeat the nothing-but-ism of the past.

CONCLUDING COMMENT

Wilson's advocacy of the "postulational-deductive approach" in the study of social behavior echoes Hull's advocacy of the "hypothetico-deductive method" in the study of learning. Indeed, the extolling of method has been a recurrent theme in the history of psychology, at least since Bacon (1620/1858) claimed that his program for science would obviate reliance on "the sharpness and strength of men's wits." From Descartes to Mill, from Wundt to Watson, we find what Peters (1962) called "dogmatic methodism—the view that success in science is the result of following a definite method [p. 336]." Of course method is important; methodological reform and innovation have repeatedly turned science aside from blind alleys and led it into new regions of conquest. But history also shows that those who put their faith in method alone doom themselves to myopia and sterility. To Bacon's (1620/1858) famous four classes of *idola* there can be added a fifth class, which Bacon himself worshipped and which, I suggest, can be described as idols of the kitchen, for faith in them vests authority in formulae or recipes.

The idols of the kitchen are false gods for three connected reasons. First, scientific study has to begin with an idea; second, the methods of science are means of testing ideas, rather than means of generating ideas; third, different kinds of ideas require different kinds of methods for their testing. Lorenz's (1950) assertion that, "It is an inviolable law of inductive natural science that it has to *begin* with pure observation totally devoid of any preconceived theory and even working hypothesis [p. 232]" is nonsense if taken literally. Without prior assumptions or expectations of some sort to focus attention, rule what is relevant, and even fix the form of the facts, the scientist could never get started on his observation, and if he did he could never come to the end of it (Popper, 1959, 1963). As Lorenz's own work amply illustrates, what the scientist perceives, what presents itself to him as a question, and what he aims at as a solution depend on his initial perspective. As in ordinary perception, he has to project vision onto the world, not just passively receive impressions from it.

Comparative psychology and comparative ethology derived from different traditions—associationistic psychology in the one, comparative anatomy and natural history in the other—but they also had a common grandparent in Darwinism. The Darwinian strain in comparative psychology is expressed most strongly in the influence of the ideas of continuity and adaptation; in comparative ethology it is even more obvious in the concern with phylogeny and adaptation. The differences of perspective can be seen in comparative psychology's preoccupation with the search for general laws and the study of learning, compared to comparative ethology's preoccupations with behavioral diversity and genetic determination. But there are differences of perspective within each of these schools as well and hence diversity in the kinds of behavior observed, the kinds of question raised, and in the kinds of methods used. The differences have often been ignored, with consequent muddle and confusion. Results arrived at by one method have been the basis for invalid inference to conclusions about matters requiring a quite different approach.

Although a perspective is necessary to the conduct of scientific investigation, it need not be fixed or unresponsive to what it brings to light. Points of view can move as conception encounters fact in reciprocal interplay. Consequently, schools of thought that might have been far apart at one time may converge or overlap at another; streams of thought within a school can join or separate as they flow in the shingle-bed of their history. Comparative psychology appears to have recovered something of the Darwinian perspective that its concern with continuity had carried it progressively away from. Partly as a consequence of its own discoveries, partly through influences from ethology, comparative psychologists are now more attentive to the differences between different kinds of animals, and between different kinds of behavior, than they used to be. And they are again interpreting what they find in terms of evolutionary adaptation. Developments in ethology's traditional concern with adaptation has brought it even closer to its always close sister science of ecology. Together with population genetics the two have converged on the study of social behavior to such a dramatic effect as to be identified collectively by a new name: sociobiology. It is perhaps ironic that this elevation of the evolutionary perspective in ethology appears in some quarters to be having the opposite effect to that in comparative psychology: Instead of broadening the view it seems to be narrowing it. But the comparative study of animal behavior is in such flux that the present lines between perspectives are unlikely to remain where they are for long.

REFERENCES

Angell, J. R. *Psychology*. New York: Holt, 1904.

Angell, J. R. The province of functional psychology. *Psychological Review,* 1907, *14,* 61–69.

Atz, J. W. The application of the idea of homology to behavior. In L. R. Aronson, E. Tobach, D. S. Lehrman, & J. S. Rosenblatt (Eds.), *Development and evolution of behavior.* San Francisco: Freeman, 1970.

Bacon, F. *Novum organum* (J. Spedding, trans.). In R. L. Ellis & D. D. Heath (Eds.), *The works of Francis Bacon* (Vol. 4). London: Longmans, 1858. (Originally published, 1620.)

Baerends, G. P. Comparative methods and the concept of homology in the study of behavior. *Archives Neerlandaises de Zoologie,* 1958, *13,* 401–417.

Beach, F. A. The descent of instinct. *Psychological Review,* 1955, *62,* 401–410.

Beach, F. A. Hormonal factors controlling the differentiation, development, and display of copulatory behavior in the ramstergig and related species. In E. Tobach, L. R. Aronson, & E. Shaw (Eds.), *The biopsychology of development.* New York: Academic Press, 1971.

Beer, C. G. Diversity in the study of the development of social behavior. In E. Tobach, L. R. Aronson, & E. Shaw (Eds.), *The biopsychology of development.* New York: Academic Press, 1971.

Beer, C. G. A view of birds. In A. D. Pick (Ed.), *The Minnesota Symposia on Child Psychology* (Vol. 7). Minneapolis: University of Minnesota Press, 1973.

Beer, C. G. Species-typical behavior and ethology. In D. A. Dewsbury & D. A. Rethlingshafer (Eds.), *Comparative psychology—A modern survey.* New York: McGraw-Hill, 1974.

Beer, C. G. Some complexities in the communication behavior of gulls. *Annals of the New York Academy of Sciences,* 1976, *280,* 413–432.

Beer, C. G. What is a display? *American Zoologist,* 1977, *17,* 155–165.

Bell, C. *The anatomy of the brain explained in a series of engravings.* London: Longmans & Rees, 1802.

Bitterman, M. E. Phyletic differences in learning. *American Psychologist,* 1965, *20,* 396–410.

Bitterman, M. E. Thorndike and the problem of animal intelligence. *American Psychologist,* 1969, *24,* 444–453.

Black, M. *Models and metaphors.* Ithaca, NY: Cornell University Press, 1962.

Blest, A. D. The concept of ritualization. In W. H. Thorpe & O. L. Zangwill (Eds.), *Current problems in animal behaviour.* Cambridge: Cambridge University Press, 1961.

Bolles, R. C. Species-specific defense reactions and avoidance learning. *Psychological Review,* 1970, *77,* 32–48.

Breland, K., & Breland, M. The misbehavior of organisms. *American Psychologist,* 1961, *16,* 681–684.

Broadbent, D. E. *Behaviour.* London: Eyre & Spottiswoode, 1961.

Cullen, E. Adaptations in the Kittiwake to cliff-nesting. *Ibis,* 1957, *99,* 275–302.

Cuvier, G. *Le Règne animal distribué d'après son organisation.* Paris: Fortin, 1828.

Daanje, A. On locomotory movements in birds and intention movements derived from them. *Behaviour,* 1950, *3,* 48–98.

Darwin, C. *The origin of species.* London: Murray, 1859.

Darwin, C. *The expression of the emotions in man and animals.* London: Murray, 1872.

Dawkins, R. *The selfish gene.* Oxford: Oxford University Press, 1976.

Dewey, J. The reflex arc concept in psychology. *Psychological Review,* 1896, *3,* 357–370.

Dunlap, K. Are there any instincts? *Journal of Abnormal Psychology,* 1919, *14,* 307–311.

Eibl-Eibesfeldt, I. *Grundriss der vergleichenden Verhaltensforschung.* Munich: Piper, 1967.

Eisenstein, E. M., & Cohen, M. J. Learning in an isolated prothoracic insect ganglion. *Animal Behaviour,* 1965, *13,* 104–108.

Eliot, G. *Middlemarch.* London: Penguin Books, 1965.

Fentress, J. C. Simpler networks and behavior. Sunderland, MA: Sinaeur, 1976.

Frye, N. *Anatomy of criticism.* Princeton, NJ: Princeton University Press, 1971.

Garcia, J., McGowan, B. K., & Green, K. F. Biological constraints on conditioning. In A. Black & W. F. Prokasy (Eds.), *Classical conditioning two: Current theory and research.* New York: Appleton-Century-Crofts, 1972.

Gray, P. H. Comparative psychology and ethology: A saga of twins reared apart. *Annals of the New York Academy of Sciences,* 1973, *223,* 49–53.

Gruber, H. E., & Barrett, P. H. *Darwin on man.* New York: Dutton, 1974.

Haekel, E. *Generelle Morphologie der Organismen: Allgemeine Grundzüge der organischen Formen-Weissenschaft, mechanisch bergrundet durch die von Charles Darwin reformirte Descendenz-Theorie.* Berlin: George Reimer, 1866.

Hailman, J. P. Homology: Logic, information, and efficiency. In R. B. Masterton, W. Hodos, & H. Jerison (Eds.), *Evolution, brain, and behavior: Persistent problems.* Hillsdale, NJ: Lawrence Erlbaum Associates, 1976.

Hall, G. S. *Adolescence, and its relations to physiology, anthropology, sociology, sex, crime, religion, and education.* New York: Appleton-Century-Crofts, 1904.

Hebb, D. O. *The organization of behavior: A neurophysiological theory.* New York: Wiley, 1949.

Hebb, D. O. Drives and the CNS (conceptual nervous system). *Psychological Review,* 1955, *62,* 243–254.

Heinroth, O. Beitrage zur Biologie, namentlich Ethologie und Psychologie der Anatiden. *Verhandlungen vor dem Internationale Ornithologie Kongress,* Berlin, 1911.

Hinde, R. A. (Ed.). *Non-verbal communication.* Cambridge: Cambridge University Press, 1972.

Hodos, W. Evolutionary interpretation of neural and behavioral studies of living vertebrates. In F. O. Schmitt (Ed.), *The neurosciences: Second study program.* New York: Rockefeller University Press, 1970.

Howard, H. E. *Territory in bird life.* London: Murray, 1920.

Hull, C. L. The conflicting psychologies of learning—a way out. *Psychological Review,* 1935, *42,* 491–516.

Hull, C. L. *Principles of behavior: An introduction to behavior theory.* New York: Appleton-Century-Crofts, 1943.

Huxley, J. Courtship activities in the red-throated diver (*Colymbus stellatus* Pontopp.); Together with a discussion of the evolution of courtship in birds. *Proceedings of the Zoological Society of London,* 1923, *35,* 253–292.

Huxley, J. (Ed.). *T. H. Huxley's diary of the voyage of H. M. S. Rattlesnake.* Garden City, NY: Doubleday, 1936.

James, W. *The principles of psychology.* New York: Holt, 1890.

James, W. *Memories and studies.* New York: Longmans, 1924.

Jennings, H. S. *Behavior of the lower organisms.* New York: Columbia University Press, 1906.

Kandel, E. R. An invertebrate system for the cellular analysis of simple behaviors and their modifications. In F. O. Schmitt & F. G. Worden (Eds.), *The neurosciences: Third study program.* Cambridge, MA: MIT Press, 1974.

Kaplan, A. *The conduct of inquiry.* San Francisco: Chandler, 1964.

Karten, H. J. The organization of the avian telencephalon and some speculations on the phylogeny of the amniote telencephalon. *Annals of the New York Academy of Sciences,* 1969, *167,* 164–179.

Kelvin, William Thomson, Lord. *Popular lectures and addresses.* London: Macmillan, 1891–1894.

Kirby, W. *On the power, wisdom, and goodness of God as manifested in the creation of animals, and in their history, habits and instincts.* London: Pickering, 1835. *(The 7th Bridgewater Treatise.)*

Klopfer, P. H. Does behavior evolve? *Annals of the New York Academy of Sciences,* 1973, *223,* 113–119.

Klopfer, P. H. Evolution, behavior and language. In M. E. Hahn & E. C. Simmel (Eds.), *Communicative behavior and evolution.* New York: Academic Press, 1976.

Krebs, J. R. The significance of song repertoires: The Beau Geste hypothesis. *Animal Behaviour,* 1977, *25,* 475–478.

Kühn, A. *Die Orientierung der Tiere im Raum.* Jena: Fischer, 1919.

Lehrman, D. S. A critique of Konrad Lorenz's theory of instinctive behavior. *Quarterly Review of Biology,* 1953, *28,* 337–363.

Lehrman, D. S. Ethology and psychology. *Recent Advances in Biological Psychiatry,* 1964, *4,* 86–94.

Lehrman, D. S. Behavioral science, engineering and poetry. In E. Tobach, L. R. Aronson, & E. Shaw (Eds.), *The biopsychology of development.* New York: Academic Press, 1971.

Loeb, J. *Einleitung in die vergleichende Gehirnphysiologie und vergleichende Psychologie mit besonderer Berücksichtigung der wirbellosen Tiere.* Leipzig: Barth, 1899.

Lorenz, K. Z. Der Kumpan in der Umwelt des Vogels. *Journal für Ornithologie,* 1935, *83,* 137–213; 289–413.

Lorenz, K. Z. Uber die Bildung des Instinktbergriffs. *Naturwissenshaften,* 1937, *25,* 289–300; 307–318; 324–331.

Lorenz, K. Z. Vergleichende Bewegungsstudien an Anatiden. *Journal für Ornithologie,* 1941, *89* (Sonderheft, 19–29).

Lorenz, K. Z. The comparative method in studying innate behaviour patterns. *S. E. B. Symposia,* 1950, *4,* 221–268.

Lorenz, K. Z. The evolution of behavior. *Scientific American,* 1958, *199,* 67–78.

Lorenz, K. Z. *On aggression.* New York: Harcourt, Brace & World, 1963.

Lorenz, K. Z. Analogy as a source of knowledge. *Science,* 1974, *185,* 229–234.

Lorenz, K. Z., & Tinbergen, N. Taxis und Instinkthandlung in der Eirollbewegung der Graugans. I. *Zeitschrift für Tierpsychologie,* 1938, *2,* 1–29.

Maier, N. R. F., & Schneirla, T. C. *Principles of comparative psychology.* New York: McGraw-Hill, 1935.

Maynard Smith, J. Game theory and the evolution of fighting. In J. Maynard Smith, *On evolution.* Edinburgh: Edinburgh University Press, 1972.

Maynard Smith, J. The theory of games and the evolution of animal conflict. *Journal of Theoretical Biology*, 1974, *47*, 209–221.

Maynard Smith, J. Evolution and the theory of games. *American Scientist*, 1976, *64*, 159–175.

Maynard Smith, J., & Price, G. R. The logic of animal conflicts. *Nature*, 1973, *246*, 15–18.

McDougall, W. *Psychology: The study of behaviour.* London: Williams & Norgate, 1912.

McKinney, F. The evolution of duck displays. In G. P. Baerends, C. G. Beer, & A. Manning (Eds.), *Function and evolution in behaviour—Essays in honour of Professor Niko Tinbergen.* Oxford: Clarendon Press, 1975.

McKinney, F. Comparative approaches to social behavior in closely-related species of birds. *Advances in the Study of Behavior*, 1978, *8*, 1–38.

Mills, J. A. The influence of age and pair-bond on the breeding biology of the Red-billed Gull *Larus novaehollandiae scopulinus. Journal of Animal Ecology*, 1973, *42*, 147–162.

Morgan, C. L. *An introduction to comparative psychology.* London: Walter Scott, 1894.

Morris, D. *The naked ape.* London: Jonathan Cape, 1967.

Moynihan, M. Notes on the behavior of some North American gulls: IV. The ontogeny of hostile behavior and display patterns. *Behaviour*, 1959, *14*, 214–239.

Owen, R. *On the archetypes and homologies of the vertebrate skelton.* London: Richard & John Taylor, 1848.

Paley, W. *Natural theology; or, evidence of the existence and attributes of the deity collected from the appearances of nature.* London: Faulder, 1802.

Pavlov, I. P. *Lectures on conditioned reflexes.* New York: International Publishers, 1928.

Peters, R. S. *The concept of motivation.* London: Routledge & Kegan Paul, 1958.

Peters, R. S. (Ed.). *Brett's history of psychology.* London: Allen & Unwin, 1962.

Pope, A. Essay on man. In A. Williams (Ed.), *Poetry and prose of Alexander Pope.* Boston: Houghton Mifflin, 1969. (Originally published, 1773.)

Popper, K. *The logic of scientific discovery.* London: Hutchinson, 1959.

Popper, K. *Conjectures and refutations.* London: Routledge & Kegan Paul, 1963.

Romanes, G. *Animal intelligence.* London: Kegan Paul, 1882.

Russell, E. S. *Form and function.* London: Murray, 1916.

Schiller, C. (Ed.). *Instinctive behavior.* New York: International Universities Press, 1957.

Schneirla, T. C. Levels in the psychological capacities of animals. In R. W. Sellars, V. J. McGill, & M. Farber (Eds.), *Philosophy for the future.* New York: Macmillan, 1949.

Schneirla, T. C. L'apprentissage et la question du conflict chez la fourmi. Comparison avec le rat. *Journal de Psychologie*, 1959, *57*, 11–44. (a)

Schneirla, T. C. An evolutionary developmental theory of biphasic processes underlying approach and withdrawal. In M. R. Jones (Ed.), *Nebraska Symposium on Motivation* (Vol. 7). Lincoln, NB: University of Nebraska Press, 1959. (b)

Schneirla, T. C. Aspects of stimulation and organization in approach/withdrawal processes underlying vertebrate behavioral development. *Advances in the Study of Behavior*, 1965, *1*, 1–74.

Seligman, M. E. P. On the generality of the laws of learning. *Psychological Review*, 1970, *77*, 406–418.

Seligman, M. E. P., & Hager, J. L. (Eds.). *Biological boundaries of learning.* New York: Appleton-Century-Crofts, 1972.

Selous, E. The earlier breeding habits of the red-throated diver. *Wild Life*, 1914, *3*, 206–213.

Selous, E. *The evolution of habit in birds.* London: Constable, 1933.

Skinner, B. F. *The behavior of organisms.* New York: Appleton-Century-Crofts, 1938.

Skinner, B. F. Are theories of learning necessary? *Psychological Review*, 1950, *57*, 193–216.

Small, W. S. An experimental study of the mental processes of the rat. *American Journal of Psychology*, 1899, *11*, 133–165; 1901, *12*, 206–239.

Smith, W. J. *The behavior of communication.* Cambridge, MA: Harvard University Press, 1977.

Spencer, H. *The principles of psychology,* London: Longmans, 1855.

Spencer, H. *An autobiography*. London: Williams & Norgate, 1904.

Taylor, C. *The explanation of behaviour*. London: Routledge & Kegan Paul, 1964.

Thayer, G. H. *Concealing coloration in the animal kingdom*. New York: Macmillan, 1909.

Thorndike, E. L. Animal intelligence: An experimental study of the associative processes in animals. *Psychological Review: Series of Monograph Supplements*, 1898, *2* (4, Whole No. 8).

Tinbergen, N. *The study of instinct*. Oxford: Clarendon Press, 1951.

Tinbergen, N. Derived activities: Their causation, biological significance, origin, and emancipation during evolution. *Quarterly Review of Biology*, 1952, *27*, 1–32.

Tinbergen, N. *The herring gull's world*. London: Collins, 1953.

Tinbergen, N. Comparative studies of the behaviour of gulls (*Laridae*): A progress report. *Behaviour*, 1959, *15*, 1–70.

Tinbergen, N. On the aims and methods of ethology. *Zeitschrift für Tierpsychologie*, 1963, *20*, 410–433.

Tinbergen, N. Ethology in a changing world. In P. P. G. Bateson & R. A. Hinde (Eds.), *Growing points in ethology*. Cambridge: Cambridge University Press, 1976.

Tinbergen, N., Broekhuysen, G. J., Feekes, F., Houghton, J. C. W., Kruuk, H., & Szulc, E. Egg shell removal by the black-headed gull, *Larus ridibundus L.*; A behaviour component of camouflage. *Behaviour*, 1962, *19*, 74–117.

Titchener, E. B. Structural and functional psychology. *Philosophical Review*, 1899, *8*, 290–299.

Tolman, E. C. The determiners of behavior at a choice point. *Psychological Review*, 1938, *45*, 1–41.

Toulmin, S. *Philosophy of science*. London: Hutchinson, 1953.

Trivers, R. L. Parental investment and sexual selection. In B. Campbell (Ed.), *Sexual selection and the descent of man*. Chicago: Aldine, 1972.

Vowles, D. M. Neural mechanisms in insect behaviour. In W. H. Thorpe & O. L. Zangwill (Eds.), *Current problems in animal behaviour*. Cambridge: Cambridge University Press, 1961.

Watson, J. B. *Animal education: The physical development of the white rat*. Chicago: Chicago University Press, 1903.

Watson, J. B. Review of *Behavior of the lower organisms* by H. S. Jennings. *Psychological Bulletin*, 1907, *4*, 288–291. (a)

Watson, J. B. Kinaesthetic and organic sensations: Their role in the reactions of the white rat in the maze. *Psychological Monographs*, 1907, *8* (No. 33). (b)

Watson, J. B. The behavior of noddy and sooty terns. *Papers from Tortugas Laboratory, Carnegie Institute of Washington*, 1908, *2*, 189–255.

Watson, J. B. Psychology as the behaviorist views it. *Psychological Review*, 1913, *20*, 158–177.

Watson, J. B. What the nursery has to say about instincts. *Pedagogical Seminary*, 1925, *32*, 293–327.

Watson, J. B., & Lashley, K. S. Homing and related activities of birds. *Carnegie Institute of Washington*, 1929 (No. 211).

Watson, J. B., & McDougall, W. *The battle of behaviorism*. New York: Norton, 1929.

White, G. *The natural history and antiquities of Selbourne, in the county of Southampton; With engravings and an appendix*. London: Benjamin White, 1789.

Whitman, C. O. Animal behavior. In *Biological lectures delivered at the Marine Biological Laboratory at Woods Hole in 1898*, 1899.

Whitman, C. O. The behavior of pigeons. *Carnegie Institute of Washington*, 1919 (No. 257).

Wickler, W. Okologie und Stammesgeschichte von Verhaltensweisen. *Fortschriften für Zoologie*, 1961, *13*, 303–365.

Wickler, W. Vergleichende Verhaltensforschung und Phylogenetik. In F. Herberer (Ed.), *Die Evolution der Organismen*. Jena: Fischer, 1967.

Willey, B. *The eighteenth century background studies on the idea of nature in the thought of the period*. London: Chatto & Windus, 1940.

Wilson, E. O. *Sociobiology.* Cambridge, MA: Harvard University Press, 1975.

Wollheim, R. Giovanni Morelli and the origins of scientific connoisseurship. In R. Wollheim, *On art and the mind.* London: Allen Lane, 1973.

Zahavi, A. Mate-selection—A selection for a handicap. *Journal of Theoretical Biology,* 1975, *53,* 205–214.

3 Developmental Comparisons

Alfred L. Baldwin
University of Rochester

Thomas M. Achenbach
National Institute of Mental Health

DEVELOPMENTAL COMPARISONS:
I. HISTORY AND THEORY
Alfred L. Baldwin

INTRODUCTION

The International Biological Programme, which operated in the decade from 1964 to 1974, was constituted to survey aspects of human welfare. Because one of the important indexes of the health status of a community or country is the growth of its children, one of the Programme's research efforts was directed at a worldwide investigation of these variables. The Programme's report can serve as a model of the comparative study of development (see Eveleth & Tanner, 1976).

If the height of a sizable sample of children at each age from birth to 19 years is measured, the results, as shown in Figure 3.1 are typical (Tanner, Whitehouse, & Takaishi, 1966). (These data are for boys, but the curves for girls are not strikingly different.) What is most apparent about these curves is their orderliness. The range of heights at any age is small by comparison with the total variation in height from birth to maturity. The shortest 19-year-old is taller than the tallest 11-year-old. Worldwide variation is relatively small. And, the predictability of adult height from the child's height (even before the beginning of the growth spurt) is high, approximately .80.

Environmental, especially nutritional, factors influence children's growth in height. There are also clear secular trends in stature. Moreover, different

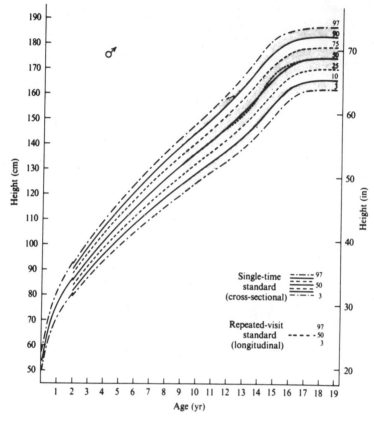

FIG. 3.1.   The growth curve for boys' height. (British data from Tanner et al.,
1966.)

populations living under comparable environmental conditions show
somewhat different growth curves because of genetic differences. However,
all these differences are relatively small.

What is clearly behind this impressive and orderly set of developmental
results is the fact that growth in height is produced by a powerful biological
mechanism that is only moderately influenced by environmental conditions
and that does not vary much among the populations of the world. In this
sense, the data on physical growth nearly ideally represent the case of
maturational development. Indeed, the growth process is so fixed—
predetermined—that it evidences self-correcting mechanisms. Children who
grow slowly for a period of time because of illness or malnutrition grow more
rapidly than normal afterward and catch up to a growth channel that is
apparently normal for them. This phenomenon has been called *canalization*
(Waddington, 1966).

This beautiful array of findings makes the developmental psychologist wish longingly for some equally orderly body of data about the development of psychological functions. It is not that growth in height does not have all the complications of psychological data, but as far as stature is concerned these complicating factors appear more as perturbations of a reasonably clear developmental process, whereas in psychological development the perturbations and the process are so confounded that often one cannot tell what is process and what is perturbation.

The study of physical growth serves to illustrate some major issues of developmental research where the primary comparisons are change within humans over time or between humans of different ages. Change with time is the basic phenomenon for a developmentalist to explain. Because chronological age, by itself, does not explain anything, the developmentalist tries to ascertain what processes occurring over time may be directly responsible for change or growth. In the growth of stature, this process is the cumulative effect over time of the secretion of the growth hormone. Once the underlying developmental process for normal growth of stature is clear, then a variety of other comparative studies round out the picture. These studies include comparison of development in disease and in health, comparison of possible differences in the gene pools, and comparison of different effects of culture (see Bornstein, in this volume).

The first section of this chapter surveys comparative approaches to psychological development. The main sections define development and review major theories of development. In the context of this theoretical treatment, dispositional and situational variables are compared, and the influences of heredity and experience on development are discussed.

DEFINITION AND SCOPE

Developmental psychology was at one time identified with child psychology. However, as early as 1954 the American Psychological Association officially recognized the two as separate disciplines. Child psychology is concerned with explaining a child's behavior at a given time—in current connotation with an emphasis on psychopathology and therapy—whereas developmental psychology is concerned with similarilties and differences in behavior over the life cycle.

Defining development opens a Pandora's box of problems. The broadest definition would include all changes over time in behavior in a given situation. Changes in behavior from one situation to another are not thought of as developmental changes. Such a broad definition then includes physical growth as well as other, more typically psychological behaviors. Though development implies change, developmental psychology is also concerned with dispositions (in Ryle's [1949] sense of the term), viz. relatively invariant characteristics of the individual that do not change from one situation to another or one age to another but are constant properties of the person.

Some developmental psychologists focus on maturation as a source of change, but learning theorists view much of development as learning. These two views together motivate much developmental research. Thus the study of psychological development involves two different types of theory building, one a theory of behavior and the other a theory of change. Developmental theories assume the validity of one or another underlying theory of behavior and behavior change. Development might be predominantly genetic, and change maturational (like height). Development might reflect systematic learning, and change the accretion of associations (like vocabulary). However, development might also reflect interaction of the two over time. The central task of developmental psychology is to account for behavior and behavior change over time.

Not all developmental change implies individual development. Children today are, on the average, about 2.5 cm taller than their parents once they reach adult height. This change reflects in part a secular trend, or *cohort* effect (see Achenbach, in this chapter). Cohort effects, we see later, complicate and limit developmental studies in psychology.

In short, the study of development assumes that there are both dispositional variables and mechanisms of learning that underlie behavior. Developmental psychology is concerned with the explanation and prediction of stability or change in behavior during the course of ontogenesis.

DEVELOPMENTAL THEORY AND
COMPARATIVE RESEARCH

The major types of theories of development include: (1) development as a maturational process; (2) development as learning; (3) development as an interaction of maturation and learning; and (4) development as qualitative change in the individual in transaction with the environment. Each of the different types of theory has implications for comparative studies of humans at different developmental levels.

The Maturation Hypothesis

What is impressive about the data on growth in height is that a fundamental growth process shines through despite perturbations related to age, culture, etc. One can easily picture a growth equation in which variations among growth curves would be accounted for by changing the values of these parameters of the equation.

Growth of stature is predominantly a maturational phenomenon in that it depends on the time since conception and the cumulative effect of the growth hormone produced during that time. Thus for growth there is a framework of invariance that permits deviation to be quantified. Fortunately, few variations (e.g., illness, genetic differences, nurtrition, or the timing of the growth spurt) alter development sufficiently to hide the essential invariant ground plan, the growth curve. Nobody under any conditions has a growth curve that jumps to adult height by age 2 and remains constant thereafter. (Even the "growth spurt" that produces the most noise in an otherwise orderly picture appears to be describable in terms of a second hormonal contribution to growth that is partially independent of the first.)

Physical growth was, perhaps for self-evident reasons, among the first developmental characteristics to be scrutinized. In many ways it provides a model for other maturational processes and for the application of genetic theory to development. Further, quantification of growth plays a valuable role in establishing descriptive norms. Although regularity discovered in physical growth certainly encouraged the maturational point of view in early psychology, the history of developmental psychology shows that the maturational theme in fact presupposed collection of physical growth data. Darwinism is based on inheritance of such characteristics, and Darwin (1897) wrote about the developing mental abilities of man (and monkey) in extending phylogeny to ontogeny. Galton (1883), in turn, devoted himself to the study of individual differences in human beings and to their measurement in objective ways, and he seems not to have expressed the slightest doubt that such differences were hereditary in nature. A capacity in which Galton seems to have had particular interest was intelligence. Others who followed Galton developed tests to track the maturation of intelligence. Although Binet (Binet & Simon, 1905) seems not to have believed firmly that intelligence was inherited, Terman (1916) and others in the mental-testing movement seem to have espoused the view that intelligence represented the maturation of an innate genetic characteristic.

One of the modern consequences of a belief in maturation and the predictability of growth in general was the founding of several longitudinal projects—for example, the Fels Study (Sontag, 1946), the Berkeley Growth Study (Jones & Bayley, 1941), and others—each devoted to multivariate assessment of factors from birth to adulthood. These projects were founded in the faith that the careful plotting of individual growth curves of intellectual ability, for example, would yield mental-growth curves. Bayley (1955) has plotted data from the Berkeley study and derived an average mental-growth curve shown in Figure 3.2. (The unit in this figure is the standard deviation of a 16-year-old sample.) Some individual-growth curves are shown in Figure 3.3; these tend to be much more variable than physical-growth curves. Case 13 F attained by age 9 the amount of growth that case 1 F required 21 years to attain. Although Figure 3.2 is merely an average growth curve, the fact that it indicates more rapid growth in early childhood than in adolescence suggests that maturation affects the growth of intelligence despite the fact that many other factors also contribute.

Although a curve of mental growth was the original primary objective of longitudinal studies, and longitudinal studies provided an immense amount of valuable information about the course of natural development of normal, unselected children, the focus of developmental study soon changed. During the 1930s and 1940s, additional variables intruded on developmental thinking: The behavior of parents and the quality of the child's home environment became important. With the growing popularity of psychoanalytic theory, data from growth studies were applied retrospectively. In general, the effects of early experience on development came to be regarded as critical.

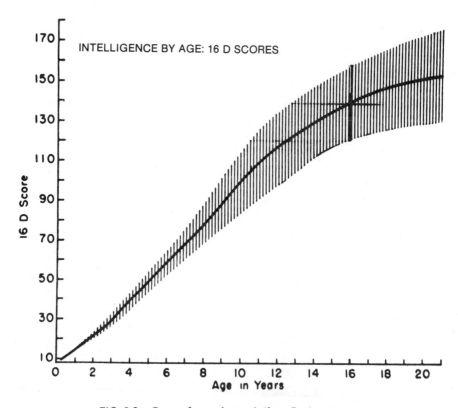

FIG. 3.2. Curve of mental growth (from Bayley, 1955).

INDIVIDUAL CURVES OF 16 D SCORES (INTELLIGENCE)

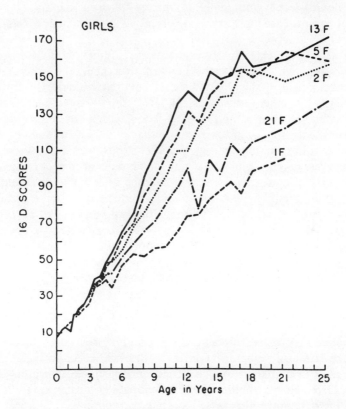

FIG. 3.3.   Individual curves of intellectual growth for five girls from 1 month to 25 years (from Bayley, 1955).

Development and Learning

Learning theory, like maturational theory, has a venerable history in philosophy and in developmental psychology. John Locke (1693), among other empiricist philosophers who were forerunners of contemporary learning theorists, was committed to a belief that the association of ideas based on their contiguity in experience is a mechanism underpinning mental development. Although Locke did not rule out the influence of congenital or constitutional characteristics on behavior, he championed the importance of experience, for example, in teaching children moral principles. The research that clarified the mechanisms for associative learning was embodied in Pavlov's (1927) studies of conditioning. Pavlov's standard was seized and applied to development by Watson (1913) who used it to start a behaviorist revolution in the United States in 1913. Watson himself conducted research on conditioning fear in young children, and in 1928 wrote a landmark book of advice for parents based on learning theory, *Psychological Care of Infant and Child.*

If one adopts the extreme position that development completely results from learning, two facts may be invoked to explain the orderliness of development and its predictability. First, all children live in the same physical world subject to the same physical laws; thus they all learn under approximately the same contingencies. Second, within any culture there is a well-established sequence of socialization that can create uniformity in the behavior. of children at the same age. In other words, learning curves replace growth curves. From a purely learning standpoint, proper developmental study consists of comparisons among children after different amounts of practice, after different amounts of reinforcement, or after exposure to different amounts of experience. Learning theory predicts that if we compose a group of children all with equivalent exposure and experience we would find less variance in performance than if we simply compose the group to be of equivalent age. However, probably no developmental learning theorist actually espouses such an extreme learning point of view.

Interaction of Maturation and Learning

Development may depend on maturation, or it may depend on learning and experience. In fact, development is probably independent of neither. A simple example will help to illustrate. A strictly maturational interpretation of semantic development would imply that children of the same age (or level of maturity) would have the same vocabulary regardless of exposure to language. This extreme position can be rejected out of hand. A strictly learning interpretation would predict that children's vocabularly is predictable from the total corpus of words to which they have been exposed since birth, regardless of age. This interpretation is equally untenable. It seems almost certain, in fact, that exposure to words at age 3 has enhanced effects over exposure to words during the first year of life, even though exposure during the first year may have some effect. Experience interacts with maturation. With this example in mind we can turn to the question of how maturation and experience interact.

Gottlieb (1976) has pointed out that experience actually influences maturation in only a small number of ways. His evidence is derived from studies of animal behavior but is directly relevant for understanding human development (see Marler, Zoloth, & Dooling, in this volume). In particular, Gottlieb distinguishes among three functions of experience: maintenance, facilitation, and induction. For the *maintenance* of normal functioning, for example, a minimal amount of sensory input is required. (The effects of sensory deprivation on efficient behavioral functioning have been outlined by Bexton, Heron, and Scott [1954].) Experience maintains behavior by preventing tissue disintegration and is necessary for the achievement or attainment of a minimal level of functioning.

Sometimes experience does more than merely maintain normal functioning; it may *facilitate* development. In the absence of experience, the organism may be less efficient or effective or advanced. Zelazo, Zelazo, and Kolb (1972) report that if the reflexive stepping movements of young human infants are encouraged and practiced between birth and 8 weeks of age, infants will walk independently earlier. The Zelazo study suggests that early experience facilitates development, but it does not say whether experience affects the eventual efficiency of functioning. Other examples of behavioral development show that experience may influence the level of final achievement. Tees (1974), for example, showed that dark-reared rats do not develop the fineness of depth perception (as shown in their behavior on the "visual cliff") achieved by light-reared rats. The dark-reared rats avoid the deep side of the cliff—therefore light rearing is not necessary for the discrimination to appear—but their threshold of discrimination between the deep and the shallow side is impaired. Experience may accelerate development, or improve the level of final achievement, or both.

In many studies one cannot discern whether the effect of environmental enrichment is to prevent deterioration or facilitate development. To do so, experimental and control subjects must be assessed both before and after an intervention because assessment of an experimental group may affect development. For such studies, Solomon and Lessac (1968) have recommended four groups of subjects, two assessed at the beginning of treatment and the other two not. One assessed and one control group experience the intervention, deprivation or enrichment, and all four groups are assessed at the end of the experiment. In this way one can identify, in instances where there is some effect of the intervention, whether enrichment facilitates development or merely prevents deterioration, or whether deprivation results in actual deterioration or merely prevents an improvement found in the control group.

The third role of experience described by Gottlieb is *induction*, or actual initiation of a developmental process. Lack of experience can prevent the appearance of behavior. To exemplify induction, Wiens (1970) analyzed the preference of frogs for certain patterns. The usual environment of the red-legged frog (*Rana aurora*) is a pond with weeds and cattails that cast a generally striped pattern of shadows on the bottom. Wiens reared three groups of tadpoles, one in each of three habitats: a striped pattern on the substrate, a checkerboard pattern, or a featureless substrate. The tadpoles were tested before metamorphosis by being placed in a pan of which half the bottom was striped and half was checkered to see how much time they spent over each pattern. The "stripe-raised" group preferred the striped pattern; the "checker-raised" group only marginally preferred the checkered pattern; and the "featureless-raised" group showed no preference. When tested as frogs, the stripe-raised group showed a strong preference for the striped pattern; the checker-raised group showed an increased preference for the checkered pattern (although still not significant); and the control group continued to show no preference. Thus the pattern on the substrate of the pond in which the tadpole was reared induced a preference for substrate pattern in the frog (because the featureless-raised group showed no preference).

This experiment also illustrates that a preference for stripes in frogs—which is a characteristic condition of their natural environment—is more easily and efficiently induced than a preference for the less natural checkerboard pattern. Whereas it may be easy to demonstrate that experience can induce various "unnatural" behaviors, it is considerably more difficult to confirm induction in normal development. Lorenz's (1970) experiments showing that young birds can be imprinted on individuals other than the mother clearly demonstrate the inductive effects of the imprinting experience on cross-species following and preference, but to conclude that normal intraspecies preference is also induced it must be shown that the preimprinted bird has a completely neutral preference. Usually, there is a preexisting species preference that may be actively modified by an unnatural imprinting experience, but normal intraspecies preference is not solely the result of imprinting.

Unfortunately, studies of the effects of environmental experience (or lack of it) on human developement are seldom if ever controlled sufficiently to distinguish clearly among maintenance, facilitation, and induction. Because deprivation of human beings can be studied only where it occurs in natural circumstances (e.g., in physical disabilities such as blindness or in the occasional child who is discovered to have been severely deprived), most studies of the influence of experience on development of humans have sought to determine how much enriched learning opportunities can modify the "natural" course of development. In one of the classical studies of this type, Gesell and Thompson (1929) gave one of a pair of identical twins extra training in a variety of skills. This twin (T) was trained, for example, to climb stairs, between 46 and 53 weeks of age, whereas another twin (C) received no training. When twin C first attempted to climb stairs at 53 weeks she did better than twin T had on her first trial, but not nearly as well as twin T was doing at 53 weeks. However, within two weeks twin C had caught up and was climbing just as well as twin T. This finding—which was generally replicated by other investigators giving (or withholding) practice in different skills—was interpreted to confirm the maturation hypothesis. Certain skills could be temporarily reduced by deprivation or enhanced by enrichment, but afterward the child might fall back into a predetermined maturational channel.

To return to our hypothetical investigation of acquisition of vocabulary, one would expect that the contrast between children exposed to a rich vocabulary and those exposed to a meager one would be smaller in the first year of life than after the child reached the age of 3 or 4 and that the difference would increase with age (at least up to some point).

Assume the relatively simple model that the child's speed of learning increases with maturity. Children who are exposed to learning opportunities at different ages profit more from them if they are relatively mature, and the achieved level of performance is a function of the amount of learning opportunity in interaction with the age at which those opportunities are available. This simple example approximates a basic behavioral phenomenon linking organism and environment interactively, the *critical period*. There have been numerous demonstrations of a critical period in the behavioral development of infrahuman species and in neurological development. Organisms seem *prepared* to learn or to change during a critical period, but are less so beforehand and afterward. In human studies, research on the effects of maternal separation from the child suggests that there is a critical period for the development of the child's attachment to the primary care giver (Bowlby, 1969; Klaus, Jerauld, Kreger, McAlpine, Steffa, & Kennell, 1972). Lenneberg (1967) also suggested that there is a critical period in language development.

The critical-period approach to assessing the effects of experience on human development has been applied in three kinds of situations: first to assess how much the influence of the early environment can be reversed by a permanent change in the environment. Although previously it was believed that the effects of early experience were permanent (e.g., Goldfarb, 1943), recently considerable evidence has been marshalled that shows early effects can be reversed (Clarke & Clarke, 1976). Second, the approach has been applied to assess whether transient early experience can have long-lasting effects. The bulk of the evidence suggests that the nature of the intervening experience determines its effect. Third, the critical-period approach has been applied to assess the effectiveness of long-term experience applied late in development. Outcome here again seems to depend on the duration and degree of the intervention.

Interactional interpretations of development sometimes call on heredity and environment in novel ways. For example, some theoreticians have suggested that maturational factors may dominate in development to a certain age after which learning accounts for development (or vice versa). Others have suggested that the relative influence of heredity and experience varies with the behavior being considered. Still others have suggested that the two vary with task requirements. Eclecticism seems indigenous to interactional developmental theorizing.

Transaction Between Individual and Environment

Recent thinking in developmental psychology has produced a theory of the developmental process enhanced over the simple models of interaction just described. This theory is defined as qualitative growth of an active organism in a continuing transaction with the environment.

The view has identifiable origins in Rousseau (1762/1911) and Baldwin (1895); with Piaget (1970), Werner (1948, 1957), Riegel (1975), von Bertalanffy (1968), Sameroff (1975), and developmental biologists counted among its modern exponents. In *Emile,* Rousseau (1762/1911) formulated the idea that development proceeds in a series of stages that arise in an invariant sequence. He described the child as an active learner who develops by exercising psychological capabilities to achieve at every age an equilibrium (although Rousseau did not use the word) that is natural for him at that stage of life. More than a century later, Baldwin (1895) wrote about development as an active process that proceeded by assimilation, accomodation, and circular response, concepts that Werner and Piaget still later developed more thoroughly in theories of orthogenetic development and genetic epistemology. In modern times, embryology and developmental biology have characterized development more as a series of qualitatively different stages than as a quantitative growth process. Although an embryo or organ increase in size, the striking changes are qualitative, from gastula to blastula for example, and the initiation of qualitative changes is governed by the interaction of genetic factors with the environment.

In brief, three principles of development are chief among contemporary proponents of this view:

Stages. A distinction between qualitative change, implying discontinuous stage-like development, and quantitative growth, implying continuity, has been made, although it is difficult to define precisely the meaning of either. Stages differ with respect to many attributes, and qualitative growth involves simultaneity of change across a constellation of attributes rather than accretion to a single attribute. Development is conceived to be genuinely discontinuous like discontinuities in a mathematical function that are sudden and without intermediate transition. Though reorganization need not necessarily occur instantly, stage theorists suggest that it usually occurs over relatively or proportionately brief periods, for example, age 5 to 7 in cognitive development (White, 1965). The transition from one stage to another is therefore not a steady, gradual process but is believed to be a period of confusion and unpredictability until the new organization becomes clarified. A flash of insight into a problem, in the aftermath of which there is an immediate cognitive reorganization toward the problem, represents such a genuine discontinuity.

Not all stage theories are congruent, however. Of many such theories, Erikson's (1953) theory of social development and Piaget's (1970) theory of cognitive development are among the most prominent. Aside from content, the two differ in interesting meta-theoretical ways. In Erikson's (1953) theory, human beings pass through a series of stages but need not resolve satisfactorily the social crisis associated with each. Erikson believes that failure at a given stage distorts the development of personality in later stages, but it does not prevent development. For Erikson, therefore, each stage does not necessarily imply the attainment of a psychosocial equilibrium. For Piaget (1970), on the other hand, attaining a new stage implies cognitive equilibrium. Some stage theories (Eriksonian) are therefore not dependent on the same internal homogeneity as are others (Piagetian). Further, Piagetian stages are defined by level of achievement not merely by description.

In concrete form, transactional theories often carry additional assumptions. For example, Werner (1948) theorized that development proceeds through differentiation toward more complex hierarchical organizations of behavior, and Piaget (1970) theorized that cognitive development proceeds through an invariant sequence of stages.

Saltatory development constrains ontogenetic study. For example, group comparisons are appropriate between stages because children at one stage are not necessarily all the same chronological age nor do they share equal exposure to learning opportunities. As a consequence, for two samples of children selected to be of different developmental stages, variance between samples ought to be larger than variance within samples.

Dialectics.   The initiation of psychological development from one stage to another is thought to result from conflict or inconsistency or psychological "disequilibrium" arising from the individual's attempt to cope with (assimilate) environmental experience on the basis of faulty or inadequate understanding at a given stage of development. For "pure" dialectical theorists (e.g., Riegel, 1975), conflict is inherent in every stage of development (see also Sameroff & Harris, 1979). Attainment of a higher stage (temporarily) resolves disequilibrium. Thus, in Piaget for example, every stage before that of formal operations is inadequate in some respects. Because formal operations represents the cognitively mature view of the world, there is no further necessity to develop fundamentally new ways of thinking. By contrast, for the pure dialectician there is no final stage of development; life is constantly posing new conflicts that require new adaptations.

Transaction. Sameroff (1975) has characterized development from the perspective of systems theory (von Bertalanffy, 1968) as a reciprocal interactional process in which the organism and its physical and social environment reciprocally influence each other at every stage. The child's behavior influences other people or things whose (re)action influences the child, who in turn again influences the environment. Growth and development in the family context exemplify such social transactions (Cole, Kokes, Harder, Baldwin, Strauss, & Baldwin, 1977).

In summary, development is today conceived of as transaction between a qualitatively changing active organism and environment. Developmental psychologists study both the nature and nurture of this transaction.

CONCLUDING REMARKS

Comparative study of stature provides orderly developmental data. These are the sorts of findings—even though they provoke many unanswered questions—that developmentalists would be delighted to duplicate in studying psychological variables.

Developmental comparison in psychology focuses on stability or change in behavior over time. The study of development implies both a theory of behavior and a theory of behavior change. Four major approaches have guided developmental study over the last hundred years. The first is concerned with maturation based on programs. The second is concerned with learning based on experience. Maturation and learning have long been combined into interactional approaches, but these fail to take adequate account of development *over time.* Contemporaneous theorizing in developmental psychology emphasizes qualitative rather than quantitative change that is initiated by dialectical challenges and conflicts that themselves result from the reciprocal transaction over time of an organism actively involved with its physical and social worlds. Each of these theories has implications for the comparative study of development. Though transaction mimics reality most faithfully, developmental psychologists are often unfortunately only in a position to assess static interaction in studying development.

REFERENCES

Baldwin, J. M. *Mental development in the child and the race.* New York: Macmillan, 1895.
Bayley, N. On the growth of intelligence. *American Psychologist,* 1955, *10,* 805–818.
Bexton, W. H., Heron, W., & Scott, T. H. Effects of decreased variation in the sensory environment. *Canadian Journal of Psychology,* 1954, *8,* 70–76.

Binet, A., & Simon, T. [The development of intelligence in children.] *L'Année Psychologique,* 1905, *11,* 163-244.

Bowlby, J. *Attachment and loss (Vol. 1: Attachment).* New York: Basic Books, 1969.

Clarke, A. M. N., & Clarke, A. D. B. *Early experience: Myth and evidence.* New York: Free Press, 1976.

Cole, R. E., Kokes, R. F., Harder, D. W., Baldwin, A. L., Strauss, J. B., & Baldwin, C. P. *Relation of family interaction to parent psychopathology.* Paper presented at the meeting of the American Psychological Association, San Francisco, August 1977.

Darwin, C. R. *The descent of man, and selection in relation to sex.* New York: Appleton, 1897.

Erikson, E. Growth and crisis in the healthy personality. In C. Kluckholm, H. A. Murray, & D. M. Schneider (Eds.), *Personality in nature, society, and culture.* New York: Knopf, 1953.

Eveleth, P., & Tanner, J. M. *Worldwide variation in human growth.* Cambridge: Cambridge University Press, 1976.

Galton, F. *Inquiries into human faculty and its devlelopment.* New York: Macmillan, 1883.

Gesell, A., & Thompson, E. Learning and growth in identical infant twins: An experimental study by the method of co-twin control. *Genetic Psychology Monographs,* 1929, *6*(Whole No. 1).

Goldfarb, W. The effects of early institutional care on adolescent personality. *Journal of Experimental Education,* 1943, *12,* 106-129; 309-310.

Gottlieb, G. The roles of experience in the development of behavior and the nervous system. In G. Gottlieb (Ed.), *Neural and behavior specificity (Vol. 3: Studies on the development of behavior and the nervous system).* New York: Academic Press, 1976.

Jones, H. E., & Bayley, N. The Berkeley growth study. *Child Development,* 1941, *12,* 167-173.

Klaus, M. H., Jerauld, B. S., Kreger, N. C., McAlpine, W., Steffa, M., & Kennell, J. H. Maternal attachment: Importance of first post-partum days. *New England Journal of Medicine,* 1972, *286,* 460-463.

Lenneberg, E. *Biological foundations of language.* New York: Wiley, 1967.

Locke, J. *Some thoughts concerning education.* London: Churchhill, 1693.

Lorenz, K. [Companions as factors in the birds' environment.] In K. Lorenz (R. Martin, trans.), *Studies in animal and human behaviour.* Cambridge, MA: Harvard University Press, 1970. (Originally written, 1935.)

Pavlov, I. P. *[Conditioned reflexes]* (G. V. Anrep, Ed. and trans.). London: Oxford University Press, 1927.

Piaget, J. *Genetic epistemology.* New York: Columbia University Press, 1970.

Riegel, K. F. (Ed.). *The development of dialectical operations.* Basel: Karger, 1975.

Rousseau, J. J. *Emile, or on education.* London: Dent, 1911. (Originally published, 1762.)

Ryle, G. *The concept of mind.* London: Hutchinson's University Library, 1949.

Sameroff, A. J. Transactional models in early social relations. In K. F. Riegel (Ed.), *The development of dialectical operations.* Basel: Karger, 1975.

Sameroff, A. J., & Harris, A. Dialectical approaches to early thought and language. In M. H. Bornstein & W. Kessen (Eds.), *Psychological development from infancy.* Hillsdale, NJ: Lawrence Erlbaum Associates, 1979.

Solomon, R. L., & Lessac, M. S. A control group design for experimental studies of developmental processes. *Psychological Bulletin,* 1968, *70,* 145-150.

Sontag, L. W. *The Fels Research Institute for the Study of Human Development.* Yellow Springs, OH: Antioch College, 1946.

Tanner, J. M., Whitehouse, R. H., & Takaishi, M. Standards from birth to maturity for height, weight, height velocity and weight velocity: British children 1965. *Archives of Disease in Childhood,* 1966, *41,* 454-471; 613-635.

Tees, R. C. Effect of visual deprivation on development of depth perception in the rat. *Journal of Comparative and Physiological Psychology,* 1974, *86,* 300-308.

Terman, L. M. *The measurement of intelligence.* Boston: Houghton Mifflin, 1916.

von Bertalanffy, L. *General systems theory.* New York: Braziller, 1968.

Waddington, C. H. *Principles of development of differentiation.* New York: Macmillan, 1966.

Watson, J. B. Psychology as the behaviorist views it. *Psychological Review,* 1913, *20,* 158–177.

Watson, J. B. *Psychological care of infant and child.* New York: Norton, 1928.

Werner, H. *Comparative psychology of mental development.* Chicago: Follett, 1948.

Werner, H. The concept of development from a comparative and organismic point of view. In D. Harris (Ed.), *The concept of development.* Minneapolis: University of Minnesota Press, 1957.

White, S. Evidence for hierarchical arrangement of learning processes. In L. P. Lipsitt & C. C. Spiker (Eds.), *Advances in child development and behavior* (Vol. 2). New York: Academic Press, 1965.

Wiens, J. A. Effects of early experience on substrate pattern selection in *Rana aurora* tadpoles. *Copeia,* 1970, *3,* 543–548.

Zelazo, P. R., Zelazo, N. A., & Kolb, S. "Walking" in the newborn. *Science,* 1972, *176,* 314–315.

DEVELOPMENTAL COMPARISONS:
II. METHODOLOGY AND RESEARCH
Thomas M. Achenbach[1]

INTRODUCTION

Virtually by definition, the focus of developmental research is on comparisons between observations of individuals at different levels of development. However, this simple formulation masks a host of complexities concerning the purposes of the comparisons, the nature of the observations, the selection of subjects, the specification of the conditions under which they are studied, the definition of developmental level, and the interpretation of findings. The purposes of Section II of this chapter are to appraise some of the difficulties involved and to discuss how to contend with the difficulties without obscuring or trivializing the questions that inspire interest in development. Three major sources of developmental questions are outlined, and then the relevant strategies of comparison are surveyed. Finally, the methodological problems arising in developmental comparisons are analyzed, and solutions to these problems are considered.

SOURCES OF DEVELOPMENTAL RESEARCH QUESTIONS

Theoretical Questions

Although not all developmental research is specifically designed to test or extend theory, theoretical assumptions—either implicit or explicit— inevitably shape the questions asked, the methods chosen, and the conclusions drawn. All research is rooted in theory because research procedures are by-products of the theoretical evolution of the field. Thus, the questions asked, the ways in which they are formulated, and the tools for answering them reflect theories of knowledge and behavior that originated long before the canons of scientific method or the technology of contemporary behavioral research. The apparent inescapability of certain theoretical issues despite advances in methodology is underlined by the

---

[1]This chapter was written by Dr. Achenbach in his private capacity. No support or endorsement by the Public Health Service was involved or should be inferred.

persistence of conflicting themes that were evident in philosophical views of development long predating empirical research.

Empiricist-Associationist versus Nativist-Structuralist Views. The most fundamental theoretical polarity is represented at one extreme by a view that can be traced from the *tabula rasa* conception of the infant proposed by Aristotle through a long line of British philosophers—including Locke, Hume, James Mill, and John Stuart Mill—and that was translated into the format of twentieth-century stimulus-response (S-R) psychology by Pavlov, Watson, Hull, and Skinner, among others. This tradition can be characterized as *empiricist-associationist* in recognition of its emphasis on (1) sensory *experience* as the source of knowledge and behavior, and (2) the formation of *associative bonds* as the mechanism of behavioral change. The opposite extreme is represented by a view that can be traced from Plato's conception of ideal forms through Kant's theory of innate categories, that has been translated into Gestalt psychology's model of perception and Chomsky's theory of grammar. This tradition can be characterized as *nativist-structuralist* in recognition of its empahsis on (1) *innate* determination of mental functioning, and (2) the primacy of mental *structure* or organization in psychological processes.

Developmental versus Nondevelopmental Theory. It is important to note the degree to which epistemological viewpoints affect both what is common to most developmental research and what produces disparities—sometimes subtle and unrecognized—among approaches to a particular topic. As an example, Piaget's (1970) theory has been a major source of research questions for developmentalists of many theoretical persuasions. The theory itself is rooted in the nativist-structuralist tradition, in that it places heavy emphasis on cognitive structure. However, innate determinants are given a far weaker role than in purer versions of nativist-structuralist theory. Although Piagetian theory allows for genetic shaping of the general modes of adaptive functioning and of species-specific growth plans, it excludes on two grounds the type of innate determination of psychological structure that Gestalt and Chomskyian theory dictate. First, because psychological structures are unlikely to exist in their mature form at birth, it postulates developmental mechanisms to account for their emergence. Second, because there appear to be qualitative differences in functioning between adults and children of various ages, it postulates an ordered sequence of stages that culminate in adult structures. Research based on Piagetian theory is therefore shaped by (1) definitions of variables in terms of structural constructs, (2) a focus on the ways in which structures emerge, and (3) the assumption of an ordered sequence of structural stages.

The two grounds on which Piagetian theory opposes its intellectual kin of that nativist-structuralist tradition illustrate how developmental theories in general differ from most psychological and philosophical theories. Whereas nondevelopmental theories focus on attained modes of functioning—typically in adults—developmental theories focus on the sequence and process of changes in functioning that occur over relatively long periods. The research questions posed by nondevelopmental theories thus concern the principles governing existing psychological systems and their responses to specific inputs. By contrast, the research questions posed by developmental theories concern the principles and sequence of *change* in psychological systems that occur over the life span.

Although the contrast between Piagetian and other theories rooted in the nativist-structuralist tradition highlights the difference in research questions generated by developmental and nondevelopmental theories that share the same epistemological heritage, it is also important to note the disparities between research questions arising from theories that share a developmental focus on change and sequence but that have very different epistemological assumptions. In terms of the volume of developmental research generated, the S-R descendants of the empiricist-associationist tradition offer the most points of comparison with research generated by Piagetian theory.

Unlike the Piagetian focus on constructs of cognitive organization, the S-R focus is on the learning of specific behavioral responses to specific stimulus situations. In most versions of S-R theory, the general mechanisms of change in S-R associations are assumed to be the same for organisms of all ages, and the sum total of change over any particular period is assumed to reflect merely the accumulation of associative bonds over that period. However, the obvious changes in biological and behavioral levels from birth to maturity have persuaded S-R researchers who study children to adapt their paradigm to the parameters of functioning that characterize their particular subjects. Consequently, the behavior studied, the means of studying it, and the environmental contingencies assumed to be relevant differ greatly according to the age and ability of the subjects.

Furthermore, in order to conceptualize apparent developmental changes in learning and to study phenomena uncovered by approaches such as Piaget's, S-R researchers have invoked constructs of mediating responses and cognitive organization to such a degree that much S-R research on children's learning is better labeled as "cognitive-behavioral" rather than purely behavioral (see Achenbach, 1978; Berlyne, 1965; Gagné, 1968; Kendler & Kendler, 1970; Mischel & Mischel, 1976). Thus, in its application to developmental research, the S-R paradigm is characterized by (1) modifications to take account of the dramatic differences in subjects of different ages, (2) the assumption that environmental contingencies nevertheless determine associative bonds, and (3) the assumption that these bonds are governed by the same general principles at all ages, even if mediating constructs are used to conceptualize the specific variables to which the principles apply.

To recapitulate, theoretical questions inevitably affect developmental research because our research procedures have been devised to perform tasks defined by theoretical views and these views continue to affect the ways in which research questions are formulated. As examples, the Piagetian and S-R approaches reflect contrasting epistemological views of psychological variables and their determinants; yet they also share a common interest in the mechanisms and sequences of change in psychological functioning. It is as conceptual models for the mechanisms and sequences of change that general theories of development explicitly serve as sources of research questions, but as sources of methods and ways of framing research questions they also implicitly shape the research on topical questions and social issues to be discussed next.

Topical Questions

By topical questions, I mean those that concern a particular aspect of psychological functioning and/or a particular period of development, rather than the broad course and mechanisms of development with which the general developmental theories deal. A look at recent issues of the major journals in developmental psychology shows that the majority of studies are of this sort. In some cases, they deal with a very specific accomplishment characteristic of subjects of particular ages, such as children's understanding of particular terms, concepts, or relations; in other cases, they deal with descriptions of a general class of behavior, such as social interactions; in still others, they attempt to elucidate a particular facet of a major phenomenon, such as the acquisition of language or of perceptual constancies. Topical studies often draw on general theories of development for their conceptual and methodological underpinnings, but they rarely test or extend these theories per se. Instead, the theoretical implications of topical studies tend to be confined to testing or extending "miniature" theories propounded to explain very specific phenomena. Miniature theories often reflect the assumptions and explanatory constructs of the general theories, but the credibility of the general theories is seldom affected much by the fate of the miniature theories, which come and go with considerable rapidity.

According to Kuhn's (1970) interpretation of the history of science, the influence of general theoretical paradigms appears to depend more on their heuristic value for researchers active during a particular stage in the evolution of a science than on decisive tests of their validity. Thus, even though most topical studies and miniature theories do not individually have much bearing on the major paradigms, the degree to which topical studies and miniature theories draw on a particular paradigm reflects the implicit influence of that paradigm in the thinking of active researchers. However, because the links between topical research and general theoretical paradigms in developmental psychology are often tenuous, and because the general paradigms themselves spawn a variety of interpretations and subtheories, topical research may appear to contribute little to the advancement of developmental psychology as a discipline.

Because no science can be completely mapped out in advance, it is not surprising that linear trends in the advancement of developmental knowledge are difficult to discern in topical studies. Yet it may be worth asking whether these studies merit attention beyond the small circle and short period in which a particular topic is popular. Since the tremendous expansion of developmental research in the 1960s, there have been successive waves of interest in topics that have generated a great deal of research for a relatively short period but then have crested and all but disappeared. The demise of popular topics has often seemed to result more from researchers' efforts to ride a new wave of interest than from completion of definitive research on earlier topics.

It should of course be recognized that, lacking prophetic foresight, researchers must explore many blind alleys before they find major payoffs, and that this exploration is an essential step in building a viable methodology and in restructuring research questions into more answerable forms. But even allowing for such factors, it is difficult to see much contribution to cumulative knowledge from many of the studies generated by temporary interest in particular topics. A central issue is, therefore, whether generalizable inferences about development can be drawn from studies of specific topics that neither explicitly contribute to an overall theory of development nor culminate in definitive conclusions about the specific topic itself.

Social Questions

In addition to theoretical and topical questions, attempts to obtain socially beneficial knowledge have been a major source of developmental research. In fact, American developmental research originated primarily with G. Stanley Hall's (e.g., 1914) questionnaire efforts to gather information about children on which to base educational reforms. From the beginning of Hall's work in the 1880s, students of child psychology shared a conviction that increased knowledge of development would have beneficial applications to childrearing and education. As a consequence, advice flowed freely (though in contradictory directions) from experts as diverse as Hall's student Arnold Gesell, the archbehaviorist John B. Watson, and the psychoanalytic followers of Freud. However, it was mainly through the efforts of an economist,

Lawrence K. Frank, that developmental research achieved an identity of its own, separate from experimental education and the mainstream of psychology (Senn, 1975). Based on the belief that research was needed to guide childrearing and education, Frank in the early 1920s persuaded the Laura Spelman Rockefeller Foundation to fund interdisciplinary child study institutes at several universities. The sense of mission shared by researchers at these institutes was given organizational form in 1933 with the founding of the Society for Research in Child Development, which then provided the primary channels for communication of developmental research through its journals and meetings.

Social Policy Issues. Despite the practical intent of the child study institutes, it was not until the 1950s that knowledge of child development was more widely sought in relation to important questions of social policy. The 1954 Supreme Court decision outlawing segregated schools was based in part on research indicative of harm to black children's self-concepts, but it was the success of the Soviet Sputnik in 1957 that triggered the first large-scale federal efforts to utilize developmental research to promote specific social goals. The responses to Sputnik were directed mainly at enhancing development of mathematical and scientific thinking in order to catch up with the Soviets. Thereafter, the National Institute of Child Health and Human Development was established in 1963 to provide a permanent base for research on children. This was followed by a host of War on Poverty and Great Society programs, such as Project Head Start and Project Follow Through, into which developmental research was incorporated in recognition of how little was known about enhancing children's development and well-being. Developmental research has also been called on to answer other important social questions, such as how to utilize television to benefit children; how children are affected by violence seen on television; how to promote the welfare of the increasing number of children placed in daycare; how to improve mental health services to children; how to optimize education for handicapped and disturbed children; and how to protect children from abuse and neglect.

Practical Utilization of Research. Unlike research generated by theoretical and topical questions, research instigated by social questions can seldom be molded neatly into preexisting definitions of variables and standardized procedures for studying them. First, important social questions are typically posed in such a general way as to invite only the most speculative of answers. It is therefore necessary to translate them into specific independent and dependent variables about which testable hypotheses can be stated. Second, it is necessary to define levels or values of the variables to be tested. Third, it is necessary to find or create measures of the variables in order to determine how they covary with one another. Fourth, it is necessary to identify conditions under which the covariation of variables can be assessed in ways that are not confounded with variation in other variables.

The foregoing requirements have counterparts in most theoretical and topical research, but research designed to answer social questions is further complicated by the fact that the answers must be applicable to complex real-world situations. Although laboratory conditions can sometimes be used to assess the relations among variables hypothesized to be relevant to particular social questions, the ultimate test must be made under conditions where many variables cannot be controlled and in less time than needed for programmatic basic research. Furthermore, to affect social policy decisions, research instigated by social questions must be communicable in a compelling fashion to people who are neither researchers nor more sensitive to research findings than to political and economic pressures, the opinions of nonresearch constituencies, or their own prejudices (see Achenbach, 1978, chapter 8, for illustrations).

The recent history of developmental research has exposed numerous gaps between the social questions asked and the tools available for answering them. Despite the applied emphasis of traditional child psychology in the United States, the social questions raised have cut across so many theoretical and topical areas as to defy adequate formulation within preexisting paradigms. When attempts were made to apply such paradigms, it became clear that a great deal of ad hoc engineering was necessary to adapt their constructs and methods to the conditions and populations about which the questions were asked. Unlike the physical sciences, developmental psychology had neither the long accumulation of applied technology nor the cadres of engineers required to put theory into practice. This has contributed to disillusionment with the ability of behavioral sciences to solve important social problems.

STRATEGIES OF COMPARISON

Longitudinal versus Cross-Sectional Comparisons

Developmental questions arising from all the sources just outlined concern stability and change in individuals as they age. The most obvious way to answer such questions is by studying the same individuals continuously as they grow older, i.e., to study them *longitudinally*. Indeed, the hope of being able to glean from longitudinal studies a total picture of development inspired major investments in longitudinal projects during the emergence of developmental research in the 1920s. Several of the early longitudinal studies have in fact yielded massive data on people followed from early childhood well into adulthood (e.g., Bayley, 1970; Kagan & Moss, 1962). However, as is discussed in the following sections, a variety of methodological and practical constraints have prevented these studies from providing the definitive conclusions originally anticipated.

Because longitudinal research takes so long and requires such sustained commitments of resources, researchers, and subjects, a far more common strategy for answering developmental questions is to compare individuals who differ in developmental level but who are assumed to be similar in other respects. If the assumption of similarity is valid, this *cross-sectional* strategy is expected to reveal how less developed individuals will be when they reach the developmental levels already attained by the more advanced group with whom they are compared. The goal is to derive inferences about the course of development from the level represented by the less-advanced subjects to the level represented by the more-advanced subjects without having to wait for the development to occur. However, because each developmental level is represented by different individuals, it can never be known for certain whether differences obtained between cohorts in fact reflect a course of development that both cohorts are following, or whether the obtained differences reflect characteristics that are peculiar to one cohort but not the other.

The difficulty in insuring that different age cohorts are following such a similar developmental path that phenotypic differences between them can be attributed exclusively to the different points they have reached on that path limits the power of the cross-sectional strategy for delineating the course and mechanisms of development. Yet the severity of the limitations depends on the variables and developmental periods in question and on the possibilities for corroborating conclusions through convergent operations. As with the longitudinal strategy, the virtues and weaknesses of the cross-sectional strategy are not absolute but are relative to the questions asked and to the other alternatives for answering them.

Correlational versus Experimental Comparisons

Although the independent variable of most general interest is age (or developmental level otherwise defined), many other independent variables are relevant to developmental change. Like age, some of these—such as gender, race, socioeconomic status, birth order, and family constellation—cannot be deliberately manipulated. These variables can therefore only be studied in a *correlational* fashion by comparing individuals who already differ on them but who are assumed to be similar in other important respects. The effects of other molar variables—such as educational curricula, daycare, clinical interventions, and methods of discipline—may potentially be manipulated and assessed through *experimental* studies in which similar individuals are subjected to differing levels of the independent variable. Likewise, experimental studies may be used to manipulate more molecular variables in order to test hypothesized mechanisms of functioning and change, typically under laboratory conditions where all other important variables are assumed to be controlled. This has been the preferred strategy of S-R researchers who extrapolate from laboratory experimental studies to more molar phenomena occurring under naturalistic conditions. The effects of experimental manipulations are usually studied over relatively short periods in cross-sectional samples or samples assumed to represent only a single developmental level. Most longitudinal studies employ correlational analyses to assess the effects of independent variables. Each strategy is vulnerable to sources of error that are unlikely to be overcome by means of that strategy alone. Some of the most salient sources of error will be delineated in the following sections.

A CRITICAL WEAKNESS IN DEVELOPMENTAL COMPARISONS

The Ceteris Paribus Requirement

A basic prerequisite for confirming inferences about causal relations between variables is that the dependent variable must be measured under conditions in which all other variables are held constant except the hypothesized independent variable. If the dependent variable consistently changes with changes in the independent variable, ceteris paribus (other things being equal), this implies that changes in the independent variable cause changes in the dependent variable. Furthermore, because almost any variable of interest is likely to be affected by more than a single hypothesized independent variable, causal generalizations must also be qualified with the ceteris paribus clause—i.e., once covariation between the independent and dependent variable has been satisfactorily established, it can only be precisely generalized to conditions where all other relevant variables remain constant.

The classic method for studying causal relations between individual independent and dependent variables is, of course, the laboratory experiment in which the independent variable is deliberately manipulated in order to track concomitant changes in the dependent variable. However, even when all relevant environmental variables can be controlled, the impossibility of directly controlling all relevant characteristics of living organisms requires experimenters to approximate the ceteris paribus requirement by using samples of subjects selected to be representative of the larger populations of interest, although it is recognized that the causal relations between independent and dependent variables may not be identically manifested in every individual of the sample or population. A further concession to the impossibility of meeting the *ceteris paribus* requirement in the study of living organisms is that data obtained on groups of subjects are evaluated by means of statistical tests in order to separate variance associated with hypothesized independent variables from variables not associated with these variables. Causal inference thus rests most directly on ratios obtained between the variance in an independent variable that is attributable to specific independent variables and the total variance of the dependent variable; the obtained ratios are then judged for significance in terms of how rarely they could occur by chance if there were in fact no reliable covariation between the independent and dependent variables (see Seitz, in this volume).

Obstacles to Fulfilling the *Ceteris Paribus* Condition

Despite the concessions to uncontrollable complexity made by conducting experiments on samples of subjects and evaluating the results statistically, laboratory experiments designed to study relations between a manipulable independent variable and a behavioral response can adequately approximate the *ceteris paribus* requirement for inferring causality, at least when both the independent and dependent variable are assessed within an interval during which all other relevant variables remain controlled. However, consider the problem posed by developmental research questions. Because the focus is on changes in the behavior of organisms as a function of their developmental level, the dependent variable of interest must be compared cross-sectionally in subjects who represent different developmental levels or longitudinally in the same subjects as they reach different developmental levels. Whenever a variable as complex and intrinsically unmanipulable as developmental level—or gender, race, socioeconomic status, birth order, etc.—is of primary interest, there is little hope of approximating the *ceteris paribus* requirement purely by means of the laboratory experimental approach. Although this approach may still be useful for comparing developmentally grouped subjects on specific dependent variables and for studying interactions between developmental level and manipulable independent variables, there are at least two major obstacles to meeting the *ceteris paribus* requirement when developmental level is treated as an independent variable.

Unmanipulability of Developmental Level. The most obvious obstacle is the difficulty in experimentally manipulating developmental level in order to insure that changes in dependent variables can be inferred to result from changes in developmental level, *ceteris paribus*. A possible loophole is to define developmental level so narrowly that it is equated with independent variables that are in fact manipulable, but this precludes too much of interest to developmental researchers to be an acceptable solution.

Difficulty of Operationally Defining Developmental Level. The second major obstacle concerns the operational definition of developmental level. Although chronological age (CA) is by far the most widely used index of developmental level, it is generally regarded merely as a convenient proxy for a host of biological, cognitive, social, emotional, and experiential variables that are assumed to correlate with age. Unfortunately, such correlations as exist are likely to vary greatly with other characteristics of the populations from which subjects are drawn and with the particular ages studied. For example, some biological characteristics—such as sexual maturity—covary with CA in different ways for populations having different gene pools, nutrition, and environmental climates. Moreover, even within a single population, sexual maturity has negligible correlations with CA prior to the ages at which a substantial proportion of children are pubescent and following the CA at which most are mature, but moderate correlations during the period when most attain puberty. Similarly, the relations between cognitive developmental level and CA may vary greatly with genetic and environmental variables, as well as with the effects of disease and neurological damage.

For certain aspects of development, reliable indices exist that can provide adequate operational rankings of individuals within a particular population: For biological development, bone age provides such an index; for cognitive development, mental age (MA) does; and for educational development, achievement tests do. Yet the far-from-perfect correlations among measures of even a single aspect of development leave much uncontrolled variation among subjects equated on these measures. In view of the additional effects imposed on behavior by social, emotional, motivational, and experiential variables that—though likely to be correlated with development—are as yet far less scalable in developmental terms, the problem of meeting the *ceteris paribus* requirement with respect to developmental level is enormous. There is simply no one operational definition of developmental level that can (1) provide a manipulable independent variable for purposes of experimental research and/or (2) provide the index of development with which to identify individuals who differ in developmental level, and *only* in developmental level, for purposes of correlational research.

Problems Arising from Failure to Meet the *Ceteris Paribus* Requirement

The problems created by failure to meet the *ceteris paribus* requirement with respect to developmental level can be seen in almost all phases of developmental research. For example, a particular stimulus situation may be construed very differently by subjects who differ in biological, cognitive, and other aspects of development and whose past experience leads them to respond differently to the demand characteristics of the situation. Likewise, the topography and meaning of subjects' responses vary with developmental level, therefore requiring different measurement procedures, or at least an adjustment for the differing distributions of responses and their different implications.

In addition to the *differences* between responses by subjects differing in developmental level, it is also necessary to take account of the fact that overt *similarities* in behavior by subjects of different levels may mask very different underlying determinants and processes. Furthermore, overtly similar behaviors treated as dependent variables may have developmentally different patterns of covariation with one another, such that they collectively comprise a single variable at one age but are independent of one another at another age. The function of particular behaviors may also change radically with development, causing behaviors that are highly adaptive at one period to become maladaptive or superfluous at another period. Unlike the short-term laboratory experiment, research on behavioral change occurring over developmentally significant periods is thus greatly complicated by the need to adjust research settings, definitions and measures of variables, and interpretations of findings to developmentally different subjects among whom comparisons are made. In short, so many developmental variables covary in such complex, inconsistent, and possibly unknowable ways as to make achievement of the *ceteris paribus* requirement for causal inference seem nearly hopeless.

SOLUTIONS TO PROBLEMS OF DEVELOPMENTAL COMPARISON

Life-Span Analyses: Effects of Age, Cohort, and Time of Assessment

If the variables of greatest interest to developmentalists are not amenable to causal analysis by studying them one at a time while all other variables are held constant, what are the alternatives? One approach has been proposed by life-span developmental psychologists in response to problems arising in the interpretation of findings on individuals of different birth cohorts who were assessed at different ages. As an example, the norms of the Wechsler Adult Intelligence Scale (WAIS; Wechsler, 1955) were based on cross-sectional samples of people aged 25 to 64. Because it was found that scores were negatively correlated with age in these samples, it was originally concluded that adults' WAIS performance declines as they grow older. However, this conclusion has been contradicted by later findings that WAIS performance *improves* significantly with age when the *same* adults are retested at intervals long enough to avoid practice effects (e.g., Kangas & Bradway, 1971). The negative correlation between scores and age in Wechsler's cross-sectional samples may therefore have been due to differences in educational and cultural experiences that were correlated with the historical epochs in which the different birth cohorts developed, rather than with declines in the performance of individual adults as they aged.

Although longitudinal studies might appear to avoid the confounding of age and cohort differences to which cross-sectional studies are so vulnerable, conclusions drawn from age changes in a single cohort studied longitudinally are vulnerable to another type of confounding between age and the characteristics of particular cohorts. Even if sampling biases, selective attrition, and the effects of repeated assessment can be controlled sufficiently to insure that results obtained on a longitudinal sample are representative of the cohort from which the sample is drawn, it is possible that changes in behavior from one age to another reflect either trends unique to that cohort or trends that are occurring at other ages in other cohorts in response to general cultural-historical conditions. An example of the latter was evident in a study by Nesselroade and Baltes (1974), who compared age changes in personality test scores obtained over a 2-year period by cohorts ranging from 13 to 16 years in initial age and 15 to 18 in final age. All four cohorts were found to decline in superego strength and social-emotional anxiety. As a result, the scores of the youngest adolescents resembled those of the oldest adolescents at the end of the study rather than resembling the scores of the oldest as they had been at the beginning of the study. The findings thus appeared to reflect similar responses by all four cohorts to changing cultural conditions; a study of only one cohort would have led to the erroneous conclusion that the observed changes were a function of age per se.

In order to delineate effects associated with cohort, age, and time of assessment, Schaie (1965) has proposed a life-span analysis whereby these variables are treated as separate sources of variance, as shown in Table 3.1. According to the table, a simple *cross-sectional* study comparing 5-, 7-, and 9-year-olds in 1980 would require children from cohorts born in 1975, 1973, and 1971, respectively. However, differences found between the age groups could be attributable to differences in their cohorts as well as to age per se. A simple *longitudinal* study of the 1977 birth cohort at ages 5, 7, and 9 would require assessing the cohort in 1982, 1984, and 1986, respectively. In this case, differences between the same children assessed at different ages could reflect general cultural-historical changes or age changes unique to their cohort as well as age changes generalizable to other cohorts. A third conventional design, the *time-lag design,* could be used to assess cultural-historical effects by comparing subjects from different cohorts when they reach the same age in different years. For example, the 1971, 1973, 1975, and 1977 cohorts can be compared when they reach the age of 11 in 1982, 1984, 1986, and 1988,

TABLE 3.1
Interrelations Among
Time and Age Variables Involved
In Developmental Analyses

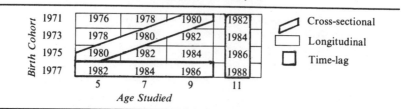

Note. Figures in table are the years in which each birth cohort would be studied at each age listed below the table (adapted from Achenbach, 1978).

respectively. However, this design confounds possible differences in cohorts with differences associated with the year of assessment.

Sequential Designs

It is clear from Table 3.1 that at least two sources of variance are inevitably confounded in conventional longitudinal, cross-sectional, and time-lag designs. In efforts to separate the confounded sources of variance, life-span developmental psychologists have proposed combinations of the conventional designs known as *longitudinal sequential, cross-sectional sequential,* and *time-lag sequential* designs (Baltes, 1968; Buss, 1973). The longitudinal sequential design is exemplified by the Nesselroade-Baltes (1974) study cited earlier in which four cohorts of adolescents were compared as they aged over a period of two years. By studying different cohorts over the same longitudinal period, it is possible to do cross-sectional comparisons at any point in the study, longitudinal comparisons of the course of development followed by each cohort during the study, and time-lag comparisons among cohorts as they reach a particular age in successive years, as illustrated in Table 3.2a.

In the *cross-sectional sequential design,* cross-sectional samples are drawn from several birth cohorts at successive points in time. As illustrated in Table 3.2b, this design follows much the same pattern as the longitudinal sequential design, *except* that the assessments on each occasion are made on *different* samples from the same cohort, rather than being made on the same samples followed longitudinally. Because cross-sectional sequential designs do not require preservation of the same samples, their samples are not vulnerable to the effects of initial selection for expected long-term availability, of attrition, or of repeated assessment. On the other hand, the lack of longitudinal assessment means that changes in individuals cannot be identified over time

TABLE 3.2
Longitudinal Sequential, Cross-Sectional Sequential, And Time-Lag Sequential Designs

Legend: □ indicates cohort ┊ indicates separate samples within cohort

[a] Longitudinal Sequential Design

Birth Cohort	5	6	7	8	9
1973			1980	1981	1982
1974		1980	1981	1982	
1975	1980	1981	1982		

Age Studied

[b] Cross-Sectional Sequential Design

Birth Cohort	5	6	7	8	9
1973			1980	1981	1982
1974		1980	1981	1982	
1975	1980	1981	1982		

Age Studied

[c] Time-Lag Sequential Design

Birth Cohort	7	8	9
1973	1980	1981	1982
1974	1981	1982	1983
1975	1982	1983	1984

Age Studied

[a]Longitudinal sequential design in which three 2-year longitudinal studies are coordinated to study development between ages 5 and 9. The same subjects within each cohort are studied on three occasions from 1980 to 1982.

[b]Cross-sectional sequential design in which three samples are drawn from each of three cohorts on three occasions from 1980 to 1982.

[c]Time-lag sequential design in which three samples from each of three cohorts are compared on three occasions from 1980–1982, 1981–1983, and 1982–1984. (adapted from Achenbach, 1978).

95

and that fluctuations in sampling among occasions of assessment may be confounded with the age and cohort effects of interest.

In the *time-lag sequential design* (Buss, 1973), assessments of two or more samples from each of several cohorts are made as they reach two or more age levels in different years. As illustrated in Table 3.2c, this is intended to focus on cultural-historical changes in the behavior of individuals at particular ages by comparing members of different cohorts as they reach a particular age in different years.

The sequential designs just outlined have been proposed as ideal models for disentangling major sources of variance in developmental studies. However, their requirements for interlocking observations on different birth cohorts, spread over intervals long enough to be developmentally significant, are difficult to implement, especially because interactions with other major variables—such as gender, socioeconomic status, and intelligence—would typically be of interest as well. Furthermore, as Table 1 shows, only two of the three variables of age, cohort, and time of assessment can be separated from one another. By specifying the age and birth cohort to be studied, the time of assessment is automatically specified, because a particular cohort attains a particular age in only one particular year. Likewise, specifying the year and age of assessment automatically specifies the cohort, and specifying the cohort and time of assessment automatically specifies the age of assessment.

Because all three variables cannot be fully separated from one another, variance attributed to any one could be inextricably confounded with variance due to at least one other. Critics have in fact shown that the idealized life-span designs, as well as their implementation in practice by life-span researchers, fall far short of the claims made for them (Adam, 1978; Horn & Donaldson, 1976, 1977). However, because any research design represents more of an ideal model to facilitate the pursuit of particular goals than a guarantee of perfection, the practical difficulties and apparently intrinsic weaknesses of the life-span designs should not preclude consideration of the potential contributions made by life-span analyses. The possible influences of the cohort and time of assessment on developmental comparisons should certainly be taken into account wherever relevant, and the sequential designs offer clearer specification of more sources of variance than do the conventional cross-sectional, longitudinal, and time-lag designs. Perhaps the major lesson to be drawn from the hopes raised and the shortcomings detected in the life-span analyses is that optimal use should be made of even partial solutions that contribute to knowledge incrementally, despite their failure to provide decisively unambiguous answers. The following sections therefore outline other partial solutions that may collectively advance our knowledge of development.

DESCRIPTION AND EXPLANATION

In debates over the value of life-span designs, a primary issue has been the degree to which they provide a basis for *description* or *explanation* of developmental change. In attempting to reconcile their different views of life-span designs, Schaie and Baltes (1975) agreed that certain of the designs can be employed alone to describe the course of developmental change in individuals and that others can be used to describe changes in populations over time, but that combinations of the designs are necessary simultaneously to describe individual developmental change and changes in populations over time. Despite agreement on the descriptive capabilities of their life-span designs, Schaie and Baltes nevertheless disagree on whether the designs permit what they call "explanatory inferences about genetic and environmental agents of change [p. 387]." Schaie contends that the sources of variance purported to be separable in life-span designs can be interpreted as representing different classes of determinants, such as the genetic and environmental; whereas Baltes contends that other approaches are needed to measure or manipulate these variables.

Description as Explanation

Where major independent variables of interest can be either directly manipulated or sufficiently isolated to approximate the *ceteris paribus* condition, an accurate description of the functional relations between particular independent variables and particular dependent variables can in some cases qualify as an explanation. For example, if the function relating the pressure of a gas to its temperature is known, increases in temperature "explain" increases in pressure, *ceteris paribus*. Having a descriptive explanation of this sort does not preclude a search for more molecular explanations (e.g., What is it about heat and the composition of gases that produces the observed relation?), but its extreme precision, testability, and replicability render superfluous any quibbles over whether it is really an explanation or "merely" a description. If developmentalists had many functional statements approaching the elegance and accuracy of the equation describing the relations between the temperature and pressure of gases, the question of description versus explanation would probably be forgotten.

Unfortunately, owing to the paucity of developmental variables that can be both operationally defined and compared as they take on different values, the question of description versus explanation is likely to persist until descriptions are achieved that permit identification of reliable functional relations among well-described variables. However, it should be remembered that the great power and elegance of physical laws are products of milennia of trial-and-error tinkering with translations of everyday experience into hypothetical variables, on the one hand, and practical measures of these variables, on the other. The fact that developmentalists have not yet formulated laws to rival the gas laws implies neither that they must adopt the types of constructs and measures so successful in physics, nor that they are overlooking a magical philosopher's stone that will obviate the need for trial-and-error struggles to forge constructs and measures appropriate to their subject matter. More productive than either a slavish imitation of other sciences or debates over total solutions would be programmatic efforts to define and measure variables in ways that permit tests of their functional relations to other variables of interest.

Unlike the benign ambiguity of the descriptive versus explanatory status of the gas laws, the ambiguity about what is descriptive and what is explanatory in developmental research may be a serious handicap. With the aid of hindsight, it is easy to categorize attempts to formulate measuring procedures for temperature and pressure as being directed toward operational description of variables, whereas attempts to identify functional *relations* between measurable variables have more of an explanatory orientation. Although the same researchers often attempt both types of enterprise at the same time, and an interplay of the two is mutually beneficial and a common feature of "normal science" (Kuhn, 1970), the continuing confusion between descriptive and explanatory objectives evident in much developmental theory and research may be less beneficial. The persistence of such confusion is perhaps forgivable in light of the relative youth of the field, the intrinsic difficulty of controlling developmental variables, and the heuristic influence of grand but difficult-to-operationalize theories. However, it may be time to acknowledge that theoretical explanations even as elementary as the gas laws are dependent on operational definitions of variables. This is no trivial enterprise either, because to achieve scientifically useful descriptions of developmental phenomena will require more sophistication in the definition and measurement of variables than most of our grander theoreticians have displayed. Furthermore, precise documentation of developmental change in well-operationalized variables is likely to require a coordination of more diverse contextual variables and research strategies than even the life-span proponents have advocated, as the confounding of sources of variance in their designs undermines not only the explanatory goals championed by Schaie but the more modest descriptive goals offered by Baltes (Schaie & Baltes, 1975).

Descriptive Strategies

If reliable description and measurement of developmental variables are accepted as important prerequisites to verifiable causal explanation, how might the descriptive enterprise best proceed? I suggested earlier that we already have reliable indices of certain aspects of biological development (e.g., bone age), cognitive development (e.g., MA), and educational development (e.g., achievement tests) with which to rank individuals within a particular population. The value of these measures is not lessened by the fact that they reflect only limited aspects of development and that they are affected in complex ways by genetic and environmental variation within and between populations. Recognition of both the specificity and the vulnerability of these indices should help to cure any undue hubris regarding the possibilities for indexing other aspects of development, but their limitations also suggest what can be realistically expected—i.e., that developmental indices must be quite specific, that they are unlikely to be universally applicable without adjustments for individual and population parameters, and that their value will depend on networks of interlocking relations with other variables.

Convergent Operations. The dependence of developmental indices on relations with other variables represents a crucial key to the dilemmas raised by the difficulty in meeting the *ceteris paribus* condition. Rather than expecting truth to emerge from single studies of single variables indexed by single measures, developmentalists need multiple convergent operations both for the measurement of variables and for the verification of hypothesized relations among variables. Convergent operations directed at triangulation of variables and their interrelations are essential in most sciences, but they may be needed in the most elementary aspects of developmental description rather than being deferred until more advanced explanatory research. In terms of nonquantitative description of variables, such as Gesell's (1928) and Piaget's (1970) descriptions of infant development, this means extensive replication and cross-validation of observations, coupled with comparisons across ages and populations, plus experimental analysis of the effects of manipulable variables on the behavior of interest. The replicability and age calibration of at least some of the phenomena already identified through nonquantitative descriptions of infant development (e.g., Piagetian object permanence, infant development test performance) and of responses to standardized cognitive test items at older ages (e.g., conservation problems, IQ test items) provide one prototype.

Multivariate Data Reduction. A more quantitative approach that may be preferable in noncognitive areas is the use of multivariate statistical methods such as factor analysis and cluster analysis to reduce multiple imperfect measures to summary descriptions of behavioral patterns and to categorize individuals who can then be compared over time (see Achenbach, 1978, chapter 6; Seitz, in this volume). However, the power of multivariate statistics to reduce large masses of data to more manageable units should not be allowed to obscure their weaknesses as inferential procedures. Because multivariate statistics optimally weight data to maximize the strength of the targeted relations, replication and external validation of multivariate findings are especially necessary. In fact, Cooley and Lohnes's (1971) formulation, "multivariate heuristics," nicely conveys the nature of the contribution that multivariate data reduction can most effectively make at the present stage of developmental research: Variables and relations derived from multivariate analyses should be regarded as suggestive of hypotheses that must then be further tested and triangulated.

In addition to summarizing multiple imperfect measures of complex behavior, certain multivariate approaches may help in choosing among hypotheses about relations among variables over time. Cross-lagged panel analysis and path analysis, for example, can help to elucidate covariation among variables measured at different points in time. However, correlational analyses of this sort cannot substantiate causal inferences unless the *ceteris paribus* condition is adequately approximated or unless multiple findings converge sufficiently to rule out alternative explanations for the obtained relations. These methods can be used to help sharpen or choose among specific hypotheses, but not as definitive evidence for causal relations.

Developmental versus Trait Variance. A further aspect of developmental description concerns the separation of behavioral variation that is attributable to developmental level from variation attributable to individual differences that persist despite developmental changes. As an example, impulsivity-reflectivity has been studied as a dimension of cognitive style that correlates with other putative individual difference variables in children. However, impulsivity-reflectivity also correlates with CA and MA. This raises the question of whether variance in impulsivity-reflectivity is best ascribed to an enduring trait that persists as development progresses, to intraindividual developmental progressions, or to both (see Baldwin in Section I, this chapter).

In order to separate cognitive developmental variance from trait variance that might persist as development progresses, Achenbach and Weisz (1975) obtained measures of preschoolers' MA and impulsivity-reflectivity on two occasions 6 months apart. Although there was a significant correlation between initial and final scores for impulsivity-reflectivity, considerably more of the variance in the final scores could be accounted for by MA than by the initial scores for impulsivity-reflectivity. Furthermore, a significant correlation between impulsivity–reflectivity and hypothesis usage—a behavior assumed central to cognitive style (Kagan & Kogan, 1970)—was reduced to nonsignificance when MA was partialled out. For children of the age range tested, it thus appears that cognitive development—as indexed by MA—accounts for much of the variance that has been ascribed to the trait of impulsivity-reflectivity. A similar lack of independence from general cognitive development has likewise been demonstrated for measures of field independence (Weisz, O'Neill, & O'Neill, 1975) and moral judgment (Taylor & Achenbach, 1975). A major task of descriptive developmental research is therefore to distinguish between variance ascribable to developmental dimensions already indexed by measures such as MA and variance ascribable to traits that persist as development progresses. Failure to separate developmental from trait variance invites a proliferation of "traits" that can be more parsimoniously conceptualized in terms of general indices of development.

THEORY AND RESEARCH

The emphasis on descriptive research in the preceding discussion does not imply a rejection of theory. As pointed out at the beginning of this Section, developmental research is rooted in theoretical assumptions. Descriptive research is inevitably shaped by the researcher's assumptions about what is worth describing, how to describe it, the developmental periods over which to describe it, and the conclusions to draw from the descriptions. This being the case, it is important to make the links between research and theory as explicit as possible in order to expose the effects of researchers' conceptual frameworks on their findings and to maximize the utilization of findings to test, revise, and extend theory.

It is perhaps ironic that our heritage includes such massive theoretical edifices as the psychoanalytic, Piagetian, and S-R theories, but that so little developmental research is explicitly directed at testing, revising, extending, or comparing these theories. It may be a sign of maturity in behavioral sciences that the era of grand, "simple and sovereign" theories is giving way to more specialized miniature theories of very specific phenomena. Yet in many areas of behavioral science, including developmental psychology, it is difficult to distinguish between bona fide efforts to further miniature theories and efforts prompted more by enthusiasm for a passing fad. As a result, the rapid turnover of miniature theories and popular topics is leaving in its wake little evidence of advancement beyond the simple and sovereign theories.

Of the theoretical issues that attract much attention, too many seem to be formulated in terms of such sweeping, popularized, and essentially false dichotomies as to offer neither the possibility of empirical test nor a heuristic impetus to more refined theory. Recent examples include the nature versus nurture debate with respect to IQ (see Jensen, 1973), the social ecology versus laboratory approaches to developmental research (see Bronfenbrenner, 1977), and the continuity versus discontinuity interpretations of development (see Kagan, 1976). Although each reflects legitimate disagreements of theoretical interpretation, they have done more to spur debate than to foster differentiated and researchable approaches to important theoretical questions. In the absence of programmatic advancement of either the grand or the miniature theories of development, more explicit attention may need to be paid to the interplay among theory as a conceptual organizer, basic research as the means for programmatically testing and extending theory, and applied research as the means for providing real-world challenges to the simplified worlds of theory and basic research. The fact that many important human developmental variables are unlikely to be fully operable under the controlled conditions of basic research dictates that applied research should play a central role in the construction of developmental theory as well as in its utilization (see Achenbach, 1978, chapter 8).

SUMMARY

Developmental research focuses on comparisons among individuals at different levels of development for purposes of answering theoretical, topical, and social questions. Although much developmental research is not designed to test or extend theory, the influence of theory pervades the formulation of research problems and choices of methods. Opposing views of development represented by the empiricist-associationist and nativist-structuralist traditions have had an especially persistent influence. Developmental theories in general are distinguished from nondevelopmental theories by their emphasis on the mechanisms and sequences of change over the life span.

Despite the grounding of developmental research in theory, many current topical studies have only tenuous links to major developmental theories and only slightly more explicit links to miniature theories of specific phenomena. The miniature theories often draw on the major theories but rarely contribute to testing or extending these theories. Social questions have long kindled interest in developmental research, but recent efforts to answer important questions of social policy have exposed broad gaps between the questions and the theory, methods, and personnel available for answering them.

Strategies of developmental comparison can be distinguished according to whether they are longitudinal or cross-sectional, and according to whether they are experimental or correlational. A critical weakness in developmental comparisons of all types is that different values of the independent variable of greatest interest—developmental level—can rarely be compared under conditions where all other independent variables are held constant. The difficulty of approximating this *ceteris paribus* prerequisite for causal inference stems from the impossibility of manipulating developmental level for purposes of experimental research and the lack of unitary indices of development that can be used operationally to define developmental level unconfounded with variation in other variables for purposes of correlational research.

Lacking any total solution to the problem of approximating the *ceteris paribus* condition, developmentalists must rely on coordination of multiple partial solutions in order to identify variables and their interrelations by means of convergent operations. Among these partial solutions are life-span designs that—despite their limitations as a basis for inference—help to make explicit more sources of variance than do simpler designs; clear distinctions between description and explanation, with increased efforts to obtain reliable and differentiated descriptions through convergent operations and multivariate data reduction; separation of developmental variance from trait variance; and more explicit attention to the interplay between theory and research, both basic and applied.

REFERENCES

Achenbach, T. M. *Research in developmental psychology: Concepts, strategies, methods.* New York: Free Press, 1978.

Achenbach, T. M., & Weisz, J. R. Impulsivity-reflectivity and cognitive development in preschoolers: A longitudinal analysis of developmental and trait variance. *Developmental Psychology*, 1975, *11*, 413-414.

Adam, J. Sequential strategies and the separation of age, cohort, and time-of-measurement contributions to developmental data. *Psychological Bulletin*, 1978, *85*, 1309-1316.

Baltes, P. B. Longitudinal and cross-sectional sequences in the study of age and generation effects. *Human Development*, 1968, *11*, 145-171.

Bayley, N. Development of mental abilities. In P. Mussen (Ed.), *Carmichael's manual of child psychology.* New York: Wiley, 1970.

Berlyne, D. E. *Structure and direction in thinking.* New York: Wiley, 1965.

Bronfenbrenner, U. Toward an experimental ecology of human development. *American Psychologist*, 1977, *32*, 513-531.

Buss, A. R. An extension of developmental models that separate ontogenetic changes and cohort differences. *Psychological Bulletin*, 1973, *80*, 466-479.

Cooley, W. W., & Lohnes, P. R. *Multivariate data analysis.* New York: Wiley, 1971.

Gagné, R. M. Contributions of learning to human development. *Psychological Review*, 1968, *75*, 177-191.

Gesell, A. *Infancy and human growth.* New York: Macmillan, 1928.

Hall, G. S. *Aspects of child life and education* (T. L. Smith, Ed). Boston: Ginn, 1914.

Horn, J. L., & Donaldson, G. On the myth of intellectual decline in adulthood. *American Psychologist*, 1976, *31*, 701-719.

Horn, J. L., & Donaldson, G. Faith is not enough: A response to the Baltes-Schaie claim that intelligence does not wane. *American Psychologist*, 1977, *32*, 369-373.

Jensen, A. R. *Educability and group differences.* New York: Harper & Row, 1973.

Kagan, J. Emergent themes in human development. *American Scientist*, 1976, *64*, 186-196.

Kagan, J., & Kogan, N. Individuality and cognitive performance. In P. Mussen (Ed.), *Carmichael's manual of child psychology.* New York: Wiley, 1970.

Kagan, J., & Moss, H. A. *Birth to maturity.* New York: Wiley, 1962.

Kangas, J., & Bradway, K. Intelligence at middle age: A thirty-eight year follow-up. *Developmental Psychology*, 1971, *5*, 333-337.

Kendler, T. S., & Kendler, H. H. An ontogeny of optional shift behavior. *Child Development*, 1970, *41*, 1-27.

Kuhn, T. S. *The structure of scientific revolutions.* Chicago: University of Chicago Press, 1970.

Mischel, W., & Mischel, H. N. A cognitive social-learning approach to morality and self-regulation. In T. Likona (Ed.), *Moral development and behavior.* New York: Holt, Rinehart & Winston, 1976.

Nesselroade, J. R., & Baltes, P. B. Adolescent personality development and historical change: 1970-1972. *Monographs of the Society for Research in Child Development,* 1974, *39*(1, Serial No. 154).

Piaget, J. Piaget's theory. In P. Mussen (Ed.), *Carmichael's manual of child psychology.* New York: Wiley, 1970.

Schaie, K. W. A general model for the study of developmental problems. *Psychological Bulletin,* 1965, *64,* 92-107.

Schaie, K. W., & Baltes, P. B. On sequential strategies in developmental research and the Schaie-Baltes controversy: Description or explanation? *Human Development,* 1975, *18,* 384-390.

Senn, M. J. E. Insights on the child development movement in the United States. *Monographs of the Society for Research in Child Devleopment,* 1975, *40,* (3-4, Serial No. 161).

Taylor, J. J., & Achenbach, T. M. Moral and cognitive development in retarded and nonretarded children. *American Journal of Mental Deficiency,* 1975, *80,* 43-50.

Wechsler, D. *Manual for the Wechsler Adult Intelligence Scale.* New York: Psychological Corporation, 1955.

Weisz, J. R., O'Neill, P., & O'Neill, P. C. Field dependence-independence on the Children's Embedded Figures Test: Cognitive style or cognitive level? *Developmental Psychology,* 1975, *11,* 539-540.

4 Cross-Cultural Comparisons

Gustav Jahoda
University of Strathclyde

INTRODUCTION

Over a century ago James Hunt (1867/1934) uttered the following prophetic words in the course of an address to the Anthropological Society of London: "After a time, I think it will be found that the study of physical anthropology will be followed by researches in psychological anthropology [p. 67]." Curiously enough it was his nephew W. H. R. Rivers who, together with some other members of the 1898 expedition to the Torres Straits, was to make this prophecy come true. In recent years the label "psychological anthropology" has been reinvented and applied to a special field within anthropology. Perhaps it would be more accurate to say American anthropology, for few anthropologists elsewhere seem to have taken to it. The classical work of Rivers on perception would probably not fall within the area of psychological anthropology as currently understood, but it would clearly be an example of cross-cultural psychology. There is no sharp boundary between the two, and how one perceives their relationship depends to some extent on the perceiver's own disciplinary affiliation. Although this issue is more fully pursued later, it should already have become evident that the term "cross-cultural psychology" does not stand for any simple, clear-cut entity; in fact, like much of psychological terminology it eludes formal definition. Most writers (including the present one) have therefore dodged the issue by either confining themselves to rather vague indications or ignoring it altogether. Two notable exceptions are Price-Williams (1975), who provided a thoughtful discussion of cross-cultural psychology as a domain, and Brislin, Lonner, and Thorndike (1973), who were bold enough to put forward what they modestly called a working definition. It will serve as a useful starting point for considering some basic problems of comparative study in this sphere.

The core of their definition runs as follows: "Cross-cultural psychology is the empirical study of members of various culture... groups who have had different experiences that lead to predictable and significant differences in behavior [p. 5]." Leaving aside for the moment the vexed question of what is meant by "culture," the emphasis on *differences* should be noted. This is understandable historically where, as is shortly shown, the primary interest has always been how "others" are different from "us." The concern with differences has also almost exclusively dominated empirical studies until fairly recently: A common procedure is to apply some kind of test or task to members of two or more cultures and to record the differences obtained. A notorious example, illustrating the dangers of such an approach, is the application of intelligence tests to what used to be called various "races." Because the outcome of such efforts may be a function of the deficiencies or inappropriateness of the measures employed, the blind search for differences of any kind is risky and generally unprofitable. It is presumably for this reason that Brislin et al. (1973) referred to "predictable" and "significant" differences. Predictability implies the existence of a theoretical framework linking "different experiences" with differences in behavior; whether or not this is an essential prerequisite of cross-cultural work is one of the issues that will be considered. Another question prompted by the formulation of the definition is "What are *significant* differences?" The term is clearly not intended in the trivial statistical sense, but points to the fact that one has to select from a potentially infinite array those differences which the investigator regards as substantive and important. The criteria used involve a consideration of the objectives of cross-cultural studies, and this immediately brings out an important limitation of the one-sided stress on differences. Any comparisons between two (or more) objects, persons, or events presuppose that they have certain attributes in common; no meaningful statement can be made about relationships if this is not the case. As Wittgenstein (1961) put it, "There is no possible way of making an inference from the existence of one situation to the existence of another, entirely different situation [p. 77]." Of course, among members of the human species, even though they may belong to different cultures, similarities vastly outweigh differences; and from a biological standpoint, many of the differences encountered in cross-cultural psychological studies are relatively minor, often requiring sensitive as well as appropriate instruments in order to be firmly established.

Although it is true that the most frequent objective of cross-cultural comparisons is to show the effect of different experiences, it is also true that one may sometimes wish, in the words of Strodtbeck (1964), "to demonstrate that culture does not matter [p. 224]." In other words, there has been an interest in identifying culturally invariant aspects of behavior, i.e., universals. It should perhaps be mentioned here that similarities and differences are of course governed not merely by life experiences but also by genetic factors. As Brislin, Lonner, and Thorndike's definition implies, these are rarely invoked by cross-cultural researchers whose primary concern is with environmental influences in the broadest sense.[1]

It should be evident by now that "differences" and "similarities" are not simple and objective "facts"; as stressed by Popper (1959), they "always presuppose the adoption of *a point of view* [p. 421]." The salient interest of the researcher usually constitutes such a point of view, which will determine the selection of relevant data. It is probably no accident that the first psychologists to move into the cross-cultural field tended to be social psychologists, as cultural differences tend to be most striking in such spheres as social behavior and attitudes. As one moves toward more specialized segments of behavior, such as cognition or even physiological aspects of behavior, it is the similarities that are most visible to the naked eye and the differences correspondingly harder to detect. However, all this relates to the merely descriptive level, which is necessary but not sufficient. The aim of science, as Poincaré said, is to uncover similarities concealed beneath surface differences. Thus even when faced with the immensely rich variety of culturally patterned social behavior, the effort should be directed at isolating the common underlying elements, some of which we appear to share with the primates. Cross-cultural psychologists could also study the way in which culture-specific social behavior comes to be transmitted, but the nature of the sociocultural system itself is within the domain of anthropologists. Insofar as they regard it as their task to engage in comparative studies (and not all of them do), anthropologists are concerned with similarities and differences of sociocultural *systems*. The relationship between the two disciplines is another theme that I discuss in this chapter.

Lastly, there is the general question as to *why* one should make cross-cultural comparisons, to which some answers will be considered. The simple one, though, is that people have always been fascinated with human differences and their implications. Moreover, some of the problems that we still seek to resolve today were first posed a long time ago.

---

[1]Although this is a perfectly defensible position, ideological considerations or the fear of being branded with a "racist" label may not be altogether unconnected. The reluctance to consider even the possibility of genetic involvement is probably a weakness, especially as this has often no conceivable connection with any "racism." For instance, Das (1973) pointed out that some of the cognitive differences between Bramin and Harijan in India might have a genetic basis because these have been for many generations purely bred subpopulations.

HISTORICAL BACKGROUND

There is practically no field of study whose origin cannot be traced back to Aristotle, and cross-cultural comparisons are no exception. He discussed ethnic differences in temperament and abilities and was the first to put forward a climatic theory, attributing the alleged lack of intelligence of north European "barbarians" to the cold. Aristotle also anticipated Darwin by placing man squarely among the animals. The exigencies of space require us to skip the Middle Ages and to come to Descartes (1637/1937), who took a remarkably modern view of man:

> In the course of my travels I remarked that all those whose opinions are decidedly repugnant to ours are not on that account barbarians and savages, but on the contrary that many of these nations make an equally good, if not a better, use of their reason than we do. I took into account also the very different character which a person brought up from infancy in France or Germany exhibits, from that which, with the same mind originally, this individual would have possessed had he lived always among the Chinese or with savages [p. 14].

Hume, in his *Essays* (1826), sought to refute the climatic theory of "national character" on empirical grounds. He argued that some large nations like the Chinese with varied climate have a uniform character, whereas small neighboring ones with the same climate often differ considerably. He concluded that "physical causes have no discernible operation upon the human mind [p. 231]." Instead, he proposed a quasi-Freudian infantile determinism—such early "impressions" persisting for life. However, he did not reconcile this belief with the prevalence of social change, of which he was well aware. There were of course numerous other eighteenth-century writers preoccupied with the influences that shaped humanity; prominent among them is Rousseau, whom Lévi-Strauss (1962) acknowledged as his intellectual ancestor. All this is well known and is merely prehistory from the present standpoint because psychological aspects were only dealt with peripherally. The real history of cross-cultural perspectives begins in the nineteenth century, and it does not seem to have been recognized that John Stuart Mill may be regarded as the founding father of cross-cultural psychology.

In his *System of Logic,* Mill (1879) analyzed the conditions of a science of human nature. He divided the subject into two parts, the first being concerned with basic or universal "laws of mind," which apply to all humans everywhere. He argued that these must be abstracted from the numerous influences acting on men in the course of their lives; and unless one establishes the nature and operation of these influences, generalizations about human behavior are difficult if not impossible:

Suppose that all which passes in the mind of man is determined by a few simple laws: still, if those laws be such that there is not one of the facts surrounding a human being, or of the events which happen to him, that does not influence in some mode or degree his subsequent mental history, and if the circumstances of different human beings are extremely different, *it will be no wonder if very few propositions can be made respecting the details of their conduct or feelings, which will be true of all mankind* [p. 451; italics mine].

Mill therefore proposed the establishment of a science of the formation of human character to which he gave the name "ethology." Needless to say, this has little to do with the current technical meaning of the term, but it corresponds fairly closely to what is now known as cross-cultural psychology. What Mill essentially argued was that generalizations about human nature are culturally biased, but that cultural effects are themselves lawful and capable of being studied:

Mankind have not one universal character, but there exist universal laws of the Formation of Character. And since it is by these laws, combined with the facts of each particular case, that the whole of the phenomena of human action and feeling are produced, it is on these that every rational attempt to construct the science of human nature in the concrete, and for practical purposes, must proceed [p. 452].

Note the emphasis on applications in the last sentence! Because Mill was concerned with character, though in a very broad sense, he did not regard it as possible to proceed experimentally, for this would involve bringing up children in different and strictly controlled circumstances and noting the outcomes. Instead, he suggested an observational and statistical approach: "observing in what state of previous circumstances it is found that certain marked mental qualities and deficiences *oftenest* exist [p. 454]." From a hypothetical example given of English, French, and Italian people being compared on some "particular mental tendency," it is clear that Mill merely expected to obtain some ordinal measure as the outcome. The logical status of "ethological" principles thus arrived would be that of "middle principles," intermediary between mere empirical generalizations and the higher-order "laws of mind."

Mill also laid down some general guidelines for the conduct of ethological inquiries, noting that progress within the discipline depended on a "double process":

First, that of deducing theoretically the ethological consequences of particular circumstances of position, and comparing them with the recognised results of common experience; and secondly the reverse operation; increased study of the various types of human nature that are to be found in the world: conducted by persons not only capable of analysing and recording the circumstances in which these types severally prevail, but also sufficiently acquainted with psychological laws, to be able to explain and account for the characteristics of the type, by the peculiarities of the circumstances [p. 462].

It would seem that Mill was here perhaps not entirely consistent, for in order to be able to deduce theoretically the consequences of particular environmental factors or account for them ex post, the relevant principles must surely be already available; but possibly he was thinking of a continuous process of successive approximation. There are indications that, at least with regard to thought, he felt deduction to be possible from general psychological laws. Mill was fully aware of the complexity of the problems with which the "most imperfect" science would have to deal, but he felt hopeful that its findings could be applied in practice, especially in education.

This brief sketch will, it is hoped, have demonstrated that Mill provided an astonishingly detailed blueprint of what was later to become comparative cross-cultural psychology. He shrewdly foresaw both its potential value and inevitable weaknesses; but of course he remained at the purely theoretical and speculative level.

Although Mill seems to have been the only one who had a vision of something closely approximating cross-cultural psychology, many others discussed problems that were later to become the subject of cross-cultural studies. Hence, this presentation is highly selective, and to some extent arbitrary. The figure towering above all was of course Darwin, who contributed in two different ways. First of all he revolutionized thinking in the social sciences about man's place in nature, thereby influencing the cross-cultural approach among others. Quite recently, for instance, a Darwinian analysis of the culture-personality relationship has been proposed by LeVine (1973). Darwin also dealt with some specific issues in the area, such as the facial expression of emotions, for which he recommended what we would now call cross-cultural comparisons; about a century later his lead was systematically followed, particularly by Ekman (1973).

An evolutionary framework was employed by the classical anthropologist Tylor (1871/1958), who held the view that anthropological studies could contribute to psychological understanding. Thus on the very first page of *Primitive Culture* he wrote,

The condition of culture among the various societies of mankind, in so far as it is capable of being investigated on general principles, is a subject apt for the study of laws of human thought and action.

Underlying Tylor's scheme of the evolution of human culture is the notion of a "psychic unity of mankind" first put forward by Bastian (1860). The concept as used then concerned potentiality rather than actuality and did not imply that all peoples were regarded as psychologically similar. In fact, Tylor broadly agreed with those who likened the mentality of "savage" adults to that of "civilized" children. His view was that given a lengthy period of historical development all peoples were innately capable of responding to environmental challenges and gradually becoming the psychological equals of Victorian civilized man. Meantime, "primitive" adults had modes of thinking that were undeveloped, involving for example rudimentary errors of reasoning that one can also observe in civilized children. This view of Tylor's was vigorously attacked by Lévy-Bruhl who has been much maligned and misrepresented. Lévy-Bruhl (1923/1966) pointed out that there was evidence of many primitive people being in some respects highly intelligent, so that it would be ludicrous to liken them to children; and yet in other respects their thinking was so strange and different from our own that we cannot make sense of it. He proceeded to analyze this in terms of "collective representations"—i.e., as a social phenomenon—in opposition to Tylor who regarded the question as a matter of individual psychology. Lévy-Bruhl (as he himself finally recognized) was at fault in exaggerating the contrast between the degrees to which primitives and ourselves are influenced by social-emotional factors in our thinking. But he grappled with a genuine problem, related to that of the psychic unity of mankind. The question of the extent to which basic psychological processes are common to mankind is still perhaps *the* major one being pursued in cross-cultural psychology.

Returning briefly to Tylor, I should mention that he pioneered the analysis of institutions by classifying and tabulating them for almost three hundred cultures. This statistical approach was a forerunner of the *hologeistic* method, and its possible shortcoming, pointed out by Galton and known as "Galton's problem," has still to be reckoned with. Galton made much use of the comparative method in relation to the varied issues which occupied his versatile mind. Although a convinced hereditarian, he was not a naive one as shown by his discussion of the mental abilities of Negroes: "If the negro race in America had been affected by no social disabilities, a comparison of their achievements with those of the whites in their several branches of intellectual effort, having regard to the total number of their respective populations, would give us the necessary information. As matters stand, we must be content with much rougher data [Galton, 1869/1914]."

Galton was generally interested in what he called "the mental peculiarities of different races," and in the context of his studies of the "visualizing faculty" (by which he meant more or less what we would term "space perception"), he referred to the outstanding abilities in this respect of African Bushmen and Eskimos; his observations have since been confirmed by recent empirical studies of hunting and gathering peoples (see Berry, 1971). One could cite many more examples of Galton's "cross-cultural" interests, but I should like to conclude with one that is little known because it is an unpublished plan for a study that does not seem to have been completed; it illustrates Galton's methodological ingenuity and is reported by Pearson (1924, pp. 352-353). This is a questionnaire entitled "Ethnological Inquiries on the Innate Character and Intelligence of Different Races." Its aim was apparently to assess the relative influence of heredity and training on character and behavior. The questionnaire was intended to be completed by Europeans in contact with non-European subjects "who have been reared since childhood in European or American schools, families, asylums or missionary establishments. By this restriction it is hoped to eliminate all peculiarities that are due to the abiding influence of early education, and to the manners and customs of their own people." Respondents were expected to answer with the *average* Anglo-Saxon character as a standard, keeping in mind such factors as sex, age, education, and social position. In the absence of any *decided* departure from this standard, respondents were advised to reply "ordinary." The questionnaire, an interesting early example of this method, is reproduced as an Appendix.

Apart from Galton, the other great figure in nineteenth-century psychology who engaged in comparative studies was Wundt. However, his massive five volumes of *Völkerpsychologie* ("folk psychology") can hardly be regarded as an ancestor of cross-cultural pscyhology; judged from our present position, it was a dead-end. Wundt (1916) argued that there are "collective mental products" such as language and religion that cannot be explained in a reductionist fashion in terms of individual consciousness. It is therefore necessary to look at the findings of ethnologists and interpret these psychologically, as a kind of secondary analysis. This hopefully would throw light on the mental development of the human species. "Our first task, then, would be the investigation of *primitive man*. We must seek a psychological explanation of the thought, belief and action of primitive man on the basis of the facts supplied by ethnology [p. 7]." Nowhere does Wundt suggest that psychologists ought to investigate primitive man at first hand, and the broad oversimplified evolutionary scheme with which he ends up is not really any advance over the more direct contribution of Tylor; on the contrary, it was distinctly more shallow.

Before concluding this historical sketch, I should like to draw attention to a different kind of predecessor who is commonly and unjustly neglected, namely the missionary. The reports of missionaries tend to be lumped together with "travellers' tales" and dismissed as anecdotal. Now it is certainly true that some missionaries were bigoted and viewed "savages" from the superior vantage point of their own enlightenment. However, there were others who saw it as their business to make intensive, objective, and yet sympathetic studies of the peoples among whom they lived. Their reports are well worth close scrutiny by cross-cultural psychologists because they worked at a time when Western influences were as yet negligible. In order to illustrate this, I refer to the writings of a Scottish missionary from what is now Malawi, the Reverend Duff MacDonald (1882/1969). He provided a highly sophisticated discussion of methodological problems in studying African beliefs and behavior, which can still be read with benefit by cross-cultural psychologists. MacDonald raised the general question why one should bother to carry out detailed investigations of native customs and beliefs and answered it by stating that such studies could throw important light on "the science of the human mind." In a period when "savages" were generally regarded as stupid and irrational, he had this to say about their intellect:

> Many facts that I shall lay before the reader will seem so strange that he may doubt whether these savages have the same minds as Europeans, whether they reason or think in the same way at all. It is true, however, that after one places oneself in their circumstances, and tries to see and feel as they do, he will understand all their strangeness; he will even see that it would have been still more strange if their reasonings and conclusions had been different [p. 10].

More than half a century later the same views were expressed by the distinguished anthropologist Evans-Pritchard (1937): "I found it strange at first to live among Azande and listen to naive explanations of misfortunes which, to our minds, have apparent causes, but after a while I learnt the idiom of their thought and applied notions of witchcraft as spontaneously as themselves in situations where the concept was relevant [p. 65]."

"CULTURE" AND THE "EMIC-ETIC" ISSUE

Those early writers who were content to attribute psychological differences to "race," in the sense of inheritance, felt that they had a straightforward and satisfying explanation. Mill, as has been shown, was not so naive and, like contemporary cross-cultural psychologists, relegated genetic factors to a residual category. Evan Galton, who was a convinced hereditarian, saw the need to take account of environmental factors and clearly perceived the difficulties involved in doing this adequately. It was Tylor who introduced the word "culture" as a quasitechnical term into the social sciences. The qualification "quasi" points to the fact that, although it has become universally accepted, the term still lacks a generally agreed meaning. Kroeber and Kluckhohn (1952), after critically reviewing some 160 definitions, attempted to extract their quintessence, which runs as follows:

> Culture consists of patterns, explicit and implicit, of and for behavior acquired and transmitted by symbols, constituting the distinctive achievement of human groups, including their embodiments in artifacts; the essential core of culture consists of traditional (i.e., historically derived and selected) ideas and especially their attached values; culture systems may, on the one hand, be considered as products of action, on the other as conditioning elements of further action [p. 181].

The reason for quoting this definition is that it was adopted by Brislin et al. (1973) as the basis of their own definition of cross-cultural psychology, discussed in the Introduction. They provided no explication, and it is doubtful whether the Kroeber and Kluckhohn definition would be more than a piece of turgid jargon for anyone who has not carefully studied the original monograph. However, Brislin et al. must be given credit at least for the attempt, because most cross-cultural psychologists do not feel it incumbent on them to say what they mean by "culture." On the other hand, there has been a great deal of discussion of the related "emic versus etic" issue in comparative research, summarized by Brislin (1976) thus:

> Briefly, the distinction relates to two goals of cross-cultural research. One is to document the valid principles that describe behavior in any one culture under study, taking into account what the people themselves value as meaningful and important. This is an emic analysis; the term comes from phonemic analysis in linguistics which refers to the documentation of meaningful sounds in any one language. The second goal of cross-cultural research is to make generalizations across cultures that take into account all human behavior. The goal, then, is theory building. This would be an etic analysis; the term comes from phonetic analysis in linguistics which refers to the development of a general system which takes into account all meaningful sounds in all languages [p. 217].

Although much play is usually made of the linguistic antecedents, it is rarely mentioned that the emic-etic distinction, like the notion of culture, has been borrowed (and substantially changed in the process) from anthropology. It is also not widely known among psychologists that the topic is a rather controversial one, as indicated by the title "Anemic and Emetic Analysis in Social Anthropology" (Berreman, 1966; see also discussions by Harris, 1968; Pelto, 1970). A more detailed critique from the psychological perspective has been provided elsewhere (Jahoda, 1977); here I argue that the relative neglect of a careful analysis of culture has probably led to widespread confusions about the emic-etic issue in discussions of comparative psychological studies. As a start, therefore, the contrasting ways in which anthropologists and psychologists concern themselves with culture must be briefly examined.

As the Kroeber-Kluckhohn definition indicates, anthropologists view particular human cultures as coherent and patterned wholes that cannot be dissociated from the societies of which they are an essential attribute. As Nadel (1951) expressed it, society and culture are both "abstractions evolved from the same observational data—individuals in co-activity [p. 80]." What is most salient for anthropologists is that culture constitutes a *system*, or rather a set of closely related systems in such areas as kinship, political power, religion, and so on. Because such sociocultural systems are obviously highly complex, the theoretical orientation of the anthropologists governs the selection of subsystems to concentrate on. Thus *functionalists* in the tradition of Malinowski (1922) will observe face-to-face interactions in everyday life, note the customary behavior associated with specific roles and statuses, and on this basis construct a model of the system. On the other hand, *structuralists* like Lévi-Strauss and to some extent Evans-Pritchard concentrate more on ideas and values obtained mainly from verbal statements of informants. However, the object is again to arrive by analysis at superordinate structures, and what informants say is merely the raw material. This sketch is so brief as to be a caricature, in the sense of exaggerating salient features. In actual fact the two approaches overlap and are complementary; but even where they diverge the ultimate aim of constructing a coherent system, in terms of which the behavior of the actors can be understood, is a common one.

Psychologists, on the other hand, generally have no coherent conception of culture relevant to their specific theoretical aims. Feeling obliged to say something, they usually borrow some definition from anthropology and then pass on hastily without bothering about it any more. Their usage also tends to be very loose, and culture often includes "ecology" as in the well-known work by Segall, Campbell, and Herskovits (1966). For many cross-cultural psychologists, culture appears to be a category conceptualized much like "social class," i.e., a term summarizing a bundle of rather ill-defined antecedent variables that usually "make a difference." At a more sophisticated level, illustrated later, certain variables are singled out, but this does not affect the main point concerning the way culture is conceptualized. The point is brought out very clearly by the previously quoted working definition offered by Brislin et al.: It simply omits all the complications of the anthropological definition and focuses on "*different experiences.*" This in fact is the crux of the matter in comparative psychological studies and is a perfectly defensible position; only psychologists ought to be clear about it and refer to "cultural variables" rather than "culture." With the exception of the culture-personality area (significantly known as "psychological anthropology"), it cannot be claimed that psychologists study cultures as systems.

It is now possible to return to the emic-etic issue to regard it from a more informed perspective. When one is dealing with a cultural system, as is the case with anthropologists, it makes good sense at least in principle to maintain that a particular word, phrase, piece of ritual behavior, or artifact cannot be understood in isolation, outside the cultural framework—in other words, it forms part of an "emic" description. In practice, though, it is often hard to be certain which aspects of a given structure, such as a kinship system, are emic and which are etic. It is noteworthy that even among anthropologists it is mainly those who are specializing in "ethnoscience" or "cognitive anthropology," i.e., fields allied to linguistics, who emphasize the emic approach. Moreover, some of them insist that their task is not merely to describe accurately the informant's "inside view," but also to be able to convey this by means of an appropriate metalanguage to outsiders.[2] The metalanguage itself would of course be regarded as etic. Within the structural anthropology of Lévi-Strauss, the objective is "the reduction of manifest or emic reality to latent or etic infrastructure [Scholte, 1973, p. 683]." There is, as has already been indicated, a good deal of controversy, particularly among American anthropologists, mainly about the relative emphasis to be placed on emic or etic approaches, not how one gets from one to the other.

Whereas the concepts of emic and etic are clearly applicable to anthropological material, it is very doubtful whether this is true of the bulk of cross-cultural comparisons in psychology. As stressed in the previous discussion, psychologists do not normally study any one culture as a system; what they typically do is make comparisons, often of rather narrow segments of behavior, across two or more cultures. Hence one cannot really apply the term "emic" within such a context without unduly stretching its meaning. The kinds of examples of emics and etics usually given by psychological methodologists favoring them are a good indication of this. Some have been discussed elsewhere (Jahoda, 1977), and here it will be sufficient to bring out a typical aspect of those provided by Brislin (1976): The authors of the comparative researches cited did not themselves find it necessary to resort to the emic-etic terminology! It was Brislin who laboriously, and perhaps mistakenly, *reinterpreted* findings in terms of what he understands by emics and etics. In most cases where such terminology is employed in comparative psychological studies, the intended notions would be more correctly expressed by such descriptions as culturally familiar or unfamiliar, or culture-specific versus universal. The game is actually being given away in an article whose title promises to provide "a solution of the etic-emic dilemma [Davidson, Jaccard, Triandis, Morales, & Diaz-Guerrero, 1976, p. 1]," which contains the following sentence: "The components of the model are assumed to be universal (etic), however, the operationalization of the variables is culture specific (emic) [p. 3]." The words in parentheses could have been left out without any loss of meaning.

Let me summarize the arguments of this section. I have contended that cross-cultural psychologists tend to assume erroneously that they are employing a model of culture identical to that used by anthropologists, when in fact they deal mainly with cultural variables and tend to ignore the structural element

---

[2]This sometimes takes curious forms, as in the example of Goodenough's work cited by Harris (1968). One of Goodenough's componential (i.e., metalanguage) definitions runs roughly as follows: "A kinsman at less than two degrees collateral distance; at two units of genealogical distance; in lineal relationship; in a senior generation; of male sex; in the presence of a marital tie; senior party involved, senior party being the first person in the particular relationship to become known to the junior party [p. 573]." The reader is invited to guess what relationship within the American kinship system is described here. There might be some difficulty in getting the correct answer, which is "grandmother's second husband"!

vital for anthropologists. Consequently, they may sometimes fail to grasp the full implications of the emic-etic distinction and usually misapply them in a manner that makes them redundant.

THEORY-TESTING: A CONTROVERSY
OF FUNDAMENTALS

"The extensive theoretical interest in cross-cultural psychology in the last decade has ... come from the realization by psychologists that psychological theories cannot be regarded as 'universal' until they have been extensively tested cross-culturally [Dawson, 1971, p. 291]." "Cross-cultural researchers in psychology either aim right for the jugular vein of a theory to see if the theory can survive rigorous tests in other cultures, or they simply add important data to a common pool of knowledge about a theoretical stance [Brislin et al., 1973, p. 143]."

These two quotations are characteristic of the views of cross-cultural psychologists who feel that testing the universal validity of psychological theories is one of their major tasks. Not surprisingly, the claim that theories ought to be regarded as tentative until they have, in Campbell and Naroll's (1972) characterization, passed through the "crucible" of cross-cultural verification is not always welcomed. For if accepted, the onus of showing that the predictions from a theory hold up across the main culture areas of the world would impose a heavy burden on theorists. However, it is necessary to distinguish between practical obstacles and the issue of principle; and if the claim is valid, means would have to be found to overcome the obstacles. Confronted with this challenge, many psychologists simply choose to ignore it, quietly continuing to cultivate their own particular corner of the garden. Others feel an obligation to make some kind of rational defense of their position, and the gist of the usual argument is contained in this candid passage by Gerard and Conolly (1972):

'How can you generalize from the behavior of college sophomores?' ... Unfortunately, we are subjected to the same sort of critical attack from misguided individuals within our own discipline. They ask that experiments be replicated with different subject populations, not only within our own culture but cross-culturally as well. ... [There follows an account of the problems and difficulties of cross-culture work.] Fortunately, there is a nice shortcut to all of this. Given the abiding faith in basic universals of humankind, the social psychologist might just as well work with a subject population he knows something about and that is close at hand—the students in his class [p. 242].

This kind of defense is not hard for the cross-cultural psychologist to counter. Granted that comparative studies are tricky and laborious, this in itself is insufficient reason to deny the need for them; that case rests on "faith in the basic universals of humankind." Quite apart from the inappropriateness of such faith in what purports to be a scientific discipline, it presupposes not merely a knowledge of what precisely these "basic universals" are, but also how they relate to the kinds of behavior under study. There is no need to labor over this line of argument, which is rather unconvincing as stated.

In contrast with such petty pinpricks, Faucheux (1976) mounted a massive counterattack aimed right at the jugular vein of cross-cultural comparisons. He questions the whole rationale of "theory-testing," which is one of the main planks of cross-cultural psychology. The fact that two notable exponents (Taft, 1976; Triandis, 1976) were asked to prepare replies indicates that Faucheux's arguments demand most careful consideration. I therefore propose to discuss them in some detail, because they deal with some of the key issues of the present chapter. Moreover, although Taft (1976) and Triandis (1976) attempted to refute Faucheux and made many points with which I am in full agreement, they did so in rather general terms; it is also necessary to examine some of his concrete examples, and my contribution to the debate therefore complements theirs.

Although his article is entitled "Cross-cultural Research in Experimental Social Psychology," Faucheux merely takes this as his starting point and arrives at general conclusions regarding cross-cultural research. His declared intention in the first part of the essay is to show that "experimental cross-cultural replications are delusive [p. 272]." He chooses as his example the replication by Schachter, Nuttin, de Monchaux, Maucorps, Osmer, Duijker, Rommetveit, and Israel (1954) of an American laboratory study on communication, deviation, and rejection in several European countries. As the study dates back more than two decades, a brief reminder may be useful. Small groups of subjects were brought together and given a hypothetical problem about a delinquent, and their task was to agree on how to deal with the case. Three stooges were planted, one of whom agreed with the majority, another was deviant at the outset and then joined the rest, whereas a third critical one stuck to an extreme position. The theory predicted that the group would begin by directing extra communications to the deviant and, when this failed, reject him. Schachter et al. saw the purpose of the replications as that of assessing the limits of generalizability of the propositions.

Now Faucheux points out that this implies making a distinction between *universal* and *culturally determined* relationships, which he questions: "If the theory of social influence is meant to have a universal validity, how then could it be 'culture-bound' [p. 274]?" He suggests that there could be only two reasons: (1) the theory is "a highly idiosyncratic product of American culture [p. 274]," and so nobody else will understand it anyway; or (2) the Americans are totally different from anyone else, in which case it would be meaningless to replicate. He goes on: "But to the extent that a theory is understandable by researchers from other cultures, and *assuming that a universal theory of human social behavior is possible,* it is not immediately clear why a theory aiming at formulating universal propositions and being experimentally substantiated in a given culture should need further testing in other cultures [p. 274; italics mine]."

A crucial part of Faucheux's argument is that a theory always implicitly defines the proper conditions for its testing, and this means that in a different cultural setting the actual procedure might have to be substantially modified. He takes as an imaginary example an African community where debates are conducted along what one might call Quaker lines, and raises the question whether in such a culture it would make sense to talk about "rejection of the deviant." His answer is that if one can find any area of behavior such as the violation of religious taboos where deviancy would be possible, and anthropologists would confirm that there *always* are such areas, then the universal psychological law could in principle be shown to hold there as anywhere else: "If a relationship has been established in one culture, the conceptually correct, specific operationalization which will verify the relationship in another culture will always be found if the effort to do so is great enough [p. 280]."

It follows from this that the theorist who goes to other cultures in order to replicate his work is performing a pointless task. For once the relationship has been established in any one culture, failure to do so elsewhere can only mean that the specific operationalization has not been properly done. All this will appear somewhat strange to the ears of conventional cross-cultural researchers, and it does in fact reflect a very different stance in the philosophy of science. Faucheux castigates those misguided enough to seek for universals through empirical generalizations, describing them as old-fashioned Aristotelians:

[They remain] at the level of phenomena instead of attempting to construct the universal theoretically in order to account for both similarities and differences. Finally, it means that cultures are considered different species, almost as different "natures," instead of accepting that *human reality is the same everywhere* and has to be apprehended beyond the phenomena.... The intention of distinguishing between the cultural and the universal is part of the illusion of an obsolete epistemology [p. 278; italics mine].

Faucheux then goes into minute details of another set of comparative experiments, which need not detain us, and this leads to a discussion of the implications of studies dealing with the perception and language of colors. Here again his aim is to oppose the empiricists who attempt to relate the objective characteristics of the physical world to the discriminations made in various cultures according to their needs. Although language is based on experience, experiences differ, and so "universality must be sought elsewhere than in the phenomena of the senses [p. 293]." It is therefore not a matter of studying "the mechanisms of perception of 'physical' reality [p. 294]," but rather of reality as experienced and represented. Faucheux recommends that we analyze the cognitive structures and categories in terms of which different cultural groups interpret reality. "Only then does it become possible to find out what are the universal laws which govern the genesis, structure and dynamics of underlying social representations [pp. 293–294]."

Finally, Faucheux describes in some detail an approach which, in his view, fulfills all these requirements, namely the early work of Berry (1966).

Obviously this highly condensed presentation does scant justice to Faucheux's elaborate arguments, but I hope it does not seriously distort them. If he is right, then a majority of the cross-cultural comparisons that have been and are being undertaken must be regarded as misconceived and futile. Faucheux's example of what he calls "the generalization fallacy" is the attempt by Schachter et al. to replicate a social-psychological experiment in several European countries. There are several reasons, which it is instructive to examine, why this was not a good choice. First of all, replication of American work in Europe is not very representative of cross-cultural studies because both places form part of the Western industrialized world; it has in fact been suggested that such studies would be more aptly described as "cross-national" (Frijda & Jahoda, 1966). Having said this, I must add that it does not affect the issue of principle with which Faucheux was concerned.

More important is the choice of a social-psychological experiment. This is a form of activity that, I would submit, is closely tied to the characteristics of Euramerican culture. In its "laboratory" form, it entails bringing together strangers (so as to control for prior relationships) on a short-term basis. Such a temporary aggregation of individuals, graced by the name of "group," is faced with some joint task to perform; the task more often than not is hypothetical in nature and known, or at least surmised to be such, as the participants are aware that they are acting within the framework of an experiment. Now a moment's reflection will make it apparent that such a game could not be played in a small, close-knit traditional community. Faucheux was of course well aware of this, but it is perhaps worth making the general observation that "classical" experimental social psychology would find it extremely difficult, if not impossible, to divest of its Euramerican cultural features so that the study could be replicated in traditional cultural systems.

This last statement of course contradicts Faucheux's claim that it can always be done if one tries hard enough. The onus is on him to show *how* it could be done, and he makes an effort to do so: Because in all cultures some behaviors are regarded as deviant, the theoretical proposition would seem to make sense and to hold anywhere. But note that there has been a shift in the *content* of the theoretical proposition. The original one by Schachter et al. (1954) referred to an increase in communication directed at the deviant, followed by rejection, and all this within the context of a small-group situation. The argument seems to have shifted toward the more general proposition that "deviants are rejected"; and such rejection can of course take numerous forms, from the imposition of mild sanctions to exclusion from the community or even death. Because such consequences are more or less implicit in the very concept of deviance, it looks as though the statement has become trivial if not tautological. There is clearly no need for replication in order to demonstrate the existence of deviance in this vague sense; but by the same token the original experiment was redundant.

The scrutiny of this example brings out one important flaw in Faucheux's argument: He treats all "theory" as a homogenous category, irrespective of the phenomena to which it relates, and as panhuman in range of application by definition. As Triandis (1976) rightly points out, this is an unrealistic conception. It is not helpful to say, as Faucheux does, that theories deal with "the same human reality" everywhere, unless one specifies the nature of this reality. This he obviously cannot do, for if he could the problem of universals would have been solved.

Given these limitations, it may be useful to make some broad distinctions between various kinds of phenomena with which theories are concerned. One made long ago is that of Laswell (1935) who posited that "if an act conforms to culture, then it is conduct, if not, then it is behavior." Conduct, i.e., behavior governed by rules and norms, is mainly within the province of anthropology and is normally analyzed within the framework of a cultural system; and one of the reasons why Faucheux's example was unsuitable and certainly atypical is that deviance tends to fall under the rubric of conduct. However, the large majority of cross-cultural studies is concerned with behavior rather than conduct. Although behavior in this sense is not normally prescribed, it is of course in varying degrees a function of cultural and ecological factors. Many cross-cultural comparisons are confined to the study of similarities and differences resulting from these factors; and, because they tend to be atheoretical, Faucheux characterizes them as "playful researches."

The notion involved in the "playful" style is that culture "is to be defined as particular, accidental, and contingent [p. 278]," in opposition to the universal that is the regular and common. Faucheux rejects such an opposition, proposing that universal relationships should be theoretically formulated in a manner that includes the relevant cultural aspects as an integral element. Without accepting that all theory must be of this kind, I would agree that, as exemplified by Berry (1966), it is a highly desirable model for cross-cultural research. However, I believe that Faucheux is mistaken when he asserts (p. 278) that the psychologist's theoretical handling of culture is or ought to be the same as that of the anthropologist.

In an earlier section, I have pointed out that culture can be conceptualized in two fundamentally different ways, namely as a system or a set of variables. The anthropologist, concerned with conduct, operates with culture-as-system; the psychologist, focusing on behavior, works nearly always with culture-as-variables. Insofar as this is the case, psychologists' culture does have the appearance of the accidental and contingent of which Faucheux complains. The question as to whether psychologists *should* endeavor to incorporate culture-as-system in their theories is one to which I intend to return; but in any case I would maintain that it is perfectly legitimate to treat culture as a set of variables for certain purposes provided one is clear what one is doing and does not, like some of the emic-etic enthusiasts, labor under the illusion that one is having it both ways.

After this preliminary clearing of the ground one is in a better position to consider Faucheux's crucial statement that it is not admissible to distinguish between universal and culturally determined relationships because "a theory is universal by definition [p. 314]." It has already been pointed out that Faucheux is highly restrictive in his concept of a theory; the same seems to apply to his view about the areas in which we should seek for "universal laws." Thus, in his discussion of the language and perception of color, now badly dated, he suggests that one should not be concerned with the mechanisms of perception of "physical reality," but concentrate on cognitive structures "in the very terms and categories used by the subjects themselves [p. 293]." This is very much in line with the current approach of cognitive anthropologists who also seek universals at that level and regard it as unnecessary to conduct cross-cultural comparisons: "One can reveal this universal on the basis of one culture or language without necessary recourse to other systems, mainly on the grounds that the analyst himself operates within the confines and constraints of a similar system that is derived from the same underlying universals [Durbin, 1973, p. 469]." It is not certain that Faucheux would also concur with the curt dismissal of the question of the psychological validity of their methods!

Now the kind of theory hinted at earlier by Faucheux and explicitly advocated by cognitive anthropologists involves the conception of culture-as-system; and in such cases it certainly does not make sense to separate universal from cultural elements, because both constitute integral parts of the system under consideration. At the risk of becoming tiresome, it must be stressed once more that psychological theories are not of this type. They treat cultural features (not culture!) as variables, and as such one can reasonably single out their effects. Note that strictly speaking this is being done not in contrast with universals, but with universals plus such other cultural elements as remain outside the theoretical scheme. There are of course very few theories with built-in cultural variables, the vast majority being constructed by and for the industrialized world, often (judging by the textbooks) with the tacit assumption of universality. Yet they often embody unrecognized or at least unacknowledged culture-specific elements that make universality impossible in principle. For instance, Guilford's (1959) theory of the intellect presupposes that everybody is literate. Theories concerned with personality, social attitudes, and group behavior are particularly vulnerable in this respect. Schachter's theory of social influence, which Faucheux cited as an example of universality, on the contrary illustrates a theory with a limited cultural range.

It might be argued that these are deficiencies in theory construction, which, in cases like that of Guilford, could easily be avoided. However, this is often just not true for two reasons. First, one cannot expect Euramerican psychologists to be acquainted with the vast range of human cultures so that they could take account of variations in cultural characteristics when constructing their theories. Even supposing that they had this vast store of information at their disposal, the amount yet to be discovered as far as psychological functions are concerned is probably much greater. Cultural influences on mental processes such as perception, thinking, or remembering are usually subtle and not detectable by casual observation, nor could they be readily deduced from any existing theory. For instance, memory theorists have shown that clustering is a feature of free recall, and it would be eminently reasonable to assume this to be a universal characteristic of the organization of information coding in memory. Yet Cole and Gay (1972) discovered this *not* to be a normal feature of recall among the Kpelle of Liberia.

One may conclude, therefore, that Faucheux is wrong to suggest that cross-cultural replications are sophistic and is wrong to castigate those engaged in such an enterprise as Aristotelian victims of an obsolete epistemology. After all, one can hardly accuse Piaget of being a mere crude empiricist; in a well-known article (Piaget, 1966), he advocated cross-cultural comparisons for the specific purpose of testing the range and extent of validity of his theory.

A substantial amount of space has been devoted to this discussion because an important issue of principle is at stake. If theory-testing were not a legitimate objective of cross-cultural comparisons, a large part of the effort in this sphere would stand condemned as futile. An attempt has therefore been made to demonstrate that Faucheux's arguments are misleading in this respect and partly arise from an ambiguity in the concept of culture. One can share Faucheux's ideal of aiming at the elucidation of universal laws, without admitting that studies that fall short of that ideal or have different objectives are thereby ruled out of court. On the other hand, one can place too much emphasis on theory testing, and I hope to show that cross-cultural comparisons also have other useful functions.

CONTRASTING STYLES: CROSS-CULTURAL PSYCHOLOGY AND PSYCHOLOGICAL ANTHROPOLOGY

The thrust of Faucheux's polemic was directed chiefly at cross-cultural psychology, and he made brief mention of the major approach in psychological anthropology only to reject it. Because there exists now a very substantial body of comparative work produced by this approach, it cannot be neglected here. Moreover, one of its main declared aims is once again the "appraising of rival theories to discover their potential for explaining behavior in cultural contexts [Honigmann, 1975, p. 619]." The term "appraising" as applied to theories, compared with more tough-minded "testing" commonly used by cross-cultural psychologists, indicates the softer style of some psychological anthropology. Its origins go back to writings of

Benedict and Mead in the 1930s, the founders of what came to be known as the "culture and personality" school. Beginning on a basis of anthropological observation, it was elaborated by Kardiner (1945) along more directly psychological (strictly neopsychoanalytic) lines, involving the use of detailed biographies of individuals and the application of projective techniques. Kardiner sought to build an overarching theory that would integrate culture and personality as interacting systems, a highly ambitious undertaking because both personality and culture constitute exceedingly complex systems. It is therefore not surprising that he must be regarded as having failed, though the problem remains a challenge (LeVine, 1973; see Barnouw, 1973, for a critical survey).

A radically new departure was made by Whiting and Child (1953) who pursued a similar though more modest aim, employing an extremely powerful tool developed by Murdock (1940). This is the cross-cultural survey, recently rechristened the "hologeistic" method based on the Human Relations Area Files. These consist of ethnographic materials drawn from cultures all over the world and divided into some 710 content categories. A few years ago there were 267 files in existence, totaling over half a million text pages, which indicates the scale of the enterprise. An efficient retrieval system places this vast store of information at the disposal of cross-cultural researchers, though if they wish to obtain data outside the standard content categories they have to extract them from the original texts. Since Whiting and Child's (1953) pioneering work, the hologeistic method has become by far the dominant one in psychological anthropology, and the present discussion therefore focuses on it exclusively.[3]

The use of the Human Relations Area Files (HRAF) is by no means universally favored. It has been severely criticized by (mainly European) anthropologists for treating culture as an aggregate of traits rather than a system, an issue that will be familiar by now; Leach (1965) went so far as to call its products "tabulated nonsense."[4] This need not unduly trouble psychologists, who routinely treat cultural features as variables. There are, however, technical and methodological problems that are highly relevant, and differ substantially from those encountered in cross-cultural psychology. They are tabulated in broad outline in the following, and the remainder of this

---

[3]A general account of the cross-cultural survey is to be found in Naroll (1973); hologeistic theory testing is specifically dealt with by Naroll, Michik, and Naroll (1974); and a broad survey including other approaches in psychological anthropology is provided by Williams (1975).

[4]See also Lévi-Strauss (1953) and Hallpike (1971); currently there are signs that the opposition is weakening, and one prominent British anthropologist has actually made use of the HRAF (Goody, 1977)!

section will be devoted to a more detailed examination of the respective strengths and weaknesses of these contrasting modes of comparison.

Cross-Cultural Psychology	*Psychological Anthropology* (hologeistic)
Data obtained by direct study of subjects in different cultures with a psychological objective.	Data collected by ethnographers and others for their own purposes.
Major topics for comparison: perception, cognition, attitudes, etc.	Major topics for comparison: socialization, motives, personality.
Sampling of individuals within cultures.	Sampling of cultures.
Types of design: descriptive, correlational, experimental, and quasiexperimental.	Types of design: descriptive and correlational.
Types of methodological problems: cultural appropriateness of measures, functional and conceptual equivalence, influence of situational factors, language and translation, etc.	Types of methodological problems: "Galton's problem," nature of unit, data quality control, availability of relevant information, reliability of categorization and coding, etc.

The outstanding contrast is in the ways data are obtained, and most of the other differences stem from this basic one. Cross-cultural psychologists collect their own data, applying whatever measures seem appropriate for the particular questions they are asking. Hologeistic researchers are, as it were, parasitic of ethnographers, anthropologists, missionaries, or travellers who reported from their own standpoint and through the selective screen of their personal and professional interests on what they observed in a culture; moreover, the emphasis is not on the particular or individual variations but on what appears characteristic of the culture as a whole.

The fact that the raw material is almost invariably observational and collected by nonpsychologists helps to account for the topics of major concern. There are few adequate measures of personality even for populations in industrialized, let alone non-Western cultures; and therefore with some notable exceptions (e.g., Holtzman, Diaz-Guerrero, & Swartz, 1975) cross-cultural psychologists tend to fight shy of this area, being only too well aware of the numerous pitfalls besetting it. They more often concentrate on such topics as perception, learning, thinking, memory, language, and attitudes where suitable measures can be more readily adapted or devised, though not without tricky problems. Ethnographers and other observers, on the other hand, are rarely concerned with psychological processes as such. When they come across a striking incident, e.g., people not being able to understand a picture, they may report it, but these are exceptions. On the other hand, most of them do comment on prevailing ways of rearing children and the dominant features of adult behavior, including beliefs, customs, and institutions. It is these materials with which the hologeistic researchers have to work. (See Bornstein, in this volume.)

The most common strategy they employ is to look at theoretically relevant aspects of reported child-rearing practices and link these to features of adult behavior also predicted on theoretical grounds. An intervening hypothetical construct is then postulated that is used to explain the link. Various theories may be resorted to for this purpose, including behavior theory; but owing to its range and flexibility (which is often regarded as a major weakness), the most popular is psychoanalytic theory. Very considerable ingenuity tends to be deployed in this procedure, which sometimes commands admiration but may occasionally stretch credulity.

It will have become clear that cross-cultural psychologists do their main work in the field, hologeistic researchers at home with files and the computer. It does of course not necessarily follow from this that one is better than the other. Field work is expensive in time and cost, so that a researcher may be content to administer a test of some kind to two cultural groups, which in the past was all too frequently done. In that case he offends against Campbell's famous canon that "a comparison of a single pair of natural objects is nearly uninterpretable [Campbell & Naroll, 1972, p. 449]." The hologeistic researcher samples many cultures and so is never in danger of falling into this particular trap, though there are plenty of others that threaten. The cross-cultural researcher samples individuals within cultures and here meets the difficulty that the requirements of representativeness and comparability often conflict; this will be obvious if one thinks of predominantly literate and illiterate populations. (For a fuller discussion of these issues see Berry, 1969; Brislin et al., 1973; Frijda & Jahoda, 1966.) Fieldworkers have considerable freedom in choosing a design suitable for their purpose. Apart from the standard correlational versus experimental dichotomy, the cross-cultural field provides an opportunity for taking advantage of natural experiments (e.g., Jahoda, 1972) or devising quasiexperiments whereby cultural variables near the extremes of a range are taken as experimental treatments (e.g., Berry,

1966). The hologeistic researcher lacks this freedom, being confined to the correlational approach, which tends to be causally interpreted with varying degrees of justification.

In choosing appropriate tests or tasks and conducting work with subjects, the cross-cultural psychologist is beset by a variety of problems, some of which are listed previously and all of which are discussed in detail in the literature cited. More is to be said of the hologeistic problems, which are of a very different nature. There is first of all "Galton's problem," which is that of discriminating "historical" associations (due to diffusion and therefore a source of bias) from "functional" association in cross-cultural surveys that are the ones of interest. Faucheux cited this as an objection, but there are now several elegant solutions. There is the question of the nature of the cultural unit and how to delimit its boundaries, which remains largely unresolved. Another problem arises from the fact that the raw material, i.e., reports of ethnographers and others, tends to be of varying quality and uneven in its range of coverage. The first of these can be dealt with by ingenious methods of quality control, whereby comparative and internal checks on accuracy can be undertaken; there is no solution to problems of omission, and cultures for which relevant material is not available just have to be excluded from the sample. Lastly, there are problems of reliability in categorization and coding, especially when material not originally included in the standard coding has to be specifically extracted. It should be added that hologeistic researchers are of course fully aware of these issues and make strenuous efforts to overcome these various obstacles.

There is yet another issue concerning research strategy at the initial planning stage that affects cross-cultural researchers more than hologeistic ones: This is whether it is preferable to start with dependent or independent variables, a problem that has been carefully considered by LeVine (1970). He points out that if one starts with an independent variable, such as the kibbutz mode of childrearing, one runs a risk; in attempting to establish its effects, the outcome may be trivial or uninteresting and account for so small a fraction of the total variance that an enormous amount of labor will have been largely wasted. On the other hand, I would suggest that there are some independent variables of such crucial importance, e.g., infantile malnutrition, that the effort is still worth making. The disadvantages of beginning with a dependent variable, i.e., the kind of behavior explained, are less fully set out by LeVine; but they are equally vexing. I illustrate this by reference to a comparative study of separation protest in Guatemalan and U.S. infants (Lester, Kotelchuck, Spelke, Sellers, & Klein, 1974). It would seem that Guatemalan subjects exhibited far less concern than American ones at the departure of the father. The authors suggest as the cause that "Latin fathers spend even less time with their infants than do American fathers," but this interpretation was not verified. Now it may be that, if it were, the hunch would turn out to be correct, but the odds are against it. This is because cultures vary simultaneously along many different dimensions; moreover, environmental elements often seem to interact in a complex manner, and the effects of this cannot be easily ascertained. Any attempt to track down the causes of such a difference unguided by any theory (and in this context Faucheux's strictures certainly apply) would entail a large and in the end probably fruitless undertaking. It is not surprising, therefore, that many of what Faucheux would call "playful" researches confine themselves to the ascertainment of similarities and differences. This is not to say, as is shown later, that such a procedure is always objectionable—under certain circumstances it can fulfill a useful purpose. Here I merely wish to point out that the hologeistic researcher need not be unduly troubled by such considerations. Whatever the starting-point, the researcher can draw on appropriate data from a large range of cultures either to examine the effects of a particular independent variable or set of variables, or to search for independent variables associated with a type of behavior whose antecedents are to be explored.

So far the discussion has been conducted as though the two comparative methods were mutually exclusive, and in practice this is approximately true because researchers tend to favor one or another style. However, there is no reason why they should not be combined, and this has in fact been done by several researchers (e.g., Munroe, Munroe, & Whiting, 1973; Rohner, 1975; Sutton-Smith & Roberts, 1967). This permits a trade-off of the respective strengths and weaknesses of the two types of comparative method, and convergent findings resulting from these contrasting approaches will greatly enhance any confidence in their validity.

MAJOR TYPES OF CROSS-CULTURAL COMPARATIVE STUDIES

Cross-cultural comparisons are undertaken in many different ways and for many different purposes. Hence it is hard to reduce such a rich and heterogeneous field of activity to some kind of more or less coherent order, but an attempt is made to provide a broad overview. Some of the obvious criteria of classification, such as topic or method, were considered only to be rejected. Instead, a more arbitrary mode has been adopted, which has the advantage of bringing out the primary purpose of the studies, to throw some light on the nature of their contribution to the general store of psychological knowledge and understanding. Each category is illustrated with some examples, but here again the caveat is necessary that some studies could easily fit into more than one category, and again some rather arbitrary decisions had to be made. However, this should not affect the general picture, which I believe reflects the dominant characteristics of cross-cultural comparative studies.

The Unacceptably "Playful" Style

This consists of one-shot, entirely atheoretical comparisons of the performance of samples of subjects from two cultures on some limited test or task, ending up with a statement of the existence of differences. As has already been explained, such findings are usually quite uninterpretable as the difference could have arisen from a variety of different causes. Comparisons of this kind are wasted efforts adding almost nothing to the pool of knowledge. In the early years of cross-cultural research, such studies were frequent, if not the norm. Unfortunately, they have by no means entirely ceased, because editors are still sometimes willing to publish papers about "interesting" differences. I cite no examples, but looking through the literature it should not be hard to pick some out.

Systematic Comparative Studies of Similarities and Differences

This is obviously a very wide category, ranging from the observational/ descriptive to highly elaborate experimental studies concerned with causal relationships. Although not usually associated with a particular theory, most do have theoretical implications in a general sense; and, unlike the isolated forays of the "playful" comparison, they can serve as points of departure for further research.

There has long been in psychology, unlike anthropology, a strong bias against "merely" descriptive studies. Admittedly there has been a recent change of outlook in some areas, but by and large the complaint made by LeVine (1970) is still justified when he wrote about "the greatest weakness of the psychological sciences in general and cross-cultural studies in particular: there is a lack of a body of well-documented variations to explain [p. 566]." One important source of evidence is of course the HRAF, but as previously mentioned it suffers from the shortcoming that its material was not collected on a uniform basis, nor even with the needs of psychological studies in mind. Given the prevailing climate of opinion, and the fact that the systematic collection of descriptive data on a large scale is extremely laborious, the pursuit of such an activity has been and remains unrewarding. Hence it is not surprising that few recent examples can be found, among them being an ethological study of sex differences in the behavior of London and Bushmen children (Blurton-Jones & Konner, 1973).

In order to find a model for this approach, one has to go back a long way to the famous pioneering study of Rivers (1901). He and his colleagues examined most of the males of a small community in Murray Island and some other locations over a period of several months. Owing to the fact that it was the work on visual illusions that happened to be followed up half a century later, Rivers is mainly remembered as an illusion researcher by psychologists (he was also an anthropologist who made a distinguished contribution in that field as well). It is therefore worth pointing out that his studies comprised a very substantial range of topics, including color vision, hearing, smell and taste, tactile acuity, reaction time, time estimation, memory, etc. In spite of the mass of material accumulated, Rivers regarded the findings as mere raw materials to be more fully exploited after subsequent research:

> Nearly all the methods used by us were modified in some way to meet the special conditions, and others were entirely new or had not been employed on any large number of individuals. Consequently much of our work is at present in the form of mere facts which will only acquire interest and importance when we have examined a considerable number of Europeans and people of other races by the same methods [p. 2].

It will be evident from these remarks that Rivers, far from being a "playful" researcher, had a methodological and theoretical sophistication lacking in many of those who followed him. In fact, his discussion of the problems and pitfalls of experimentation in what we would now call the cross-cultural field still deserves careful reading.[5]

One of the major contributions of Rivers and the other members of the Torres Straits Expedition (McDougall, Myers, and Seligman) was to provide evidence indicating the falsity of certain beliefs about non-European peoples that were widely prevalent at the time, e.g., that their sensory acuity is greatly superior to that of Europeans. On the other hand, they were children of their time inasmuch as they took it for granted that "savages" were inferior in "higher mental development." Although this assumption has long been abandoned, the fact remains that on many cognitive tasks people in traditional cultures differ in their performance from Euramericans, mostly in the direction of doing less well. The interpretation of such differences is still a moot issue, and although seldom attributed to genetic factors, they are sometimes taken as reflecting fundamental differences in cognitive processes resulting from cognitive development within differing ecocultural settings. On this issue the mantle of Rivers has been donned by Cole and his associates, whose extensive studies among the Kpelle of Liberia have been largely devoted to collecting evidence against such a view.

---

[5]Some of the incidents described are highly amusing. For instance, the people from one particular village seemed most reluctant to be tested. On inquiry it was discovered that one overzealous subject had tried to impress the importance of truthfulness vis-à-vis the investigators by announcing that if they told lies Queen Victoria would send a man-of-war to punish them!

Cole and his associates (Cole, Gay, Glick, & Sharp, 1971; Cole & Scribner, 1974; Gay & Cole, 1967) explored in depth the similarities and differences in cognitive performance of Kpelle and American subjects. They took the point made by anthropologists that the experimental procedures of Western psychologists are inapplicable in their normal form for the purpose of cross-cultural comparisons, so that results obtained in this manner cannot be taken at face value. Cole proposed a new approach, which he called "experimental anthropology." This involves radical modification of experimental procedures designed to adapt the tasks required of the subjects so that they more closely related to their particular mode of cognitive functioning in everyday life. For example, contrary to notions about the exceptional rote memory of traditional nonliterate peoples, Cole and Gay (1972) found that illiterate Kpelle children did more poorly on a free recall task than Californian children. Instead of accepting this as evidence of a cognitive deficit, as some "playful" researchers would have done, they made it the starting point for a systematic search for the conditions that favored or inhibited free recall among the Kpelle; and they were able to show that under certain culturally appropriate circumstances the Kpelle do at least as well as American children. The general conclusion reached was that "cultural differences in cognition reside more in the situation to which particular cognitive processes are applied than in the existence of a process in one cultural group and its absence in another [Cole et al., 1971, p. 233]." The emphasis is therefore on *situational* factors that are regarded as modifying the outcome of what are essentially the same "basic component cognitive processes [Cole & Scribner, 1974, p. 193]." Although there are some problems with such a formulation (Jahoda, 1978), the work of Cole and his colleagues constitutes a substantial advance in cross-cultural comparative studies.

The examples cited in this section so far concern ethological and experimental studies, but there are other forms that belong here, and a prominent one that might be selected is the Six Cultures study of Whiting and Whiting (1975). It consisted of the systematic observation of the social behavior of children secured by time-sampling, the material being allocated to twelve basic categories. For the purpose of analyzing cross-cultural similarities and differences, the scores of the children on each of the categories were pooled within each of the six cultures, thereby averaging individual differences and yielding a net residual attributable to culture. The resulting cultural medians were then found to be related to the socioeconomic systems and the household structures characteristic of the cultures. This is the kind of empirical generalization frowned on by Faucheux but which I would regard as not merely defensible but valuable. Admittedly, the end point is of the nature of a hypothesis that needs to be tested by further comparisons with other cultural samples; yet it does hold out the promise of new insights.

Before concluding the discussion of this category of studies, I should mention that even routine comparisons of similarities and differences can sometimes serendipitously yield fresh discoveries. Thus, when Hudson was engaged in the administration of a pictorial test to African factory workers, he noted a substantial number of odd responses implying complete misunderstanding of a particular picture. This led him to the problem of pictorial depth perception (Hudson, 1960), which opened up an entirely new field of inquiry.

Testing of Theories or Hypotheses

It has already been said that the testing of important theories, such as those of Piaget, is a major focus of cross-cultural comparisons. Because most of this work is well known (see Bornstein, in this volume), the illustration chosen concerns theories of intergroup relations. In social psychology there is a plethora of such theories, based in the main on laboratory or, less frequently, natural groups, mainly in America or Europe. Most of the studies have involved pairs of groups, larger numbers being very rare. Moreover, when natural groups are involved, studies tend to concentrate on one group's attitudes to the other, and reciprocal relations are less often examined. The reason is that it is difficult to find a variety of groups, each with a well-defined identity, in mutual contact; in the United States the black-white dichotomy is usually the dominant theme. Under these circumstances the testing of theories yielding conflicting predictions tends to be difficult and largely inconclusive.

Brewer and Campbell (1976) decided to take advantage of the fact that one can find a wide range of culturally varied tribal groups with a strong sense of their identity within confined geographical areas in Africa. Their design was fairly simple in principle, though of course considerable practical problems had to be overcome. They devised a survey interview dealing essentially with interethnic contacts and attitudes, including own-group attitudes. Interviews were conducted with members of thirty different groups in a region where three countries border one another. The questions always concerned thirteen different outgroups and their own. The analysis of this material was complex, and the results were probably unique, inasmuch as significance tests were based on Ns consisting of ten to thirty groups. The outcome of this work was not merely the separation of theoretical chaff from wheat, and incidentally the casting of doubt on the alleged motivating force of cognitive inconsistency, but also some fresh light on the factors governing intergroup relations.

Another more contentious example concerns the hologeistic approach. Recall that this involves the use of psychological hypotheses for predicting relationships between, in the main, socialization variables and subsequent adult behavior. Such hypotheses are then tested by means of the material in the HRAF. Now the most popular source of hypotheses is psychoanalytic theory, and it is argued by Kline (1977) that such studies in effect constitute tests of aspects of Freudian theory. There are some reasons for questioning this, discussed in more detail elsewhere (Jahoda, 1978); in short, many if not most of the relationships obtained are open to alternative interpretations. Whatever the force of this particular objection, the hologeistic method is essentially a tool for hypothesis-testing and has been fruitfully employed for this purpose. One area, for instance, is that of the antecedents of heavy alcohol use, which has been extensively studied. Thus, Barry (1976) postulated on the basis of an eclectic theoretical mix that heavy drinking is in part a manifestation of a dependency conflict, and he predicted that it would be associated with childrearing conditions predisposing toward such a conflict. Cross-cultural comparisons did in fact yield substantial associations between such variables as "high amount of crying during infancy" and a high frequency of drunkenness across a variety of cultures.

There is in practice no sharp dividing line between research mainly concerned with the testing of formal theories or hypotheses and more exploratory work that yet has unquestionable theoretical relevance; hence it is also briefly illustrated in relation to the problem of pictorial recognition. This has the virtue of drawing attention to the fact that problems of a fundamental kind, even in experimental psychology, sometimes became first apparent within the cross-cultural sphere. Thus it has been noted from the nineteenth century onwards by travellers, missionaries, and, recently, anthropologists (e.g., Forge, 1970) that people in nonliterate traditional societies in various parts of the world are apt to have difficulties in understanding pictures. Now putting it rather crudely, two different stances have been adopted in relation to this issue. One is that of Hochberg and Brooks (1962), who, from a well-known study with $N = 1$, concluded that pictorial recognition is "an unlearned ability"; accordingly, they cast doubt on the observation. Against this, Miller (1973) suggested that "the ability to perceive anything in a pictorial representation requires some experience with pictures [p. 148]." An empirical attack on this problem obviously demands a pictorially impoverished environment. Deregowski, Muldrow, and Muldrow (1972) tracked down a remote pictureless population and tested them, confirming that difficulties were experienced, but their extent had probably been exaggerated in some of the reports. With regard to the recognition of pictures of simple objects, Jahoda et al. (1977) were able to replicate Hochberg and Brooks's (1962) finding with young children almost entirely devoid of exposure to pictures. Through these and similar studies, surveyed by Hagen and Jones (1977), the problem area becomes more clearly defined, which is a step toward a more adequate theory of pictorial perception.

It should be added that the foregoing is merely an instance of a whole class of problems that, for practical and/or theoretical reasons, cannot easily be explored without cross-cultural work. Among the most important issues of this kind are the effects of malnutrition (e.g., Klein, Irwin, Engle, &

Yarborough, 1977) or formal schooling (e.g., Super, 1977) on mental development.

Cross-Cultural Theories and the Quest for Universals

According to Faucheux, any proper theory is ipso facto universal in its range, and if this were so then it would not make sense to distinguish cross-cultural from other kinds of theories. However, I have argued at some length that his view is not strictly tenable; and if this is accepted it becomes reasonable to make such a distinction. Hence, I propose that a cross-cultural theory is one embodying *explicit statements* about cultural variables, either specifying the relevant ones or (in the case of universals) stating that they make no difference.

The earliest and best-known of the former type is the work of Segall et al. (1966) dealing with visual illusions, which followed up and formalized the findings of Rivers mentioned earlier. Applying to these the Brunswikian concept of "ecological cue validity," they postulated a set of ecological characteristics that would differentially affect susceptibility to several kinds of visual illusions. Although their predictions were only partially borne out, the theoretical approach was most fruitful in stimulating research in this complex area, which is now much better understood (Deregowski, 1978).

A far more comprehensive ecocultural theory has recently been put forward by Berry (1976). It is based on Witkin's theory of psychological differentiation, whose relative freedom from culture-specific content makes it eminently suitable as a conceptual tool in cross-cultural comparisons (Witkin & Berry, 1975). Berry (1976) constructed an elaborate theoretical model in which the physical environment is linked through cultural features to a variety of behaviors. Thus, the physical environment imposes certain constraints on modes of subsistence and demographic characteristics, which in turn lead to certain kinds of social organization favoring particular forms of childrearing that make for relatively field-dependent or field-independent adults. This is of course a gross over-simplification, as the model also deals with external cultural influences and incorporates numerous feedback loops. Given the complexity of the model and the difficulties involved in testing it, the extent to which it is supported by empirical data is remarkable. Since the demise of the old culture-and-personality school, global theories have been at a discount, and Berry's demonstration that it is possible to test such a theory with some rigor therefore opens up an important avenue for future comparative studies.

Social change is one of the salient aspects of the modern world, and it has been pointed out that it is featured in Berry's model. Others have focused more narrowly, but in greater detail, on the psychological consequences of social change as it impinges on the individual. Although these approaches are perhaps more in the nature of empirical studies of processes than theories in the strict sense, they are mentioned here because the concept of "modernity" with which they operate does represent a theoretical and, to some extent, controversial construct. An outstandinding example of such an approach is the work of Inkeles and Smith (1974) who attempt to assess the relative influence of such institutions as school and factory on attitudes and personality in a variety of cultural contexts. Whether or not individuals from traditional societies are really "homogenized" into "modern" men remains a moot issue, but there can be little doubt that substantial changes do occur. Thus, one of the theoretically interesting by-products of this type of comparative study is the evidence it provides that some crucial modifications of psychological characteristics, falling squarely within the rubric of "personality," can and do take place well after infancy and childhood. This is in accordance with other kinds of evidence (see Clarke & Clarke, 1976).

Theoretical approaches concerned with universals are of two main types: One deals with what might be called underlying *structural uniformities,* whereas the other postulates common *basic processes.* The first usually involves multivariate, the second mainly experimental methods. An outstanding example of the first type is the work of Triandis (1972) on what he calls "subjective culture," by which he means the way people perceive and think about their social environment. More recently, Triandis (1977) has developed his approach further and proposed a set of universal dimensions of social behavior involving binary oppositions. These are Association versus Dissociation, roughly equivalent to cooperation versus conflict; Superordination versus Subordination, which refers to relative status in an interaction; Particularism versus Universalism, which denote a personal or impersonal transaction, respectively; and lastly, Overt-Covert, External Behavior versus Internal Feelings. Triandis suggests that any given piece of social behavior may be regarded as a point in four-dimensional space; cultural variations will appear as differential densities of points in the several regions of this space. (A somewhat similar model has been elaborated, and tested cross-culturally, by Foa and Foa [1974].)

Attempts to tease out underlying uniformities have not been confined to the sphere of social behavior. In particular, Vandenberg (1973) has posited that the fundamental structure of mental abilities is the same in all human cultures, and he has provided some impressive evidence.

The last approach of this type to be mentioned is that of Osgood, which, somewhat confusingly, also bears the label of "subjective culture." Osgood was concerned with the proposition that what he calls "affective meaning systems," i.e., the affective and connotative aspects of language, are cross-culturally invariant. The outcome of what must be one of the most extensive comparative studies ever undertaken provided strong support for this position (Osgood, May, & Miron, 1975). In view of what follows, it might be noted that Osgood paid particular attention to colors, which he used as an illustration of the general format of the semantic differential *Atlas* that was produced. Thus, in terms of the usual EPA scheme (the rating of attributes or objects as evaluative, potent, and active), BLUE was found E + and BLACK E-; RED was P + and A + , whereas WHITE was P-; these are examples of "universals" as defined by a statistical criterion and of course within the range of samples covered by the studies. Where geographically neighboring communities exhibited similar patterns, these were termed "sub-universals," and naturally there were also many "uniquenesses." Componential analysis was applied to the data in order to discover "underlying cognitive bases for the differential distribution of affect [p. 290]," and an attempt was made to relate the findings to the work of Berlin and Kay (1969). It is suggested that the salient results, such as the universal tendency to evaluate brightness positively, have a biological basis; and it is even speculated that "the *feelings* associated with referents of color signs do indeed contribute to the cultural evolution of color lexicons [p. 334]." Osgood and his associates thus tried to build a bridge between the purely semantic approach and the more direct studies of the categorization to which I now turn.

Color is of course only one of innumerable kinds of categorization in terms of which humans structure their world, but it has been a major battlefield between the relativists and their opponents. Relativists, such as Leach (1976, p. 33), maintain that the slicing up of the physical world into objects and their attributes has to be *taught* to the child and is thus relative to culture and essentially arbitrary. The opposite theoretical standpoint is that biological organisms are programmed from birth to make certain distinctions, including those of color. The development of the argument, illustrating the manner in which cross-cultural research can contribute to psychological theory, has been lucidly summarized by Rosch (1977):

> Cross-cultural research began with the observations of naive observers placed in cross-cultural contexts who reported what they noted—differences in colour names between cultures. However, such unlimited relativism violated another cross-cultural observation, namely that it appeared possible to communicate cross-culturally about colour regardless of differences in naming.
>
> Given [this] empirical description of possible universals in colour naming, Rosch sought psychological principles which might underlly the universals. ... Cross-cultural tests were always of hypotheses which predicted differences within, not between cultures, thereby avoiding the pitfalls of uncontrolled variables in performance on tests between cultures [p. 17].

With regard to color, the universalist case was clinched by Bornstein, Kessen, and Weiskopf (1976) who were able to demonstrate categorical perception of hue in 4-month-old infants, which illustrates the potentialities of fruitful interplay between cross-cultural and developmental studies in advancing psychological theory (see Bornstein, in this volume). Rosch herself went on to elaborate a wider theory of categorization tested so far only with American subjects, which will require further verification in a cross-cultural context.

Finally, there is the area of facial expressions of emotion where Darwin's universalist theory gave way to the view expressed by Klineberg (1935): "There is no doubt that emotional expression, apparently so natural and so direct, is to a large extent a learned reaction—a bodily language which must be known if it is to be understood. Under the controlling influence of tradition and training, it may vary so greatly in nature and in amount as to make the overt behavior of two different groups mutually unintelligible [p. 287]."

It was Ekman (1973) who vindicated Darwin by showing that in spite of culturally variable "display rules" a common set of facial muscular movements are involved in the expression of particular emotions across all cultures investigated. He achieved this by making strenuous efforts to avoid the blends of different emotions that characterized most of the previous work. Thus, just as in the case of colors where the universal elements were ascertained by concentrating on "focal" colors, so the universal aspects of emotional expression were established by singling out relatively "pure" emotions and carrying out cross-cultural tests with these.

RETROSPECT AND PROSPECT

Cross-cultural comparisons in psychology have a respectable ancestry dating back to the beginnings of empirical psychology itself. Yet after an initial brilliant start in the Torres Straits, cross-cultural work went into the doldrums for almost a half century. It is a fascinating question why this should have happened, and perhaps a little speculation may be permitted. The answer is probably to be sought in two directions: (1) changes in the broad intellectual climate; and (2) psychology viewed from the perspective of the sociology of science. With regard to the former, the end of the nineteenth century was dominated by the idea of evolution, including mental evolution, which was discussed by Galton, Romanes, Tylor, and Spencer, and the report of the Torres Straits Expedition reflects this preoccupation. It must be understood that at that time it was not a simplistic notion of inborn differences but a search for subtle connections that might account for the ways in which mental evolution occurs. For instance, Rivers (1901) put forward the following chain of arguments: Hypermetropia is more frequent in "savage races" and leads to more extensive use of visual accommodation; this is related to close observation of the minutiæ of nature, requiring predominant attention to concrete sense objects; this in turn means that less attention can be paid to "the more serious problems of life" and thereby constitutes an obstacle to higher mental development. From our current perspective it is of course not hard to spot the flaws in the argument, but what matters here is that it was a strenuous attempt to understand complex causal relationships. This impetus was lost early in the twentieth century, when the reaction against social Darwinism swept away the good together with the bad. As far as psychology was concerned it was only the bad that remained, namely a crude notion of genetically determined "race differences," mainly in "intelligence"; and this persisted until well after Klineberg (1935) had begun to turn the tide. An intellectual climate in which the main task was seen as that of establishing an inventory of supposedly immutable race differences was clearly not favorable to cross-cultural comparisons along the lines pioneered by Rivers.

The second aspect mentioned is perhaps best conveyed by means of a parable. This is about a branch of science called animology, concerned with the study of the behavior of animals. The practical problems that contributed to the rise of the new discipline were those of cattle breeders, farmers, pet owners, proprietors of zoos, and trainers of circus animals. It is therefore not surprising that they concentrated on the study of domesticated animals and those wild ones that are kept in zoos. Animology spread and flourished, becoming an established field of study in universities. Animologists developed theories and related applications, gaining recognition and rewards. Occasionally the odd animologist went to work with wild animals and ventured to suggest that theories ought to take their specific characteristics into account. Such eccentric individuals were regarded with tolerant interest, but the established textbooks ignored their work and few followed their example. Studies of wild animals are troublesome, difficult, and expensive; and after all, domesticated animals are also *animals,* so why bother when the potential payoff is so meager in proportion to the effort? Yet while animologists were contentedly pursuing their work, even more rapid changes took place in the outside world. At first, practical men in response to economic and political pressures had begun partially to domesticate many species of wild animals everywhere. This led the wild ones to appreciate the comforts of a domesticated life, so that more and more of them clamored for the benefits of domestication without wishing to abandon all the advantages of a precarious freedom. This produced conflict and problems in the whole social fabric, eventually leading to changes in the behavior of domesticated animals as well, who became less docile. Animologists were called in to help, but whereas they had previously been fairly effective in routine situations, they now found it hard to cope. At long last this made them realize the importance of studying the behavior of wild animals as well, but they were rather late; for by that time there were few really wild animals left in the world (see Jahoda, 1973).

The parable should not be taken too literally. Its intention is merely to hint at the factors that first retarded and then encouraged the growth of cross-cultural comparisons. It is not my contention that they have in the past yielded some startling revelations about human nature, or are likely to do so in the future. On the contrary, systematic comparative description has, more often than not, brought out basic similarities underlying superficial contrasts; and this has contributed to the increasing realization that the image of people in other cultures as strange and inscrutable is a false one, and that we are all variations on a common theme. On the other hand, such comparisons have also uncovered unsuspected differences not readily discernible by superficial observation, though often they are of considerable practical as well as theoretical importance (e.g., pictorial depth perception).

Although cross-cultural comparisons have made a solid contribution, there are no grounds for complacency. The kinds of topics studied by means of cross-cultural comparisons have, in historical perspective, paralleled or followed those dominant in psychology at the time. If this continues, cross-cultural comparisons will be confined to the theory-testing and other useful functions described in this chapter and will remain what Bochner, Brislin, and Lonner (1973) called a "meta-method." Alternatively, it is not inevitable that this should be so, and some recent trends point to the possibility of an independent contribution, of taking the lead in some respects instead of merely tagging along. In my view the main key to such progress lies in the fact that cross-cultural comparisons are at the interface between psychology and anthropology, but so far the opportunities arising from this have been insufficiently exploited. It seems to me that there are at least three main ways in which this might be done.

The first is more extensive cultivation of existing areas of common interest between the two disciplines. This has been done by Berry (1976) who drew extensively on anthropological sources when elaborating his eco-cultural model; Cole described his own work as "experimental anthropology," basing it squarely on both psychological *and* anthropological research. Lastly, Bornstein (1975) produced a remarkable synthesis of psychological, anthropological, and linguistic approaches to the domain of color which directly inverts the Whorfian thesis. All these are examples of genuinely innovative results of cross-cultural comparisons, drawn from the fields of personality and cognitive style, thinking and memory, and perception. Paradoxically it would be difficult to cite examples where, on the face of it, one would expect most overlap, namely social behavior and attitudes. The probable reasons for this are instructive and lead to the second point.

Cross-cultural comparisons in the social-psychological sphere concerned with attitudes, values, norms, roles, and such are almost invariably characterized by an exclusive focus on the *individual* in isolation from the social and cultural setting. The aim is usually to distill from the material those elements that remain invariant across cultures, and it unavoidably follows that the outcome tends to consist of high-level abstractions unrelated to any cultural features. This is in complete contrast with the style of anthropologists who always treat individual social behavior, perceptions of roles and norms, etc. as primary data that require a set of *secondary* concepts before one can make sense of the data; these concepts usually relate to the social system to which the individual informants belong. Cross-cultural comparisons, if any, are made between *systems* rather than aggregates of individuals. Hence, the results of social psychological and anthropological comparisons are nearly always totally incommensurable. This lack of contact is of course undesirable for both disciplines, but being in each case based on long tradition it would not be easy to change. What seems to be needed is some kind of *tertium quid* that capitalizes on the strengths of both. Because the issue is being presented here from the psychological standpoint, I venture to suggest that the adoption of a modified "systems" approach might prove beneficial for cross-cultural comparisons, and not only in the social-psychological sphere. Such a proposal is neither as radical nor, alas, original as I thought when first writing it, as it has been put forward in a different context by Bronfenbrenner (1977), who in passing also made remarks pertinent to this discussion:

> The first [strategy] is the comparison of existing systems that embody markedly differing patterns of social organization. Cross-cultural studies are the most common form of this type of investigation. Unfortunately, many of these researches focus attention almost exclusively on the characteristics of individuals rather than on the social contexts in which these individuals are found [p. 527].

It is only when such a systems approach has been adopted (and Berry's model is so far the closest approximation to it) that the emic-etic terminology will become appropriate and meaningful. (Certain subsystems like childrearing or modes of subsistence do form part of some cross-cultural theories, but it should be pointed out that they are treated as quasivariables in such cases.)

The third and last comment relates to areas of anthropological study that are highly germane to the interests of psychologists but have been largely ignored by them. There is only space to cite one particularly striking instance of this, namely symbolism. Most psychologists tend to associate this term mainly with psychoanalysis and are disposed to relegate it to the category of antiquated intellectual lumber. On the other hand, the fact that symbolism in some form features prominently in most modern anthropological theories should give us pause. Although it is true that the intellectual roots of current anthropological usage of the term "symbolism" go back to Freud, it has become so extensively modified as to bear only slight traces of its original ancestry. Given the volumes that have been written on the subject it would be presumptuous to pretend that I could offer a full or even adequate discussion of this exceedingly complex topic. All I can hope to achieve is to say enough to persuade readers that it is an important one.

The giant, albeit controversial, figure of Lévi-Strauss (e.g., 1966) must be mentioned first. For him the opposition between nature and culture is bridged by unconscious symbolism, cognitive in character, which can be interpreted because it is based on a universal logic shared by all humans. The unconscious symbolic structures are not static but may be regarded as a self-regulating system of transformations somewhat like those conceived by Piaget. The structures uncovered by Lévi-Strauss's "structural analysis" are claimed to enable us to understand social reality, partly by bringing out the underlying categories in terms of which people think and act in relation to nature and culture. (For a fuller discussion of some of the psychological assumptions made by Lévi-Strauss, see Jahoda [1970].) If this sounds like obscure verbiage, the fault is no doubt partly mine; but some anthropological critics have been hardly more charitable, without however questioning the key role of symbolism. Lévi-Strauss is also unusual that he is only concerned with cognition; most anthropologists stress also the emotional aspects of symbols (see Lewis, 1977). Few anthropologists subscribe to an extreme structuralist position, and one of the eclectic ones most prominent in the study of symbolism is worth quoting. Turner (1968) states:

> I have long considered that the symbols of ritual are... "storage units," into which are parked the maximum amount of information. They can also be regarded as multi-faceted mnemonics, each facet corresponding to a specific cluster of values, norms, beliefs, sentiments, social roles and relationships within the total cultural system of the community performing the ritual. In different situations, different facets... tend to be prominent.
>
> Each type of ritual... represents a storehouse of traditional knowledge. To obtain this knowledge one has to examine the ritual in close detail and from several standpoints [pp. 1-2].

Although the passage is specifically concerned with ritual symbols, a context wherein they are especially potent, the import is general. In common with others, Turner holds that symbols are products of social interactions that come to embody "images, meanings, and *models for behaviour* which constitute the cognitive and ethical landmarks of the culture [p. 5; italics mine]." In this view there is at least partial awareness of the meaning of the symbols among the members of the culture, though it is not readily verbalized and often finds its main expression in action. Tough-minded psychologists might react sceptically to all this, finding it vague and unsatisfactory; but anyone who has closely witnessed traditional rituals and talked to the participants can attest that it is a very real phenomenon.

Anthropologists are of course interested in symbolism as a means of exploring cultural systems, but when writing about them they cannot avoid using strikingly psychological language. It is equally justified to consider symbolism as a psychological process sufficiently diverse in character to appeal to the interests of cognitive, developmental, personality, and social psychologists; as yet, no one seems to have begun to take it seriously as a field of psychological research. Because its manifestation can be most clearly observed in various traditional cultures around the world (see Willis, 1975), symbolism offers a challenge for cross-cultural comparisons. No doubt it would be a difficult challenge requiring more than paper-and-pencil methods that lend themselves to mass production, and cooperation with anthropologists would probably be essential. On the other hand, there would be a rich reward if cross-cultural comparative studies led to the opening up of a significant new field for psychology at large.

Perhaps all this is excessively optimistic, and John Stuart Mill's blueprint of a "frontier" science based on cross-cultural comparisons will not be realized. What is certain is that even in its more modest role as a "meta-method," cross-cultural comparisons have a valuable contribution to make to the advancement of psychological knowledge.

REFERENCES

Barnouw, V. *Culture and personality.* Homewood, IL: Dorsey Press, 1973.

Barry, H., III Cross-cultural evidence that dependency conflict motivates drunkenness. In M. W. Everett, J. O. Waddell, & D. B. Heath (Eds.), *Cross-cultural approaches to the study of alcohol.* The Hague: Mouton, 1976.

Bastian, A. *Der Mensch in der Geschichte: Zur Bergrundung einer Psychologischen Weltanschauung.* Leipzig: Wigand, 1860.

Berlin, B., & Kay, P. *Basic color terms: Their universality and evolution.* Berkeley: University of California Press, 1969.

Berreman, G. D. Anemic and emetic analysis in social anthropology. *American Anthropologist,* 1966, *68,* 346–352.

Berry, J. W. Temne and Eskimo perceptual skills. *International Journal of Psychology,* 1966, *1,* 207–229.

Berry, J. W. On cross-cultural comparability. *International Journal of Psychology,* 1969, *4,* 119–128.

Berry, J. W. Ecological and cultural factors in spatial perceptual development. *Canadian Journal of Behavioral Science,* 1971, *3,* 324–336.

Berry, J. W. *Human ecology and cognitive style.* New York: Wiley, 1976.

Blurton-Jones, N. G., & Konner, M. J. Sex differences in the behavior of London and Bushmen children. In R. P. Michael & J. H. Crook (Eds.), *Comparative ecology and behaviour.* London: Academic Press, 1973.

Bochner, S., Brislin, R. W., & Lonner, W. J.   Introduction. In R. W. Brislin, S. Bochner, & W. J. Lonner (Eds.), *Cross-cultural perspectives on learning.* New York: Wiley, 1973.

Bornstein, M. H.   The influence of visual perception on culture. *American Anthropologist,* 1975, *77,* 774–798.

Bornstein, M. H., Kessen, W., & Weiskopf, S.   The categories of hue in infancy. *Science,* 1976, *191,* 201–202.

Brewer, M. B., & Campbell, D. T.   *Ethnocentrism and intergroup attitudes.* New York: Wiley, 1976.

Brislin, R. W.   Comparative research methodology: Cross-cultural studies. *International Journal of Psychology,* 1976, *11,* 215–229.

Brislin, R. W., Lonner, W. J., & Thorndike, R. M.   *Cross-cultural research methods.* New York: Wiley, 1973.

Bronfenbrenner, U.   Toward an experimental ecology of human development. *American Psychologist,* 1977, *32,* 513–531.

Campbell, D. T., & Naroll, R.   The mutual methodological relevance of anthropology and psychology. In F.L.K. Hsu (Ed.), *Psychological anthropology.* Cambridge, MA: Schenkman, 1972.

Clarke, A., & Clarke, A.D.B. (Eds.).   *Early experience: Myth and evidence.* London: Open Books, 1976.

Cole, M., & Gay, J.   Culture and memory. *American Anthropologist,* 1972, *74,* 1066–1084.

Cole, M., Gay, J., Glick, J., & Sharp, D. W.   *The cultural context of learning and thinking.* New York: Basic Books, 1971.

Cole, M., & Scribner, S.   *Culture and thought.* New York: Wiley, 1974.

Das, J. P.   Cultural deprivation and cognitive competence. In N. R. Ellis (Ed.), *International review of research in mental retardation.* New York: Academic Press, 1973.

Davidson, A. R., Jaccard, J. J., Triandis, H. C., Morales, M. L., & Diaz-Guerrero, R.   Cross-cultural model testing: Toward a solution of the etic-emic dilemma. *International Journal of Psychology,* 1976, *11,* 1–13.

Dawson, J.L.M.   Theory and research in cross-cultural psychology. *Bulletin of the British Psychological Society,* 1971, *24,* 291–306.

Deregowski, J. B.   Perception. In H. C. Triandis, W. Lonner, & A. Heron (Eds.), *Handbook of cross-cultural psychology* (Vol. 2). Boston: Allyn & Bacon, 1978.

Deregowski, J. B., Muldrow, E. S., & Muldrow, W. F.   Pictorial recognition in a remote Ethiopian population. *Perception,* 1972, *1,* 417–425.

Descartes, R.   *A discourse on method.* London: Dent, 1937. (Originally published, 1637.)

Durbin, M.   Cognitive anthropology. In J. J. Honigmann (Ed.), *Handbook of social and cultural anthropology.* Chicago: Rand McNally, 1973.

Ekman, P. (Ed.).   *Darwin and facial expression.* New York: Academic Press, 1973.

Evans-Pritchard, E. E.   *Witchcraft, magic and oracles among the Azande.* London: Oxford University Press, 1937.

Faucheux, C.   Cross-cultural research in experimental social psychology. *European Journal of Social Psychology,* 1976, *6,* 269–322.

Foa, U. G., & Foa, E. G.   *Societal structures of the mind.* Springfield, IL: Charles C. Thomas, 1974.

Forge, A.   Learning to see in New Guinea. In P. Mayer (Ed.), *Socialization.* London: Tavistock, 1970.

Frijda, N., & Jahoda, G.   On the scope and methods of cross-cultural psychology. *International Journal of Psychology,* 1966, *1,* 109–127.

Galton, F.   *Hereditary genius.* London: Macmillan, 1914. (Originally published, 1869.)

Gay, J., & Cole, M.   *The new mathematics and an old culture.* New York: Holt, Rinehart & Winston, 1967.

Gerard, H. B., & Conolly, E. S.   Conformity. In C. G. McClintock (Ed.), *Experimental social psychology.* New York: Holt, Rinehart & Winston, 1972.

Goody, J. *Production and reproduction.* Cambridge: Cambridge University Press, 1977.

Guilford, J. P. The three faces of intellect. *American Psychologist,* 1959, *14,* 468–479.

Hagen, M. A., & Jones, R. K. Cultural effects on pictorial perception. In H. Pick & R. Walk (Eds.), *Perception and experience.* New York: Plenum Press, 1977.

Hallpike, C. R. Some problems in cross-cultural comparisons. In T. O. Beidelman (Ed.), *The translation of culture.* London: Tavistock, 1971.

Harris, M. *The rise of anthropological theory.* London: Routledge & Kegan Paul, 1968.

Hochberg, J., & Brooks, V. Pictorial recognition as an unlearned ability: A study of one child's performance. *American Journal of Psychology,* 1962, *75,* 624–628.

Holtzman, W. H., Diaz-Guerrero, R., & Swartz, J. D. *Personality development in two cultures.* Austin: University of Texas Press, 1975.

Honigmann, J. J. Psychological anthropology: Trends, accomplishments and future tasks. In T. R. Williams (Ed.), *Psychological anthropology.* The Hague: Mouton, 1975.

Hudson, W. Pictorial depth perception in sub-cultural groups in Africa. *Journal of Social Psychology,* 1960, *52,* 183–208.

Hume, D. *Philosophical works* (Vol. 3). Edinburgh: Adam Black & William Tait, 1826.

Hunt, J. *Anthropological Review* (Vol. 5). Quoted in A. C. Haddon (Ed.), *History of anthropology.* London: Watts, 1934. (Originally published, 1867.)

Inkeles, A., & Smith, D. H. *Becoming modern.* Cambridge, MA: Harvard University Press, 1974.

Jahoda, G. A psychologist's perspective. In P. Mayer (Ed.), *Socialization.* London: Tavistock, 1970.

Jahoda, G. Social expectations and the development of personality. In S. H. Irvine & J. T. Sanders (Eds.), *Cultural adaptation within modern Africa.* New York: Teachers College Press, 1972.

Jahoda, G. Psychology and the developing countries: Do they need each other? *International Social Science Journal,* 1973, *25,* 461–474.

Jahoda, G. In pursuit of the emic-etic distinction. In Y. H. Poortinga (Ed.), *Basic problems in cross-cultural psychology.* Amsterdam: Swets & Zeitlinger, 1977.

Jahoda, G. Theoretical and systematic approaches in cross-cultural psychology. In H. C. Triandis, W. W. Lambert, & J. W. Berry (Eds.), *Handbook of cross-cultural psychology* (Vol. 1). Boston: Allyn & Bacon, 1978.

Jahoda, G., Deregowski, J. B., Ampene, E., & Williams, N. Pictorial recognition as an unlearned ability. In G. E. Butterworth (Ed.), *The child's representation of the world.* London: Plenum Press, 1977.

Kardiner, A. *The psychological frontiers of society.* New York: Columbia University Press, 1945.

Klein, R. E., Irwin, M., Engle, P. L., & Yarborough, C. Malnutrition and mental development in rural Guatemala. In N. Warren (Ed.), *Studies in cross-cultural psychology* (Vol. 1). London: Academic Press, 1977.

Kline, P. Cross-cultural studies and Freudian theory. In N. Warren (Ed.), *Studies in cross-cultural psychology* (Vol. 1). London: Academic Press, 1977.

Klineberg, O. *Race differences.* New York: Harper, 1935.

Kroeber, A., & Kluckhohn, C. Culture. *Papers of the Peabody Museum,* 1952, *47* (No. 1).

Laswell, H. D. Collective autism as a consequence of culture contact. *Zeitschrift für Sozialforschung,* 1935, *4,* 232–247.

Leach, E. R. Comment. *Current Anthropology,* 1965, *5,* 299.

Leach, E. *Culture and communication.* Cambridge: Cambridge University Press, 1976.

Lester, B. M., Kotelchuck, M., Spelke, E., Sellers, M. J., & Klein, R. E. Separation protest in Guatemalan infants: Cross-cultural and cognitive findings. *Developmental Psychology,* 1974, *10,* 79–85.

LeVine, R. A. Cross-cultural study in child psychology. In P. Mussen (Ed.), *Carmichael's manual of child psychology* (Vol. 2). New York: Wiley, 1970.

LeVine, R. A. *Culture, behaviour and personality.* London: Hutchinson, 1973.

Lévy-Bruhl, L. [*Primitive mentality*] (L. Clare, trans.). Boston: Beacon Press, 1966. (Originally published, 1923.)

Lévi-Strauss, C. Social structure. In A. L. Kroeber (Ed.), *Anthropology today.* Chicago: University of Chicago Press, 1953.

Lévi-Strauss, C. Rousseau: The father of anthropology. *UNESCO Courier,* 1962, *16,* 10–14.

Lévi-Strauss, C. *The savage mind.* Chicago: University of Chicago Press, 1966.

Lewis, I. *Symbols and sentiments.* London: Academic Press, 1977.

MacDonald, D. *Africana, or the heart of heathen Africa.* London: Dawsons of Pall Mall, 1969. (Originally published, 1882.)

Malinowski, B. *The Argonauts of the western Pacific.* London: Routledge & Kegan Paul, 1922.

Mill, J. S. *A system of logic* (Vol. 2). London: Longmans, Green, 1879.

Miller, R. J. Cross-cultural research in the perception of pictorial materials. *Psychological Bulletin,* 1973, *80* 135–150.

Munroe, R. L., Munroe, R. H., & Whiting, J.W.M. The couvade: A psychological analysis. *Ethos,* 1973, *1,* 30–74.

Murdock, G. P. The cross-cultural survey. *American Sociological Review,* 1940, *5,* 261–370.

Nadel, S. F. *The foundations of social anthropology.* London: Cohen & West, 1951.

Naroll, R. The culture-bearing unit in cross-cultural surveys. In R. Naroll & R. Cohen (Eds.), *A handbook of method in cultural anthropology.* New York: Columbia University Press, 1973.

Naroll, R., Michik, G. L., & Naroll, F. Hologeistic theory testing. In J. G. Jorgensen (Ed.), *Comparative studies by Harold E. Driver and essays in his honor.* New Haven, CT: HRAF Press, 1974.

Osgood, C. E., May, W. H., & Miron, M. S. *Cross-cultural universals of affective meaning.* Urbana: University of Illinois Press, 1975.

Pearson, K. *The life, letters and labour of Francis Galton.* (Vol. 2). Cambridge: Cambridge University Press, 1924.

Pelto, P. J. *Anthropological research: The structure of inquiry.* New York: Harper & Row, 1970.

Piaget, J. Necessité et signification des recherches comparatives en psychologie genetique. *International Journal of Psychology,* 1966, *1,* 3–13.

Popper, C. R. *The logic of scientific discovery.* London: Hutchinson, 1959.

Price-Williams, D. R. *Explorations in cross-cultural psychology.* San Francisco: Chandler & Sharp, 1975.

Rivers, W.H.R. *In Reports of the Cambridge anthropological expedition to Torres Straits* (Vol. 2). Cambridge: Cambridge University Press, 1901.

Rohner, R. P. *They love me, they love me not.* New Haven, CT: HRAF Press, 1975.

Rosch, E. Human categorization. In N. Warren (Ed.), *Studies in cross-cultural psychology* (Vol. 1). London: Academic Press, 1977.

Schachter, S., Nuttin, J., de Monchaux, C., Maucorps, P., Osmer, D., Duijker, H., Rommetveit, R., & Israel, J. Cross-cultural experiment on threat and rejection. *Human Relations,* 1954, *7,* 403–440.

Scholte, B. The structural anthropology of Claude Lévi-Strauss. In J. J. Honigmann (Ed.), *Handbook of social and cultural anthropology.* Chicago: Rand McNally, 1973.

Segall, M. H., Campbell, D. T., & Herskovits, M. J. *The influence of culture on visual perception.* Indianapolis: Bobbs-Merrill, 1966.

Strodtbeck, F. L. Considerations of meta-method in cross-cultural studies. *American Anthropologist,* 1964, *66,* 223–229.

Super, C. M. *Who goes to school and what do they learn?* Paper presented at the meeting of the Society for Research in Child Development, New Orleans, 1977.

Sutton-Smith, B., & Roberts, J. M. Studies of an elementary game of strategy. *Genetic Psychology Monographs,* 1967, *75,* 3–42.

Taft, R. Cross-cultural psychology as a social science: Comments on Faucheux's paper. *European Journal of Social Psychology,* 1976, *6,* 323–330.

Triandis, H. C. *The analysis of subjective culture.* New York: Wiley, 1972.

Triandis, H. C. On the value of cross-cultural research in social psychology: Reactions to Faucheux's paper. *European Journal of Social Psychology,* 1976, *6,* 331–341.

Triandis, H. C. *Interpersonal behavior.* Monterey, CA: Brooks/Cole, 1977.

Turner, V. W. *The drums of affliction.* Oxford: Clarendon Press, 1968.

Tylor, E. B. *Primitive culture.* New York: Harper & Row, 1958. (Originally published, 1871.)

Vandenberg, S. G. Comparative studies of multiple factor ability measures. In J. Royce (Ed.), *Multivariate analysis and psychological theory.* New York: Academic Press, 1973.

Whiting, B. B., & Whiting, J.W.M. *Children of six cultures.* Cambridge, MA: Harvard University Press, 1975.

Whiting, J.W.M., & Child, I. L. *Child training and personality.* New Haven, CT: Yale University Press, 1953.

Williams, T. R. (Ed.). *Psychological anthropology.* The Hague: Mouton, 1975.

Willis, R. (Ed.). *The interpretation of symbolism.* London: Malaby Press, 1975.

Witkin, H. A., & Berry, J. W. Psychological differentiation in cross-cultural perspective. *International Journal of Psychology,* 1975, *6,* 4–87.

Wittgenstein, L. *Tractatus logic-philosophicus.* London: Routledge & Kegan Paul, 1961.

Wundt, W. *The elements of folk psychology.* London: Allen & Unwin, 1916.

APPENDIX

The questionnaire reproduced here was planned by Galton (1869/1914) for use in his "Ethnological Inquiries on the Innate Character and Intelligence of Different Races." Because he did not leave any papers explaining its rationale, one can only venture some speculations concerning the reasons that led to this particular form.

The major underlying assumption was presumably that if children of "primitive" races are brought up from an early age in a "civilized" European setting, those aspects of their behavior ascribable to environmental influences will become adapted to the norms of that setting; on the other hand, such differences as persist will be attributable to innate dispositions. The first six questions were clearly designed to probe genetic and environmental background factors. The bulk of the remaining questions concerns intelligence and character, apart from two (questions 7 and 19), which cover what would nowadays be labeled "modernity" (see Inkeles & Smith, 1974).

With regard to intelligence and special aptitudes (questions 8, 10, 11, and 33), Galton attempted to provide guidelines for the respondent so that the answers would be based on specific observations rather than broadly based judgments of "clever" versus "stupid." Question 33 anticipates verbal intelligence tests. The idea that the thinking of "primitive" children ceases to develop at an early stage is an old one, frequently reported by travellers. Although the phrasing of question 10 is heavily loaded, Galton did at least make some effort to verify this notion.

The many questions on character constitute, to our minds, a rather odd mixture. In particular, the emphasis on moral and religious topics, including even original sin, seems most intriguing. One might be inclined to put it down to typical Victorian moralism and religiosity; however, this would be quite out of character for someone like Galton, who scandalized some of his contemporaries by conducting an experiment on the efficacy of prayer! In *Hereditary Genius* (1869/1914), where Galton developed a theory about the responses of "savages" to the impact of civilization, he postulated a relationship between the character of the "savage" and the "savage's" religious feelings. A key passage setting out one of the hypotheses reads: "The newly reclaimed barbarian, with the impulsive, unstable nature of the savage, when he also chances to be gifted with a peculiarly generous and affectionate disposition, is of all others the man most oppressed with a sense of sin [p. 336]." I suggest that a number of Galton's questions may be better understood if one supposes that Galton put them in for the purpose of hypothesis testing. Whether or not this interpretation is correct (and there is unfortunately no means of verifying it), the chances are that there is more behind this questionnaire than would appear on the surface. Such a view certainly complements what we do know about Galton's scientific ingenuity and his extraordinary versatility.

Galton's questionnaire is reproduced in the following:

1. Signature, title and full address of the sender of the information.

2. Name or initials, sex and age of individual whose character is described.

3. His (or her) country and race. State specifically if his race is known to be pure, if not describe the admixture.

4. Age at which he was removed from his parents and people, also particulars showing the extent to which he has since been separated from their influence.

5. What language, or languages, does he commonly speak? Does he retain the use of his native tongue?

6. State any circumstances that may or may not justify his being considered a good typical specimen of his race.

7. Is he capable of steady and sustained hard labour; or, is he restless and irregular in his habits?

8. Is he capable of filling responsible situations? Does he show coolness of temper when in difficulty? (It is said that Hindoos are incapable of steering large ships, that is, of acting as quartermasters; while in British vessels the duty is commonly performed by native Christians of the Philippines.)

9. Is he docile or obstinate?

10. Children of many races are fully as quick, and even more precocious than European children, but they mostly cease to make progress after the season of manhood. Their moral character changes for the worse at the same time. State if this has been observed in the present instance.

11. Has he any special aptitudes, or the reverse, such as in mimicry, sense of the ludicrous, taste in colours, music, poetry, dancing, calculating power, keenness of sight or hearing, quickness of observation, manual dexterity, horsemanship, ability to tend cattle?

12. Is he naturally polished and self-composed in manner or rude and awkward?

13. Is he modest and self-reliant, or servile and cringing? Is he vain?

14. Is he solitary or sociable; morose or cheerful?

15. Is the passion of sexual affection strongly developed in him, or the reverse?

16. Is he fond of children, and are children fond of him?

17. Does he cherish malice for long periods, or does he forgive frankly?

18. Is he liable to outburst of rage?

19. Did he for long show uneasiness at the restrictions of civilised life, or did he readily accept them; such as keeping regular hours, acting on a steady system, wearing shoes and other clothing?

20. Children of savages, who have been reared in missionary families, have been known to throw off their clothes, and quit the house in a momentary rage, and go back to their people, among whom they were afterwards found in apparently contented barbarism. State authentic instances of this, if you know of any, with full particulars.

21. Has he a strong natural sense of right and wrong, and a sensitive conscience?

22. Does he exhibit to his religious teachers any strong conviction of an original sinfulness in his nature, or the reverse?

23. Is he much influenced by ceremonial observances, such as those of the Roman Catholic Church?

24. Is he a willing keeper of the Sabbath?

25. Has he any strong religious instinct; is he inclined to quiet devotion?

26. Is he ascetic, self-mortifying and self-denying, or the contrary?

27. Is he inclined to be unduly credulous or unduly sceptical?

28. Is he active or impassive in social duties?

29. Is he much governed by superstitious feelings, such as [are indicated by the use of] charms or omens of good or ill luck?

30. Has he any tendency to be sanctimonious and hypocritical?

31. Is he honest, truthful and open, or cunning and intriguing?

32. Is he grateful or ungrateful?

33. Does he, in conversation, make frequent use of abstract terms? Does he adequately understand their meaning when he employs them?

34. Are there any other marked peculiarities in his character or intellect?

Please address copies to
FRANCIS GALTON,
42 Rutland Gate,
London

5 Statistical Issues and Comparative Methods

Victoria Seitz
Yale University

INTRODUCTION

Statistical theory is often directly relevant to the comparative approach in psychology. The comparison of treatment groups with control groups is central to classical experimental design. The comparison of groups in nonexperimental contexts (e.g., comparing the two sexes or different ethnic groups) has also engendered a substantial literature, some of which we consider later in this chapter.

As every psychologist soon discovers, there is often a gap between the ideal theoretical examples on textbook pages and the less than ideal data that are actually available for analyses. The purpose of the present chapter is to discuss the fit between statistical theory and the realities of data generated in the group comparisons of importance to psychologists. Clearly it is impossible to go into much detail in a short chapter, but I attempt to discuss some broad issues in a nontechnical way and to provide references to indicate where more technical presentations may be found. The first section of the chapter is devoted to general considerations. The second section considers problems that are especially common in the cross-species, developmental, and cross-cultural approaches discussed throughout this book.

GENERAL ISSUES

On the Need—Or Lack of Need—for Statistical Comparison

In general, the usefulness of statistical methods in comparing groups depends on the magnitude of the difference between the groups. If groups differ enormously, one has little need for statistical methods to document the fact. If they differ very little, statistical procedures may have insufficient power to detect the difference. To phrase this more technically, the usefulness of statistical comparison is partially dependent on the size of the effect to be detected.

Before further considering when statistical group comparisons are most useful, it would be worth examining briefly how such comparisons are typically made. Fundamental to almost all statistical procedures in wide usage is the assumption that a simple additive, linear model can be used to represent the relationship between outcome measures and predictor variables (Searle, 1971). That is, it is assumed that a predictive equation can be written in which exponents larger than one are not needed (e.g., no squared or cubed values) and in which all terms can be connected by plus or minus signs. Use of the additive, linear model represents a decision at the philosophical level as much as it does a statistical convenience. The scientist is in effect committed to a search for the smallest number of explanatory variables as well as a simple relationship among them.

It may seem surprising that a simple model can ever be useful in a complex world. In trying to explain the incidence of child abuse, for example, a theorist might easily postulate a number of causes, from social and economic pressures to psychological events such as parental hostility and the parents themselves having been abused as children. The expectation that somehow one can create a theory in which measures of the presumed causative events can be related in an additive, linear fashion might seem to strain credulity. In fact, however, solutions to complex mathematical problems can often be approximated reasonably well by simple equations. Although more complex models are mathematically feasible, by a principle of parsimony, simpler models are preferred so long as they function well. The additive, linear model has proved to have a surprising utility in dealing with a wide range of statistical problems. It is the basis for both experimental and correlational designs, and it is adaptable to both univariate cases (where there is a single outcome measure) and to multivariate problems (with multiple outcome measures).

Within the additive, linear model, there are a number of procedures for comparing groups. Perhaps the simplest such procedure is the well-known "*t*-test," based on a rationale originally published by W. S. Gossett under the modest anonymity of the pseudonym "Student" (1908) and later refined by Fisher (1925). The logic underlying this simple, familiar inferential statistic is so elegant and lucid that it deserves restatement here as providing the ideal textbook case against which we can assess real data. From the two-group comparison of the t-test, there is no basic change in logic needed to progress to the multiple-group comparisons of the analysis of variance (ANOVA) or to the many correlational methods that are derived from the additive, linear model.

To determine whether two groups differ reliably, Gossett showed, we need to have a standard of unreliability against which to compare an observed difference. That is, we need to know the reasonable limits of chance variation. The determination of these limits can be made on the assumptions that one has random samples drawn from populations with homogeneous (equal) variance, and that the measured event is normally distributed in each population. Given that these conditions are reasonable, the t-test produces the desired yardstick for deciding whether an observed mean difference between two groups should be regarded as a real difference rather than as a sampling accident.

The decision may be wrong in two ways. First, we may decide that the groups differ more than can reasonably be expected from sampling error, yet in fact sampling error has caused the difference. This "Type I" decision error is well known, and it is customary to set a fixed, low probability of committing this error. The second, "Type II," error is unfortunately given much less attention: The failure to detect a true population effect is a real and common problem in comparisons of groups on psychological variables. The probability of avoiding a Type II error is referred to as the "power" of a statistical test.

As suggested earlier, the approach just described is most useful when groups being compared arise from populations in which the average differences are neither extremely large nor small. As an example of a small effect, suppose that two populations have equal variances and normal distributions, but differ only slightly in their means—say, about two-tenths of a standard deviation's difference. With IQ scores from the Wechsler Intelligence Scale for Children, where the standard deviation is assumed to be about 15 points, the mean difference we are describing would be only three points. As Cohen (1977) points out, small differences of this kind are often the focus of psychological research. Two actual examples of such small effects are the difference in mean IQ between twins and nontwins (a difference favoring nontwins), and adult sex differences on the Wechsler Adult Intelligence Scale (favoring men) on the Information and the Picture Completion subtests. True population differences of this magnitude may be of value in building or testing theories. However, detecting them may require large numbers of observations that—particularly with human subjects and in cross-cultural applications—may be ethically impossible or prohibitively expensive to obtain. Also, with small effects, statistically significant results are unlikely to have much practical significance. However, small effects are to be expected in new fields of inquiry where there is little theoretical guidance to help the investigator sharpen the hypothesis.

To consider the opposite case, where effect size is very large, the question may be raised as to why one should apply statistical techniques at all. If there is minimal overlap between the distributions of two populations, one may, as Tukey has phrased it, be seeking "statistical sanctification." It is perhaps for this reason that ethologists have often eschewed statistics, finding that effects involved in phenomena such as imprinting were so obvious that they met Leonard Savage's "inter-ocular-traumatic" test—where you know what the data mean because they leap up and hit you between the eyes.

The most fertile ground for statistical comparisons of groups lies in detecting moderate population differences. Although this concept is somewhat difficult to define, a reasonable approach has been offered by Cohen (1977), who suggests that a difference in population means of half a standard deviation is a "medium effect." In correlational terms, the magnitude of this effect does not seem impressive: If one expresses as a correlation the t-test information from a comparison of groups differing by half a standard deviation, the value is .24, indicating that only about 6% of the variance is accounted for by group membership. However, if one examines the overlap of the two populations being compared, the practicality of the difference is more obvious. With a medium-effect size as just described, and given normal distributions and equal variances, almost 70% of the individuals in the lower population (e.g., a control group) would fall below the median for the upper population (e.g., an experimental group). This is a reasonably useful difference, yet not such an obvious one that it is visible to the naked eye.

Because we usually do not know the size of the effect in the population, it might seem that this discussion of power is pointless. However, usually it is possible to produce at least an educated guess about population differences. Conceptualizing theoretical questions in terms of population effects can lead both to a more thoughtful decision as to whether statistics are necessary and to the design of experiments with sufficient power in those cases where statistical methods are useful. Cohen (1977) provides detailed advice concerning the design of experiments when the investigator desires to take both Type I and Type II errors into account.

Because it is so commonly used in psychology, a few comments on the analysis of variance might also be of value here. The analysis of variance represents a technique for comparing three or more groups, rather than the two to which t-test comparisons are limited. ANOVA designs also permit groups to be classified simultaneously on two or more dimensions and comparisons to be made along any of the dimensions. An example of an

ANOVA design and the benefits to be gained from it is provided by Ressler's (1963) experiment on foster mothering in mice. Ressler took two groups representing different genetic strains of mice and randomly assigned half the newborn pups in each group to be reared by foster mothers of the opposite genetic strain. The remaining half of the pups was also given to foster mothers, but of their same genetic strain. After the pups had matured, Ressler measured such outcomes as survival, weight at weaning, and visual exploration of unfamiliar environments. (Ressler's design also included a third classifying variable that I ignore here for simplicity's sake.)

The design just described produces four groups of subjects (type A pups with type A mothers; type A pups, B mothers; B pups, A mothers; B pups, B mothers). The procedure known as a one-way analysis of variance could be used to compare the means of these four groups. With a logic similar to that described for the t-test, a statistical test can be made to determine whether the four observed means could reasonably be expected to occur in samples drawn randomly from four equivalent populations (e.g., with normal distributions, equal means, and equal variances). If the four groups being compared were related on only one dimension—if, for example, they had been groups of the same kind of mice reared under four different conditions—the analysis would be terminated at this point. A signficant F-test result from the ANOVA would indicate that at least one of the four means was unusual relative to the others. A procedure of comparing all pairs of groups would then be undertaken to determine whether each group was different from each of the others. With four groups, there are six possible two-group comparisons, and a significant overall F guarantees that at least one of the six t-test comparisons will be significant.

However, in our present example, the four groups can be classified along two dimensions (type of pup and type of mother). For this reason, the extra information is taken into account in the analysis. Rather than interpreting the overall F value, the variability across groups is partitioned into a portion due to type of pup, a portion due to type of mother, and a remainder, which is a portion due to interaction. (The technique for such partitioning is a matter of algebra based on the additive, linear model.) At this point it might be instructive to consider Table 5.1 and three hypothetical outcomes of this experiment.

Case 1 in Table 5.1 represents a situation in which the four group means differ very little. The variability across the groups is much less than the variability within each group. Performance on the outcome measure is not predictable from knowledge about a subject's group membership. Cases 2 and 3 represent an opposite extreme where the group means are very different from each other. Overlap among the four groups is small in either outcome situation, and a subject's performance could be predicted from knowledge of group membership with much better than chance accuracy. Case 2 differs

TABLE 5.1
Several Possible Results of a 2 × 2 Analysis of Variance of Data from a
Foster-Mothering Experiment

	Experimental Group			
	A pups, A mothers [N = 50]	A pups, B mothers [N = 50]	B pups, A mothers [N = 50]	B pups, B mothers [N = 50]
Case 1				
Mean	94	95	95	96
Standard Deviation	10	10	10	10
Case 2				
Mean	80	100	90	110
Standard Deviation	10	10	10	10
Case 3				
Mean	100	80	90	110
Standard Deviation	10	10	10	10

from Case 3, however, in the information gained from partitioning the variance of the four groups. In Case 2, there are simple effects for pups and for type of mothers: Type B pups have higher scores than type A pups regardless of the kind of mother; type B mothers do a better job than type A mothers regardless of the kinds of pups they are rearing. In Case 3, the same scores arranged in a different pattern indicate an effect for type of pups (the means are 90 versus 100 for type A and B pups, respectively), but no effect for type of mother (the mean is 95 for both types of mother). However, the key finding is the interaction: Each type of mother does best raising her own genetic strain of pup. In general, what a significant interaction indicates is that the results are not simple: One cannot safely generalize about the effects of either variable without providing information about the other. (In the present example, although Case 3 might seem more likely to occur in nature, in fact, Ressler's data more nearly resembled Case 2. However, the data in Table 1 are fictional.)

On the Importance of Satisfying Assumptions

A major consideration in employing statistical tests is *robustness*. Robustness refers to how well a statistical procedure can survive the translation from theoretical cases to real data, which almost always violate pristine textbook assumptions in some way, no matter how carefully the scientist has collected them. In the present discussion we cannot consider all possible assumptions in all statistical tests, but we focus only on the most common assumptions. We first consider the problem of how less than interval scale measurement of data may affect the accuracy of statistical conclusions. Next, we examine effects of violations of assumptions of normality, homogeneity of variance, linearity, and randomness and independence of sampling. Finally, we consider parametric versus nonparametric techniques.

Scale of Measurement. The most frequently employed statistical tests often presume the existence of at least interval-scale measurement, whereas most of the measurements in behavioral science cannot be proved to have a better than ordinal relationship to the underlying property being measured. A statistical purist, such as S. S. Stevens (1951, 1968), would therefore categorically rule out the use of the most common and powerful statistical techniques with most of the data gathered by psychologists, sociologists, and anthropologists.

The present author is in agreement with Harris (1975) and with Baker, Hardyck, and Petrinovich (1966) that the purist position is far too extreme and should not be adopted as dogma. As Harris points out, the validity of statistical computations depends on how well the numbers being analyzed meet distributional assumptions (normality and homogeneity of variance), and not on the scaling procedures involved in obtaining the numbers. One may safely conclude that a significant difference in, say, "masculinity of interests" scores does exist between a group of men and a group of women if the data are from random groups, if they meet the distributional assumptions, and if that is what one's *t*-test result indicates. It is only at the point of making theoretical statements—of interpreting the data—that scale of measurement becomes an important consideration. However, here one can often apply tests of "reasonableness" that permit reasonable interpretations. We return to this point in a moment.

It is also noteworthy that alternative statistical procedures that are supposed to be appropriate for noninterval-scale numbers often yield very similar results to those designed for interval scale data. Consider the case of the Pearson product-moment correlation coefficient (*r*). There are several alternative formulas, such as Spearman's *rho* (to relate ordinal scale variables), point-biserial *r*'s (for relating dichotomous nominal-scaled variables to continuous equal-interval variables), and the *phi* correlation coefficient (for relating two dichotomized, nominal variables). These special formulas in fact produce results identical to those obtained by using the Pearson *r* formula on the same data expressed in ranks (for Spearman's *rho*) or with nominal variables coded as zero and one (for the point-biserial and the *phi* coefficients). Furthermore, the significance levels of the four types of correlation are nearly identical. Even with so few as five degrees of freedom, the value of a signifcant correlation coefficient is .75, .79, .75, and .74 for Pearson *r*, Spearman *rho*, point-biserial *r*, and the *phi* coefficient, respectively. When there are more degrees of freedom, the correspondence is even better (e.g., .38 for all four types of correlation with 25 degrees of freedom). The present author agrees with Harris (1975) that "searching out statistical procedures and measures of relationship especially designed for nominal or ordinal data is usually a waste of time [p. 228]."

This does not mean that the question of level of measurement is meaningless. Let us now turn to the issue of how one makes valid generalizations from one's findings. Harris provides the following guideline:

> Consider the range of possible transformations, linear or otherwise, which you could apply to your data without changing any important properties or losing any of the useful information "stored" in your numbers. Then restrict your generalizations and theoretical statements to those whose truth or falsehood would not be affected by the most extreme such permissible transformation [p. 228].

Consider, for example, the set of numbers shown in Table 5.2, representing, say, attitudes toward making contraceptives available to unmarried persons (where increasing numbers denote decreasingly favorable attitudes). The transformation rule in Table 5.2 is to preserve the rank order of the data and to make the largest value many times larger than all others. One may use statistical procedures such as a *t*-test to determine whether the two means from either the original or transformed data are significantly different. However, if the relationship between the numbers and the conceptual variable the researcher was attempting to assess were truly as weak as suggested by the above transformation, then generalization from these data to the external state of nature would not be acceptable.

Most researchers would immediately protest that this was not a reasonable transformation. Although the numbers are ordinal, they do convey some information about the relative distance between pairs of numbers. The difference between attitudes of 9 and 10 is almost certainly not 10 times as large as that between 8 and 9. Usually a researcher knows *something* more

TABLE 5.2
Example of Transformation of Data

	Original Data	$\bar{X}$	Transformed Data	$\bar{X}$
Urban housewives	1, 2, 10, 3, 4	4.0	1, 2, 100, 3, 4	11.0
Rural housewives	5, 6, 6, 7, 8	6.4	5, 6, 6, 7, 8	6.4

than just rank order from the numbers. If it is possible to specify in advance of performing statistical analyses what the most extreme *reasonable* monotonic transformation would be for all possible observations that may be found, the researcher should be able to apply this transformation to the actual data and determine whether it is reasonable to generalize the findings at the conceptual level. (It may be reassuring to observe that the most common transformations employed to render data more normal in distribution, for example logarithmic, square root, and inverse sine transformations [Winer, 1971, pp. 397–402], frequently have little effect on the resulting significance levels of standard statistical tests.)

There are occasions when a researcher may be limited in generalizability by the ordinal properties of the data. The shape of a distribution (for example a bar graph) is very easily altered by changing category boundaries. If, for example, one is trying to determine whether the social class distribution in a society is rectangular or nonrectangular, it is essential to employ numbers bearing an interval-scale relationship to social class. Cross-cultural comparisons are also often problematical because the data are at best ordinal. For example, attempts to determine whether Piagetian stages occur at the same ages in other cultures are seriously hampered when children's ages can only be estimated. It is common to find reports of retardation from two to seven years in the ages at which children in other cultures reliably demonstrate conservation on Piagetian tasks (Kamara & Easley, 1977). The interpretation of this fact depends on how adequately the age estimates approximate the interval-scale nature of actual ages. As Kamara and Easley (1977) point out: "If there are systematic errors in ages reported, the amount of retardation is affected; if there are random errors, the confidence in the difference is affected [p. 30]." (See also Bornstein, in this volume.)

Another area in which caution is needed is in the interpretation of interactions. Monotonic transformations may cause statistical interactions to appear or to disappear, leaving one to wonder whether there is a real interaction at the conceptual level. As Stanovich (1976) has warned, "To the extent that the dependent variable employed in a particular study is chosen arbitrarily, rather than from a direct theoretical link to the underlying construct of interest, any interactive effects can be removed or produced by equally arbitrary monotonic transformations of the dependent variable [p. 395]." Here it is worth noting that if the interaction is of the "crossover" variety, where the direction of one variable's effect is actually reversed at different levels of the other variable, one need not be concerned. No monotonic transformation of the data will affect the conclusion that such an interaction exists. But interactions that indicate a difference in degree but not in direction of effect should be very carefully interpreted using Harris's guideline of the most extreme reasonable transformation.

Other Assumptions.   Many statistical tests require the assumptions of normality and homogeneity of variance in the populations from which the sample observations were drawn. For univariate statistics, the literature on robustness is now quite well known. As Harris (1975) points out, the data cited earlier on the robustness of Pearson *r* under violations of scale of measurement assumptions also illustrate the amazing robustness of Pearson *r* under violations of the assumptions of normality. Ranked data have a rectangular distribution, and dichotomized data have a binomial distribution; yet in most circumstances, the use of Pearson *r* yields results virtually identical with those from formulas designed especially for less-than-interval data. Havlicek and Peterson (1977) have recently demonstrated empirically that "the Pearson *r* is insensitive to extreme violations of the basic assumptions of normality and of the type of measurement scale [p. 373]," and similar reassurances exist for the *t*-test (Boneau, 1960; Havlicek & Peterson, 1974). Except for cases where one's samples are very small and/or unequal in size or where one wishes to use one-tailed tests, one usually need not be greatly concerned about violations of the normality and homogeneity assumptions. Harris (1975) advises:

> As a general guideline, normal-curve-based tests on a single correlation coefficient can be considered valid for almost any unimodal X and Y population for any number of observations greater than about 10; while normal-curve-based *F* or *t*-tests can be considered valid for even U-shaped population distributions so long as two-tailed tests are used; the ratio between the largest and smallest sample variance is no greater than about 20 to 1; the ratio between the largest and smallest sample size is no greater than about 4; and the total degrees of freedom for the error term is 10 or more [p. 231].

Bock (1975, pp. 104–112) has pointed out that there is also good reason to believe that most behavioral data do in fact satisfy at least the normality assumption. Bock argues that there are three sources of variation in behavioral data: individual differences (the result of genetic differences, individual learning histories, and idiosyncratic accidents of development), response error (trait instability), and measurement error (variation reflecting the measuring instrument itself). Bock provides a detailed consideration of each source of variation and concludes that they are likely to result cumulatively in normal distributions for most behavioral data.

Not all statistical procedures are robust. A commonly used procedure that yields inaccurate results under commonly occurring conditions is the analysis of variance with repeated measures. As McCall and Appelbaum (1973) have pointed out, when there are three or more measures per subject, the resulting covariance matrices for measures across time often do not meet the homogeneity requirements. The consequence is that the *F*-tests assessing change over occasions are overly sensitive—too likely to indicate a significant change where none exists. The fact of this violation by no means rules out the use of this statistical analysis, however. All one need do is modify the critical value of the F-ratio that is used to determine significance. Winer (1971, p. 523) provides a procedure for estimating whether one has minimal, moderate, or maximum heterogeneity and for adjusting the F value accordingly. Because a maximally conservative estimate can easily be generated, a researcher can first check the results to determine whether they are significant against this stringent criterion. Although the most stringent estimate is easy to establish, it is *very* conservative. If the results do not meet this criterion, it is worth generating an estimate of the actual degree to which the homogeneity assumption has been violated. Alternatively, as McCall and Appelbaum (1973) suggest, the researcher may wish to employ a multivariate analysis of variance (MANOVA), treating the repeated measures as if they were from separate tests made at one time. MANOVA programs are increasingly available as standard statistical packages at computer centers, so that this is a reasonable alternative.

As described earlier, the linearity assumption is that the relationship among the raw scores for the variables of interest can be expressed in an additive equation with no exponents larger than one. As Harris (1975) points out, the linearity requirement might seem to have a quality of wishful thinking about it, but in fact many variables do have a reasonably linear relationship to each other across most of their range. It is possible to examine data both visually and statistically to determine whether their relationship departs markedly from linearity, and it is usually possible to find a transformation of the raw data yielding linearly related transformed scores suitable for analysis if the original data are not linear. For example, although Einstein's famous $e = mc^2$ is not a linear equation, a logarithmic transform would produce a linear equivalent. Because the techniques for dealing with nonlinearity are discussed in most statistical textbooks, and because they differ for different measures, they are not further considered here.

Two other assumptions that are fundamental to almost every statistical procedure are that one's samples are randomly taken from the population to which one wishes to generalize and that all observations are independently taken. Violation of these assumptions raises problems that no statistical manipulations or adjustments can remedy. Asking a sample of New Yorkers emerging from St. Patrick's Cathedral on Sunday morning for their attitudes concerning abortion will not permit one to generalize to the population of all American adults no matter what kind of statistical witch-doctoring procedure is attempted. Statistics cannot compensate for inadequate experimental design and poor data.

However, again, there is a danger of adopting the purist position that all imperfect designs and samples are equally imperfect. This is not the case. As

Campbell and Stanley (1966) have so carefully documented, some flaws are more fatal than others. As researchers have become increasingly interested in studying behavior in its broad social context (see Bronfenbrenner, 1977; Zigler & Seitz, 1978), the methodological problems of conducting research in naturalistic settings have drawn correspondingly increased attention. Because of the extensive treatment of this topic elsewhere (Campbell & Boruch, 1975; Campbell & Stanley, 1966; Kenny, 1975a), I limit my comments to agreeing with these theorists that science can progress by a kind of converging operations approach when a number of research projects, all slightly flawed but in somewhat different ways, can be pieced together to yield a coherent, consistent conclusion. For example, some studies may have adequate initial sampling but a differential attrition problem. Others may have biased samples but little attrition. It may therefore be possible to estimate the probable magnitude of attrition effects in the first set of studies from the data in the second and vice versa. Given enough studies and enough convergence in findings across a number of settings, it may be possible to arrive at an accurate assessment of the effects of the program being evaluated. It is rapidly becoming a fine art to tease out meaning from a mass of somewhat imperfect studies (Glass, 1976; Guttentag & Struening, 1975; Struening & Guttentag, 1975).

Parametric versus Nonparametric Statistical Methods.   Both for reasons of concern about the level of measurement employed and because of concern about whether the necessary distributional requirements have been met, some researchers have sought to employ nonparametric procedures with their data. Several sourcebooks exist (e.g., Hollander & Wolfe, 1973; Marascuilo & McSweeney, 1977; Siegel, 1956), and recently texts are becoming available to extend nonparametric techniques to multivariate analyses (Krishnaiah, 1969).

Data in cross-group comparisons often take the form of contingency tables where independent variables (which may include group status such as gender or ethnic group) are the bases of classification and the dependent variable consists of frequency counts. Data of this sort have typically been difficult to approach in an efficient manner.

Recent techniques permit as systematic an analysis as is provided by the usual factorial ANOVA. The log-linear approach, using an ANOVA following a logarithmic transformation of the cell counts, and additional analytic procedures for contingency table data have recently been described by Bishop, Fienberg, and Holland (1975); a very technical discussion is provided in Krishnaiah (1969). Winer (1971, pp. 855–859) describes a method that can be employed without transformations to "partition" chi-square data. These techniques provide a straightforward method of analysis for what would otherwise require the calculation of a number of nonindependent chi-square values. Furthermore, they permit the assessment of interactions among the classifying variables. The availability of these techniques will doubtless increase the enthusiasm of researchers for analyzing their heretofore aggravating nominal-level, frequency-count data.

However, in general, nonparametric techniques suffer from very low power. Given the fact that much psychological research is conducted with small samples and is aimed at detecting relatively small true population effects, the use of nonparametric techniques may virtually guarantee that nothing short of the most obvious facts that could easily have been detected without statistical help will be judged significant. Under most circumstances, it would seem far better to apply thoughtful consideration to whether one's data are reasonably ordinal, reasonably normal, reasonably homogeneous, and so forth than to choose automatically a nonparametric technique.

If an investigator is in doubt, a useful strategy is to employ both parametric and nonparametric analyses to determine whether the conclusions are similar. Bock (1975, p. 15) presents a simple nonparametric procedure that can be used for this purpose. Bock suggests a randomization test in which the data are partitioned in all possible ways subject only to the restriction that each experimental group continues to have the same original number of observations. The test statistic is calculated for all these random partitions and the percentile rank for each value of the statistic is recorded. As Bock notes, "if the percentile rank [of the actual experiment] is extreme, tending toward 0 or 100 percent, it is easier to believe that the statistic is reflecting the systematic effects of the conditions than that it is a fortuitous result of the random assignment of the subjects [p. 15]." In this test, values outside 2.5% or 97.5% are conventionally considered significant. With the wide availability of computers, this procedure is now quite feasible.

One of the best safeguards against misanalyzing one's data—either by taking too much or too little from them—is the practice of "living with" them for a time. Routinely scatterplotting variables against each other, examining the data against many possible confounding factors such as order of collection, recasting one's dependent measures in several forms to see if some variates have particularly desirable qualities (e.g., lack of floor or ceiling effects) are procedures that are increasingly recommended by statisticians (Anscombe, 1973; Daniel & Wood, 1971; Mosteller & Tukey, 1968). The selection of the best, or most reasonable, measure should be made on such thoughtful, logical bases before statistical analyses are employed. Given such care in the selection of measures, it is likely that one will come to statistical conclusions that will stand the test of replicability.

Multivariate versus Univariate Statistical Procedures

Another problem in the applicability of statistics concerns the multidimensional nature of data. Statistical theory has long been able to deal with the effects of multidimensionality of both independent and dependent variables. Practical application of theory had to await the development of modern computers. Twenty years ago, one could have spent a lifetime solving the equations necessary for the solution to even a relatively simple multidimensional problem. Understandably, few scientists were eager to ask statistical questions that would require them to spend years at a calculator performing tasks analogous to writing out the nine million names of God in longhand (tasks with perhaps more appeal to an Oriental metaphysician). The fact that activities once requiring years can now be performed by a computer in less than a second must rank as one of the greatest revolutions in the history of technology. That this revolution has had repercussions in everyday statistical techniques is certainly not surprising.

Techniques for dealing with multiple simultaneous interactions among many variables are now becoming commonplace. This is not the place to go into detail regarding multivariate techniques, as a number of texts now exist for this purpose (Bock, 1975; Harris, 1975; Morrison, 1976; Namboodiri, Carter, & Blalock, 1975; Overall & Klett, 1972; Tatsuoka, 1971; Timm, 1975). It is, perhaps, the place to comment on the usefulness of these techniques. The danger exists that as multivariate procedures become more readily available they will be used relatively thoughtlessly. The same thoughtfulness needs to be exercised in selecting a set of variables to be analyzed as is exercised in selecting variables for univariate analyses. Multivariate assumptions are often relatively straightforward generalizations of the univariate case (e.g., multivariate normality and homogeneous covariance matrices). The robustness of multivariate procedures is not yet as fully documented as is the case for univariate procedures. There are some indications that at least some multivariate tests are reasonably robust provided that sample sizes are equal (Ito & Schull, 1964) or fairly large (Ito, 1969), but that the requirement of homogeneity of covariance may be somewhat more important for multivariate than for univariate tests (Korin, 1972). The use of multivariate procedures at this still relatively early stage of widespread availability thus carries some risk that the procedures may eventually be found to be less robust than desired.

Little guidance is provided by authors of texts on multivariate procedures regarding the number and nature of variables that should be included in a multivariate analysis. Several principles are useful here. First, the number of variables should not exceed the number of subjects in the smallest cell of the design, and a wiser practice is that it not exceed half the number of subjects in the smallest cell. In practice, the number of variables that interest the researcher may easily exceed the number of subjects in the study. However, as the number of variables increases, so does the probability that one is adding redundancy. It is rare, if not impossible, that one can obtain more than 20 mutually uncorrelated scores, and there is much to be said for reducing one's data set, if it is gargantuan, to something in the realm of plausibility.

Another principle is that none of the variables may be linearly dependent, as is the case, for example, when one variable is the sum of the remaining variables, or if two variables are so highly correlated as to be virtually identical. Finally, although few texts state this principle in quite this way, one's dependent variables should be of roughly equivalent quality. The inclusion of any and all variables of interest in a MANOVA results in a virtual garbage bag of information, thus making it difficult to understand how any valid conclusion could emerge. A good choice for a MANOVA might be, for example, scores on several subtests of an intelligence, personality, or ability test. These scores are likely to be moderately, but not perfectly, correlated, and the MANOVA corrects, as it is intended to, for the correlation among the dependent measures. Conversely, a MANOVA mixing nominal with ordinal measures, reliable with unreliable scores, and measures meeting the requirements of normality with highly skewed variables will not provide an adequate test of whether the groups in question differ on the vector of dependent measures.

In general, the use of multivariate analyses other than those based on correlation matrices is still relatively new. The existing literature suggests that many multivariate techniques may be reasonably robust. However, researchers should be especially careful in employing these techniques and should not view them with great awe as somehow representing a fundamentally different kind of procedure from the more familiar univariate techniques.

PROBLEMS IN DEVELOPMENTAL AND INTACT-GROUP COMPARISONS

In the topics described elsewhere in this book two particularly difficult problems of group comparisons frequently arise: the assessment of developmental change and the comparison of groups whose defining characteristic has not been assigned at random but instead is some inherent quality such as gender or ethnic group. We now consider these special problems of statistical group comparisons.

The Problem of Assessing Change

An understanding of the nature of developmental change has proved to be difficult both conceptually and statistically. A key problem in measuring change is that no fully satisfactory theoretical model of developmental change is available against which to compare empirical data. Most statistical tests of change are made with the presumption that change is linear over time; this assumption is disquieting to the developmentalist, who sees spurts and plateaus and even temporary regressions in the growth curve for almost any function. Yet for groups of children, the curve describing the mean is likely to show a reasonably smooth increment over a long period of time, and the growth between any two points may often be reasonably linear. It is probably for these reasons that statistical tests of change presuming linearity often work reasonably well.

A more satisfying state of affairs would exist if statistical models of change could be specified that permitted genuinely interactive contributions of endogenous and exogenous factors in development rather than presuming that all factors necessarily could be combined in an additive fashion. The "interaction" term in the analysis of variance is an additive leftover of the amount of variance not accounted for by main effects. This is not a good representation of interaction at the biological level in an epigenetic model of development where both organism and environment change as does the relationship between them (see Kessen [1968] for a detailed presentation of this view and the embryological evidence on which it is based). Scarr-Salapatek (1976) and Sameroff and Chandler (1975) present similar views in describing the "canalization" of development and a "transactional" model, respectively. A fully adequate statistical model of developmental change will probably have to depart from the additive, linear model.

McCall (1977) has recently pointed out that the developmental psychologist is faced with the perplexing statistical tasks of describing both the lawful pattern of change in mean performance over time and the degree of stability or instability in individual differences over time. The first aim—to define the "developmental function" as Wohlwill (1973) has termed it—requires the normative procedure of describing typical behavior at different ages. Piaget's descriptions of the course of cognitive development are illustrative of this approach. Numerous other theorists have also provided conceptualizations of developmental change that stress the necessity of obtaining developmental functions (Buss & Royce, 1975; Coombs & Smith, 1973; Emmerich, 1968; Flavell, 1972; Van den Daele, 1969, 1974; Wohlwill, 1973). Illustrative of the second approach are the many existing longitudinal studies of stability and change in physical characteristics, IQ-test performance, and personality characteristics (reviewed in Bloom, 1964). As McCall (1977) points out, the two approaches have different statistical implications. Correlational methods are of little value in the normative approach because correlations are insensitive to differences in mean values across time. Correlational methods are fundamental to the individual-differences approach because correlations preserve information about rank order at all testings.

It would clearly be of much interest to attempt to join the two approaches, as in determining whether there are individual differences in developmental functions. McCall and his colleagues (McCall, Eichorn, & Hogarty, 1977) have attempted this by identifying groups of subjects whose pattern of IQ performance across time was similar for the subjects within the groups but different from that of subjects in other groups. Theirs is only one of many techniques that attempt to define clusters of subjects. For those seeking detailed information of the many methods of cluster analysis, several recent texts are available (e.g., Anderberg, 1973; Bailey, 1974; Everitt, 1974; Hartigan, 1975); Blashfield (1976) provides an excellent brief review and critical comments on the state of the art. The present author concurs with McCall (1977) in recommending the cluster analysis technique developed by Tucker and Messick (1963) known as "Three Mode Factor Analysis" (Tucker, 1963). (A similar procedure has also been developed by Jöreskog [1969].) Because this method allows factors for persons, variables, and time of measurement (the three factors for which it is named), it provides an efficient way of describing patterns of change for different clusters of individuals across time. This approach is described more fully later in this chapter in the discussion of scaling techniques.

Whether one is seeking to define the developmental function or to investigate the stability of individual differences or both, the basic design for the developmentalist is longitudinal. Only by observing that particular individuals show the same pattern of development, as revealed in longitudinal data, is a developmentalist convinced that the actual pattern of development has been described. However, as a number of methodologists have pointed out (Baltes & Schaie, 1973; Nesselroade & Baltes, 1974; Schaie, 1965), the single most serious problem of the longitudinal method is that it produces results specific to a particular cohort measured at particular times. (The term "cohort," derived from the Roman term describing legions of soldiers who fought together, implies equivalence of birth year. In a broader sense, the term could also represent a sample from a particular ethnic group or culture.) Whatever group one chooses to study longitudinally may differ, for both genetic and environmental-cultural reasons, from other groups one might have studied.

Ordinarily there is probably not a great deal of genetic difference between cohorts that are only a few years apart in birth year, but the possibility of genetic change does exist. Given changes in immigration policies, abortion practices, prenatal care, radiation, sampling procedures, and so forth, one may be dealing with a somewhat different gene pool in studying children born in the 1970s as opposed to those who participated in the growth studies of the 1930s. Much less arguably, cultural shifts create variations in the life experiences of persons born at different times (or in different countries). Preschool children of the 1940s were not raised with television; preschool children of the 1970s spend many hours a week with this electronic companion (Kaye, 1974). Studies of social and cognitive development in present-day preschoolers might therefore yield somewhat different conclusions from earlier studies.

As developmentalists have become more interested in the entire life span, the methodological problems of longitudinal research have become the focus of increasingly critical scrutiny. Studying changes over a 30- to 40-year period makes the problem of cohort differences very apparent. In response to the need, several designs have been suggested to untangle cohort from age effects. Schaie (1965) proposed several designs that could deal with any two of the three factors that vary in a developmental study—age, cohort, and time of measurement. As Wohlwill (1970) has pointed out, time of measurement is less important conceptually to the developmentalist than the other two, and the problem of being unable to separate time of measurement from cohort or age differences generally does not trouble the developmental theorist. Schaie's collection of designs therefore can be reduced to two strategies that seem particularly useful. The first of these is simply a replication strategy in which a researcher performs the same longitudinal study, but with two or more separate cohorts. This strategy is essentially Schaie's (1965) "cohort-sequential" design as well as Baltes's (1968) bifactorial model and Cattell's (1970) Age × Cohort bifactorial. A second of Schaie's designs, also advocated by Buss (1973a, 1973b), is the replication of a cross-sectional study at two different times. This design is particularly useful to ascertain whether cohort differences have occurred. (See also Achenbach, in this volume.)

Two other common problems of the longitudinal method are selective attrition and the possibility that repeated testing itself causes changes in behavior. However, not all longitudinal studies suffer from attrition, and in those which do it is sometimes possible to estimate the extent of the effect and correct statistically for it. Repeated testing probably has its greatest effect from the first to the second test and relatively little effect thereafter. If this is so, establishing numerous control groups to assess the effects of being tested for all possible times of testing would represent an unnecessary investment. Despite the many criticisms of longitudinal studies, I agree with McCall (1977) that thoughtful use of longitudinal studies, including replication with other samples from other cohorts and cultures, is ultimately the developmentalist's most powerful method.

Turning now to methods of analyzing longitudinal data in order to assess change, an almost bewildering number of methods are available. Such a multiplicity of approaches is testimony to the fact that there is no one best solution to this vexing statistical problem. If one is interested in determining whether the mean level of performance has changed over time (i.e., determining the shape of the developmental function), the statistical procedure involves some variation of performing a t-test on correlated observations (for two testing occasions) or an ANOVA with repeated measures or MANOVA (for more than two testing occasions). If one is interested in the stability of individual differences, many correlational techniques exist for analyzing longitudinal data. Kraemer and Korner (1976) have reviewed statistical alternatives for assessing reliability across time and have recommended the intraclass correlation coefficient for parametric data and the coefficient of concordance for nonparametric data. (Formulas for the intraclass correlation coefficient are available in Haggard [1958] and Hays [1973]; the latter source, as well as Kendall [1962] and Siegel [1956], provide the formula for the coefficient of concordance.) A technical treatment of reliability is provided by Cronbach and his associates (Cronbach, Gleser, Nanda, & Rajaratnam, 1972). Reviews of the many factor-analytic approaches that examine either changes in factor scores or factor loadings across time have been provided by Bentler (1973) and by Nesselroade (1970). As mentioned earlier, if one is interested in both the developmental function and individual differences, Tucker's (1963) or Jöreskog's (1969) method is recommended.

A number of theorists have suggested statistical means for teasing out causative information from longitudinal data. Methods based on multiple regression or partial correlation tend to have been favored by sociologists and economists (Bohrnstedt, 1969; Goldberger, 1971; Heise, 1970; Pelz & Andrews, 1964), although descriptions are also available in the psychological literature (Duncan, 1969). Nonparametric methods suitable for nominal data are also available (Goodman, 1973; Lazarsfeld, 1973; Yee & Gage, 1968).

Kenny (1975b) suggests that cross-lagged panel correlation is often a good choice for ascertaining the possible causes of change in the behavior of a longitudinally studied sample. As Kenny points out, multiple regression presumes causative relationships between predictors and the criterion and is vulnerable to measurement error and to unmeasured third variables. Cross-lagged panel correlation presumes both measurement error and unmeasured third variables and attempts to deal with them. For those desiring considerable detail on the use of the method, a number of sources are available (Campbell & Stanley, 1966; Kenny, 1973, 1975b; Rickard, 1972; Rozelle & Campbell, 1969).

Cross-lagged correlation can be defined as a difference between two particular correlation coefficients obtained as follows (for simplicity's sake assume all correlations are positive): If two events, X and Y, are measured on two occasions, one computes the correlation between the first occasion values of X and the second occasion values of Y. Next, one computes the correlation between the first occasion values of Y and the second occasion values of X. If the first of these two computed correlations is significantly larger than the second, X is said to cause Y. If the reverse is true, Y causes X.

The two principal assumptions required in order to employ this method are "synchronicity" and "stationarity." Synchronicity is the requirement that X and Y be measured at the same time, a requirement which is not met when one of the variables is an average (such as a grade point average) or when it is a retrospective report. However, synchronicity can be achieved in many research projects, as in assessing the number of hours of televised aggression a child watches weekly and the child's level of overt aggressive behavior (Eron,

Huesmann, Lefkowitz, & Walder, 1972). The second requirement, stationarity, is the assumption that whatever is causing X and Y continues to do so in the same way at all times of measurement. It is not necessary to assume that X and Y have a direct causal effect on each other—a third variable may be causing both—but the causal equation must remain constant. This assumption can be a problem in developmental studies if children enter new stages of development during the course of the study. (The requirement of stationarity also may be questionable during periods of rapid growth.) Although stationarity is not the same as the simple reliability of the two variables, the causal equation may be affected by changes in reliability of either X or Y. In practice, one of the most serious problems with the cross-lagged method is that changes in reliability can be mistaken for cause and effect relationships. In practice also, the method often has low power.

With all these caveats, the reader may wonder why the method is recommended at all. The principal reason is that it appears to be the best available procedure for gaining some hint of the nature of causative relationships from correlational data. The method is recommended relatively early in the theory building of a science, somewhere between simple correlational analysis and the testing of a well-elaborated causal theory. If the causal relationships suggested by cross-lagged correlational analysis are true, the results should be replicable across different time lags, different groups of subjects, and different operational measures of the same constructs. If it is ethical and practical to manipulate the variables in question, some experimental tests of the causal relationships suggested by the cross-lagged analysis may also be possible as a later step in the research strategy.

If one has clear theoretical reason to expect observed change to show a well-defined function across time—for example, if change can be predicted to be linear, quadratic, or oscillating—one can test this theory directly. Many statistical texts provide detailed consideration of trend analyses. Two good treatments may be found in Hays (1973) and in Kirk (1968). For relatively complex functions, the reader is referred to Glass, Willson, and Gottman (1975). Bryk and Weisberg (1976) also provide suggestions for conceptualizing patterns of natural growth and possible statistical ways of analyzing such pattern data.

The Problem of Comparing Naturally-Formed Groups

Stated very simply, many of the problems raised by developmental and cross-cultural studies occur because the data are correlational (see Bornstein, in this volume). As Kenny (1975b, p. 888) so aptly puts it, variables "attached to rather than assigned to" the organism are the focus of much psychological interest. In contrast, researchers studying animals are often in the position of being able to assign experimental conditions randomly to groups that are either randomly formed or that represent clearly defined populations. Where subjects are assigned randomly, research can yield information about causes of group differences. Where subjects are well-defined groups, research can permit specification of different developmental functions or reaction patterns for the groups. By employing purebred strains of dogs and mice, for example, researchers have been able to show the existence of genotype-environment interactions in young organisms' responses to a number of early environmental influences (Freedman, 1967; Ressler, 1963; Scott & Fuller, 1965). Such research essentially accomplishes the aims of a cluster analysis, as described earlier, in which groups whose performance is homogeneous within but heterogeneous across group membership can be isolated and described.

In developmental and cross-cultural research, group membership often cannot be assigned. One cannot by definition randomly assign individuals to be adolescents or infants or to be !Kung Bushmen or Navajos. The causes of group differences are therefore difficult to ascertain by statistical means. It is possible to investigate whether different groups respond differently to the effects of a treatment if the treatment can be given to some randomly chosen members of each group. If we cannot assign a treatment at all, we can explore through purely correlational techniques the differences between the groups. In cross-cultural and cross-ethnic group comparisons, this latter situation is by far the most common. If !Kung mothers in the Kalahari Desert nurse their infants for three to five years, whereas Hasidic Jewish mothers in Brooklyn do not, it is unlikely that one can persuade a random half of the mothers in each group to change their early-feeding practices. Group comparisons in such cases must necessarily be correlational ones.

Much is made, and rightly so, of the distinction between experimental and correlational studies. What is often overlooked is that the distinction is methodological rather than statistical. Whereas one can compare a group of males with a group of females by employing a t-test, it is equally feasible to calculate a correlation coefficient to describe the relationship between sex and performance. All that is necessary is to assign numerical values to the sex "variable" (e.g., zero = male, one = female, or vice versa) and to compute the correlation between sex coded in this manner and performance scores. Similarly, analysis of variance problems can be analyzed as multiple regression problems (an extension of simple correlational analysis) by assigning numerical values to different levels of the classifying variables. A Sex × Race ANOVA design might thus be recast as a multiple regression, predicting performance from sex and racial group membership. The choice of code values is a matter of some controversy because different coding systems can lead to different conclusions about the relative importance of the predictor variables. In principle, however, as Cohen (1968) has documented, there is an intimate statistical relationship between ANOVA and multiple regression. What must not be forgotten is that data obtained by correlational sampling procedures (e.g., from groups where membership cannot be randomly assigned) are correlational regardless of how they are analyzed, and the usual cautions in interpretation of correlational data should apply. We consider some common interpretational pitfalls shortly.

The Control of Correlated Variables. A common problem in comparing naturally-formed groups is determining how to control for the effects of a known "nuisance" variable. Suppose, for example, one wishes to compare children from two social classes on a measure of creativity. It is likely that children of the same age from different socioeconomic backgrounds will differ significantly on measures of cognitive ability, such as IQ tests, and thus will differ on mental age. If performance on creativity tests is influenced by general cognitive level (as indexed by mental age), some method is needed to deal with this correlated nuisance variable. One strategy is to match the groups for mental age and compare the performance of the resulting matched groups. Another strategy is to sample randomly from the two populations, then employ a covariance analysis to control statistically for the mental age difference. In one case one controls experimentally, in the other statistically. Does it make a difference?

The problems with matching procedures have been discussed extensively (Campbell & Boruch, 1975; Campbell & Erlebacher, 1970; Campbell & Stanley, 1966; Meehl, 1971; Rubin, 1973). The chief difficulty is that if two populations differ on a variable, the selection of matched samples matched on this variable will produce atypical groups that are unrepresentative of the populations to which the researcher wishes to generalize. One could match groups of same-aged lower- and middle-class children on mental age, for example, by selecting only average-IQ children (in the range of 90-110) for the study. This procedure would be likely to result in a group of lower-SES children with relatively high IQs compared to their classmates and a group of higher-SES children for whom the reverse is true. To whom, one may wonder, could the results of such a study be generalized? Although one might wish the answer to be "children of average intellect who happen to have been raised in different socioeconomic circumstances," it is clear that this may not be true. The effects of social comparisons with the peer group, for example, might have given both groups of children somewhat peculiar life experiences relative to other children of their same socioeconomic standing.

A related problem of matching is that atypical samples are likely to be subject to unequal regression effects that make it difficult to study change over time. In this context, "regression" refers to the tendency for any group that is selected on the basis of extreme performance to perform in a more average manner when retested. Because, as just discussed, matching procedures often involve selecting samples that are not average, regression effects are a common problem with matched samples. The more extreme the sample relative to its parent population, the greater is the expected regression. For example, taking a cutoff point of 145 on an IQ test and defining children with IQs above this point as "gifted" is a procedure virtually guaranteed to result in a group that will perform more poorly when retested. This statistical effect can easily be mistaken for a change produced by some treatment procedure.

Furby (1973) has provided a thoughtful and relatively nontechnical discussion of the regression problem and the reasons for its occurrence. Briefly, regression occurs because extreme performance on any occasion is the consequence of a number of unlikely events occurring simultaneously (for example, the child was feeling especially alert when tested, had just studied the topics presented on the test, etc.). The likelihood is low that over a large number of subjects all of the factors contributing to extreme performance will continue to do so in additional testings. As this suggests, regression is a phenomenon of groups rather than individuals. Particular individuals may perform in a manner still more extreme in a second testing, but large numbers of individuals are unlikely to do so. With matched groups, if one sample is above average for its population and the other is below average for its population, the two groups will show regression effects in opposite directions, making the assessment of change over time particularly difficult.

A common alternative to matching has been to obtain representative samples and to employ a covariance analysis. In our present example, we could obtain creativity measures from typical samples of lower- and middle-class children and perform an analysis of covariance with mental age (MA) as the covariate. As Harris (1975, p. 21) succinctly defines it, "A covariate is a variable which is related to (covaries with) the predictor and/or the outcome variables, and whose effects we wish to control for statistically as a substitute for experimental control." An analysis of covariance is essentially a two-step analysis of variance. In the first step, one uses the covariate alone to predict the outcome of the experiment: If MA is correlated with creativity, one can predict creativity scores from MA. These predicted scores can then be used in the second step, a regular analysis of variance of these predicted, or "adjusted," scores.

However, there are a number of problems with covariance analyses, and the procedure has generated considerable discussion (Bryk & Weisberg, 1977; Campbell & Erlebacher, 1970; Cronbach & Furby, 1970; Evans & Anastasio, 1968; Kenny, 1975a; Linn & Werts, 1977; Lord, 1960, 1967; Overall & Woodward, 1977; Porter, 1967; Werts & Linn, 1970). Much of this discussion is overly technical to be considered here. However, in general, cases frequently arise where further statistical adjustments must be made. This is true, for example, if the covariate is not reliably measured. Given measurement error in the variable being predicted and measurement error in the covariate—and therefore the necessity of making adjustments on adjustments—one's confidence in the analysis can become rather tenuous.

Because neither matching nor covariance provides an unequivocally best solution to the problem of the correlated nuisance variable, the investigator might well be perplexed as to the best strategy to pursue. In a thoughtful consideration of this problem, Meehl (1971) has cut the Gordian knot, recommending that a researcher should pursue both the matched- and the typical-samples strategies simultaneously. As Meehl observes, "But surely we know more if we have both to think about [p. 147]." The feasibility of Meehl's strategy has recently been tested in a study by Yando, Seitz, and Zigler (1978). The results of the study supported Meehl's argument by permitting fuller interpretation than would have been possible by using either matched or typical samples alone. With samples of children matched on age and IQ, there were few differences among social class and ethnic groups on a large battery of personality and motivational measures. With typical samples and a covariance analysis, there were many differences. Some variables showed significant group differences regardless of the sampling procedure employed. In general, the effort needed for such a double study seems to be justified by the strength of the conclusions one can draw from it.

The "Pseudo-orthogonal" Design.   One problem of typicality of samples is sometimes disguised within a seemingly straightforward ANOVA design in studies comparing natural groups. In cases where cells are not equally easy to fill (e.g., a Social Class × IQ design), the likelihood exists that certain cells may be atypical samples of their populations. There is now a substantial literature on the problems associated with the "pseudo-orthogonal" design— a design where equal numbers of subjects are employed in each cell, but the classifying variables are correlated (Appelbaum & Cramer, 1974; Gocka, 1973; Humphreys & Dachler, 1969; Keren & Lewis, 1976, 1977; Overall & Spiegel, 1969; Overall, Spiegel, & Cohen, 1975; Wolf & Cartwright, 1974).

An example of a pseudo-orthogonal design is provided by Humphreys and Dachler (1969) using academic test data for a population of nearly 12,000 ninth-grade boys. In this reasonably typical, unselected population, the sizes of the cells, divided at the median for social class (SES) and IQ, were markedly unequal, with approximately 5,000 cases each of high SES-high IQ and low SES-low IQ, and approximately 1,000 cases each in the other two cells. These data may be analyzed within an ANOVA design either by ignoring the different cell sizes (performing an "unweighted means" analysis) or by weighting each cell mean in proportion to its size (performing a "least squares" analysis). The results of the two procedures are quite different. For sentence memory data, for example, Humphreys and Dachler found that weighting the cells in proportion to their size reversed the direction of the main effect for SES as well as the sign of the SES × IQ interaction in comparison with the unweighted means procedure.

The pseudo-orthogonal design may also be analyzed as a multiple regression problem. By the choice of coding values, one can weight unequal-sized groups either differentially (Overall & Spiegel, 1969; Overall et al., 1975) or equivalently (Gocka, 1973; Wolf & Cartwright, 1974) with consequences similar to those just described in choosing between least squares and unweighted means ANOVA solutions, respectively. As Keren and Lewis (1976) comment in a recent review of coding procedures, "There is a large degree of arbitrariness to the choosing of weights, but it is the same kind of arbitrariness that already exists in experimental design [p. 826]." Keren and Lewis point out that one should distinguish experimental from correlational types of samples and choose one's coding system accordingly, a position with which I strongly concur. Equal weights are appropriate for randomly assigned group membership. Unequal weights may be necessary with correlational data.

Thoughtfully interpreted, the results of properly coded multiple regression and properly chosen ANOVA should not contradict each other. But it is perhaps easier to remain aware with a multiple regression analysis that one is dealing with correlational data. Remaining alert to whether each of the variables has adequate sampling, whether its relationship with the criterion is approximately linear, whether there is adequate range, and so forth, may seem more natural to the person who is attempting to interpret the results of the study than when the data are analyzed as an ANOVA, comparing means. (Comprehensive treatments of multiple regression are provided by Cohen and Cohen [1975], Darlington [1968], and Kerlinger and Pedhazur [1973].)

The implications for practice are that these and all correlational designs must be interpreted with great care. If the cell sizes are considered to be equal, either by employing an unweighted means ANOVA when the cells have typical subjects but are unequal or by exerting great effort to find enough subjects to fill the "difficult" cells of a pseudo-orthogonal design, then one is answering one kind of question. (For example, "if the effects of IQ are held constant, is there any difference between SES groups?") If one employs a weighting procedure, one is asking a different question (for example, "among the typical populations in the real world is there an SES difference in the variable I am examining?"). Both answers may be useful, but for different purposes. The pseudo-orthogonal procedure is deliberately peculiar for the purpose of attempting to disentangle causative factors. Results from this procedure may be useful in theory building but cannot be directly generalized to real populations. The problem is the same as that already described for the control of nuisance variables, and Meehl's recommendation that we consider both kinds of answers is a good one.

The Assessment of Differential Change in Noncomparable Groups. An extremely difficult problem is the investigation of whether two or more nonequivalent groups differ significantly in amount of change over time. One approach to this problem is to employ the paradigm of the nonequivalent control-group design (Campbell & Stanley, 1966). There now exists a considerable statistical literature on how to analyze effects of a treatment given to an experimental group when that group is known to have differed from a control group at the start of the treatment. In this design, pretest and posttest data are available for both groups. This familiar "quasi-experimental" design can be adapted to the problem of comparing diverse groups if we recognize that administering an experimental treatment is not an essential part of the design. All that is essential is that measures of the same variable on two or more occasions be available for two or more groups. We can interpret a significant "treatment" effect in analyzing results from such a study as indicating significant differences across groups in change over time.

As Kenny (1975a) points out, there are four possible methods of analyzing data from the design we have just described: (1) analysis of covariance; (2) analysis of covariance with correction for the unreliability of the covariate; (3) raw change score analysis; (4) standardized change score analysis. The covariance methods are appropriate only when the groups being compared were actually selected on the basis of the pretest score. Although this is not usually true in developmental and cross-cultural research, because there may occasionally be cases where intact groups can be considered to have been formed on the basis of pretest values, we consider this case here.

Despite the many warnings on the use of covariance (Campbell & Erlebacher, 1970; Evans & Anastasio, 1968; Lord, 1960, 1967), recent statistical opinion favors its use in certain contexts (Bryk & Weisberg, 1977; Kenny, 1975a; Linn & Werts, 1977; Overall & Woodward, 1977). If group selection is based directly on the pretest scores, then a conventional analysis of covariance with the pretest as the covariate is recommended (Kenny, 1975a; Overall & Woodward, 1977). If selection is based on a true but unmeasured pretest value for which the measured pretest is an unreliable estimate, then an analysis of variance employing a Lord (1960) or Porter (1967) correction for the unreliability is recommended. If the analysis results in a nonsignificant group by time interaction following the statistical control for initial group differences, then the two groups may be considered not to differ in their degree of change over time.

More commonly, selection is based not on some pretest value but instead on a demographic, psychological, or sociological criterion. There is no clear consensus on how best to analyze such data, but Kenny (1975a) provides a thoughtful argument that a change score analysis is the method of choice. Again, despite the widely cited criticisms of change score analysis (Cronbach & Furby, 1970; Werts & Linn, 1970), there are occasions when the use of change scores is defensible. Kenny offers recommendations for analyzing changes in raw scores, or in standardized scores if the variance on the two occasions needs to be equalized. The interested reader is referred to Kenny (1975a) for further details. The reader is also referred to Linn and Werts (1977) and to Overall and Woodward (1977) for discussion of assumptions required in interpreting results from such analyses. All of these analyses presume the linearity of change over time, as described in an earlier section.

The Usefulness of Scaling Procedures.   For certain questions, cross-group comparisons can benefit from psychophysical scaling procedures that include recognition of the existence of individual differences in perceptual viewpoints. The goal of psychophysical scaling is to represent meaningfully the amount of perceived similarity among stimuli as distances between points in space (Torgerson, 1958). The task is as if a person were shown the stimuli to be scaled and were asked to place these stimuli in such a manner that the physical distances among them corresponded to the perceived "psychological distances" among them. If a person could perform this task directly, and if there were no more than three dimensions necessary, the investigator could then easily determine how many dimensions had been used as well as the nature of the dimensions. However, as just described, the task would be very difficult even for adult subjects within one's own culture and perhaps meaningless to ask of small children or of adults in other cultures. Instead of requiring people to perform such a task directly, therefore, the amount of psychological distance between stimuli is usually inferred from similarity judgments that an individual makes about a small number of stimuli on each trial. Numerous forms of judgmental tasks and methods for estimating psychological distances from them exist in the literature. Some are simple enough to be appropriate even with young children (Seitz, 1971).

A common assumption in scaling has been that all persons view the stimuli in the same manner, and judgments have often been pooled across subjects in order to obtain estimates of the psychological differences among stimuli. In cross-group comparisons, a modification of this assumption has sometimes been that individuals within a particular group will view stimuli homogeneously in one way, whereas individuals in another group will view them in another way. Bornstein (1973), for example, describes nine studies in which color vision has been scaled comparatively for persons of different nationalities or ethnic groups. However, in addition to such intact-group comparisons, a useful scaling procedure in group comparisons would be one in which both subjects and stimuli are scaled—that is, where groups of individuals who view the world differently can be identified empirically rather than on the assumption of within-group homogeneity of groups established on an a priori basis.

Tucker's Three Mode Factor Analysis (1963) is suitable for this aim. As Tucker (1964) has pointed out, it would be chaotic to assume that each individual's perceptions are unrelated to those of other individuals, but the assumption that each individual is like every other is a gross over-simplification. A compromise that is probably nearer the true state of affairs is that there are subgroups of individuals with a high degree of within-group similarity but differing markedly from other subgroups. As Tucker and Messick (1963) state, Three Mode Factor Analysis was developed as:

> a procedure for uncovering differential perceptual spaces that does not require sorting of individuals into subgroups on the basis of variables *presumed* to differentiate between perceptual structures, but one that would instead... first isolate *empirically* any consistent individual viewpoints about stimulus differences and would then provide for the derivation of separate multidimensional spaces for each viewpoint [p. 334; emphasis added].

The "factor space of individuals" in this procedure is of key interest because it can be inspected to determine which individuals are similar to each other in their judgments—in effect to determine how subjects "cluster" together in groups. To the extent that clusters do exist, Tucker (1964) has proposed choosing an "ideal subject" to represent the cluster as a whole; judgments of this ideal subject may be studied more economically than studying the judgments of all the subjects in the cluster. A standard multidimensional scaling can then be performed to obtain the perceptual space (i.e., to describe the number and nature of dimensions the subject has used to judge the stimuli and the distances between them) for each subject of interest.

The results being compared in such a cross-group scaling study would be the degree of homogeneity within each culture (the degree to which there really was an identifiable cultural viewpoint) and the degree of overlap between the two groups—for example, whether perhaps 10% of one group and 50% of the other shared some particular common viewpoint. This type of multidimensional scaling approach can be applied to attitudes, food preferences, and other psychological data as well as to presumably more physiologically based variables such as color perception.

CONCLUSION

In the present chapter I have discussed a number of basic assumptions and special problems in the statistical comparison of groups. The position was taken that although many assumptions basic to the statistical method are not fully satisfied by real data, the fit between assumptions and reality is usually sufficient to justify most common statistical procedures. In the second part of the chapter, two particularly difficult statistical problems raised by group comparison data were discussed: the measurement of developmental change and the comparison of groups that cannot be formed experimentally. The theme in this discussion was that there is no single, best solution to these problems. Because for ethical and logical reasons correlational methods will remain the major technique available in developmental and cultural investigations, the challenge is to interpret correlational data fully without being misled by them. A further goal in comparing groups is to identify meaningful clusters of individuals who have different developmental functions or who respond to stimuli in different ways. A scaling procedure that takes individuals, variables, and testing occasions into account was recommended for this purpose.

REFERENCES

Anderberg, M. R. *Cluster analysis for applications.* New York: Academic Press, 1973.

Anscombe, F. J. Graphs in statistical analysis. *American Statistician,* 1973, *27,* 17–21.

Appelbaum, M. I., & Cramer, E. M. Some problems in the nonorthogonal analysis of variance. *Psychological Bulletin,* 1974, *81,* 335–343.

Bailey, K. D. Cluster analysis. In D. R. Heise (Ed.), *Sociological methodology 1975.* San Francisco: Jossey-Bass, 1974.

Baker, B. O., Hardyck, C. D., & Petrinovich, L. F. Weak measurements vs. strong statistics: An empirical critique of S. S. Stevens' proscriptions on statistics. *Educational and Psychological Measurement,* 1966, *26,* 291–309.

Baltes, P. B. Longitudinal and cross-sectional sequences in the study of age and generation effects. *Human Development,* 1968, *11,* 145–171.

Baltes, P. B., & Schaie, K. W. On life-span developmental research paradigms: Retrospects and prospects. In P. B. Baltes & K. W. Schaie (Eds.), *Life-span developmental psychology: Personality and socialization.* New York: Academic Press, 1973.

Bentler, P. M. Assessment of developmental factor change at the individual and group level. In J. R. Nesselroade & H. W. Reese (Eds.), *Life-span developmental psychology: Methodological issues.* New York: Academic Press, 1973.

Bishop, Y.M.M., Fienberg, S. E., & Holland, P. W. *Discrete multivariate analysis: Theory and practice.* Cambridge, MA: MIT Press, 1975.

Blashfield, R. K. Mixture model tests of cluster analysis: Accuracy of four agglomerative hierarchical methods. *Psychological Bulletin,* 1976, *83,* 377–388.

Bloom, B. S. *Stability and change in human characteristics.* New York: Wiley, 1964.

Bock, R. D. *Multivariate statistical methods in behavioral research.* New York: McGraw-Hill, 1975.

Bohrnstedt, G. W. Observations on the measurement of change. In E. F. Borgatta (Ed.), *Sociological methodology 1969.* San Francisco: Jossey-Bass, 1969.

Boneau, C. A. The effects of violations of assumptions underlying the *t* test. *Psychological Bulletin,* 1960, *57,* 49–64.

Bornstein, M. H. Color vision and color naming: A psychophysiological hypothesis of cultural difference. *Psychological Bulletin,* 1973, *80,* 257–285.

Bronfenbrenner, U. Toward an experimental ecology of human development. *American Psychologist,* 1977, *32,* 513–531.

Bryk, A. S., & Weisberg, H. I. Value-added analysis: A dynamic approach to the estimation of treatment effects. *Journal of Educational Statistics,* 1976, *1,* 127–155.

Bryk, A. S., & Weisberg, H. I. Use of the nonequivalent control group design when subjects are growing. *Psychological Bulletin,* 1977, *84,* 950–962.

Buss, A. R. A conceptual framework for learning effecting the development of ability factors. *Human Development,* 1973, *16,* 273–292. (a)

Buss, A. R. An extension of developmental models that separate ontogenetic changes and cohort differences. *Psychological Bulletin,* 1973, *80,* 466–479. (b)

Buss, A. R., & Royce, J. R. Ontogenetic changes in cognitive structure from a multivariate perspective. *Developmental Psychology,* 1975, *11,* 87–101.

Campbell, D. T., & Boruch, R. F. Making the case for randomized assignment to treatments by considering the alternatives: Six ways in which quasi-experimental evaluations in compensatory education tend to underestimate effects. In C. A. Bennett & A. A. Lumsdaine (Eds.), *Evaluation and experiment: Some critical issues in assessing social programs.* New York: Academic Press, 1975.

Campbell, D. T., & Erlebacher, A. How regression artifacts in quasi-experimental evaluations can mistakenly make compensatory education look harmful. In J. Hellmuth (Ed.), *Compensatory education: A national debate* (Vol. 3 of *The disadvantaged child*). New York: Brunner/Mazel, 1970.

Campbell, D. T., & Stanley, J. C. *Experimental and quasi-experimental designs for research.* Chicago: Rand McNally, 1966.

Cattell, R. B. Separating endogenous, exogenous, ecogenic, and epogenic component curves in developmental data. *Developmental Psychology,* 1970, *3,* 151–162.

Cohen, J. Multiple regression as a general data-analytic system. *Psychological Bulletin,* 1968, *70,* 426–443.

Cohen, J. *Statistical power analysis for the behavior sciences* (Rev. ed.). New York: Academic Press, 1977.

Cohen, J., & Cohen, P. *Applied multiple regression/correlation analysis for the behavioral sciences.* Hillsdale, NJ: Lawrence Erlbaum Associates, 1975.

Coombs, C. H., & Smith, J. E. K. On the detection of structure in attitudes and developmental processes. *Psychological Review,* 1973, *80,* 337–351.

Cronbach, L. J., & Furby, L. How we should measure "change"—or should we? *Psychological Bulletin,* 1970, *74,* 68–80.

Cronbach, L. J., Gleser, G. C., Nanda, H., & Rajaratnam, N. *The dependability of behavioral measurements: Theory of generalizability for scores and profiles.* New York: Wiley, 1972.

Daniel, C., & Wood, F. S. *Fitting equations to data: Computer analysis of multifactor data for scientists and engineers.* New York: Wiley, 1971.

Darlington, R. B. Multiple regression in psychological research and practice. *Psychological Bulletin,* 1968, *69,* 161–182.

Duncan, O. D. Some linear models for two-wave, two-variable panel analysis. *Psychological Bulletin,* 1969, *72,* 177–182.

Emmerich, W. Personality development and concepts of structure. *Child Development,* 1968, *39,* 671–690.

Eron, L. D., Huesmann, L. R., Lefkowitz, M. M., & Walder, L. O. Does television violence cause aggression? *American Psychologist,* 1972, *27,* 253–263.

Evans, S. H., & Anastasio, E. J. Misuse of analysis of covariance when treatment effect and covariate are confounded. *Psychological Bulletin,* 1968, *69,* 225–234.

Everitt, B. S. *Cluster analysis.* London: Halsted Press, 1974.

Fisher, R. A. Applications of "Student's" distribution. *Metron,* 1925, *5,* 90–104.

Flavell, J. H. An analysis of cognitive-developmental sequences. *Genetic Psychology Monographs,* 1972, *86,* 279–350.

Freedman, D. G. The origin of social behavior. *Science Journal,* November 1967, pp. 69–73.

Furby, L. Interpreting regression toward the mean in developmental research. *Developmental Psychology,* 1973, *8,* 172–179.

Glass, G. V. (Ed.). *Evaluation studies review annual* (Vol. 1). Beverly Hills, CA: Sage, 1976.

Glass, G. V., Willson, V. L., & Gottman, J. M. *Design and analysis of time-series experiments.* Boulder: Colorado Associated University Press, 1975.

Gocka, E. F. Regression analysis of proportional cell data. *Psychological Bulletin,* 1973, *80,* 25–27.

Goldberger, A. S. Econometrics and psychometrics: A survey of communalities. *Psychometrika,* 1971, *36,* 83–107.

Goodman, L. A. Causal analysis of data from panel studies and other kinds of surveys. *American Journal of Sociology,* 1973, *78,* 1135–1191.

Guttentag, M., & Struening, E. L. (Eds.). *Handbook of evaluation research* (Vol. 2). Beverly Hills, CA: Sage, 1975.

Haggard, E. A. *Intraclass correlation and the analysis of variance.* New York: Dryden Press, 1958.

Harris, R. J. *A primer of multivariate statistics.* New York: Academic Press, 1975.

Hartigan, J. A. *Clustering algorithms.* New York: Wiley, 1975.

Havlicek, L. L., & Peterson, N. L. Robustness of the *t* test: A guide for researchers on effect of violation of assumptions. *Psychological Reports,* 1974, *34,* 1095–1114.

Havlicek, L. L., & Peterson, N. L. Effect of the violation of assumptions upon significance levels of the Pearson *r. Psychological Bulletin,* 1977, *84,* 373–377.

Hays, W. L. *Statistics for the social sciences.* New York: Holt, Rinehart & Winston, 1973.

Heise, D. R. Causal inference from panel data. In E. F. Borgatta & G. W. Bohrnstedt (Eds.), *Sociological methodology 1970.* San Francisco: Jossey-Bass, 1970.

Hollander, M., & Wolfe, D. A. *Nonparametric statistical methods.* New York: Wiley, 1973.

Humphreys, L. G., & Dachler, H. P. Jensen's theory of intelligence. *Journal of Educational Psychology,* 1969, *60,* 419–426.

Ito, K. On the effect of heteroscedasticity and nonnormality upon some multivariate test procedures. In P. R. Krishnaiah (Ed.), *Multivariate analysis—II.* New York: Academic Press, 1969.

Ito, K., & Schull, W. J. On the robustness of the T_o^2 test in multivariate analysis of variance when variance-covariance matrices are not equal. *Biometrika,* 1964, *51,* 71–82.

Jöreskog, K. G. Factoring the multitest-multi-occasion correlation matrix. *Educational Testing Service Research Bulletin,* RB-69-62, 1969.

Kamara, A. I., & Easley, J. A., Jr. Is the rate of cognitive development uniform across cultures?—A methodological critique with new evidence from Temne children. In P. R. Dasen (Ed.), *Piagetian psychology: Cross-cultural contributions.* New York: Gardner Press, 1977.

Kaye, E. *The family guide to children's television: What to watch, what to miss, what to change, and how to do it.* New York: Pantheon Books, 1974.

Kendall, M. G. *Rank correlation methods.* New York: Hafner, 1962.

Kenny, D. A. Cross-lagged and synchronous common factors in panel data. In A. S. Goldberger & O. D. Duncan (Eds.), *Structural equation models in the social sciences.* New York: Seminar Press, 1973.

Kenny, D. A. A quasi-experimental approach to assessing treatment effects in the nonequivalent control group design. *Psychological Bulletin,* 1975, *82,* 345–362. (a)

Kenny, D. A. Cross-lagged panel correlation: A test for spuriousness. *Psychological Bulletin,* 1975, *82,* 887–903. (b)

Keren, G., & Lewis, C. Nonorthogonal designs: Sample versus population. *Psychological Bulletin,* 1976, *83,* 817–826.

Keren, G., & Lewis, C. A comment on coding in nonorthogonal designs. *Psychological Bulletin,* 1977, *84,* 346–348.

Kerlinger, F. N., & Pedhazur, E. J. *Multiple regression in behavioral research.* New York: Holt, Rinehart & Winston, 1973.

Kessen, W. Comparative personality development. In E. F. Borgatta & W. W. Lambert (Eds.), *Handbook of personality theory and research.* Chicago: Rand McNally, 1968.

Kirk, R. E. *Experimental design: Procedures for the behavioral sciences.* Belmont, CA: Brooks/Cole, 1968.

Korin, B. P. Some comments on the homoscedasticity criterion M and the multivariate analysis of variance tests T^2, W and R. *Biometrika,* 1972, *59,* 215–216.

Kramer, H. C., & Korner, A. F. Statistical alternatives in assessing reliability, consistency, and individual differences for quantitative measures: Application to behavioral measures of neonates. *Psychological Bulletin,* 1976, *83,* 914–921.

Krishnaiah, P. R. (Ed.). *Multivariate analysis—II.* New York: Academic Press, 1969.

Lazarsfeld, P. F. Mutual relations over time of two attributes: A review and integration of various approaches. In M. Hammer, K. Salzinger, & S. Sutton (Eds.), *Psychopathology: Contributions from the social, behavioral, and biological sciences.* New York: Wiley-Interscience, 1973.

Linn, R. L., & Werts, C. E. Analysis implications of the choice of a structural model in the nonequivalent control group design. *Psychological Bulletin,* 1977, *84,* 229–234.

Lord, F. M. Large-sample covariance analysis when the control variable is fallible. *Journal of the American Statistical Association,* 1960, *55,* 307–321.

Lord, F. M. A paradox in the interpretation of group comparisons. *Psychological Bulletin,* 1967, *68,* 304–305.

Marascuilo, L. A., & McSweeney, M. *Nonparametric and distribution free methods for the social sciences.* Monterey, CA: Brooks/Cole, 1977.

McCall, R. B. Challenges to a science of developmental psychology. *Child Development,* 1977, *48,* 333–344.

McCall, R. B., & Appelbaum, M. I. Bias in the analysis of repeated-measures designs: Some alternative approaches. *Child Development,* 1973, *44,* 401–415.

McCall, R. B., Eichorn, D. H., & Hogarty, P. S. Transition in early mental development. *Monographs of the Society for Research in Child Development,* 1977, *42* (3, Serial No. 171).

Meehl, P. E. High school yearbooks: A reply to Schwarz. *Journal of Abnormal Psychology,* 1971, *77,* 143–148.

Morrison, D. F. *Multivariate statistical methods.* New York: McGraw-Hill, 1976.

Mosteller, F., & Tukey, J. W. Data analysis, including statistics. In G. Lindzey & E. Aronson (Eds.), *The handbook of social psychology* (Vol. 2). Reading, MA: Addison-Wesley, 1968.

Namboodiri, N. K., Carter, L. F., & Blalock, H. M., Jr. *Applied multivariate analysis and experimental designs.* New York: McGraw-Hill, 1975.

Nesselroade, J. R. Application of multivariate strategies to problems of measuring and structuring long-term change. In L. R. Goulet & P. B. Baltes (Eds.), *Life-span developmental psychology: Research and theory.* New York: Academic Press, 1970.

Nesselroade, J. R., & Baltes, P. B. Adolescent personality development and historical change: 1970-1972. *Monographs of the Society for Research in Child Development,* 1974, *39* (1, Serial No. 154).

Overall, J. E., & Klett, C. J. *Applied multivariate analysis.* New York: McGraw-Hill, 1972.

Overall, J. E., & Spiegel, D. K. Concerning least squares analysis of experimental data. *Psychological Bulletin,* 1969, *72,* 311–322.

Overall, J. E., Spiegel, D. K., & Cohen, J. Equivalence of orthogonal and nonorthogonal analysis of variance. *Psychological Bulletin,* 1975, *82,* 182–186.

Overall, J. E., & Woodward, J. A. Nonrandom assignment and the analysis of covariance. *Psychological Bulletin,* 1977, *84,* 588–594.

Pelz, D. C., & Andrews, F. Detecting causal priorities in panel study data. *American Sociological Review,* 1964, *29,* 836–848.

Porter, A. C. *The effects of using fallible variables in the analysis of covariance.* Unpublished doctoral dissertation, University of Wisconsin, 1967.

Ressler, R. H. Genotype-correlated parental influences in two strains of mice. *Journal of Comparative and Physiological Psychology*, 1963, *56*, 882-886.

Rickard, S. The assumptions of causal analyses for incomplete causal sets of two multilevel variables. *Multivariate Behavioral Research*, 1972, *7*, 317-359.

Rozelle, R. M., & Campbell, D. T. More plausible rival hypotheses in the cross-lagged panel correlation technique. *Psychological Bulletin*, 1969, *71*, 74-80.

Rubin, D. B. The use of matched sampling and regression adjustment to remove bias in observational studies. *Biometrics*, 1973, *29*, 185-203.

Sameroff, A. J., & Chandler, M. J. Reproductive risk and the continuum of caretaking casualty. In F. D. Horowitz, E. M. Hetherington, S. Scarr-Salapatek, & G. M. Siegel (Eds.), *Review of child development research* (Vol. 4). Chicago: University of Chicago Press, 1975.

Scarr-Salapatek, S. Genetic determinants of infant development: An overstated case. In L. P. Lipsitt (Ed.), *Developmental psychobiology: The significance of infancy*. Hillsdale, NJ: Lawrence Erlbaum Associates, 1976.

Schaie, K. W. A general model for the study of developmental problems. *Psychological Bulletin*, 1965, *64*, 92-107.

Scott, J. P., & Fuller, J. L. *Genetics and the social behavior of the dog*. Chicago: University of Chicago Press, 1965.

Searle, S. R. *Linear models*. New York: Wiley, 1971.

Seitz, V. Multidimensional scaling of dimensional preferences: A methodological study. *Child Development*, 1971, *42*, 1701-1720.

Siegel, S. *Nonparametric statistics for the behavioral sciences*. New York: McGraw-Hill, 1956.

Stanovich, K. E. Note on the interpretation of interactions in comparative research, *American Journal of Mental Deficiency*, 1976, *81*, 394-396.

Stevens, S. S. Mathematics, measurement, and psychophysics. In S. S. Stevens (Ed.), *Handbook of experimental psychology*. New York: Wiley, 1951.

Stevens, S. S. Measurement, statistics, and the schemapiric view. *Science*, 1968, *161*, 849-856.

Struening, E. L., & Guttentag, M. (Eds.). *Handbook of evaluation research* (Vol. 1). Beverly Hills, CA: Sage, 1975.

"Student." [W. S. Gossett]. The probable error of a mean. *Biometrika*, 1908, *6*, 1-25.

Tatsuoka, M. M. *Multivariate analysis: Techniques for educational and psychological research*. New York: Wiley, 1971.

Timm, N. H. *Multivariate analysis with applications in education and psychology*. Monterey, CA: Brooks/Cole, 1975.

Torgerson, W. S. *Theory and methods of scaling*. New York: Wiley, 1958.

Tucker, L. R. Implications of factor analysis of three-way matrices for measurement of change. In C. W. Harris (Ed.), *Problems in measuring change*. Madison: University of Wisconsin Press, 1963.

Tucker, L. R. Systematic differences between individuals in perceptual judgments. In M. W. Shelly, II & G. L. Bryan (Eds.), *Human judgments and optimality*. New York: Wiley, 1964.

Tucker, L. R., & Messick, S. An individual differences model for multidimensional scaling. *Psychometrika*, 1963, *28*, 333-367.

Van den Daele, L. D. Qualitative models in developmental analysis. *Developmental Psychology*, 1969, *1*, 303-310.

Van den Daele, L. D. Infrastructure and transition in developmental analysis. *Human Development*, 1974, *17*, 1-23.

Werts, C. E., & Linn, R. L. A general linear model for studying growth. *Psychological Bulletin*, 1970, *73*, 17-22.

Winer, B. J. *Statistical principles in experimental design*. New York: McGraw-Hill, 1971.

Wohlwill, J. F. The age variable in psychological research. *Psychological Review*, 1970, *77*, 49-64.

Wohlwill, J. F. *The study of behavioral development*. New York: Academic Press, 1973.

Wolf, G., & Cartwright, B. Rules for coding dummy variables in multiple regression. *Psychological Bulletin,* 1974, *81,* 173–179.

Yando, R. M., Seitz, V., & Zigler, E. *Social class, race, and patterns of abilities in children: An exploratory investigation.* Unpublished manuscript, Yale University, 1978.

Yee, A. H., & Gage, N. L. Techniques for estimating the source and direction of causal influence in panel data. *Psychological Bulletin,* 1968, *70,* 115–126.

Zigler, E., & Seitz, V. Changing trends in socialization theory and research. *American Behavioral Scientist,* 1978, *21,* 731–756.

II DERIVATIVE COMPARISONS

Basic to scientific evidence ... is the process of comparison ... .
—D. T. Campbell and
J. C. Stanley (1963, p. 6)

Interspecies, interage, and interculture comparisons, treated in Part I, are each self-sufficient, and each provides a critical perspective from which to view and to understand psychology. However, the ontogenetic perspective is in a sense special, in that it combines with phylogenetic and cultural comparisons to provide further, more comprehensive insights into behavior. Animal developmental and cross-cultural developmental comparisons have risen in prominence in contemporary psychology. These dyadic comparative methods are treated in Part II of this volume.

Ethology and Development

Beer (in this volume) observes that the study of animal behavior, following Darwin, bifurcated into separate schools of ethology and psychology. Both have nevertheless continued Darwin's interest in development. Ethologists, like Lorenz, have sought to study species-general principles of developmental adaptation (like the concept of "babyishness") as well as species-specific principles (like "imprinting"). Comparative psychologists, like Watson and Skinner, have likewise interested themselves in species-general mechanisms of behavior origins and developmental change (like the mechanisms of learning and association) as well as species-specific aspects of development (like special experience).

In chapter 6, Peter Marler, Robert Dooling, and Stephen Zoloth consider the study of animal ethology cum development. What are the values of combining these perspectives? How, for example, do ethologists benefit from the study of development? Two ways can be discerned. First, insofar as comparative research that crosses species investigates behavior, the origins and development of that behavior will interest animal comparativists. Second, ethologists who study development can observe among species similarities and differences of a macropsychological phenomenon, ontogeny, in addition to typical substantive micropsychological phenomena. Developmentalists benefit from the study of animal behavior in several ways, too. Studying behavioral development of different species provides an indication of developmental variability and contributes in this way to more complete behavioral description in developmental psychology. Ethological studies frequently provide developmentalists with a unique (and sometimes the only) way to answer questions that pertain to the antecedents of behavioral dispositions and to the development of behavior. This advantage derives both from animal-behavior models and from the fact that different species inhabit different ecological niches. In the same vein, animal studies help to test the generality or specificity of developmental principles and theories. Comparative studies among different animal species further help to generate new hypotheses for developmental investigators. In short, ethological developmental comparisons permit a broadened view of behavior and more advanced assessment of the hereditary and experiential forces acting on its development.

In their chapter on ethology and behavioral development, Marler and his colleagues examine three substantive areas in the ontogeny of behavior in animals. First, they highlight relations between nature and nuture, showing how hereditary status may differentially determine early behavior (e.g., of preference) or program an organism's susceptibility to experience (e.g., of imprinting). Second, they review in case-study fashion examples of experimental approaches to animal development, and they define several situations where ethologists have identified environmental and organismic determinants that underlie the emergence of behavior. Third, the authors illustrate developmental perspectives on species-specific and species-general behaviors. Throughout their treatment of these three critical issues, Marler et al. use examples of perceptual and motor development to stand for behavioral development more generally.

Ontogenetic and phylogenetic comparisons show how the same or different behaviors originating and developing in different species may reflect the forces of adaptation. Reading the chapter by Marler, Dooling, and Zoloth one quickly comes to understand ways in which the strategy of natural selection manifests itself in behavioral development. From the perspective of this comparative method, we deduce the real biological propensities in behavior and true biological constraints on learning, and we are introduced to the potentials of experience and action among different species.

Cross-Cultural Developmental Psychology

In chapter 7, Marc Bornstein presents a second derivative comparison, one that combines cultural and developmental perspectives. Again, scrutinizing what is exchanged between these two modes of study illuminates the raison d'être of comparison carried by their combination. How, then, do cross-cultural psychologists benefit from the study of development? At least two ways may be discerned. First, because psychological research that crosses cultures involves some substantive area of behavior, it follows that examination of the origins of that behavior and assessment of its development over the life span will be of interest to cross-culturalists. Second, cross-culturalists who study psychology developmentally are in an ideal position to observe interactions between behavior and culture, thus defining which human behaviors are susceptible to the influence of culture and to what degree.

Complementarily, we can ask how developmentalists benefit from the study of cross-cultural psychology—again, in several ways. Studying human behavior in different cultures gives the best indication of its true variability and thus contributes substantively to description. The cross-cultural perspective frequently provides the human developmentalist with a unique (and sometimes the only) way to answer questions pertaining to the antecedents of behavioral dispositions and to the development of behavior. Parallel to animal developmental study, variation in race and unique experience render cross-cultural findings particularly advantageous to developmentalists. Further, cross-cultural studies provide the fullest test of developmental theories and principles against reality, and they allow the applicability and typicality of behavior explanations to be assessed outside the small, select (and usually Western) group on which they are usually developed. Finally, cross-cultural studies generate hypotheses for developmentalists. Cross-cultural developmental comparison thus provides a broader view of the normative evaluation of behavior and better assessment of the nature and nurture of behavioral development among human beings.

Although early suggestions of this method are to be found in philosophy, history, and biology—especially in the "riot of parallel drawing between primitive man and child," as Kessen (1965, p. 115) characterized the intellectual aftermath of Darwin—the modern roots of this derivative comparison emerged from anthropology. In psychology, universalist theories, like those of Freud and Piaget, have generated an enormous corpus of cross-cultural developmental research. A proportion of the extant literature of experimental developmental cross-cultural comparison is unfortunately methodologically weak, and Bornstein's chapter evaluates designs and techniques contemporarily prominent in this line of investigation.

The body of the cross-cultural developmental chapter overviews the progress of cross-cultural developmental research in five areas of psychology: physical and motor behavior, perception, cognition, language, and social behavior. In each, the study of psychological development in the context of culture has supplied unique information about development, about culture, and about human psychology. These studies have provided the most comprehensive descriptions of psychological phenomena because they endeavored to examine those phenomena in the richest variety of contexts and across the human life span. Further, cross-cultural developmental studies have endeavored to identify the origins of behavior and to follow the contingent course of its development by isolating constitutional and environmental contributions. Description and explanation summate here to place this kind of psychological comparison in the best possible position to predict behavior.

In summary, the predominant derivative comparisons in psychology look at development in evolutionary and in cultural contexts. Ontogeny may be biologically ballistic, or it may be influenced by experience; inevitably, however, it reflects separate adaptations to different environments, ecological or social. In their chapter on ethology and behavioral development, Marler, Dooling, and Zoloth strongly emphasize the biological view; in the cross-cultural developmental chapter, Bornstein shows how biology dominates human development in some cases but how experience does in others. Obviously nature and nurture interact in development, and species differences help to emphasize distinctions between the two. In a curious way, these two derivative comparisons are similar: Within psychology, animal young and children sans culture have been conceived of as alike. As Kessen (1965) has said, they are often "assumed to have fewer, or more simple, units of behavior than does the full man, and their apparent simplicity may permit finding the beginning of the thread that is woven into the inexplicably complicated pattern of adult human behavior [p. 129]."

Because derivative comparisons combine principal ones, the last two chapters tend to focus on principles special to derivative comparisons. By corollary, both chapters are filled with examples and case studies from intersecting investigations of principal comparisons; and although many classical experiments are evoked in the pages that follow, clear presentation of experimental purpose and meaning is emphasized in lieu of experimental detail. Finally, as appropriate, the ethological chapter concentrates on development of infrahuman species and the cross-cultural chapter on development of human beings.

REFERENCES

Campbell, D. T., & Stanley, J. C. *Experimental and quasi-experimental designs for research.* Chicago: Rand McNally, 1963.
Kessen, W. *The child.* New York: Wiley, 1965.

6 Comparative Perspectives on Ethology and Behavioral Development

Peter R. Marler
The Rockefeller University

Robert J. Dooling
The Rockefeller University

Stephen Zoloth
University of California, Berkeley

INTRODUCTION

For animals in nature, acting appropriately in response to the environment is a matter of life and death. To the extent that genetic mechanisms aid the organism in responding with actions that maximize fitness, natural selection will play an inevitable role in strategies of behavior development.

The embryologist C. H. Waddington (1957) referred to patterns of development as "canalized." He used this term to characterize the innate tendency of developing organ systems to follow particular paths. The development of any organ reflects the influence of many competing and cooperating genes, which interact in a self-stabilizing and conservative fashion. It can be surprisingly difficult to divert such growth patterns from their developmental goals (Waddington, 1957). Behavioral development can be viewed as canalized (Bateson, 1976; Fishbein, 1976). Although the final product is not an organ but behavior with a particular form of organization, there is unquestionably interplay between genetically determined constraints and environmental influences. In this chapter we suggest that young organisms of many species come armed with programs of behavioral development that, in their own way, are as "canalized" as those for the development of a limb or a heart. Some examples from ethological studies of behavioral development include perception, patterns of action, and stimulus control.

As we conceive of such programs in the perceptual domain, they focus the developing infant's attention to particular aspects of environmental stimulation. Such innate, attentional predispositions form the fundamental building blocks of what is likely, in higher vertebrates, to be a predominantly learned perceptual organization (Marler, 1977). Among the genetic specifications for such constraints on learning, some are broad, such as those that establish levels of receptor sensitivity. Others are highly specific, allowing selective responsiveness only to certain key features of the environment. Whereas some specifications are absolute, others are relative and manifest only in choice situations. Such preferences may be durable, or they may be transient. They may be resistant to environmental influence, or as will often be the case, highly subject to learned modification. The adaptive significance of many such innate, perceptual specifications is intimately related to the nonrandom structure of natural environments. Preferences expressed in one stimulus domain, and at certain stages of life, will exert strong and pervasive influences on the likelihood of other particular stimuli being encountered, so imposing further probabilistic constraints on perceptual development. In this way, unique features of genetic constitution, social organization, and ecology, each causally related to the other in a myriad of ways, influence the development of the adult perceptual *Umwelt,* as distinct for each species as its morphology, its way of life, and its patterns of action.

The plasticity of motor patterns of behavior is vitally important for the survival of many organisms. However, much of the potential flexibility lies in the timing and orientation of actions rather than in the basic patterns of motor coordination, which may be controlled by somewhat different mechanisms. Relevant here is a distinction in classical ethology between releasing and orienting stimuli. In studies of the stimulus control of the egg-rolling response of the graylag goose *(Anser anser)* and the begging of nestling blackbirds *(Turdus merula)* the dichotomy between these two classes of stimuli was clear (Lorenz, 1937; Lorenz & Tinbergen, 1938; Tinbergen, 1973; Tinbergen & Kuenen, 1939). The distinction has implications not only for understanding the stimulus control of behavior, but also for understanding motor development.

The relative stereotypy of the basic coordinations of action that underlie the natural patterns of animal behavior was epitomized in a concept from classical ethology that could only have been derived from comparative research, that of the "fixed action pattern." Although it has undergone transformations of conception and use in the course of further research (e.g., Barlow, 1977), the main point that Lorenz and Tinbergen were seeking to make is still fundamental to the understanding of motor development. Descriptive analyses of animal actions invariably uncover patterns that are universal to all species members. Often there are clear and consistent contrasts across species, so deeply rooted in their biology that they can even be used as criteria for taxonomy. They may even provide a basis for reconstruction of phylogenetic histories (Manning, 1971), as illustrated by organisms as diverse as fruit flies (Manning, 1965; Spieth, 1952), fiddler crabs (Crane, 1975), fish (Baerends & Baerends-van Roon , 1950), ducks (Lorenz, 1941), gulls (Tinbergen, 1959), and monkeys (Gautier & Gautier, 1977). The fixed action pattern in turn became the fundamental natural unit from which to construct hierarchical models for the organization of behavior. Such models have proved especially valuable as heuristic aids in understanding the principles of neural organization that must underlie behavior (Dawkins, 1976; Hinde, 1956; Kortlandt, 1955; Nelson, 1973; Tinbergen, 1950; Wendler, 1978).

A seminal meeting held in 1950 in Cambridge, England, by the Society for Experimental Biology witnessed the juxtaposition of the current ideas of Lorenz (1950) with those of experimental embryology as represented by the work of Weiss (1950). Just as the comparative ethologist is struck by the relative stability of motor patterns across a species, so the embryologist emphasizes the remarkable ability of developing embryos to achieve stable endpoints for growth. Moreover, they achieve this in spite of the many variations and vicissitudes in the environments in which they grow, exhibiting a stability of purpose exemplified by Waddington's (1957) felicitous concept of canalization.

In past studies of the fundamental operations of the sensory systems, the emphasis in traditional psychology has been on the use of simple stimuli. The works of E. J. and J. J. Gibson illustrate the advances that ensue from appreciation of the ecological significance of stimuli employed in the analysis of perceptual development (E. J. Gibson, 1969; J. J. Gibson, 1966). The famous "visual cliff" experiments are examples (Walk, 1965; Walk & Gibson, 1961). Although a wide variety of animals will respond to a cliff edge, the cues used differ among species in ways that appear adaptive to the varying ways of life (Hinde, 1970).

Ethological studies of the stimulus control of behavior have a "Gibsonian" bias, as in use of the complex stimuli that emanate from inanimate models of members of the species in postures of display. The comparative approach is central, providing axes along which experimentally generated stimuli are varied. Instead of asking generally about what an animal will and will not respond to, experimenters ask how is it that animals of species A respond to their own signals, but not to those of cohabitating species B? In the auditory domain, recordings of natural and modified communicative sounds are often used, thus exploring the efficacy of "sign stimuli" in "releasing" natural patterns of behavior. Again the question of species-specificity, by its nature a comparative concept, has proved a fertile source of hypotheses about what parameters can fruitfully be varied in such experiments. Recent efforts to combine the viewpoints of ethological and psychological approaches, especially in studies of responsiveness to biologically significant sound, offer particular promise of new insights into the physiology and psychology of perception (Bullock, 1977).

One current theme in ethological studies of "sign stimuli" is the existence of hierarchies of responsiveness to particular features of complex stimuli. Certain stimuli are found to be optimal in achieving the release and orientation of particular behaviors. The specificity of such optimal responsiveness has been demonstrated in a wide variety of species (Tinbergen, 1951), but whereas the specificity of *optimal* stimuli for evoking certain responses is irrefutable, the class of *minimally adequate* stimuli is often large. As a result, deprivation from optimal stimuli need not by any means prohibit occurrence of the response. Instead, the organisms will respond to some less preferred stimulus. The importance of understanding the natural ecology of stimulus situations confronting different species is immediately evident. In the laboratory it is easy to overlook the varying probabilities of encountering stimulus situations in nature. Often it is only in the context of such natural, species-specific environments that genetic adaptations for behavioral development can be understood. In this selective review of ethological research on the principles that underlie behavioral development in animals, we seek to emphasize some of the ways in which innate influences make their all-important contributions. Their effects are manifest in all behavior, not the least in learned patterns of action and in learned responsiveness, both animal and human.

In this chapter, we review three major topics of ethology and behavioral development. These include genetic and experiential influences on the early development of behavior, case studies of experimental isolation of environmental determinants and species characteristics related to the emergence of behavior in the young of different species, and notions of species-specific and species-general behavior. Across these topics, we limit our review and discussion to development of perceptual and motor behaviors. In our view these areas are the vanguard of a comparative ethology of behavioral development, and they may serve as models of the development of other behaviors.

GENETIC AND EXPERIENTIAL INFLUENCES
ON BEHAVIOR

Studies of the young of a variety of infrahuman species illustrate influences of both genetic programs and experience on behavioral development. Frequently, simple innate preferences show adaptive value; more complex perceptions, such as depth, also seem to be wired in. Other behaviors, both perceptual and social, are more plastic to experience. In certain cases, the temporal course of the organism's sensitivity to that experience appears to be programmed. In this section, we examine some genetic and experiential influences on the development of behavior.

The Ecology of Perceptual Preferences

Comparative studies repeatedly uncover species differences in perceptual predispositions that are interpretable in the light of differences in their ecology. Of particular interest are cases where such predispositions interact with the readiness to learn new patterns of environmental responsiveness. Honeybees (*Apis mellifera*) can be trained to approach a great variety of scents in their search for nectar. It would be easy to conclude from laboratory experiments with odorous compounds drawn at random from the reagent shelf that the range of perceptible olfactory stimuli to which they can learn to respond is unlimited and genetically unconstrained. The lack of potential limitation may be correct. The conclusion that there are no genetic constraints would be false (Lindauer, 1970).

Olfactory Conditioning in Honeybees.   Studies with natural stimuli demonstrate that, when given a choice, honeybees respond preferentially to odors that are common components in the perfume of nectar-bearing flowers. Comparative studies reveal that the rates with which bees of different races learn to associate odors with food vary. Each race learns to respond most rapidly to odors generally characteristic of its own native flora (Koltermann, 1973).

Conditioning to odor cues is easier than to color cues, although honeybees can be trained to approach many colors when associated with food reward. Once more preference is important: Bees learn to respond more quickly to violet, blue, or yellow markings than to blue-green ones (Menzel, 1967). Again the preferences are ecologically appropriate, and different races show different learning predispositions.

More abstract learning predispositions have also been uncovered. Lauer and Lindauer (1973) have demonstrated a difference between the *Apis mellifera carnica* and *A. m. ligustica* races of honeybees in their readiness to acquire responsiveness to a visual pattern at a feeding site when it is moved independently of other environmental features. *Carnica* bees do much better under these conditions, and Lindauer (1975) explains the difference as follows:

A. m. ligustica, originating in the Mediterranean area, are able to fly in sunny weather throughout the year. Sun-compass orientation can thus be relied upon for guidance directly to the goal. *A. m. ligustica's* learning capacities themselves are focussed on the recognition of patterns. *A. m. carnica* bees, native of mid-

Europe, have to orientate themselves more often under a partially or fully overcast sky and cannot rely on the sun-compass alone; thus it is adaptive for them to use landmarks which are associated with the food goal [p. 241].

Comparative studies of honeybees thus reveal genetically controlled, ecologically appropriate stimulus preferences. Some are relatively fixed, whereas others are so malleable that experience can completely reorganize the relative ranking of different stimuli in a preference hierarchy. We believe that the principles involved here have profound implications for species-specific development and they can be extended to higher organisms with more complex perceptual organization.

The Visual Cliff. That genetic predispositions characterize behaviors more complex than simple responsiveness to particular stimuli is shown by experiments on the nature of the response to visual cliffs. Although general abilities to perceive depth appear as unlearned responses in most precocial and altricial species (Walk, 1978), comparative research reveals that more refined abilities emerge from the integration of genetic predispositions and environmental experience and that evidence of ecological adaptation emerges.

There are specific adaptations to environments that require special sensitivity to visual cliffs. Cullen (1957) described several in the Kittiwake (*Rissa tridactyla*), a gull that rears its young on narrow ledges on very steep cliffs. Adaptations in behavioral patterns of nesting, courtship, and rearing all conform to the restricted available space. Adaptations to the cliff environment also appear in the behavior of the chicks: Rather than fleeing the nest as do the chicks of ground-nesting species, Kittiwake chicks freeze on the approach of danger. Further, McLannahan (1973) demonstrated that these chicks react appropriately to a visual cliff irrespective of the environment in which they were raised. (See also Beer, pp. 54–55, in this volume.)

Smith (1966) examined responsiveness of gull chicks of four different species to the approach of a human to the nest. In this situation the willingness to flee the nest was the dependent variable. Offspring of two of the three cliff-nesting species stayed in the nest, whereas the offspring of ground-nesting gulls readily fled the nest. Because these gull chicks already had extensive experience with their respective environments, these observations are not entirely surprising. However, Smith extended his observations to cross-fostered chicks from ground and cliff environments. The results demonstrated a clear effect of the environment on patterns of flight behavior. Whereas most species behaved according to the environment in which they were reared, others such as the Thayers gull (*Larus thayeri*) and the Kittiwake acted like cliff nesters no matter what the rearing environment. In these species it appears that there is a dominant and relatively immutable genetic predisposition to respond to a visual cliff.

In species in which the response is modifiable the particular nature of the experience is likely to be important. In a now classic experiment, Held and Hein (1963) demonstrated that visual feedback from the environment alone is not adequate to develop normal behavior on visually guided tasks, including responsiveness to visual cliffs. Sensory feedback must be coupled with self-initiated movement and its accompanying feedback in order to develop normal perceptuomotor coordination. What organisms learn of an environment is thus related to how they move through that environment, and patterns of locomotion are as varied as animal morphology. Indeed, they are largely determined by morphology, and the development of species-specific structural traits is mainly under genetic control, reminding us of another route by which genes impinge on learning.

Behavioral Plasticity: Sensitive Periods

In embryological development the relative timing of events is crucial in determining the final product of processes of growth. The same is true of behavioral development, because different situations will be encountered at different stages of the life cycle. The development of the pecking of young birds illustrates how color preferences may be translated into complex-oriented behavior as a result of perceptual learning, but with modifiability varying greatly from one stage of development to another. As in the honeybee, comparative research reveals adaptive differences in innate color preferences.

Perception.   Several plant-eating ducks and pheasants have an innate tendency to peck preferentially at yellow and green (Kear, 1964). Grain-eating domestic chicks, on the other hand, are innately predisposed to peck at yellow or orange-red, depending on the strain, with green as one of the least-preferred colors (Hess, 1956; Hess & Gogel, 1954). They are also innately responsive to such features of form as grain-like shapes, three-dimensionality, and illumination from above (Goodwin & Hess, 1969). In the first minutes of visual experience, when chicks are presented with a graded series of solid forms seen through plastic, they clearly favor round over angular forms. Round solid forms are also preferred to similar flat ones, as demonstrated by Fantz in a program of comparative research that lead ultimately to the discovery of unexpected visual abilities in very young human infants (Fantz, 1957, 1965; Fantz, Fagan, & Miranda, 1975).

Notwithstanding these preferences, young chicks will peck at a wide variety of objects differing in color, texture, and shape if they fall within a certain size category. It is evident that chicks quickly come to discriminate between food and nonfood items. At least a partial explanation for the emergence of this discrimination is that the developing chicks begin to learn about two sorts of properties. In addition to the exteroceptive features we have already mentioned, at about the third day posthatching, they begin to learn to associate pecking with food ingestion. Hogan (1973) reviewed in detail the complex interrelations of these two factors.

Among chicks' innate form preferences is a tendency to peck more at circles than triangles (Hess, 1962). If naive chicks are given a choice between a white triangle on a green background and a white circle on a blue background, they clearly prefer the latter. Hess set out to modify this preference by placing seeds behind the triangle on green. Chicks quickly discovered the seeds and shifted their pecking preferences accordingly as long as seed was present. After two hours of such rewarded pecking the seed was withdrawn, and chicks were tested in extinction with the same stimuli. Persistence of the new preference was strongly dependent on the age at which this two-hour reinforcement was given, peaking sharply when this experience was given at 3 to 4 days (Hess, 1962). It is perhaps no coincidence that this is the age at which the yolk sac is finally exhausted. These data led Hess to postulate a *critical period* for the greatest modifiability of early food-object preferences.

Hogan subsequently demonstrated that the chick's abilty to recognize food is more complex than a simple critical period hypothesis would suggest. He considered three types of experience, each capable of influencing pecking: the behavior of the mother hen, responsiveness to tactile features of food objects, and long-term effects of ingestion. Several experiments suggest that the last are most influential in permanently changing the pecking preferences of young chicks. Again, the effects first appear around 3 days of age. However, a study of effects of reinforcement by forced feeding on discrimination between food and sand yielded the paradoxical result that reinforcement increased subsequent rates of pecking but did not influence the discrimination of nutritive and nonnutritive objects (Hogan, 1973). Although more work is needed, it may be that the Hess result is more concerned with learning *where* to peck for food than with *what* to peck at. Also the relative timing of perceptual experience and reinforcement is another issue inviting futher attention.

Although many questions remain, chicks obviously can acquire responsiveness to the new food items. However, one could not hope to understand the acquisition process without an appreciation of innate predispositions brought to the learning task. Chicks have innate form and color preferences (Baerends & Kruijt, 1973). The speed of learning to discriminate between colors is significantly greater if innate preferences are reinforced than otherwise. It is as though unlearned preferences bear simple additive relationships to effects of experience, a conclusion suggested by studies on readiness of chicks to approach colors (Kovach, 1971; Kovach & Hickox, 1971). There are sensitive periods for maximal modifiability by food reinforcement. In nature, these innate proclivities will have inevitable consequences for the full emergence of feeding behavior, favoring responsiveness to natural food items, while at the same time permitting survival in circumstances in which the animal can only find unpreferred stimulus situations. This flexibility is an essential feature of the operation of innate constraints on learning.

Sexual and Familial Imprinting. It is ironic that in their major contribution to the understanding of animal learning, namely the discovery and analysis of imprinting, ethologists originally underestimated the role of innate factors. At least two distinct phenomena were incorporated under the rubric of imprinting as originally defined by Lorenz. One, filial imprinting, is concerned with parent-young attachment, and the other, sexual imprinting, with sexual preferences in adulthood (Hess, 1973; Lorenz, 1935/1970).

Immelmann (1972) has reviewed numerous cases in which special rearing conditions affect mate choice, either intraspecifically or across species. Domesticated strains of ducks, chickens, pigeons, and finches, foster-reared by a different strain from their own, have been shown to exhibit a sexual preference for that strain in adulthood. In nature, different color phases of the snow goose (*Anser caerulescens*) exhibit selective mate choice, probably as a consequence of imprinting on the parental type (Cooke, 1978). By similar means, imprinted sexual attachments to members of other species have been demonstrated in many birds (review in Immelmann, 1972). The sensitive period for sexual imprinting is usually later in life than that for filial imprinting and longer exposures are required.

As Lorenz emphasized, the influence of imprinting on adult sexual behvior is preferential rather than absolute. Although the imprinted object may be preferred, sexual interaction with other partners is by no means excluded. There are many cases of ambivalent behavior in animals that breed successfully with a member of their own species while still exhibiting an abnormal imprinted preference to another. Clearly there is flexibility in the range of objects that are acceptable for sexual imprinting. Nevertheless, there are species-specific preferences for particular objects.

Immelmann (1972) concludes that birds generally imprint most easily on their *own* species. If no conspecifics are available, they imprint on species similar to their own more easily than on dissimilar ones. The lines of evidence for this conclusion derive from a variety of experiments. In a choice situation for sexual imprinting, a conspecific is often preferred. Sexual preferences for the bird's own species are always more rigid than those for another, and the time constraints on reversal tend to be more severe. With zebra finches (*Taeniopygia guttata*), Immelmann found that reversal of a sexual preference can be achieved up to about 40 days if the subject was foster-reared by another species, but only up to about 20 days if it was reared by its own species.

Schutz (1965) has provided striking evidence of a capacity for innate recognition of sexual partners in ducks, renowned for Lorenz's demonstrations of their imprintability. His work also gives a striking illustration of insights derived from adopting a comparative strategy.

Working with sexually dimorphic species in which the male has distinctive species-specific plumage patterns, Schutz found that females were not sexually imprintable. They became sexually responsive to conspecific males at maturity more or less irrespective of earlier experience. However, males were imprintable on other species, perhaps as a correlate of the greater visual similarity of female ducks of different species as compared with males. Relevance of this correlation is implied by Schutz's further finding that in a sexually monomorphic duck, the Chilean Teal (*Anas flavirostris*), females are as easily imprinted as males.

A contrasting result was obtained with the sexually dimorphic zebra finch, females being strongly imprintable on another foster species, the Bengalese finch (*Lonchura striata*) [Sonnemann & Sjölander, 1977]. Whereas males showed a clear-cut preference according to imprinting, the imprinted females still showed a considerable interest in their own species. Even imprinted males will court and breed with females of their own species if the imprinted species is not available (Immelmann, 1972).

Given the evidence that females of most imprintable species seem to have an innate capacity to recognize a conspecific sexual partner, and with the likelihood that males have at least potential access to the same information, it is legitimate to ask why learning should intrude at all in the process of selection of a reproductive mate. One answer is that there is far more to mate selection than just a preference for members of the same species. As sociobiologists have reminded us, questions of subspecies, population, age, social status, and kin relationship all bear on the appropriateness of a partner as an ideal mate, to say nothing of a multitude of individual differences that also affect or reflect a mate's fitness. Responsiveness to many of these features could only be acquired through learning.

Bateson has recently indicated one probable component of considerable subtlety. It derives from his finding that chicks respond optimally to a parent surrogate that, although very similar to the original imprinted object, nevertheless exhibits a degree of novelty, superimposed on the preference for a familiar object (Bateson & Jaeckel, 1976). Imprinting may serve to aid young in recognizing close kin, with the preference for novelty designed to strike an optimal balance between inbreeding and outbreeding (Bateson, 1978).

In considering the functional significance of filial imprinting, Bateson (1978) focuses again on the ability to recognize close kin. He pointed out that many parent birds discriminate between their own offspring and others and are ready to attack and kill alien young. Thus it behooves young birds to learn early in life to discriminate parents from other adults.

In filial imprinting there is again strong evidence of interplay between perceptual learning and innate constraints. Although the sensitive period for the first stage of the filial imprinting process is compressed in time, we can again view the organism as proceeding from innate selective responsiveness through a series of developmental stages. The simple, rather generalized, initiating stimuli are gradually succeeded and superseded by a particular complex stimulus constellation. The end result is a recognition system uniquely matched to the demands of the social environment of the young organism. Consider the preferred stimuli for the early initiation of approach and following in ducks and geese. Gottlieb (1971, 1974) has shown that ducklings are innately capable of specific responsiveness to calls of their species. In the absence of this optimal stimulation, they will also respond to a variety of other calls, as Lorenz showed with his proverbial "kom, kom, kom."

By contrast, the present picture in the visual domain is one of innate responsiveness to relatively unspecific stimuli. Certain size conditions must be met—if the moving object is too small it will evoke pecking, and if too large, fleeing (Fabricius & Boyd, 1954). There are particular color preferences, but for the most part these have not yet been found to relate in any obvious way to species-specific adult coloration. This is surprising in view of the clear evidence from sexual imprinting that this information is innately available at a later age. One wonders whether further experimentation with live parents might reveal species-specific visual contributions that have been overlooked thus far (cf. Fabricius, 1951).

Notwithstanding the evidence for innateness in responsiveness to stimuli that first evoke following in naive subjects, responsiveness is modified rapidly through learning. Individual auditory and visual recognition between parent and young arises early in many precocial species (Beer, 1970; Cowan, 1974; Evans, 1970, 1972, 1977; Evans & Mattson, 1972; Impekoven & Gold, 1973; Mattson & Evans, 1974; Miller & Emlen, 1975).

By the time a chick or duckling reaches adulthood it has acquired a great deal of perceptual information about its social companions, the vast bulk of it unquestionably learned. It is equally obvious that the direction taken by that learning is profoundly influenced by sets of innate instructions that establish selective responsiveness to particular subsets of stimuli at particular times. The selectivity is preferential and not absolute, exploiting certain probabilities inherent in the social relationship, such as the likelihood that an adult encountered by a newly hatched bird will indeed be close kin. Yet the potential plasticity is considerable, allowing for departures from the typical pattern of species-specific stimulation should they arise.

A CLOSER LOOK AT SELECT ASPECTS OF PERCEPTUAL DEVELOPMENT

Comparative ethological research with animals led Tinbergen to point out that mere knowledge of the potential capacities of the sense organs rarely enables us to identify, in any concrete case, the actual complex of stimuli responsible for the release of a reaction. Beginning in the early 1930s, ethologists developed a variety of ingenious methods for characterizing stimulus complexes found to "release" given innate responses. By disguising live animals and using experimentally modified models, experimenters found that many innate responses were triggered by a limited subset of the total array of stimuli presented by a given situation, dubbed as "sign stimuli" (Tinbergen, 1948, 1951). Tinbergen found that the red belly of a reproductive male three-spined stickleback (*Gasterosteus aculeatus*) was a sign stimulus that triggered attack in territorial males, and that the red underside would elicit this response in the face of a variety of distortions of other features of a normal male's appearance—features unquestionably visible to the fish, but ineffective in this situation.

In this section, we examine three case studies from the literature on perceptual development in human and animal young. These studies illustrate the value of controlled experimentation in defining salient features of the environment in interaction with significant characteristics of the developing organism. Our examples come from facial recognition in human infants, sign stimulus sensitivity in gull chicks, and selective learning of songs by birds.

Face Recognition in Human Infants

Among the most important and potentially informative stimuli confronting the human infant are those emanating from a parent's face. Studies of face perception by human infants have revealed that by about 7 months of age the human infant is capable of quite sophisticated visual discriminations (e.g., Fantz et al., 1975; E. J. Gibson, 1969). Patterns of differential fixation reveal that the 7-month-old infant can discriminate among photos of adult male faces and among poses of the same man's face. Furthermore, infants at this age respond to invariance in pose (Fagan, 1976) and to the sex of a face (Cornell, 1974). Interestingly enough, the method of studying face perception capitalizes on the infant's tendency to choose novel targets for inspection over more familiar ones (Fagan, 1976; Fantz, 1964), reminiscent of the greater potency of slightly novel targets used in imprinting experiments (Bateson, 1973).

How does such sensitivity come about? As in the case of imprinting, face perception by human infants is generally considered as moving from an initial sensitivity to simple features of a stimulus complex to a final, more selective sensitivity to configurational properties. There is clear evidence of an unlearned responsiveness to face-like sign-stimuli even in infants only a few minutes old (Goren, Sarty, & Wu, 1975). However, infrared corneal reflection photography used to track infants' fixations has revealed developmental trends in face scanning. The pattern that emerges from studies using both real faces and photographs is one of an initial responsiveness to the perimeter of the face in 3- to 5-week-old infants, shifting to intense concentration on internal features of the face stimulus—particularly the eyes—at about 7 weeks through 11 weeks of age (Haith, Bergman, & Mare, 1977). Hainline (1978) has shown that these increased internal fixations by 7-week infants occur to a face stimulus but not to an object stimulus matched to the face in details of contour, contrast, and symmetry. Furthermore, scanning responses to the object stimulus were different depending on whether it preceded or followed the face stimulus. Responses to the object stimulus when it followed the face stimulus were more disrupted, suggesting that infants' expectations were violated (Hainline, 1978). These differences in effects of face and nonface stimuli imply that the concept of "faceness" is achieved in infants by 7 weeks of age. Stimulus complexities such as these that confront the infant and the subsequent development of complex schemata are not unique to humans.

Sign Stimulus Sensitivity in Gull Chicks

In animal studies sign stimuli were found to be effective in a sufficient number of cases studied that dependence on them for elicitation was originally viewed as diagnostic of innate behavior. As such, this dependence was thought to differentiate innate reactions from conditioned ones, viewed as "not usually dependent on a limited set of sign stimuli, but on much more complex stimulus situations [Tinbergen,1951, p. 37]." Viewpoints on this have changed with further research, as on the issue of innate responsiveness to configurational stimuli. There is evidence of such a transition in studies of one of the most celebrated ethological subjects, namely the pecking responses of gull chicks.

As an illustration of an ethological *innate release mechanism,* Tinbergen studied the preferred visual stimuli for pecking of chicks of the herring gull (*Larus argentatus*). In the original conception, innate release mechanisms were viewed as implying innate perceptual "schemata" of stimulus objects (Lorenz, 1935/1970), in this case involving special perceptual mechanisms adapted to match responsiveness of the pecking chick to coevolved stimulus features of the parent's bill. It has gradually become evident that the term "schema," with its "image-like" connotations, is probably inappropriate. Instead one typically finds "a mosaic of extremely simple receptor correlates activated by specific key stimuli [Lorenz, 1935/1970, p. 375]."

Although innate responsiveness to these initial triggering stimuli may undergo rapid learned modification, such stimuli will be the natural precursors of early occurrences of the pecking response. It follows that they play a significant role in the chick's acquisition of learned responsiveness to selected aspects of the stimulus complex presented by the parent, and thus in the acquisition of a full, learned, parental "schema."

The herring gull feeds its young by standing above them with food. A chick pecks at its bill and eventually hits the food. Stimulus properties evoking this pecking response include a particular bill shape and a red patch at the tip, characterized by both hue and contrast. Bill orientation and patterns of movement also have an influence (Tinbergen, 1953; Tinbergen & Perdeck, 1950). In his now classical studies, Tinbergen emphasized the "relational" or configurational property of some of the effective sign stimuli, such as the position of a red spot on a head-like shape.

However, when Hailman (1967) reanalyzed this situation, taking care to control the earliest experience of his gull subjects, he found that the sign stimuli for pecking in fully naive chicks, now of the laughing gull (*Larus atricilla*) rather than the herring gull, could all be interpreted in nonconfigurational terms. For example, Tinbergen emphasized the greater valence of a red patch on the bill tip rather than on the forehead of the gull model. Hailman pointed out that the greater effectiveness of a bill-tip spot was attributable to the difference in arc traveled during pivotal movement of the stimulus model. Correcting for this, a spot on the forehead was as effective as one on the bill tip in fully naive laughing gull chicks. Optimal bill width also proved definable in absolute terms.

Hailman detected changes in the stimulus control of pecking after a week or so of normal feeding experience. Chicks were now responsive to three-dimensional properties of the parent head that were ignored by naive chicks. Most interestingly, configurational properties became significant, as though the chick was developing a more complex perceptual "schema" of the parent head. At this stage, a red forehead spot was indeed less effective than one on the bill tip, irrespective of its rate of movement. Clearly, a chick's visual perception of its parents change considerably during the first week of life, and the chick probably learns a good deal about its parents' voices as well. As in other organisms, certain preferences of young gulls are easily modified by learning, others less so. Both domestic chicks and laughing gull chicks have clear innate pecking color preferences. As we have seen, the former can be trained to shift preferences to a new color. This is possible with gull chicks (Weidmann & Weidmann, 1958), but only with considerable difficulty.

The concept of sign stimuli has application beyond innate responsiveness. When a stimulus complex to which a learned response has been established is analyzed critically, we typically find that a particular subset is most salient in its control, though the effective subset may vary from subject to subject, or in the same subject from time to time (Mackintosh, 1974). As with innate behavior, some stimulus features can be varied without affecting the response, even though they are known to be perceptible to the subject. When octopuses, goldfish, and rats are trained to respond to patterned visual stimuli and then required to generalize to other patterns that share some features with the original but differ in other respects, all prove to be responding more strongly to certain elements in the stimulus complex than to others (Lashley, 1938; Sutherland, 1968, 1973). As Mackintosh (1974) cautiously expressed it, "where several stimuli are simultaneously relevant, an increase in control by one stimulus is accomplished by a decrease in control by the remaining stimuli [p. 618]." It seems probable that all responses of organisms, innate and learned, depend most heavily on an abstracted subset of arrays of stimuli, which we may think of as sign stimuli.

The mode of stimulus control over innate and learned responses is obviously different. In the former case, given equivalent histories of experience, all individuals of a species will tend to form the same innate abstractions in species-specific fashion. In the control of learned responsiveness we may be prepared for more intraspecific variation, though here too there may be within-species and even across-species uniformities in the kinds of stimulus features on which learned responsiveness becomes dependent (Sutherland, 1973). "The similarity of the findings for species as different as the octopus, the goldfish and the rat is very much more striking than are the differences. This strongly suggests that there is some optimal way to process visual information and that this method has been discovered in the course of evolution independently by cephalopods and vertebrates [Sutherland, 1973, p. 164]." One is inevitably drawn to the implication of innate biases in the processes that underlie perceptual learning (Herrnstein, Loveland, & Cable, 1976).

Selective Learning of Birdsong

The more complex the signals used by a species in social communication, the more learning is likely to intrude in the development of responsiveness to them, and the more it will benefit from innate instructions as to how the learning should proceed. Oscine birdsongs are the most complex social stimuli known from the animal kingdom. All seem to be learned (e.g., Marler & Mundinger, 1971; Thorpe, 1961). Consider the perception of such a learned song by an adult, experienced bird. The intricate variability found within the song of any oscine bird is not accidental, but comprises a set of controlled variations that have significance and meaning to the birds themselves. These have to do with such things as species and population membership, discrimination of neighbors and strangers, varying levels of motivation, personal identity, and so on (Falls, 1969, 1978; Kroodsma, 1976, 1978). An adult's experimentally demonstrable responsiveness to such varied, subtle features of the acoustic structure of song, unique to each individual's experience, could have developed only through learning. Some involve simple properties, others complex ones; some are absolute, whereas others are configurational in nature (Thorpe & Hall-Craggs, 1976). It follows that the learned, mental imagery that a bird has of its species' song must be rich and complex.

Yet we cannot ignore *innate* influences in song learning. For one thing there are "universals" in song structure. Careful study reveals that the enormous variability of the song patterns of most birds is restricted to certain parameters of the song, with other features more stable. These universals are the features that an ornithologist relies on in identifying the species of a bird, often done more quickly and accurately by voice than by plumage.

Comparative experimentation reveals direct evidence of innate influences. If we look back into a bird's early life and examine the process by which the song was originally learned, we find an interesting paradox. Everyone knows that some birds learn sounds not only from their own species but from others as well, as in the mocking bird (*Mimus polyglottos*), the European starling (*Sturnus vulgaris*), the lyrebird of Australia (*Menura novalhollandiae*), and other famous mimics. But these are exceptions, and it is more general to find that, even in those songbirds in which a Kaspar Hauser male sings a highly abnormal song, a wild male only very rarely learns the song of other species (e.g., Baptista, 1972).

How do such birds avoid learning the wrong song? In some species this is done through a social mechanism. Young birds learn from an adult with whom they have established a particular social bond, such as the father. They learn whatever sounds he produces, and because he will normally be a member of their species, the learning process is canalized so as to preserve a certain set of species-specific characteristics. Having learned the basic features of the father's song they will then often improvise on certain aspects so that individuality comes to mingle with stereotypy (Immelmann, 1969; Nicolai, 1959).

In other species selective guidance of the learning process appears to be achieved by a physiological mechanism in possession of the individual bird (Thorpe, 1958). An example is the white-crowned sparrow (*Zonotrichia leucophrys*). Development of song in young male white-crowned sparrows illustrates three key points.

A male presented with a choice of two songs to learn during the sensitive period, one a song of his own species and the other a song of a close relative living in the same environment, will learn the conspecific model and ignore the alien one. The second key point is that the song of a Kaspar Hauser, although abnormal in many respects, has some natural features, including the presence of long-sustained whistles. Also relevant is the fact that this is a feature that distinguishes white-crowned song from song sparrow song (*Melospiza melodia*) (Marler, 1970a; Marler & Tamura, 1964). The final point of interest is that these normal features are lost if a young male is deafened early in life. The song he develops without the ability to hear his own voice is a noisy tuneless buzz (Konishi, 1965). We infer that the capacity to produce the sustained whistles rests on a perceptual ability. The very same ability would also provide a simple way of distinguishing between white-crowned song and song sparrow song. In the face of some significant natural choices, the young male attends especially closely to songs of his species.

How might this perceptual process develop? The bird behaves as though there is an innate focus of attention on a particular set of sounds. In the process of attending to "acceptable" sounds, other acoustic features are committed to memory. These include not only additional features of the species' song but also the particular dialect to which the young male has been exposed in his youth.

Like many song birds, the young male white-crown learns to sing from memory, only embarking on the gradual transition from subsong to full song after the sensitive period of the first, purely sensory phase of the learning is completed (Marler & Mundinger, 1971). In the second sensorimotor phase, the male behaves as though his next task is to match his vocal output to the memory of sections of the particular pattern of sound to which he was last exposed days, weeks, or even months earlier, during the sensitive period. This interpretation is the essence of the modifiable auditory template hypothesis for selective vocal learning in birds (Marler, 1976a). The learned auditory *engram* of song is used as a kind of template against which the young male matches his song, going through a series of increasingly accurate approximations to the pattern heard in youth until the representation of those features of the song not reserved for individual modifications and inventions is perfect.

As with an infant hearing the sounds of speech for the first time, so one may properly wonder what a bird's first perception of the song of its species is like. What is a male bird's behavior when first exposed to a medley of sounds from the environment? Is the bird equally open and responsive to stimulation by all sounds, or is there some innate perceptual selectivity at the very first exposure? He apparently rejects some sounds for the process of song learning, accepting only a limited set that have properties diagnostic of conspecific song. For an ethologist, it is initially tempting to evoke an innate release mechanism in the original Lorenzian sense. One might view the young male as possessing something equivalent to innate auditory imagery, albeit embodying only skeletal features of the song of the species. The young male would use this to select the appropriate model for learning and then pad out some of the detail through experience. To develop this train of thought further, one needs to delve more deeply into the nature and extent of the innate basis for perceptual learning (see Konishi, 1978).

What of the possibility that motor constraints are involved, so that many sounds are learned during the sensitive period for song learning, only to be subjected to severe filtering when they are transformed into motor activity? Could the syrinx of each species be differently designed so that it can only produce the song of its species? The extraordinary versatility of the songbird syrinx as a sound-producing instrument argues against this notion, but it cannot be completely discounted. If on the other hand there is innate *perceptual* selectivity, are birds responsive to the entire spectrum of species-specific traits or to some subset? In early investigations of selective learning there were no separation of sensory and motor constraints and no specification of the critical acoustic features. Moreover, there was no clear resolution of the question of innateness because the experiments were all conducted with birds taken after hatching, leaving open the possibility that responsiveness might have been shaped by prior experience.

Experiments with two species of sparrow have clarified some of these issues. The song sparrow (*Melospiza melodia*) and the swamp sparrow (*Melospiza georgiana*) were selected as ideal for the purpose. They are closely related species with overlapping breeding ranges. Within the very extensive, continent-wide range of the abundant song sparrow, the less common swamp sparrow lives in pockets, surrounded by and mingled with members of the other species. Swamp sparrows nest almost solely in marshes, whereas song sparrows nest along the edges of marshes as well as in a great variety of other habitats. In these marshy areas males of the two species often occupy adjacent or even overlapping territories. Both species learn their songs early in life. As the less common of the two, the swamp sparrow faces the problem of discriminating its own songs from those of the other species in acute form.

Borrowing techniques from speech synthesis, Marler and Peters (1977) generated a series of synthetic songs by computer. The young of both species were presented with these models during the sensitive period for song learning with surprising results. Although both species learned a great deal from the models presented, neither payed the slightest attention to the syntactical patterning. Although the two species behaved similarly in this respect, in others the outcome was different. The swamp sparrows learned highly selectively, but solely on the basis of syllabic structure. They accepted syllables derived from songs of their own species, irrespective of the temporal pattern in which they were presented. By contrast, the song sparrows were unselective, ready to learn both song-sparrow syllables and swamp-sparrow syllables. Finally, although both species were unresponsive to temporal organization of the models, the temporal organization of their songs exhibited several distinct species-specific features: The swamp sparrows gave steady trills, and the song sparrows multipartite songs. The same was true of other birds reared with no training.

There is something of a paradox here. Whereas these sparrows are unresponsive to features of overall patterns during the first, "sensory" phase of song learning, they nevertheless possess some of the necessary information about syntax. However, this only becomes manifest when they begin to sing, at which time they incorporate the syllabic structures already learned into the overall syntactical pattern. They behave as though there were an advantage in dividing the process into stages, with completion of acquisition of the smaller units before a commitment is made to the higher levels of syntactical organization.

The distinction between perceptual and motor contributions to the selective vocal learning of the swamp sparrow would be clarified if one could detect any signs of selective responsiveness at an age prior to the development of singing. Using the cardiac orienting response to sound, Dooling and Searcy (in press) found evidence that young swamp sparrows can discriminate their own vocalizations from song sparrow vocalizations even on the initial exposure to these natural songs. Swamp sparrows show cardiac deceleration more to conspecific song, suggesting a clear preference. In contrast, song sparrows discriminate more weakly if at all, which is consonant with their readiness to learn syllables of both species. Although the discrimination is weak, it shows an opposite trend from the swamp sparrows, tending to favor their conspecific song. Thus young song sparrows may have a weak ability to discriminate in favor of conspecific song in infancy, not manifest in their choice of models for learning under our test conditions.

In contrast with the infantile condition, playback studies with wild adults using synthetic songs reveal that the vocal perception of song sparrows is more elaborate in adulthood than in infancy (Peters, Searcy, & Marler, in press). What then are the factors that intervene between early infancy and adulthood resulting in this perceptual enrichment? Undoubtedly further interaction with adults of their own species and experience of their song must play an important part. However, there is another possible source of some of this information, namely feedback from the bird's own vocal production. Recall that imitated syllables were rendered into more-or-less species-specific temporal patterns.

The birds behave as though it is advantageous to withhold innate information about syntax until a still more basic issue has been dealt with, namely the acquisition of an adequate repertoire of syllabic units. Once these have been learned, then the bird can proceed to the next stage, equipped with raw materials to construct larger-scale patterns. What is the physiological origin of this syntactical information? Does it originate as a kind of endogenous motor tape, or is this a manifestation of another kind of auditory predisposition that guides motor development by sensory feedback?

Konishi (1964, 1965) has shown that there is some tendency for sparrows deafened early in life (prior to singing) to develop very elementary patterns of singing in which most species-specific features are erased. If confirmed, this finding will implicate species-specific auditory mechanisms not only in early selective responsiveness at the syllabic level but also in the later organization. How is this second auditory mechanism engaged? It might be timed to coincide with the onset of singing, or perhaps we should begin to think in terms of a motor-contingent mechanism such that special sensory predispositions are only activated as some immediate correlate of singing behavior, a notion that Held and Hein have introduced us to in their research on development of the visual control of movement in cats (Held, 1965; Held & Hein, 1963).

It appears that the development of vocal perception in sparrows proceeds in stages, with different items of innate information injected at different stages and blending with different kinds of learned information. The underlying notion of innate hierarchical programs for the development of perceptions of complex stimuli may apply more generally. Speech development is one of the most obvious cases where one can conceive of advantages to this strategy. Clearly, such programs would enable the infant to proceed quickly and surely through the stages of a very complex process. Perhaps most important of all, a hierarchical program of rule development would increase the likelihood that all human infants tackle the problem in roughly the same way. The effect will be to reduce the incidence of private, nonuniversal solutions to perceptual problems that could only be a hindrance to the free and efficient use of speaking and of speech perception for purposes of social communication.

SPECIES-SPECIFIC AND
SPECIES-GENERAL PERCEPTIONS

Although innate constraints on perceptual learning are sometimes viewed as species-specific limitations, their phylogenetic distribution often goes beyond species limits. With form vision, for example, it is reasonable to anticipate independent emergence of best solutions at more than one phyletic level (Sutherland, 1973). The same may be true for color and for select aspects of the speech signal. Whereas some perceptual characteristics are general, others arise that are unique to a species, requiring truly species-specific strategies. For example, monkeys show specific auditory processing of their own vocal sounds. In this section, we examine perceptual biases of both kinds as uncovered in comparative ethological research.

Vocal Recognition in Monkeys

Among sounds used in the communication of higher primates there is a predominance of graded signals (Green, 1975; Marler, 1965, 1970b; Struhsaker, 1975). Graded vocal systems, as contrasted with the discretely organized systems found in some primates and many birds, are those where the amount of variability both within and between categories of signals is so great that they become connected by intermediate forms. In the extreme cases of grading, especially characteristic of such higher primates as the chimpanzee (*Pan troglodytes*) (Marler, 1976b; Marler & Tenaza, 1977), it becomes difficult for the observer even to assign vocalizations to a particular category. Often such judgments are based more on the observer's own comparisons with arbitrarily selected exemplars than on a detailed analysis of vocal morphology and usage. It is quite possible that, as human observers of the communication system of another species, we misinterpret the nature of the complexity of the sound systems used.

The functional significance of highly graded vocal systems could lie in their tremendous potential for conveying detailed information to others. According to this view each variant potentially represents a unique cognitive state of the vocalizing animal. By attending to such variation, a listener could accurately predict changing probabilities in the vocalizer's subsequent behavior (Zoloth & Green, in press).

Before we can understand how primate vocal repertoires are used in communication, we must find some way to ask primates to define which properties of their vocalizations are most salient—not for us, but for them. The task is reminiscent of the problem confronting investigators of speech perception by human infants. A test is required that queries a nonlinguistic subject as to what it hears (see Snowdon, in press; Snowdon & Pola, 1978).

An investigation of vocal perception in Japanese macaques (*Macaca fuscata*) asked whether the sound features that have a natural meaning are also relevant in auditory perception of calls in a laboratory situation (Beecher, Petersen, Zoloth, Moody, & Stebbins, in press; Green, 1975). Two call variants of the macaque "coo" vocalization were selected. Each variant of the *M. fuscata's* graded repertoire is correlated with a unique, definable behavioral class (Green, 1975). As their names suggest, these calls are clear, tonal sounds with a single unbroken frequency sweep. They can be typified by the temporal position of the frequency rise of "peak." One of the coo variants, the smooth early high (SEH), is given by animals isolated from their companions and apparently desirous of making affinitive contact. The second coo variant used, the smooth late high (SLH), is given by animals that are more highly aroused and actively seeking contact. They are given most typically by estrous females in the early stage of consort formation.

Japanese macaques and monkeys of three other species, as controls, were trained to perform an operant response to playback of natural coos. Initially, it was relatively easy for all the monkeys to learn to distinguish between one SEH and one SLH in the test situation. As new examples of SEHs and SLHs were introduced, generalization proceeded readily for the Japanese macaques. On the other hand, the other species, pigtail and bonnet macaques (*M. nemestrina* and *M. radiata*) and vervet monkeys (*Cercopithecus aethiops*), found it difficult to acquire the ability to distinguish between sets of these calls, which varied considerably in acoustic dimensions other than the peak position, such as pitch, duration, and harmonic structure.

The task for each subject was to learn to identify vocalizations as belonging to the same class even though they differed along these other dimensions. The stimulus sets were so arranged as to be stable along the target dimension of peak position but not in other respects. Thus as novel instances of SEHs and

SLHs were introduced to the basic stimulus set, the animal's task changed from simple sensory discrimination of two auditory patterns to the formation of a perceptual concept about auditory patterns.

After much "remedial" training, the control-species monkeys eventually reached a performance level similar to that of the Japanese macaques. The task is not impossible for them, simply harder. Thus Japanese macaques are more capable than the other species of perceiving natural and inherent relationships among vocalizations taken from the *fuscata* repertoire.

In a second experiment, the same coo vocalizations were rearranged to present a discrimination task in which the target dimension was the onset frequency, with peak position as an irrelevant variation. Japanese macaques acquired this pitch discrimination much less easily than they solved the peak position task. However, the converse was true for the control monkeys. Vervets and pigtail macaques learned the pitch discrimination more quickly than the peak discrimination. These data again suggest that these two species are using different strategies when discriminating between *M. fuscata* vocalizations (Zoloth, Petersen, Beecher, Green, Marler, Moody, & Stebbins, 1979).

Color Categorization

Behavioral "universals" are one source of information as to how perceptual worlds are organized. Some such clues derive from cross-cultural studies of the perceptual ability of infant and adult humans, posing such questions as: What features of the environment are attention-getting? Which are discriminable? What is there in common among responses across stimuli that reveals underlying tendencies for perceptual classification?

Human color vision and color naming illustrate both the subtlety and the pervasiveness of the perceptual effects of what we may consider as predetermined constraints on sensation (Bornstein, 1979). Color naming was long thought to reflect the ultimate in environmentally determined influences on perceptual classification. The strongest statement was given by Whorf (1964), who argued that the environment has a direct influence on the labels given to various colors and that these names effectively determine perceptual organization. In opposition to Whorf's hypothesis was the viewpoint that operations inherent to the sensations of color preordain the basic color classification. Resolution of this controversy came from three lines of evidence: seminal was an increased understanding of the physiological mechanisms underlying color vision in humans and other animals (DeValois, 1973; Hurvich & Jameson, 1957; Ratliff, 1976); another important line of evidence derived from study of color naming across languages (Berlin & Kay, 1969); of equal importance were studies of the processes of color classification in young human infants (Bornstein, 1975; Bornstein, Kessen, & Weiskopf,

1976a, 1976b). Taken together, these studies demonstrate that constraints on the sensory apparatus have a strong influence on the perception of color and ultimately on the process of color naming.

When color chips of varying hue but constant saturation and brightness are presented to English-speaking adults, they are labeled as members of four basic categories: red, green, blue, and yellow. Labeling functions can also be assigned experimentally in other species as diverse as bees, pigeons, and macaques, although the actual hue categories employed by these species are, of course, different from those used by English-speaking people. Pigeons, for example, divide our visible spectrum into three primary categories with a substantially different placement of boundary wavelength values (Wright & Cumming, 1971). Whatever the differences, there seems to be a universal tendency to partition the spectrum into perceptual categories with regular boundaries between classes, a predisposition that is obviously independent of any animal ability to provide linguistic labels.

The effect of this categorization is also evident if a person is asked to discriminate between exemplars of different colors. Although we can discriminate among a great many different hues, it is possible to rank the relative ease of such discriminations. When this is done, discrimination is found to be more difficult with hue pairs near the center of the labeled color categories than with pairs across boundaries. As a result, perceptual categorization naturally imposes some restrictions on our perceptions of the visual wavelength continuum.

Research into the physiological mechanisms underlying color vision demonstrates how neural activity of the retinal cones is transformed by interactions within the retina and in higher visual centers into an opponent-process color system. Much of the evidence derives from research into visual processes in macaques (DeValois, 1973). Recordings from single units within the lateral geniculate nuclei demonstrated the existence of four types of spectrally opponent neurones (DeValois, Abramov, & Jacobs, 1966). Each type is excited by one wavelength range and inhibited by a second or opponent wavelength range. The optimal wavelength values for these neurones divide them into groups responding to two pairs of opponent hues, red versus green, and yellow versus blue. Each group contains neurones that are excited by one member of the pair and inhibited by the other. From these data and from psychophysical evidence, an explicit model of color vision can be derived that accounts for the existence of the four primary hues (Abramov, 1977).

Further evidence of the primacy of the tetrachromatic interpretation comes from cross-cultural studies of color names. Berlin and Kay (1969) investigated color naming in a large number of language groups. By interrogating native speakers about color names and using standardized color chips, they were able to determine which hues serve as best examples of the color categories and where the boundaries between the categories fall. They demonstrated eleven color categories from which most color names are drawn (Berlin & Kay, 1969). Most importantly, Berlin and Kay showed that the four color categories to appear first in any language are always the four basic ones (red, green, blue, and yellow), once names are given beyond black and white. Thus the simplest color systems have names only for black and white; those languages with three color terms have words for black, white, and red. The order of linguistic development of color terms always progresses through the primary hues before extending to names for compound colors. The regularity of color-naming systems and their parallel development across many languages suggest that this process reflects innately determined species-specific predispositions. Finally, using the Berlin and Kay cross-cultural data, Bornstein (1973) was able to show that the "best examples" they obtained for each hue are a good match with the DeValois data on the wavelength to which single neurones are most sensitive in the macaque.

In other cross-language research Rosch (1973; Heider, 1972) demonstrated that the Dani of New Guinea, whose color-naming system is organized by brightness rather than hue, were nevertheless perfectly capable of recognizing hue categories. Constructing categories around "focal colors" as defined by the Berlin and Kay study, Rosch demonstrated that these categories were learned faster and with fewer errors than categories constructed around nonfocal colors. Rosch's data show that, even when a color space is linguistically unlabeled, it does not remain undifferentiated.

Color perception clearly rests on a fundamental biological foundation, common to all members of the species rather than originating within a particular linguistic or social structure. The final piece of evidence on this issue is also the most compelling. Data gathered from prelinguistic infants strongly suggest that they perceive colors as belonging to the same categories as adults. Bornstein, Kessen, and Weiskopf habituated the fixation response of young infants to a colored stimulus by repeated presentations. Having reached a certain habituation criterion, a probe stimulus was then introduced at some other wavelength. If this were perceived by the infant as different from the first, it would produce dishabituation, and fixation would be resumed. Stimulus pairs were chosen to straddle adult color boundaries or to fall within a single adult category. The latter did not result in dishabituation, the former did, demonstrating unequivocally that infants partition the spectrum into the four basic hue categories (Bornstein et al., 1976a, 1976b). Thus the human infant brings into the world a set of innate perceptual proclivities that then serve as guidelines for any subsequent linguistic organization of color space (Bornstein, 1973, 1979).

In summary, color categories in human and nonhuman species rest on the functional organization of the visual system. The tendency to divide the spectrum into perceptual categories, with focal regions and relatively fixed boundaries, is ubiquitous in our species. As such, it provides a set of guidelines for the developing infant's organization of color space. The color-naming systems of different cultures exhibit many idiosyncracies, such as the use by the Dani of intensity dimensions of light and dark as a basis for defining color space. We are reminded that, in the ontogeny of links between color and behavior, perceptual predispositions such as we have described are not immutable but can be overridden by environmental and cultural effects. Yet we cannot begin to understand the ontogeny of color perception without taking them into account.

The coexistence of a universal set of predispositions together with the great variety of color-naming systems used in human societies illustrate the subtlety of visual constraints on the development of behavior associated with the division and labeling of color space. The "preferences" of humans for focal hues in a color-naming experiment resemble the type of animal experiment in which one aspect of a compound stimulus seems to have more salience and tends to take priority as a conditioning stimulus when choice is permitted. We have already suggested that many animal-preference experiments can be reinterpreted as providing evidence for innate guidelines for the subsequent development of learned behaviors. As the growing organism encounters new problems in visual discrimination tasks, it will tend to persevere with stimulus dimensions already successfully employed in previous discriminations and to resist transfer of control to other dimensions (Mackintosh, 1974). Thus innate stimulus preferences expressed at critical stages of behavioral development may have profound consequences for learned perceptual behavior in adulthood.

Speech Perception

It is our view that research on the perception of speech by adults and human infants provides further support for the notion of canalized perceptual learning. According to this interpretation, development of speech perception is guided first by innate responsiveness to simple stimuli, which subsequently becomes integrated into the formation of complex, learned schemata for speech sounds, the latter so complex that we still cannot fully specify the acoustic carriers of the phonetic message. Thus having shown that innate constraints are important for understanding the ontogeny of human color vision and naming, we now extend the argument to the more complex behavior of speech perception (see Bornstein, 1979).

Given the remarkable acoustic complexity of speech, it is surprising to a nonlinguist to learn that there are "universals" in certain physical features of speech patterns that define boundaries between functionally distinct patterns of sound, recurring across all languages. We can best illustrate this by reference to the distinction in many unrelated languages between critical pairs of voiced and unvoiced consonants. "Voice-onset time" has been a focus of special study as a property of speech that can be reliably measured from the frequency/time sound spectrograms on which so many bioacoustical studies are based. The cross-cultural studies of Lisker and Abramson (e.g., 1964) have shown that all languages studied employ voice-onset time (VOT) as one basis for differentiating voiced and unvoiced consonants in speech. Furthermore, when there are VOT boundaries, they always fall in approximately the same place(s). Universals have also been found in the patterns of formant onset that differentiate speech sounds produced at different points of articulation, labial, alveolar, and velar (e.g., / b/-/ d/-/ g/) (Lisker & Abramson, 1964). There is a long list of other universals (Greenberg, 1969; Studdert-Kennedy, 1977), but the voicing and formant-onset properties of consonants have the advantage that they are specific and lend themselves to precise analysis and experimental control. When such universals are discovered in ethograms of animal behavior, an ethologist is likely to entertain the possibility of genetic developmental controls. This comparative viewpoint pays dividends in the present case.

A further relevant finding is the recurrence of "categorical perception" of voicing. We have already described similar characteristics in color vision, although it was first described in speech perception (Liberman, Cooper, Shankweiler, & Studdert-Kennedy, 1967; Liberman, Harris, Hoffman, & Griffith, 1957; Liberman, Harris, Kinney, & Lane, 1961). Asked to label sounds on the VOT continuum, an English-speaking subject divides it into two parts, labeling one side /p/, the other /b/, with a sharp boundary between that coincides with the trough in VOT productions. This boundary recurs in different languages, though with details that vary consistently from one to another. In some languages, such as Thai, there is a second boundary.

If adult subjects are tested for the discriminability of sound pairs differing by small increments on the VOT continuum, they display greater sensitivity to variations in the zone of the boundary than to within-category variations (Studdert-Kennedy, Liberman, Harris, & Cooper, 1970), thus illustrating the other characteristic of categorical perception. Although within-category speech variations can be detected, especially with practice (Strange & Jenkins, 1978), adults nevertheless behave as though desensitized to them while being acutely sensitive to small changes at the boundary. The perceptual "quantization" of certain dimensions of complex stimuli contrasts with the more classical "continuous" perception of such properties of simple tones as pitch or loudness. Perceptual discontinuities, though occurring along stimulus dimensions that are acoustically continuous, seem to be a consequence of changing a subset of components in a stimulus complex while keeping the remaining components constant (Miller, Wier, Pastore, Kelly, & Dooling, 1976; Pastore, 1976).

Categorical processing is of great potential interest to the comparative ethologist, because it has the consequence of grouping stimuli into classes, imposing a particular kind of order on varying patterns of stimulation. Thus some acoustically distinct sounds are treated by the listener as functionally equivalent. Although not unique to the perception of speech sounds (e.g., Cutting & Rosner, 1974; Miller et al., 1976; Pisoni, 1977), nor, as we have seen, restricted to the auditory modality (Pastore, 1976), it is especially well exemplified in responses of human subjects to complex acoustic continua from speech. In adult humans, categorical perception may be viewed as a component in the larger issue of the perceptual constancy of speech-sound categories. It also seems to make a critical, innate contribution to the development of speech perception.

A variety of measures of human infant responses to speech sounds, including habituation of a sucking response, heart-rate changes, and evoked brain potentials, indicates responsiveness to similar boundary values between functionally distinct speech sounds to those observed by adults, in subjects as young as 1 month of age or less (Eilers & Minifie, 1975; Eimas, 1974, 1975; Kuhl, 1976; Morse, 1972). The early age at which these responses are manifest gave rise to the speculation that responsiveness to some of these boundary properties may be innate.

Still firmer evidence for an innate component was obtained in studies of speech perception in 4- to 6-month-old infants living in a Spanish-speaking environment (Lasky, Syrdal-Lasky, & Klein, 1975). There are slight but consistent differences between English and Spanish VOT boundaries in adult production and perception. These led to the prediction that infants would demonstrate boundary limits different from those obtained by Eimas (1975) with children living in English-speaking environments, if these were acquired through infantile experience of speech patterns. The infants proved to be responsive to boundaries in both regions of the VOT continuum that are universal, the so-called "English" and the "Thai" boundaries, with no sign that experience of the distributions used in Spanish had yet affected their speech perception.

Streeter (1976) conducted a well-conceived cross-cultural study in Africa. Infant perception of boundaries along the VOT continuum was studied in children exposed to Kikuyu in infancy. This language has the interesting feature that there is only one labial-stop constant, with a unique VOT boundary. These Kikuyu 2-month-olds, although lacking experience of anything equivalent to a /p/, also proved to be responsive to the "English" boundary, thus resembling infants exposed to English and various other languages. Streeter concluded that even at this early age some phonetic or acoustic discriminations are universal and innate, even though others may require appropriate experience.

The potential lability of predispositions that human infants bring to segmentation of speech-sound continua is also clear. Discriminations that are difficult at a younger age, such as those involving the fricatives /s/ and /z/, are made with ease at 6 months (Eilers & Minifie, 1975; Eilers, Wilson, & Moore, 1977). The /r/-/l/ distinction that Japanese adults find so difficult, unemployed in Japanese, is probably easier for infants, though only American infants have been tested thus far (Eimas, 1975).

The properties of speech sounds on which learned responsiveness in adulthood is based are obviously more complex and abstract than those that infants respond to, with more redundancy, perhaps involving configurational features rather than simple properties, and sometimes so changed that the original predispositions of infancy are no longer evident. Nevertheless, the latter must surely play a significant ontogenetic role in setting the trajectory of the perceptual learning process (see Pisoni, in press).

One way in which such trajectories may be achieved is indicated in a study by Kuhl and Miller (1974). The formant patterns that distinguish different vowel sounds are complicated by variations in the fundamental frequency of different voices, as between men and women. This must be a serious distraction for an infant embarking on the linguistic analysis of speech. Given the importance of vowel coding in speech, we might perhaps expect a predisposition to focus more strongly on formant patterns than on pitch in early responses. By independently varying the two features in sounds presented to infants, while monitoring high-amplitude sucking, Kuhl and Miller were able to show that variations in formant pattern are indeed more salient or arresting for human infants than variations in pitch. When formant patterns were varying randomly the infants habituated rather slowly and were more distracted from attending to a pitch change than they were in the opposite condition when required to attend to a vowel change in the face of random pitch variations. This is not to say that infants are unresponsive to pitch variation—far from it. However, the salience of pitch changes to infants of this age is lower than that of variations in vowel patterns, under these test conditions. It thus imposes some order on the process of learning to extract different features from the complex stimuli that speech sounds present, insofar as success in using this dimension in sorting speech sounds probably leads them to persevere with it, at least for a time, in further speech-sound discriminations (see Mackintosh, 1974, p. 615). Further experiments using a conditioned head-turning response suggest that by 6 months of age infants can perceive similarity between vowels produced by different size vocal tracts and between a fricative consonant when it occurs in different vowel environments and spoken by different talkers. Clearly, innate responsiveness to simple properties of vowel formants quickly becomes modified and enriched as a consequence of further experience with speech behavior.

Human infants thus bring well-defined perceptual predispositions to the task of developing responsiveness to the immensely complex pattern of sound stimuli that speech represents. Some predispositions are innately manifest in initial encounters, developing without prior experience of the stimuli involved. Although these innate contributions are clear, we are hardly tempted to view them as developmental instructions for designing infants as human automata. It seems natural to think of them as helping the infant to learn. They provide initial instructions that set the trajectory for development of learned responsiveness. Eventually, elaborate arrays of features are abstracted through learning and become embodied in mental images or "schemata" as a basis for perceiving the meaningful phonological components of mature speech.

CONCLUSION

Specialized and Versatile Perceptual Systems

As Tinbergen (1951) has indicated, early ethologists sought explanations for the selectivity of responsiveness of different animals to environmental stimulation in part by characterizing species differences in the potential capacities of their sense organs. Von Uexküll (1921) stressed the uniqueness of the perceptual world of each species, consequent on the design of its receptor systems. Even the most extreme environmentalists have always appreciated the obvious fact that no organism is potentially capable of perceiving all possible changes in the external world. Limits are set by the structure of its sense organs. Because these develop through processes of growth, in which genetic controls play a major role, no one questions the importance of innate constraints at this level.

The sensory world of an insect is obviously different from that of a mammal. The honeybee sees intricate patterns of ultraviolet coloration on flowers that are invisible to us without the trick of photographing them through a quartz lens, allowing the ultraviolet to pass (Daumer, 1956, 1958; von Frisch, 1967). It is impossible for us to imagine the subleties of ultrasonic echolocation at which bats are so incredibly adept (Griffin, 1974). There is growing evidence that birds hear infrasound, so low-pitched that we cannot hear it, and perhaps important to birds because it attenuates so little with distance, providing possible long-range cues for orientation of migration (Yodlowski, Kreithen, & Keeton, 1977). Equally mysterious for us is the electrical sense that some fish use for both object location and communication (Heiligenberg, 1975; Hopkins, 1974; Lissmann, 1958).

The literature of ethology and comparative physiology is replete with examples of specialized sensory systems so highly developed in certain species as to open up for them new sensory domains to which others, lacking such innate specializations, are insensitive or even totally blind. It is self-evident that *some* innate features pervade all perception by imposing structural limitations on the organs of sensation. Less obvious are the contributions of innate processes to the development of later phases of stimulus processing than mere sensation, phases in which impressions are organized and interpreted, reflected on, and finally manifest in some appropriate action—in other words, in the development of perception.

Being so far removed by innumerable developmental transformations from the chemistry of particular genes, and bearing in mind our ignorance as to which particular structures of an organism are responsible for the transmutations of mental imagery, we find it exceptionally difficult to get a grasp on how genes might influence the more subtle aspects of perceptual development. As we have tried to show here a *comparative* approach helps in coping with this problem.

A recurrent finding in studies of Lorenz, Tinbergen, and others is that developing young animals manifest responsiveness to particular environmental stimuli. These especially salient stimuli are associated with events that are fraught with special biological significance for all species members, such as predator detection or sexual communication. The selectivity of such innate responsiveness is sometimes such that it is hard to imagine peripheral structures that could specify responsiveness so narrowly, especially when mediated by receptor systems known to be responsive to broader ranges of stimuli. Thus the concept of innate release mechanisms as developed by Lorenz and Tinbergen (see Baerends & Kruijt, 1973; Schleidt, 1962) seeks to involve both peripheral and central influences in selective perception (Marler, 1961).

To the extent that environmental events with special significance in the life of an organism are predictable over transgenerational time, species-specific genetic control over at least some details of stimulus responsiveness is feasible. The frequency responsiveness of the auditory systems of many frogs and toads seems to be adapted to match species-specific features of the calling songs of males of the species, so that species recognition is achieved in part by a kind of complex frequency filter (Capranica, 1965; Capranica, Frishkopf, & Nevo, 1973). There are other examples from invertebrates (Marler, 1961; Marler & Hamilton, 1967) of even more specific selectivity of responsiveness imposed by adaptations of entire sensory systems; for example, mosquitoes have sound-sensitive antennae that are tuned to resonate mechanically to the wing tone of conspecific females (Roth, 1948; Tischner & Schief, 1954).

In cases such as these, where much information about stimuli is discarded in the very process of sensory transduction, the selectivity of responsiveness is obviously bought at considerable cost. This cost may be measured in terms of perceptual versatility. For an organism embarking on a stage of its life cycle dominated by a few special behavioral requirements, it will be efficient if most environmental changes impinging on its receptors are rejected or highly attenuated at an early stage. Such specialized receptor systems will serve to focus immediate attention on the subset of stimuli that is biologically appropriate, as in long-range lepidopteran olfaction, which is specialized for detection and orientation to female sex pheromones (Schneider, 1970; Shorey, 1976). However, for organisms whose structure, behavior, and ecology allow them to benefit from responsiveness to many kinds of environmental information, such a price would be exorbitant. Instead, more versatile receptor systems will be favored, as exemplified by the olfactory system of the honeybee (von Frisch, 1967).

These conditions are met in many organisms. Active, nonspecialized predators, such as octopus and dragonflies, and species with elaborate social behavior, such as the honeybee, are cases in point. Above all, most higher vertebrates qualify—especially birds and mammals—which have been the main focus of this chapter, to the neglect of a vast and important literature on the behavior in invertebrates and lower vertebrates.

The essential feature of "versatile" perceptual systems, as we have characterized them, is the dynamic quality of stimulus selectivity. Here the same receptor system can mediate selective responsiveness to many patterns of stimulation, the particular selection being adjusted according to changing needs of the organism. Sometimes these changes will reflect reversible, often cyclic changes in the hierarchically organized motivational states of an organism (Tinbergen, 1951). On other occasions there will be progressive noncyclical changes in the selectivity of responsiveness, such as accrue by learning from the cumulative experience of continuing interactions between the organism and its environment.

Although innate responsiveness plays a dominant role in the developing behavior of many animals, enrichment through learning is often extensive. In such cases the challenge is to understand how genetic and environmental influences interact. We have pressed the viewpoint here that some innate release mechanisms, as described by ethologists in experiments on the behavior of young animals, should be viewed not so much as components for designing animals as efficient automata but rather to provide developmental guidelines for learning, modifiable through experience. Thus through comparative research we seek to unify concepts developed by ethologists for understanding innate behavior with those of psychologists arising from studies of animal learning.

According to this view, young birds and mammals have the potential to acquire responsiveness to most if not all perceptible features of a stimulus object. In many circumstances they will nevertheless be prone to attend to certain features of natural situations in preference to others, as though these were endowed with an innate salience, thus serving to canalize perceptual development. In species-typical environments the consequences for adult perceptual organization may be highly predictable in certain respects. There are potentially many different types of perceptual organization, as in individuals growing up in atypical environments or having otherwise unusual individual histories. Although the diversity may be great, at a certain level of perceptual organization most species members will share similar operational rules, the degree of sharing depending on the nature and timing of innate perceptual constraints of the type we have considered.

As guidelines for perceptual learning, rather than prescriptions for automata, the effects of innate release mechanisms of higher vertebrates are often subtle. They are designed to operate in concert with stimulation from species-specific environments, physical and social, the importance of which cannot be overestimated. Out of this ecological interaction the developing organization of perception of the external world of each species emerges in orderly and predictable procession, assured of the adaptiveness of its major lineaments, yet flexible enough to allow benefit from the vagaries of individual experience and experimentation.

Development of Motor Behavior

In thinking about the development of motor patterns, it is essential to bear in mind that "the basic integrative architecture of the nervous system is organized directly in the growth process itself [Sperry, 1951, p. 237]." "The self-regulative, operational organization of the nervous system, not just the character of its protoplasm, is what enables it to utilize its experience selectively to improve upon its own structure. Complex self-regulative mechanisms must first be constructed in ontogeny before adaptation by learning can begin to take place [Sperry, 1951, p. 270]."

As research progresses on the physiological mechanisms that underlie complex motor coordinations, the evidence for endogenous patterns of neural commands from the brain as the basis for fixed-action patterns becomes more and more compelling (see reviews in Evarts, 1971; Herman, Grillner, Stein, & Stuart, 1976). This seems to be the case not only for the maintenance of the mature behavior of adult animals but also for its development, as Szekely (1976) has shown for the ontogeny of amphibian locomotion. Adjustments through experience are achieved by peripheral modulation of these autochthonous patterns of neural activity. This is true even of higher vertebrates, probably including man.

When Harlow (1965) demonstrated in his classic studies the importance of social experience in the development of the sexual behavior of rhesus monkeys (*Macaca mulatta*), he found the basic components of their sexual activity to be intact. The abnormalities arose in the patterns of sequencing in which they were assembled and in their inappropriate orientation to the partner (Harlow, 1965; Mason, 1965). In many animals social experience is vital for the development of patterns of activity and interaction that are typical of the species in all of their details. However, the effects of experience are constrained by the structure of the organism with which they interact. Thus genetic contributions to motor development are even more significant and pervasive than those to the ontogeny of perception.

Changes of behavior taking place as organisms mature often prove to be as much a function of maturation of the nervous system as of the accumulation of experience. Carmichael (1951) showed this directly in his demonstrations of quite normal locomotion in salamander embryos anesthetized through a major phase of development and thus rendered unable to "practice." Behavioral embryologists have demonstrated many correlations among behavioral changes in developing organisms, growth of the nervous system, establishment of new connections, and the onset of myelinization (Bekoff, 1978; Coghill, 1929; Gottlieb, 1973; Hamburger, 1970).

Direct genetic control over action patterns has been demonstrated in a large number of cases, both invertebrate and vertebrate (Fuller & Thompson, 1960; Manning, 1976), including such behaviors as fruitfly courtship (Ewing & Manning, 1967), lovebird nest building (Dilger, 1962), singing of doves (Lade & Thorpe, 1964), and many aspects of the behavior of dogs and other mammals (Scott & Fuller, 1965). In certain cases structural variations in the nervous system have been implicated, as in the control of species differences in cricket singing behavior (Bentley, 1971). Genetic control is implied directly in many evolutionary studies of the behavior of related species showing more divergence in areas of sympatry than allopatry (Brown, 1975).

Aspects of human behavior are encompassed by this viewpoint (Ehrman & Parsons, 1976; Hirsch, 1967; Vandenberg, 1968). In his prophetic book on the expression of emotions in man and animals, Charles Darwin (1872/1915) was clearly convinced of the overwhelming importance of genetic factors in the ontogeny of human facial expressions. This viewpoint has been sustained by subsequent work, demonstrating normal expressive development in blind infants (for example, Charlesworth & Kreutzer, 1973; Eibl-Eibesfeldt, 1972). The universal recurrence across cultures of similar patterns of expressive behavior has also been demonstrated (Ekman, 1973).

On the other hand, there are numerous illustrations of the divergence of expressive behavior between cultures. The influence of experience on the actual programming of expressive behaviors must be ubiquitous, however pervasive innate influences on the basic fixed action patterns may be. Although precursors of many mature action patterns can be discerned in the prenatal behavior of human embryos (Trevarthen, 1977), there can be no doubt as to the importance of learning in determination of the particular patterns of action in which they become incorporated. However, as with motor development in other organisms, the consequences of innate limitations on the perceptual side are not to be ignored, insofar as they provide the pathways for environmental influence on motor development.

A Last Word

The problem for the student of development is not whether behavior is learned or innate, but how genetic and environmental influences interact in the course of development. To overlook or overestimate the contribution of one or the other is to doom an investigation to failure. One achievement of lasting value, largely attributable to comparative ethology, is the reinstatement of genetic components as a key item in life's equation for ensuring the genesis of adaptive behavior through learning.

REFERENCES

Abramov, I. Interactions among chromatic mechanisms. In H. Spekreijse & L. H. van der Tweel (Eds.), *Spatial contrast: Report of a workshop.* New York: North Holland, 1977.

Baerends, G. P., & Baerends-van Roon, J. M. An introduction to the study of the ethology of cichlid fishes. *Behaviour Supplement,* 1950, *1,* 1–242.

Baerends, G. P., & Kruijt, J. P. Stimulus selection. In R. A. Hinde & J. Stevenson-Hinde (Eds.), *Constraints on learning.* Cambridge: Cambridge University Press, 1973.

Baptista, J. Wild housefinch sings white-crowned sparrow song. *Zeitschrift für Tierpsychologie,* 1972, *30,* 266–270.

Barlow, G. W. Modal action patterns. In T. A. Sebeok (Ed.), *How animals communicate.* Bloomington: Indiana University Press, 1977.

Bateson, P. P. G. Preferences for familiarity and novelty: A model for the simultaneous development of both. *Journal of Theoretical Biology,* 1973, *41,* 249–259.

Bateson, P. P. G. Rules and reciprocity in behavioural development. In P. P. G. Bateson & R. A. Hinde (Eds.), *Growing points in ethology.* Cambridge: Cambridge University Press, 1976.

Bateson, P. P. G. Sexual imprinting and optimal outbreeding. *Nature,* 1978, *273,* 659–660.

Bateson, P. P. G, & Jaeckel, J. B. Chicks' preferences for familiar and novel conspicuous objects after different periods of exposure. *Animal Behaviour,* 1976, *24,* 386–390.

Beecher, M., Peterson, M., Zoloth, S., Moody, D., & Stebbins, W. Perception of conspecific vocalizations by Japanese macaques: Evidence for selective attention and neural lateralization. *Brain, Behavior and Evolution,* in press.

Beer, C. G. Individual recognition of voice in the social behavior of birds. In D. S. Lehrman, R. A. Hinde, & E. Shaw (Eds.), *Advances in the study of behaviour* (Vol. 3). New York: Academic Press, 1970.

Bekoff, A. A neuroethological approach to the study of the ontogeny of coordinated behavior. In G. Burghardt & M. Bekoff (Eds.), *Ontogeny of behavior.* New York: Garland Press, 1978.

Bentley, D. R. Genetic control of an insect neuronal network. *Science,* 1971, *174,* 1139–1141.

Berlin, B., & Kay, P. *Basic color terms: Their universality and evolution.* Berkeley: University of California Press, 1969.

Bornstein, M. H. Color vision and color naming: A psychophysiological hypothesis of cultural difference. *Psychological Bulletin,* 1973, *80,* 257–285.

Bornstein, M. H. The influence of visual perception on culture. *American Anthropologist,* 1975, *77,* 774–798.

Bornstein, M. H. Perceptual development: Stability and change in feature perception. In M. H. Bornstein & W. Kessen (Eds.), *Psychological development from infancy.* Hillsdale, NJ: Lawrence Erlbaum Associates, 1979.

Bornstein, M. H., Kessen, W., & Weiskopf, S. The categories of hue in infancy. *Science,* 1976, *191,* 201–202. (a)

Bornstein, M. H., Kessen, W., & Weiskopf, S. Color vision and hue categorization in young human infants. *Journal of Experimental Psychology: Human Perception and Performance,* 1976, *2,* 115–129. (b)

Brown, J. L. *The evolution of behavior.* New York: Norton, 1975.

Bullock, T. H. (Ed.). *Recognition of complex acoustic signals.* Berlin: Dahlem Konferenzen, 1977.

Capranica, R. R. The evoked vocal response of the bullfrog. *Research Monographs,* 1965, *33.*

Capranica, R. R., Frishkopf, L., & Nevo, E. Encoding of geographic dialects in the auditory system of the cricket frog. *Science,* 1973, *182,* 1272–1275.

Carmichael, L. Ontogenetic development. In S. S. Stevens (Ed.), *Handbook of experimental psychology.* New York: Wiley, 1951.

Charlesworth, W. R., & Kreutzer, M. A. Facial expressions of infants and children. In P. Ekman (Ed.), *Darwin and facial expression.* New York: Academic Press, 1973.

Coghill, E. G. *Anatomy and the problem of behavior.* London: Cambridge University Press, 1929.

Cooke, F. Early learning and its effect on population structure. Studies of a wild population of snow geese. *Zeitschrift für Tierpsychologie,* 1978, *46,* 344–358.

Cornell, E. H. Infants' discrimination of photographs of faces following redundant presentation. *Journal of Experimental Child Psychology,* 1974, *18,* 98–106.

Cowan, P. J. Selective responses to the parental calls of different individual hens by young *Gallus gallus:* Auditory discrimination learning versus auditory imprinting. *Behavioral Biology,* 1974, *19,* 541–545.

Crane, J. *Fiddler crabs of the world. Ocypodidae: Genus Uca.* Princeton, NJ: Princeton University Press, 1975.

Cullen, E. Adaptations in the Kittiwake to cliff-nesting. *Ibis,* 1957, *99,* 272–302.

Cutting, J. E., & Rosner, B. Categories and boundaries in speech and music. *Perception and Psychophysics,* 1974, *16,* 564–570.

Darwin, C. *The expression of the emotions in man and animals.* New York: Appleton, 1915. (Originally published, 1872.)

Daumer, K. Reizmetrische Untersuchung des Farbensehens der Bienen. *Zeitschrift für vergleichende Physiologie,* 1956, *38,* 413–478.

Daumer, K. Blumenfarben, wie sie die Bienen sehen. *Zeitschrift für vergleichende Physiologie,* 1958, *41,* 49–110.

Dawkins, R. Hierarchical organisation. In P. P. G. Bateson & R. A. Hinde (Eds.), *Growing points in ethology.* Cambridge: Cambridge University Press, 1976.

DeValois, R. Central mechanisms of color vision. In R. Jung (Ed.), *Handbook of sensory physiology* (Vol. 7). New York: Springer-Verlag, 1973.

DeValois, R., Abramov, I., & Jacobs, G. Analysis of response patterns of L.G.N. cells. *Journal of the Optical Society of America,* 1966, *56,* 966–977.

Dilger, W. Behavior and genetics. In E. Bliss (Ed.), *Roots of behavior.* New York: Harper & Row, 1962.

Dooling, R. J., & Searcy, M. A. Early perceptual selectivity in the swamp sparrow (*Melospiza georgiana*). *Developmental Psychobiology,* in press.

Ehrman, L., & Parsons, P. A. *The genetics of behavior.* Sunderland, MA: Sinauer, 1976.

Eibl-Eibesfeldt, I. Similarities and differences between cultures in expressive movements. In R. A. Hinde (Ed.), *Non-verbal communication.* Cambridge: Cambridge University Press, 1972.

Eilers, R. E., & Minifie, F. D. Fricative discrimination in early infancy. *Journal of Speech and Hearing Research,* 1975, *18,* 158–169.

Eilers, R. E., Wilson, W. R., & Moore, J. M. Developmental changes in speech discrimination in infants. *Journal of Speech and Hearing Research,* 1977, *20,* 766–780.

Eimas, P. D. Auditory and linguistic processing of the cues for place of articulation by infants. *Perception and Psychophysics,* 1974, *16,* 513–521.

Eimas, P. D. Speech perception in early infancy. In L. B. Cohen & P. Salapatek (Eds.), *Infant perception: From sensation to cognition* (Vol. 2). New York: Academic Press, 1975.

Ekman, P. Cross-cultural studies of facial expression. In P. Ekman (Ed.), *Darwin and facial expression.* New York: Academic Press, 1973.

Evans, R. M. Imprinting and mobility in young ring-billed gulls, *Larus delawarensis. Animal Behaviour Monographs,* 1970, *3,* 193–248.

Evans, R. M. Development of an auditory discrimination in domestic chicks (*Gallus gallus*). *Animal Behaviour,* 1972, *20,* 77–87.

Evans, R. M. Auditory discrimination-learning in young ring-billed gulls (*Larus delawarensis*). *Animal Behaviour,* 1977, *25,* 140–146.

Evans, R. M., & Mattson, M. E. Development of selective responses to individual maternal vocalizations in young *Gallus gallus. Canadian Journal of Zoology,* 1972, *50,* 777–780.

Evarts, E. V. Central control of movement. *Neurosciences Research Program Bulletin,* 1971, *9,* 1–170.

Ewing, A. W., & Manning, A. The evolution and genetics of insect behavior. *Annual Review of Entomology,* 1967, *12,* 471–494.

Fabricius, E. Zur Ethologie junger Anatiden. *Acta Zoologica Fennica,* 1951, *68,* 1–178.

Fabricius, E., & Boyd, H. Experiments on the following reaction of ducklings. *Report of the Wildfowl Trust,* 1954, *6,* 84–89.

Fagan, J. F. Infants' recognition of invariant features of faces. *Child Development,* 1976, *47,* 627–638.

Falls, J. B. Function of territorial song in the white-throated sparrow. In R. A. Hinde (Ed.), *Bird vocalizations.* Cambridge: Cambridge University Press, 1969.

Falls, J. B. Bird song and territorial behavior. In L. Krames, P. Pliner, & T. Alloway (Eds.), *Aggression, dominance and individual spacing. Advances in the study of communication and affect* (Vol 4). New York: Plenum Press, 1978.

Fantz, R. L. Form preferences in newly hatched chicks. *Journal of Comparative and Physiological Psychology,* 1957, *50,* 422–430.

Fantz, R. L. Visual experience in infants: Decreased attention to familiar patterns relative to novel ones. *Science,* 1964, *146,* 668–670.

Fantz, R. L. Ontogeny of perception. In A. M. Schrier, H. F. Harlow, & F. Stollnitz (Eds.), *Behavior of non-human primates* (Vol. 2). New York: Academic Press, 1965.

Fantz, R. L., Fagan, J. F., & Miranda, S. B. Early perceptual development as shown by visual discrimination, selectivity, and memory with varying stimulus and population parameters. In L. Cohen & P. Salapatek (Eds.), *Infant perception: From sensation to cognition* (Vol. 1). New York: Academic Press, 1975.

Fishbein, H. D. *Evolution, development and children's learning.* Santa Monica, CA: Goodyear, 1976.

Fuller, J. L., & Thompson, W. R. *Behavior genetics.* New York: Wiley, 1960.

Gautier, J. P., & Gautier, A. Communication in old world monkeys. In T. A. Sebeok (Ed.), *How animals communicate.* Bloomington: Indiana University Press, 1977.

Gibson, E. J. *Principles of perceptual learning and development.* Englewood Cliffs, NJ: Prentice Hall, 1969.

Gibson, J. J. *The senses considered as perceptual systems.* Boston: Houghton Mifflin, 1966.

Goodwin, E. B., & Hess, E. H. Innate visual form preferences in the pecking behavior of young chicks. *Behaviour,* 1969, *34,* 223–237.

Goren , C. C., Sarty, M., & Wu, P. Visual following and pattern discrimination of face-like stimuli by new born infants. *Pediatrics,* 1975, *56,* 544–549.

Gottlieb, G. *Development of species identification in birds.* Chicago: University of Chicago Press, 1971.

Gottlieb, G. (Ed.). *Studies on the development of behavior and the nervous system* (Vol. 1, *Behavioral embryology*). New York: Academic Press, 1973.

Gottlieb, G. On the acoustic basis of species identification in wood ducklings (*Aix sponsa*). *Journal of Comparative and Physiological Psychology*, 1974, *87*, 1038–1048.

Green, S. Communication by a graded vocal system in Japanese monkeys. In L. A. Rosenblum (Ed.), *Primate behavior* (Vol. 4). New York: Academic Press, 1975.

Greenberg, J. H. Language universals: A research frontier. *Science*, 1969, *166*, 473–478.

Griffin, D. R. *Listening in the dark*. New York: Dover, 1974.

Hailman, J. P. Ontogeny of an instinct. *Behaviour Supplement*, 1967, *15*, 1–159.

Hainline, L. Developmental changes in visual scanning of face and nonface patterns by infants. *Journal of Experimental Child Psychology*, 1978, *25*, 90–115.

Haith, M. M., Bergman, T., & Mare, M. J. Eye contact and face scanning in early infancy. *Science*, 1977, *198*, 853–855.

Hamburger, V. Embryonic motility in vertebrates. In F. O. Schmitt (Ed.), *The neurosciences: Second study program*. New York: Rockefeller University Press, 1970.

Harlow, H. F. Sexual behavior in rhesus monkeys. In F. A. Beach (Ed.), *Sex and behavior*. New York: Wiley, 1965.

Heider, E. Universals in color naming and memory. *Journal of Experimental Psychology*, 1972, *93*, 10–20.

Heiligenberg, W. Theoretical and experimental approaches to spatial aspects of electrolocation. *Journal of Comparative Physiology*, 1975, *103*, 247–272.

Held, R. Plasticity in sensory-motor systems. *Scientific American*, 1965, *213*, 84–94.

Held, R., & Hein, A. Movement produced stimulation in the development of visually guided behavior. *Journal of Comparative and Physiological Psychology*, 1963, *56*, 872–876.

Herman, R. M., Grillner, S., Stein, P. S. G., & Stuart, D. G. (Eds.). *Neural control of locomotion*. New York: Plenum Press, 1976.

Herrnstein, R. J., Loveland, D. H., & Cable, C. Natural concepts in pigeons. *Journal of Experimental Psychology: Animal Behavior Processes*, 1976, *2*, 285–302.

Hess, E. H. Natural preferences of chicks and ducklings for objects of different colors. *Psychological Reports*, 1956, *2*, 477–487.

Hess, E. H. Imprinting and the "critical period" concept. In E. L. Bliss (Ed.), *Roots of behavior*. New York: Harper, 1962.

Hess, E. H. *Imprinting*. New York: Van Nostrand, 1973.

Hess, E. H., & Gogel, W. C. Natural preferences of the chick for objects of different colors. *Journal of Psychology*, 1954, *38*, 483–493.

Hinde, R. A. Ethological models and the concept of drive. *British Journal for the Philosophy of Science*, 1956, *6*, 321–331.

Hinde, R. A. *Animal behavior: A synthesis of ethology and comparative psychology*. New York: McGraw-Hill, 1970.

Hirsch, J. (Ed.). *Behavior-genetic analysis*. New York: McGraw-Hill, 1967.

Hogan, J. A. How young chicks learn to recognize food. In R. A. Hinde & J. Stevenson-Hinde (Eds.), *Constraints on learning*. New York: Academic Press, 1973.

Hopkins, C. D. Electric communication in fish. *American Scientist*, 1974, *62*, 426–437.

Hurvich, L., & Jameson, D. An opponent-process theory of color vision. *Psychological Review*, 1957, *64*, 383–404.

Immelmann, K. Song development in the zebra finch and other estrildid finches. In R. A. Hinde (Ed.), *Bird vocalizations*. Cambridge: Cambridge University Press, 1969.

Immelmann, K. Sexual and other long-term aspects of imprinting in birds and other species. *Advances in the Study of Behavior*, 1972, *4*, 147–174.

Impekoven, M., & Gold, P. S. Parental origins of parent-young interactions in birds: A naturalistic approach. In G. Gottlieb (Ed.), *Behavioral embryology*. New York: Academic Press, 1973.

Kear, J. Colour preference in young Anatidae. *Ibis*, 1964, *106*, 361–369.

Koltermann, R. Rassen- und artspezifische Duftbewertung bei der Honigbiene und ökologische Adaptation. *Journal of Comparative Physiology,* 1973, *85,* 327–360.

Konishi, M. Effects of deafening on song development in two species of juncos. *Condor,* 1964, *66,* 85–102.

Konishi, M. The role of auditory feedback in the control of vocalization in the white-crowned sparrow. *Zeitschrift für Tierpsychologie,* 1965, *22,* 770–783.

Konishi, M. Auditory environment and vocal development in birds. In R. D. Walk & H. L. Pick (Eds.), *Perception and experience.* New York: Plenum Press, 1978.

Kortlandt, A. Aspects and prospects of the concept of instinct (vicissitudes of the hierarchy theory). *Archives Neerlandaises de Zoologie,* 1955, *11,* 155–284.

Kovach, J. K. Interaction of innate and acquired: Color preferences and early exposure learning in chicks. *Journal of Comparative and Physiological Psychology,* 1971, *75,* 386–398.

Kovach, J. K., & Hickox, J. E. Color preferences and early perceptual discrimination learning in domestic chicks. *Developmental Psychobiology,* 1971, *4,* 255–267.

Kroodsma, D. The effect of large song repertoires on neighbor "recognition" in male song sparrows. *Condor,* 1976, *78,* 97–99.

Kroodsma, D. Aspects of learning in the ontogeny of bird song: Where, from whom, when, how many, which and how accurately? In G. Burghardt & M. Bekoff (Eds.), *Ontogeny of behavior.* New York: Garland Press, 1978.

Kuhl, P. K. Speech perception in early infancy: The acquisition of speech-sound categories. In S. K. Hirsh, D. H. Eldredge, I. J. Hirsh, & S. R. Silverman (Eds.), *Hearing and Davis: Essays honoring Hallowell Davis.* St. Louis: Washington University Press, 1976.

Kuhl, P. K., & Miller, J. D. Speech perception in early infancy: Discrimination of speech-sound categories. *Journal of the Acoustical Society of America,* 1974, *58,* Supplement 1, 56.

Lade, B. I., & Thorpe, W. H. Dove songs as innately coded patterns of specific behaviour. *Nature,* 1964, *212,* 366–368.

Lashley, K. S. The mechanism of vision. XV. Preliminary studies of the rat's capacity for detail vision. *Journal of General Psychology,* 1938, *18,* 123–193.

Lasky, R., Syrdal-Lasky, A., & Klein, R. VOT discrimination by four to six and a half month old infants from Spanish environments. *Journal of Experimental Child Psychology,* 1975, *20,* 215–225.

Lauer, J., & Lindauer, M. Die Beteiligung von Lernprozessen bei der Orientierung. *Fortschritte der Zoologie,* 1973, *21,* 349–370.

Liberman, A. M., Cooper, F. S., Shankweiler, D., & Studdert-Kennedy, M. Perception of the speech code. *Psychological Review,* 1967, *74,* 431–461.

Liberman, A. M., Harris, K. S., Hoffman, H. S., & Griffith, B. C. The discrimination of speech sounds within and across phoneme boundaries. *Journal of Experimental Psychology,* 1957, *54,* 358–368.

Liberman, A. M., Harris, K. S., Kinney, J. A., & Lane. H. The discrimination of relative-onset time of the components of certain speech and nonspeech patterns. *Journal of Experimental Psychology,* 1961, *61,* 379–388.

Lindauer, M. Lernen und Gedächtnis-versuche an der Honigbiene. *Naturwissenschaften,* 1970, *57,* 463–467.

Lindauer, M. Evolutionary aspects of orientation and learning. In G. Baerends, C. Beer, & A. Manning (Eds.), *Function and evolution in behaviour.* Oxford: Clarendon Press, 1975.

Lisker, L., & Abramson, A. S. A cross-language study of voicing in initial stops: Acoustical measurements. *Word,* 1964, *20,* 384–422.

Lissmann, H. W. On the function and evolution of electric organs in fish. *Journal of Experimental Biology,* 1958, *35,* 156–191.

Lorenz, K. Uber den Begriff der Instinkthandlung. *Folia Biotheoretica,* 1937, *2,* 17–50.

Lorenz, K. Vergleichende Bewegungs-studien an Anatinen. *Journal für Ornithologie,* 1941, *89,* 194–293.

Lorenz, K. The comparative method in studying innate behaviour patterns. *Symposium of the Society for Experimental Biology,* 1950, *4,* 221–268.

Lorenz, K. *Studies in animal and human behaviour* (Vol. 1) (R. Martin, trans.). Cambridge, MA: Harvard University Press, 1970.

Lorenz, K., & Tinbergen, N. Taxis und Instinkthandlung in der Eirollbewegung der Graugans, I. *Zeitschrift für Tierpsychologie,* 1938, *2,* 1–29.

Mackintosh, N. J. *The psychology of animal learning.* New York: Academic Press, 1974.

Manning, A. Drosophila and the evolution of behaviour. *Viewpoints in Biology,* 1965, *4,* 125–169.

Manning, A. Evolution of behavior. In J. L. McGaugh (Ed.), *Psychobiology.* New York: Academic Press, 1971.

Manning, A. The place of genetics in the study of behaviour. In P. P. G. Bateson & R. A. Hinde (Eds.), *Growing points in ethology.* Cambridge: Cambridge University Press, 1976.

Marler, P. The filtering of external stimuli during instinctive behavior. In W. H. Thorpe & O. L. Zangwill (Eds.), *Current problems in animal behaviour.* Cambridge: Cambridge University Press, 1961.

Marler, P. Communication in monkeys and apes. In I. DeVore (Ed.), *Primate behavior.* New York: Holt, Rinehart & Winston, 1965.

Marler, P. A comparative approach to vocal learning: Song development in white-crowned sparrows. *Journal of Comparative and Physiological Psychology,* 1970, *71,* 1–25. (a)

Marler, P. Vocalizations of East African monkeys. I. Red colobus. *Folia Primatologica,* 1970, *13,* 81–91. (b)

Marler, P. Sensory templates in species-specific behavior. In J. Fentress (Ed.), *Simpler networks: An approach to patterned behavior and its foundations.* Sunderland, MA: Sinauer, 1976. (a)

Marler, P. Social organization, communication and graded signals: The chimpanzee and the gorilla. In P. P. G. Bateson & R. A. Hinde (Eds.), *Growing points in ethology.* Cambridge: Cambridge University Press, 1976. (b)

Marler, P. Development and learning of recognition systems. In T. H. Bullock (Ed.), *Recognition of complex and acoustic signals.* Berlin: Dahlem Konferenzen, 1977.

Marler, P., & Hamilton, W. J., III. *Mechanisms of animal behavior.* New York: Wiley, 1967.

Marler, P., & Mundinger, P. Vocal learning in birds. In H. Moltz (Ed.), *The ontogeny of vertebrate behavior.* New York: Academic Press, 1971.

Marler, P., & Peters, S. Selective vocal learning in a sparrow. *Science,* 1977, *198,* 519–521.

Marler, P., & Tamura, M. Culturally transmitted patterns of vocal behavior in sparrows. *Science,* 1964, *146,* 1483–1486.

Marler, P., & Tenaza, R. Signaling behavior of apes with special reference to vocalization. In T. A. Sebeok (Ed.), *How animals communicate.* Bloomington: Indiana University Press, 1977.

Mason, W. A. The social behavior of monkeys and apes. In I. DeVore (Ed.), *Primate behavior.* New York: Holt, Rinehart & Winston, 1965.

Mattson, M. E., & Evans, R. M. Visual imprinting and auditory-discrimination learning in young of the canvasback and semiparasitic redhead (*Anatidae*). *Canadian Journal of Zoology,* 1974, *52,* 421–427.

McLannahan, H. M. C. Some aspects of the ontogeny of cliff nesting behaviour in the Kittiwake (*Rissa trydactyla*) and the herring gull (*Larus argentatus*). *Behaviour,* 1973, *44,* 36–88.

Menzel, R. Untersuchungen zum Erlernen von Spektralfarben durch die Honigbiene. *Zeitschrift für vergleichende Physiologie,* 1967, *56,* 22–62.

Miller, D. E., & Emlen, J. T. Individual chick recognition and family integrity in the ring-billed gull. *Behaviour,* 1975, *52,* 124–144.

Miller, J., Wier, C., Pastore, R., Kelly, W., & Dooling, R. Discrimination and labelling of noise-buzz sequences with varying noise-lead times: An example of categorical perception. *Journal of the Acoustical Society of America,* 1976, *60,* 410–417.

Morse, P. The discrimination of speech and nonspeech stimuli in early infancy. *Journal of Experimental Child Psychology*, 1972, *14*, 477–492.

Nelson, K. Does the holistic study of behavior have a future? In P. P. G. Bateson & P. H. Klopfer (Eds.), *Perspectives in ethology*. New York: Plenum Press, 1973.

Nicolai, J. Familientradition in der Gesangsentwicklung des Gimpels (*Pyrrhula pyrrhula* L.). *Journal für Ornithologie*, 1959, *100*, 39–46.

Pastore, R. E. Categorical perception: A critical re-evaluation. In S. K. Hirsh, D. H. Eldredge, I. J. Hirsh, & S. R. Silverman (Eds.), *Hearing and Davis: Essays honoring Hallowell Davis*. St. Louis: Washington University Press, 1976.

Peters, S., Searcy, W., & Marler, P. Species song discrimination in choice experiments with territorial male swamp and song sparrows. *Animal Behaviour*, in press.

Pisoni, D. B. Identification and discrimination of the relative onset time of two component tones: Implications for voicing perception in stops. *Journal of the Acoustical Society of America*, 1977, *61*, 1352–1361.

Pisoni, D. B. On the perception of speech sounds as biologically significant signals *Brain, Behavior and Evolution*, in press.

Ratliff, F. On the psychophysiological bases of universal color terms. *Proceedings of the American Philosophical Society*, 1976, *120*, 311–330.

Rosch, E. On the internal structure of perceptual and semantic categories. In T. E. Moore (Ed.), *Cognitive development and the acquisition of language*. New York: Academic Press, 1973.

Roth, L. M. A study of mosquito behavior. *American Midland Naturalist*, 1948, *40*, 265–352.

Schleidt, W. Die historische Entwicklung der Begriffe "angeborenes auslösendes Schema" und "angeborener Auslömechanismus" in der Ethologie. *Zeitschrift für Tierpsychologie*, 1962, *19*, 697–722.

Schneider, D. Olfactory receptors for the sexual attractant (bombykol) of the silk moth. In F. O. Schmitt (Ed.), *The neurosciences: Second study program*. New York: Rockefeller University Press, 1970.

Schutz, F. Sexuelle Prägung der Anatiden. *Zeitschrift für Tierpsychologie*, 1965, *22*, 50–103.

Scott, J. P., & Fuller, J. L. *Genetics and the social behavior of the dog*. Chicago: University of Chicago Press, 1965.

Shorey, H. H. *Animal communication by pheromones*. New York: Academic Press, 1976.

Smith, N. G. Adaptations of cliff nesting in some Arctic gulls (*Larus*). *Ibis*, 1966, *108*, 68–83.

Snowdon, C. The response of non-human animals to speech and to species-specific sounds. *Brain, Behavior and Evolution*, in press.

Snowdon, C., & Pola, Y. V. Interspecific and intraspecific responses to synthesized pygmy marmoset vocalizations. *Animal Behaviour*, 1978, *26*, 192–206.

Sonnemann, P., & Sjölander, S. Effects of cross-fostering on the sexual imprinting of the female zebra finch *Taeniopygia guttata*. *Zeitschrift für Tierpsychologie*, 1977, *45*, 337–348.

Sperry, R. W. Mechanisms of neural maturation. In S. S. Stevens (Ed.), *Handbook of experimental psychology*. New York: Wiley, 1951.

Spieth, H. T. Mating behavior within the genus *Drosophila* (Diptera). *Bulletin of the American Museum of Natural History*, 1952, *99*, 401–474.

Strange, W., & Jenkins, J. J. Role of linguistic experience in the perception of speech. In R. D. Walk & H. L. Pick (Eds.), *Perception and experience*. New York: Plenum Press, 1978.

Streeter, L. A. Language perception of 2-month-old infants shows effects of both innate mechanisms and experience. *Nature*, 1976, *259*, 39–41.

Struhsaker, T. T. *The red colobus monkey*. Chicago: University of Chicago Press, 1975.

Studdert-Kennedy, M. Universals in phonetic structure and their role in linguistic communication. In T. H. Bullock (Ed.), *Recognition of complex acoustic signals*. Berlin: Dahlem Konferenzen, 1977.

Studdert-Kennedy, M., Liberman, A. M., Harris, K. S., & Cooper, F. S. Motor theory of speech perception: A reply to Lane's critical review. *Psychological Review*, 1970, *77*, 234–249.

Sutherland, N. S. Outlines of a theory of visual pattern recognition in animals and man. *Proceedings of the Royal Society, B,* 1968, *171,* 297–317.

Sutherland, N. S. Object recognition. In E. C. Carterette & M. P. Friedman (Eds.), *Handbook of perception* (Vol. 3). New York: Academic Press, 1973.

Szekely, G. Developmental aspects of locomotion. In R. M. Herman, S. Grillner, P. S. G. Stein, & D. G. Stuart (Eds.), *Neural control of locomotion.* New York: Plenum Press, 1976.

Thorpe, W. H. The learning of song patterns by birds, with especial reference to the song of the chaffinch, *Fringilla coelebs. Ibis,* 1958, *100,* 535–570.

Thorpe, W. H. *Bird song: The biology of vocal communication and expression in birds.* Cambridge: Cambridge University Press, 1961.

Thorpe, W. H., & Hall-Craggs, J. Sound production and perception in birds as related to the general principles of pattern perception. In P. P. G. Bateson & R. A. Hinde (Eds.), *Growing points in ethology.* Cambridge: Cambridge University Press, 1976.

Tinbergen, N. Social releasers and the experimental method required for their study. *Wilson Bulletin,* 1948, *60,* 6–52.

Tinbergen, N. The hierarchical organisation of nervous mechanisms underlying instinctive behaviour. *Symposia of the Society for Experimental Biology,* 1950, *4,* 305–312.

Tinbergen, N. *The study of instinct.* Oxford: Clarendon Press, 1951.

Tinbergen, N. *The herring gull's world.* London: Collins, 1953.

Tinbergen, N. Comparative studies of the behaviour of gulls (Laridae): A progress report. *Behaviour,* 1959, *15,* 1–70.

Tinbergen, N. *The animal in its world* (Vols. 1 & 2). Cambridge, MA: Harvard University Press, 1973.

Tinbergen, N., & Kuenen, D. J. Uber die ausloesenden und die richtunggebenden Reizsituationen der Sperrbewegung von jungen Drosseln (*Turdus m. merula* L. und *T. e. ericetorum* Turton). *Zeitschrift für Tierpsychologie,*1939, *3,* 37–60.

Tinbergen, N., & Perdeck A. C. On the stimulus situation releasing the begging response in the newly hatched herring gull chick (*Larus a. argentatus* Pont.). *Behaviour,* 1950, *3,* 1–39.

Tischner, H., & Schief, A. Fluggerausch und Schallwarnehmung bei *Aedes aegypti* L. (Culicidae). *Verhandlungen Deutsche Zoologie Gesellschaft,* 1954, *51,* 453–460.

Trevarthen, C. Neuroembryology and the development of perception. In F. Falkner & J. M. Tanner (Eds.), *Human growth: A comprehensive treatise.* New York: Plenum Press, 1977.

Vandenberg. S. *Progress in human behavior genetics.* Baltimore: Johns Hopkins University Press, 1968.

von Frisch, K. *The dance, language, and orientation of bees.* Cambridge, MA: Harvard University Press, 1967.

von Uexküll, J. *Umwelt und Innenwelt der Tiere.* Berlin: Springer-Verlag, 1921.

Waddington, C. H. *The strategy of the genes.* London: Allen & Unwin, 1957.

Walk, R. D. The study of visual depth and distance perception in animals. In D. S. Lehrman, R. A. Hinde, & E. Shaw (Eds.), *Advances in the study of behavior* (Vol. 1). New York: Academic Press, 1965.

Walk, R. D. Depth perception and experience. In R. D. Walk & H. L. Pick (Eds.), *Perception and experience.* New York: Plenum Press, 1978.

Walk, R. D., & Gibson, E. J. A comparative and analytical study of visual depth perception. *Psychological Monographs,* 1961, *75*(15, Whole No. 519).

Weidmann, R., & Weidmann, U. An analysis of the stimulus situation releasing food-begging in the black-headed gull. *Animal Behaviour,* 1958, *6,* 114.

Weiss, P. Experimental analysis of coordination by the disarrangement of central-peripheral relations. *Symposium of the Society for Experimental Biology,* 1950, *4,* 92–111.

Wendler, G. Lokomotion: Das Ergebnis zentral-peripheren Interaktion. *Verhandlungen Deutsche Zoologische Gesellschaft,* 1978, 80–96.

Whorf, B. *Language, thought and reality.* Cambridge, MA: MIT Press, 1964.

Wright, A., & Cumming, W. Color-naming functions for the pigeon. *Journal of Experimental Analysis of Behavior,* 1971, *15,* 7–17.

Yodlowski, M. L., Kreithen, M. L., & Keeton, W. T. Detection of atmospheric infrasound by homing pigeons. *Science,* 1977, *265,* 725–726.

Zoloth, S., & Green, S. Monkey vocalizations and human speech: Parallels in perception? *Brain, Behavior and Evolution,* in press.

Zoloth, S. R., Petersen, M. R., Beecher, M. D., Green, S., Marler, P., Moody, D. B., & Stebbins, W. Species-specific perceptual processing of vocal sounds by monkeys. *Science,* 1979, *204,* 870–873.

7

Cross-Cultural
Developmental Psychology

Marc H. Bornstein
Princeton University
and
University College London

INTRODUCTION

James I of England (1566-1625) was surely among the first to propose a cross-cultural study of psychological development. Long interested in the Bible, James sought to determine man's original language, that of Adam and Eve. To do so he conceived a unique experimental situation: James proposed to place two infants on an otherwise uninhabited island in the care of a deaf-mute nurse. Doubtlessly he reasoned that if the two spontaneously developed speech, theirs would be the "natural" language of man.

This chapter focuses on psychological issues such as those implied in James's proposal. James's experiment is as unacceptable ethically as it is less than adequate methodologically. Yet his idea is seminal and implies a very important and complex type of comparison, viz. development in the context of culture.

Why make cross-cultural developmental comparisons? Several motives may be ascertained. First, many lay people are curious about human development in other cultures, and for this reason social commentary has as a matter of course included reports of child life (from the Athenian history of Spartan childrearing practices to the Spanish explorer Pedro Simon's sixteenth-century reports on head flattening of infants among the South American Panche Indians to the American journalist Hendrick Smith's [1977] recent account of Russian children in school). Thus, a major motive of cross-cultural developmental research has been to augment our understanding of other (particular) cultures.

Further, academic anthropologists, sociologists, and psychologists have long sought to compare humans of different ages from different regions of the world (e.g., Bronfenbrenner, 1970; Erikson, 1950; Kessen, 1975; LeVine, 1970; Montagu, 1974; Munroe & Munroe, 1975; Werner, 1979; Whiting & Whiting, 1960). The rationale for submitting human development in different cultures to psychological study derives from the extraordinary power cross-cultural comparisons furnish social scientific analysis.

Cross-cultural developmental *descriptions* of behavior are ipso facto the most comprehensive. Theoretically, they encompass the full spectrum of human variation at all ages under all experiences in all places. Delimiting the full range of behavior in turn permits an inclusive definition of "normal" behavior as well as the delineation of development which may be considered "atypical." Description also provides information about the degree to which psychological phenomena may be "universal" or unique to a given period in the life cycle. Further, as Achenbach in this volume suggests, description itself is prerequisite to other formal rationales, most significantly explanation.

Cross-cultural developmental analysis helps to *explain* the origins and contingent developmental course of the widest possible variety of behaviors. This type of analysis helps to distinguish behaviors that emerge and develop in a culture-dependent (*emic*) fashion from those that are independent of culture (*etic*). Further, genetic universals can be distinguished from structural ones. Finally, this analysis lays bare how forces that vary globally (e.g., family structure, degree of urbanization, nationality, religion, economic system or status, etc.) differentially mold human behavior.

Description and explanation therefore account for two major rationales motivating cross-cultural developmental study. But cross-cultural developmental comparison also *promotes psychological investigation and understanding*. For example, it provides investigators from the social and biological sciences with unique opportunities to test particular hypotheses or theoretical predictions. Through such study variables are exposed that an ethnocentric world view otherwise tends to mask. Finally, cross-cultural phenomena also often suggest developmental studies and vice versa.

Although the desire to study behavior in this way and to assess its origins and development by crossing cultures was expressed at least as early as the sixteenth century, the deed is nevertheless very modern. Today, cross-cultural developmental studies are ineluctably bound up with the substance of general psychology. The idea of discussing physical development, perception, cognition, language, or any of a variety of social behaviors in any degree of depth without making developmental comparisons that cross cultures is (charitably) thought to constitute short-sighted scholarship. A. R. Luria (1930/1978) has put the rationale and mandate most succinctly:

...no psychological function can be understood except in terms of its development (the genetic approach) and its particular social conditions (the sociological approach) [p. 45].

This chapter surveys cross-cultural developmental psychology. The questions with which is it concerned include the following. What is the history of cross-cultural developmental study? How does it proceed? With which topics it is concerned? What has a half-century of cross-cultural developmental comparison contributed to our understanding of culture, of development, and of human behavior? Finally, in which direction will future cross-cultural developmental study most profitably move?

I do not attempt here either to define or to review the concepts of "culture" or "development" as they influence psychological study because these tasks are admirably accomplished by Jahoda and by Baldwin and Achenbach in this volume. Rather, I assume and attempt to build on the reader's background familiarity with them.

The chapter is divided conceptually into two halves. The first concerns the nature and the second the substance of cross-cultural developmental comparison. In the first half, history and methodology are discussed. In the second half, the contributions of this method of comparison are illustrated through a review of selected areas of research. The chapter concludes with an assessment of past problems and future prospects for cross-cultural developmental psychology.

ORIGINS: HISTORICAL AND PHILOSOPHICAL

Cross-cultural developmental comparison has its origins in many academic disciplines, including philosophy, history, biology, and anthropology. Select highlights of each can be mentioned briefly to set this chapter in context. Romantic fancies, like Rousseau's "noble savage," derived from considerations of development in the context of alternative cultures. Epistemological inquiry provoked many other philosophers, following Bacon and Descartes (see Jahoda, in this volume), to ponder the origins and development of mind and morals under widely varying social conditons. Early historical commentary, such as that of De Toqueville, Spengler, and Huizinga, has seemed bent on analyzing the characteristics of a society or of an age, psychological characteristics that are, as Compte observed, transmitted from one generation to another.

Although Darwin commented only very little on cross-cultural developmental comparisons per se, his spiritual influence was extraordinary even in this area and inspired the widened scientific study of human development in many cultures: Galton in Great Britain on the inheritance of genius, Binet in France on testing, Hall in the United States on objective observation, and Freud in central Europe on psychosexual development all followed the naturalist's lead. Yet a second biological connection between culture and development derived from the nineteenth century view that the child and the "primitive" both recapitulated early stages of man's evolutionary history (see Endnote 1).

Historically, anthropology has contributed more to the theory and practice of cross-cultural developmental study than has any other discipline. Anthropologists have made two principal substantive contributions. First, they have systematically and nearly single-handedly widened our knowledge of child life: Anthropological ethnographies document cultural information about children the world over that might have otherwise gone unrecognized or simply been lost.[1] Second, formal observations of cultural dimensions of personality and cognition were conducted originally by anthropologists. It is out of these efforts that psychology's orientation grew most directly. For example, in the first half of this century, personality was deemed an extension of culture, and this view of its plasticity brought it appropriately under the purview of anthropological analysis. The best-known early investigations in this area included Bronislaw Malinowski's (1927/1966) studies of the universality of Freudian developmental psychodynamics, Margaret Mead's (1935) studies of the influence of childrearing patterns on the socialization of sex roles, and Ruth Benedict's (1938) studies of the mechanisms by which cultural customs, beliefs, and knowledge are transmitted across generations. Likewise, human cognition received the early attention of anthropologists. Among many others, Franz Boas (1911), Lucien Lévy-Bruhl (1923/1966), Alfred Kroeber (1948), and Claude Lévi-Strauss (1966) particulary examined and compared cultural modes of thought—rational and irrational, primitive and civilized.

Beyond these substantive contributions, anthropology first served to sensitize psychology to culture and to the limitations inherent in ethnocentric science. Writing in the *Handbook of Research Methods in Child Development,* Whiting and Whiting (1960) observed that:

> If children are studied within the confines of a single culture, many events are taken as natural, obvious, or a part of human nature and are therefore not reported and not considered as variables. It is only when it is discovered that other peoples do not follow these practices that have been attributed to human nature that they are adopted as legitimate variables [p. 933].

---

[1]It is intriguing to observe that the status of the anthropologist in the field is analogous to that of the child being socialized.

The Whitings (1960) have further observed that, "even when individual variation...within western society suggests the presence of an important variable, the range of variation is often very small in contrast with its range in the societies of the world at large [p. 933]." Thus anthropology provides knowledge of where a particular society stands in relation to the range, helping psychology (and that society) to determine norms.

Although at the beginning of this century Wundt (1916) attempted to promote an interest among psychologists in the analysis of "cultural products," neither cross-cultural experimentation nor development were his concerns. Among the earliest explicitly psycho-cultural studies of development in non-Western society was Kidd's (1906) monograph, *Savage Childhood*. Interest in cross-cultural developmental psychology has grown exponentially since the turn of the century. An analysis of publications in the psychological journal *Child Development* helps to illustrate that course of growth. Between 1930 (when the journal was founded) and 1965, an average of about two cross-cultural articles appeared every five years; the first to refer to itself specifically as cross-cultural was published only in 1945 (Bullen, 1945). Between 1965 and 1969, about one article appeared every year; in the next five years (1970-1974), about three per year were published; and in the last five-year period (1975-1979) almost two per year have appeared. Content analysis of these publications shows that most have focused on childhood, some on adolescence, very few on infancy, and none on the elderly. Further, whereas publications related to physical development predominated at the beginning, more recently a rather even distribution among studies of perception, cognition, language, and social development has prevailed.

Psychological studies that have crossed cultures have emphasized both similarities and developmental differences (see Jahoda, in this volume). When speaking of divergence, psychologists have been prone to dichotomize its sources as genetic or environmental. Although both may excite equal interest, genetic differences among groups are fixed and require less elaboration from a psychological standpoint. Environmentally determined differences are, by contrast, more tractable and amenable to psychological analysis. They may either reflect the influence of ecology, for example, population density, or an individual's differential experiences, for example, the customs, language, educational system, or particular socialization processes characteristic of a culture.

An interest in similarities and behavioral universals has persistently rivaled this focus on cultural difference. Again, genetic and environmental determinants have been invoked. Human similarities are in large part ascribable to shared genetic heritage; it is paradoxical but true that men are as much similar as they are individual and unique. As a consequence, cross-cultural developmental comparisons have recognized in genetics and man's shared biology bases for a shared psychology. Moreover, physical and social environments foster similarity. All societies require certain behaviors of their member citizens (for example, care of infants and young, socialization of children, exchange of social control and responsibility across generations, etc.), and most if not all societies differentiate among members (for example, by promoting sexual, developmental, or socioeconomic class distinctions; see Endnote 2). Further, the laws of learning, as the laws of physics, are presumably the same for all men. Unfortunately, the influences on behavior of structural determinants, whether physical or social, have been far less well-recognized or studied.

Despite emphases traditionally placed on isolated genetic or environmental factors, the phenotype at any given time actually represents a culmination of the developmental transaction between genotype and experience. Life forces promote stability or change *over time*. Unfortunately, the temporal nature of this interaction is often neglected, sacrificed, or masked in psychological study. Cross-cultural cum developmental comparison reminds us of the true temporal reality of development.

METHODOLOGY

Principles and Pitfalls

Cross-cultural developmental comparison has the potential to combine the best that cross-cultural research and developmental research can offer into a positive synergy. Unfortunately, this method is among the least practicable or feasible of comparative methods, although it is among the most demanding and complex. Moreover, cross-cultural developmental studies inherit the disadvantages of both cross-cultural and developmental methodologies. (Achenbach has already discussed the major methodological pitfalls of developmental comparison; Jahoda has done likewise for cross-cultural comparison. It is unnecessary to review these further.) However, the methods applied in tandem raise additional idiosyncratic problems. Historically, cultural and developmental comparisons have been impelled by different psychological motives, one by an assessment of social aggregate phenomena and the other by individual growth. The two approach issues at different levels of psychological analysis, one at the cultural level, and the other at the individual level. Finally, the two typically address different psychological states, static culture versus the changing individual.

Additional methodological questions, including sample representativeness, the quality of experimenter-subject communication, and population matching, challenge all comparative research but are particularly acute in cross-cultural developmental research. For all cross-cultural researchers, representativeness of the sample is an issue, but developmental investigators encounter this problem most acutely because children and the aged are often least representative within society, coming, respectively, from its most transitional and most traditional segments (for further discussions, see Brislin & Baumgardner, 1971; Frijda & Jahoda, 1966). If communication difficulties cause laboratory psychologists to question whether subjects seen on an everyday basis comprehend the nature of the experimental task or whether their responses may be faithfully given or accurately interpreted, both the cross-culturalist and the developmentalist are in more compromised positions (Campbell, 1964). Yet the cross-cultural developmentalist is additionally compromised. The passage between his Scylla and Charybdis is narrow. Investigators find it difficult to use standardized tests or apply them to children in different societies because of culture and language variation. Alternatively, those who have worked profitably with tailored or ad hoc formulations find that they have sacrificed comparability that is at the heart of cross-cultural comparison in the first place. (Cross-cultural developmentalists do well to minimize reliance on verbal instructions and responses in their experiments and to require subjects to respond adequately in pretests. In the absence of such precautions they particularly must confront questions about procedural reliability and validity.) Further complicating the cross-culturalist's practical difficulties in studying development is the fact that childrens' ages are not recorded in many cultures, and frequently it is impossible to match children in different experimental treatments or societies on this basis, on educational level (which generally varies among societies anyway; see King, 1973; Thut & Adams, 1964), or on other usual criteria (see Endnote 2). Moreover, it is little solace that children typically show the greatest variability among age groupings, so that developmental status and other difficulties usually associated with cultural bias (e.g., experimental materials, task familiarity, test sophistication, etc.) are increasingly likely to interact at younger ages. The result of these practical problems is unavoidably diminished comparability among samples in intercultural developmental comparison.

Beyond considerations germane to the conduct of experiments loom problems basic to the design and theory of cross-cultural developmental comparison. Historically, studies in this tradition have been only marginally cross-cultural or developmental in the sense of testing many cultures or many ages. Instead, investigators have typically assessed some effect, behavior, or phenomenon in the West and then tried to test it in at least one non-Western culture. Usually comparison cultures are selected because of circumstances that lead the experimenter to expect a difference; sometimes the generality of behavior is being assessed. Unfortunately, most experiments have compared only two cultures, the idea being simply to incorporate "culture" into the experimental design; yet cultures differ in more than one way (Campbell,

1961). By adopting only pairwise comparison investigators run a risk of confounding variables over which they have no control or may even have no knowledge (see Seitz, in this volume). Further, cross-cultural developmental studies have typically concentrated on a particular age (other than adulthood) in the life cycle and have qualified as "developmental" only because that focus is on infants, children, or (least frequently) the aged, and not because several points in the life span are being compared. Lloyd (1972) has imaginatively and accurately characterized cross-cultural investigators as either "explorers" who conduct one-shot studies over only a short time, or "settlers" who, by contrast, live and work intensively among the peoples they study. The traditional model in cross-cultural developmental research has been exploration; for obvious reasons truly comparative developmental research may never be done in settler fashion. There have been notable and unique efforts in this direction though: Witkin, Price-Williams, Bertini, Christiansen, Oltman, Ramirez, and Van Meel (1974), for example, cooperated internationally to study socialization and psychological differentiation (see pp. 250–251) among children of two ages in each of two villages in each of three home countries (Holland, Italy, and Mexico).

These experimental shortcomings create a dilemma. The goal of cross-cultural developmental research is to enable psychologists to study similarities and differences in the ways individuals of different ages in different cultures behave or develop. Yet practical and theoretical shortcomings permit only the most cautious conclusions about human similarity or difference to be ventured. Conclusions about cultural differences could emerge out of wholly artifactual circumstance, related to testing for example, while conclusions about intercultural similarity or universality, too, frequently rest on the results of tests or tasks that may be insufficiently sensitive to expose underlying cultural differences or alternatively provoke only situationally similar responses.[2]

Strong experimental designs therefore take into account the lessons of both cross-cultural and developmental research. As opposed to comparing one behavior in children of one age in two societies, optimal studies assess behavior with two or more converging measures, in three or more different societies, where at least two are expected to share some feature and the

---

[2]Independent of whether universals are descriptive or explanatory, questions pertaining to their psychological reality and origins are knotty. Some anthropologists, including Boas and Evans-Pritchard, have rejected altogether the possibility of cross-cultural universals; for them, the analysis of culture and behavior is sufficiently realistic and worthwhile only in local, uniquely rich forms. Other anthropologists, like Murdock, along with many psychologists argue that cross-cultural generalizations are justified so long as abstraction does not dilute reality. Further, universal, in an accepted sense of relatively common across societies, is problematical philosophically: According to Popper (1962), one exceptional case constitutes refutation of a universalist hypothesis.

other(s) not, and with humans studied longitudinally or, at a minimum, cross-sectionally at two or more developmental levels. Such designs promote confidence in reliability of assessments, allow the possibility of strong developmental inferences, and disallow oversimplified cultural contrasts. Not every experiment will attain this ideal nor will every experimenter take account of all possible precautions. The extent to which experiments fall short of these standards is reflected in the quality and the potential of their contribution to psychology.

Specialized Designs

Experimental designs in cross-cultural developmental research do not typically deviate very far from that of classical research in psychology. In addition to the standard armamentarium, cross-cultural developmentalists have utilized two more specialized approaches. The first is the "natural experiment," and the second is the "hologeistic method."

Natural Experiments.   Developmentalists are naturally interested in the effects of culture and ecology on behavior, yet unlike most other psychologists they are not in a position experimentally to manipulate the relevant independent variables because such manipulations are infeasible, impractical, or ethically unacceptable. However, much could be learned about the nature of man and the course of his development from such manipulations. To meet this need, psychologists have turned to "natural experiments." Natural experiments rest on the fortuitous occurrence of particular customs man has adopted or of particular environments in which he has evolved. For example, in a well-known report, Kagan and Klein (1973) took advantage of physical and social deprivation natural among young Guatemalan infants to test the notion of continuity in development and the lasting significance of early experience. Although Guatemalan babies lagged behind American babies on several performance measures, preadolescents in Guatemala and in the United States performed similarly on a variety of cognitive measures. Infant retardation, the investigators concluded, does not prevent the eventual emergence of species-specific competences. (See, too, Kagan et al., 1979.) Several additional examples may help to illuminate further the utility and versatility of natural experiments to the conduct, interpretation, and power of cross-cultural developmental research.

Parents in some cultures swaddle their infants. In a classic series of naturalistic studies, Dennis (1940; Dennis & Dennis, 1940) used this fact to investigate the long-term effects of physical restraint on motor development. He found that continued early confinement, which is natural among Iranian children, retarded sitting, standing, and walking even after two years. However, degree and duration of restraint were found to play an important role. Some Hopi (American Indian) infants are cradle-boarded, but not for lengthy periods, and they do not suffer permanently, but begin to walk at about the same age as Hopi children who are not cradle-boarded. (These data have parallels in the animal developmental literature; see Marler, Dooling, & Zoloth, in this volume.)

Many psychologists have suggested that the development of perception is influenced by experience. One hypothesis is that growing up in a world constructed primarily of geometric orthogonals causes individuals to make specific inferences about what they see. Based on just such experience we interpret a rotating trapezoid as oscillating instead. Allport and Pettigrew (1957) tested the experiential hypothesis concerning this illusion with urban and rural Zulu (Natal) children. Rural Zulus are reared in a curved rather than orthogonal perceptual ecology; for example, their huts are circular. In a simple test of the hypothesis, rural Zulu children saw less illusion than did urban children.

Recently, through terrible accident, the selective and deleterious effects of certain drugs on prenatal development have been exposed. In the 1960s in Europe, though not in the United States, thalidomide was widely prescribed as a sedative. Unfortunately, if the drug were ingested during the critical first trimester of pregnancy it tended to arrest limb differentiation in the developing fetus. If this morphological "natural experiment" were not enough, limbless thalidomide children in turn provided a startling additional experimental possibility to theory testing because they constituted a rather unique human sample. With them DéCarie (1969) discounted the Piagetian formulation that normal cognitive development is hierarchical and contingently dependent on normal sensorimotor experience in infancy.

How much do factors associated with the family, as opposed to those outside the family, contribute to cognitive development? In the West, the two sets of factors are typically confounded; social class and family milieu are often highly correlated. In modern Warsaw, rebuilt physically and politically since World War II, social policy has randomly distributed nonfamilial factors—dwellings, schools, and health facilities—without regard to social class, thus providing the opportunity for control of this variable on a wide scale. In a comprehensive study of cognitive development among Polish 11-year-olds, Firkowska, Ostrowska, Sokolowska, Stein, Susser, and Wald (1978) found that mental performance was regularly related to familial factors— parental education and occupation—where nonfamilial ones were equalized.

In the fall of 1944, the Axis halted all food supplies to western Hoiland, which by the end of the year suffered from severe famine. It was not liberated until the spring of 1945. During the famine, the number of Dutch births in that region fell by half, and the average weight of babies declined by 10%. This experience, unique for the fixed onset and offset of the famine, provided Stein, Susser, Saenger, and Marolla (1975) an opportunity to assess the long-term effects of early malnutrition on intellectual development. Surprisingly, a massive sample of Dutch men and women surviving that famine showed no seriously deleterious long-term mental or physical outcomes.

Western ideals of masculine and feminine have long been stereotyped as biological and hence fixed and universal. What if there existed human societies where both girls and boys were reared into the Western idea of feminine, where both girls and boys were reared into the Western idea of masculine, and where boys were reared to express prototypically feminine qualities and girls prototypically masculine ones? The consequence would turn gender biologizing on its head. Mead (1935) claimed to have found three such societies, the Arapesh, the Mundugumor, and the Tchambuli, respectively, all living in New Guinea within one hundred miles of one another.

Westernization and modernization have brought representational arts to nearly everyone living in the world. Isolated peoples therefore become important to study from the perspective of cultural development. Conklin (Anonymous, 1961), Shapiro (1960), and Deregowski (1977) conducted natural experiments when they studied artistic production and perception among different peoples who had never before held a pencil or seen two-dimensional representations. Natural experiments such as these are precious as they become less and less feasible in a quickly modernizing world.

These are invaluable examples of natural experiments covering many areas of developmental concern, including prenatal health, physical growth, perception, cognition, intelligence, socialization, and aesthetics. However, contributions of some natural experiments may be suspect and must be interpreted with caution. In fact, it is impossible to interpret behavioral etiology—a prime purpose of the natural experiment—when only a single case is implicitly contrasted with a control situation. In this sense, the design of the natural experiment is only "preexperimental." As in a true experiment, investigators may select the subject population and control the timing of the study; however, in experiments of opportunity, such as are frequent in cross-cultural developmental psychology, investigators do not exercise actual control over the stimulus or treatment (usually culture, ecology, or economy). Nor have they sampled randomly in the construction of comparison groups. Consequently, other uncorrelated variables may differentially have influenced conditions, or the two groups may not have been equivalent to begin with. These are terribly important shortcomings in experimental terms. For experimenters to assume that a target culture in a natural experiment lies toward the opposite pole from some anchor culture on a unitary dimension and that the two are otherwise equivalent may be to assume in error; people and cultures are complex entities that differ from one another in many ways. Campbell (1961; Campbell & Stanley, 1963) has extensively and critically discussed such preexperimental designs. (It is important to note that the same criticism extends to intracultural comparisons; see Endnote 3.)

Hologeistic Method. Cross-cultural developmentalists traditionally follow the methodological canons of psychological experimentation, where individual subjects serve as the units of analysis. Yet, this approach has obvious limitations for the purposes of cultural study. The effort that must be mounted to conduct a study in three or more societies at two or more stages in the life cycle approximates prohibitive. Moreover, it shakes one's faith in inference to consider that even if achieved, three societies are no more representative of global variation than two points in the life span are representative of human development.

For these reasons and others, cross-cultural developmentalists have turned to a research tactic that quantitatively analyzes reports of psychological phenomena from large numbers of field workers and that uses entire cultures as the units of analysis. The method was initiated by the anthropologist Edward Tylor (1871), but Whiting (anthropologist) and Child (psychologist) modernized the idea ingeniously in their 1953 study, *Child Training and Personality*. They argued that modal developmental behaviors (e.g., dependence in children) could be causally linked to different cultural treatments (e.g., punitiveness of child training by parents) if it could be assumed that consistent individual relationships mediated societywide effects. To prove this theory, they coded ethnographies for degrees of both parent punitiveness and child dependence and then correlated the two. (The hologeistic method uses the HRAF; see Jahoda, p. 124, in this volume.)

Two later surveys of child rearing practices further illustrate how this method works. Barry, Bacon, and Child (1957) surveyed relationships between socialization practices and manifest behavior differences between the sexes in ethnographies of 110 preindustrial cultures. They rated infant indulgence and social pressures on young boys and girls to be responsible, nurturant, obedient, self-reliant, and achieving. Barry et al. found that, in general, cultures do not differentially indulge the sexes in infancy, but by early childhood girls around the world experience greater pressure to be nurturant, obedient, and responsible, whereas boys experience greater pressure to achieve and express self-reliance.

In a second study, Rohner (1978) rated each of 101 societies for its acceptance (affection, praising, etc.) or rejection (hostility, neglect, etc.) of young children. These variables proved to be related to the level of emotional responsiveness, stability, self-evaluation, and independence that characterized adult personality types typical of a society. Moreover, psychological, social, and environmental conditions were found to induce parents the world over to behave toward their children in parallel ways.

Naroll and Cohen (1970) and Jahoda (in this volume) have assessed some of the costs and benefits of the hologeistic method. Its advantage lies in the fact that a large number of independent investigators have (usually unknowingly and hence in an unbiased way) contributed to a data base nearly representative of a world sample; it has provided invaluable descriptive data on the frequency and variety of customs, beliefs, and behaviors of peoples around the world; and studies based on this method, though inconclusive by themselves, are richly suggestive of causal relationships between culture and behavior. To its disadvantage, the hologeistic method relies on unplanned observations by investigators not seeking the occurrence of a particular behavior; it is frequently poor in data "quality control"; it does not directly measure individuals but is correlational in nature; finally, the strength of the method is determined at each link in a chain of logic between individual and culture by inference alone.

To this point I have summarized the rationales, history, and methodologies peculiar to cross-cultural developmental comparison; in the next section I treat the substance of the method. Beforehand, however, notice the rather compromised position in which this comparison as practiced finds itself; it is deficient on practical, empirical, and theoretical grounds. Nevertheless, an outline of the rationales and benefits of this mode of comparison convinces us that cross-cultural extensions to developmental psychology are mandatory, that developmental comparisons in cross-cultural psychology are invaluable, and that cross-cultural developmental psychology can provide uniquely complete and theoretically significant data about human behavior. Its shortcomings notwithstanding, past practice and future potential forge an advantage to this mode of comparison not realizable elsewhere in psychology.

ARENAS OF CROSS-CULTURAL
DEVELOPMENTAL COMPARISON

In spite of its relatively brief history, cross-cultural developmental comparison has contributed to virtually all of the traditional arenas of psychology. The second half of this chapter reviews briefly some of its principal contributions to physical and motor development, perception, cognition, language, and social behavior. Complexity and comprehensiveness are sacrificed in these treatments in at least two ways: first, not all of the history and relevant data are detailed; and second, the spectrum of perspectives and subtlety of relevant criticisms are not discussed in full. The relevant literature grows daily, and much of it (for reasons of design and the like, already discussed) has been subjected to penetrating critique (e.g., LeVine, 1970). Rather than dissect, I have elected to illustrate cross-cultural developmental comparisons by providing a broad, progressive, and frankly sanguine overview of results of the method. This approach is intended, further, to highlight its potential. Throughout, it can be seen that particular experiments exemplify the unique uses of the cross-cultural developmental method. Other, more comprehensive reviews of selected topics are noted appropriately in the text.

Physical and Motor Development

As Baldwin (in this volume) has observed, early developmentalists concerned themselves with description in the service of defining normality and identifying abnormality. Yet *normal* is a relative concept. However, before the advent of cross-cultural study, the relativity of normal seems to have been recognized by developmentalists in only small degree.

The early cross-cultural investigation of psychomotor development in infants, particularly the work of Arnold Gesell (e.g., 1946), provides a model of the pitfalls likely to beset studies undertaken in monocultural contexts. Gesell's goal was to document early physical (cum psychological) development. On the basis of extensive and careful research, he constructed detailed cinematic atlases of what normal development entailed. Further, he confidently founded developmental diagnoses of the progress and prognosis of normal and abnormal infant development. Surely universal, culture-free concerns occupied Gesell, for he worked with such young infants and on behaviors thought to be almost wholly under biological control (Ball, 1977). The regularity of motor development that he observed no doubt reinforced this belief.

Though Gesell's tests, and those of other developmentalists of the same ilk (e.g., Bayley, 1969, 1970; Griffiths, 1954), were continuously refined, only later did infant testing reach beyond the confines of the Gesell Institute in New Haven and beyond the middle- and upper-class American Caucasian society that it served. The results of cross-cultural surveys, first among American Indians and later among peoples in Bali and Africa (beginning only in the 1940s!), undermined Gesell's assumptions. These studies showed that Mongol and Negro babies deviate from the accepted norms for Caucasian babies with respect both to the stages and to the timing of motor development in the first two years. Hopi infants begin to walk alone late (Dennis & Dennis, 1940); Balinese infants follow a different set of stages on their way to walking (Mead & MacGregor, 1951); and Ghanda and Wolof infants tend to be more advanced in sensory, psychological, and motor development than Caucasian age norms would predict (Ainsworth, 1967; Geber, 1956, 1958; Lusk & Lewis, 1972). Indeed, the findings of some 50 studies have pointed to a generalized accelerated psychomotor development among non-Western infants (Werner, 1972; but see Warren, 1972, for a critique).

What is the source of this developmental difference? Gesell (Gesell & Amatruda, 1945) conceived psychomotor development to be ballistic and under unfolding genetic control; he captured this theme in one of his most influential books, entitled *The Embryology of Behavior*. In fact, some data support a hypothesis that favors genetic differences among babies. Geber and Dean (1957a, 1957b), for example, found that 9-hour-old Ghandan neonates are significantly advanced in neuromuscular standing; and Tanner (1970) found that native Africans were advanced beyond Western Caucasians in skeletal maturation and ossification at birth. Indeed, Werner's (1972) 50-study survey documents a racial hierarchy: Negro infants are most advanced in psychomotor development, and they are followed by Mongols, and last by Caucasians.

However, the majority of investigators have favored an environmentalist position on psychomotor development. Dennis and Dennis (1940), for example, suggested that Hopi locomotor retardation reflected Hopi babies' traditional early constriction on the cradle board; Mead and McGregor (1951) proposed that the manner in which Balinese mothers habitually carried their infants promoted the babies' unique motor performance; and Ainsworth (1967) attributed advanced Ghanda motor abilities to a nurturing climate of physical freedom.

The environmentalist interpretation gains more credence when one examines the evidence and the babies more closely, as Super (1976) has done. Super found advanced sitting, standing, and walking among Kenyan Kipsigis babies, but retarded head lifting, crawling, and turning over. In the absence of a "generalized precocity" among these infants, Super was led to study Kipsigis mothers, over 80% of whom deliberately taught their infants to sit, stand, and walk. Super further ascertained that these practices were widespread among native Africans, thus providing a rationale for the general findings of previous investigators. In fact, Super determined that the statistical correlation between the percentage of mothers who reported "teaching" their babies to crawl and the average age of crawling in six African societies was .77.

Manipulative and "natural experiments" further confirm the environmentalist interpretation. Zelazo, Zelazo, and Kolb (1972) showed that an early start and extra practice improved otherwise "normal" American infants. Further, Rebelsky (1967, 1972) found that Dutch infants, who are stimulated less than American infants, scored lower than Americans on infant scales of psychomotor ability. Similarly, Bovet, Dasen, and Inhelder (1974) accounted for sensorimotor retardation in Baoulé (Ivory Coast) infants relative to French children by the fact that the Africans tend to be carried on their mothers backs. Pertinently, Geber (1958) and Super (1976) found that African infants (Ghanda and Kipsigis, respectively) reared in the manner of European babies loose the advantage that their traditionally reared, genetically similar compatriots maintain.[3]

Of course, innate differences in infant psychomotor abilities still may exist, or prenatal factors, such as maternal nutrition, activity, or anxiety level, could influence development of the fetus. However, the cross-cultural data show, that psychomotor differences among infants can reflect the influence of childrearing practice. In summary, the norms of psychomotor development that Gesell strived to canonize must be viewed as plastic (within limits) to both social and cultural influences.

Cross-cultural developmentalists have compared numerous other aspects of physical development. For example, United Nations statistics show

---

[3]Although Bayley (1965) found American Negro and Caucasian infants equivalent on the mental scale of her developmental schedule, Negroes were advanced on the motor scale; her result could be accounted for in terms of social class differences in childrearing (see Endnote 3; Williams & Scott, 1953).

conclusively that rates of infant mortality vary significantly among nations (e.g., Werner, 1979). Extensive studies (e.g., Meredith, 1978) have compared physical growth and maturation of children in different cultures. Three surveys exemplify the potential contributions of such data. In one, Landauer and Whiting (1964) showed a strong, positive correlation between infantile stress and adult stature. In the others, Tanner (1970, 1978) and Roche (1979) used worldwide data to document secular trends favoring earlier maturation and to discover where (developed versus undeveloped countries) and why (nutrition, environment, heterosis) such trends occur.

In a microcosmic way, physical growth and psychomotor data adequately illustrate some of the major advantages of cross-cultural developmental comparison. Cross-cultural study is vital to delimiting the true range of human experience and to establishing realistic developmental norms, and for these descriptive functions alone it would be invaluable. The study of development across cultures is twice valuable for the check it provides against an ethnocentric world view and the implications of such a view. Following the lead of early developmentalists, our acceptance of Western norms of psychological processes seems to have been much too willing. Thus, Caucasian infants actually fall at the lower end of internationally normed standards of motor achievement, and Ghandan infants are "precocious" (by the developmentalist's common turn of phrase) only against the false Western "norm." Finally, psychological comparison in the context of culture is thrice valuable for increasing our understanding of the contributions of nature and of nurture to development. Even behaviors that are logical candidates for a strong genetic interpretation (because they display regularity and submit to normative analysis in one place) may be subject to experiential manipulation and show variability if studied in other places. Studies of early development like these provide a standard for our understanding of other cross-national differences in psychologial functions.

Perception

Classification (Serpell, 1976), the differentiation of left and right (Rudel & Teuber, 1963; Serpell, 1976), and the interpretation of depth cues (Deregowski, 1977; Jahoda & McGurk, 1974; Miller, 1973) are a few of many aspects of perception known to change during the course of development. Why? Two explanations of these effects, maturation and experience, compete.

The classic report of cross-cultural differences in perception derived from Rivers's (1901) observations that Papuans and Englishmen differed in their susceptibility to visual illusions. Such differences have since been confirmed across a wide variety of human societies (e.g., Segall, Campbell, & Herskovits, 1966). Berry (1971), Jahoda (1971), and Bornstein (1973) have provided support for various biological interpretations of this difference related to visual system function. Alternatively, Segall et al. (1966), D. Wagner (1977), and others have argued an experiential-judgmental view, suggesting that adult perceptual inferences are ecologically adaptive and environmentally conditioned. If perceptual inference is acquired in childhood, cross-cultural developmental study ought to help tease apart biological and experiential explanations. Whereas the experiential view presumes increasing susceptibility with age (to the Müller-Lyer illusion, for example), biological interpretations (related to maturation and acuity) have suggested that illusion susceptibility ought to decrease. Available developmental data support a biological view (e.g., Bornstein, 1973; Pick & Pick, 1970). Explanations of illusions are recognized to vary (Coren & Girgus, 1978), however, and it is not surprising that neither a biological nor an experiential interpretation wholly accounts for degree of illusion susceptibility. The cultural-developmental study provides demonstrably unique and important data nonetheless.

In the same way, cross-cultural developmental data have contributed singularly to our understanding of the perception of select speech sounds (see Marler, Dooling, & Zoloth, in this volume). In the vast majority of languages, voicing represents one critical dimension along which some phonemes (meaningful sounds) are differentiated. Although voicing is a physically continuous dimension, it is perceived to change more or less categorically, i.e., sounds within a phonetic category (e.g., /b/) are distinguished poorly whereas sounds between categories (e.g., /b/ versus /p/) are distinguished acutely (Liberman, Cooper, Schankweiler, & Studdert-Kennedy, 1967). Importantly, cross-language research has shown that the same three phonemic categories (prevoiced, voiced, and voiceless) regularly recur (Lisker & Abramson, 1964). Most languages (like English) use the central category and at least one other.

In a fundamental series of studies, Eimas (1975; Eimas, Siqueland, Jusczyk, & Vigorito, 1971) presumed that a phenomenon so ubiquitous and important in human behavior as categories of speech may have a biological foundation. He therefore sought to discover whether preverbal human infants would perceive acoustic changes of voicing in a manner parallel to adult phonemic perception. Eimas found that American infants discriminated between-phoneme (voiced-voiceless) but not within-phoneme changes. His developmental results strongly suggested a biological basis for perception of elementary language units, but again the addition of a cross-cultural dimension to developmental studies was necessary to separate nature and nurture and to delineate their relative influences.

Two cross-cultural developmental studies have examined infants' discrimination of voicing in communities where different patterns of voicing are present in the adult language. In one, Lasky, Syrdal-Lasky, and Klein

(1975) investigated infants from Spanish monolingual families living in Guatemala. (In Spanish, unlike English, the main boundary between phoneme pairs exists at an uncommon location on the voicing dimension [Abramson & Lisker, 1973].) Lasky et al. found that the 4- to 6-month-olds did not discriminate the Spanish voicing distinction, but they discriminated a prevoiced one. In the second study, Streeter (1976a) tested voicing discriminations among Kikuyu (Kenya) 2-month-olds. (Adult Africans who speak Kikuyu make a prevoiced distinction but do not use the voiced-voiceless contrast [Streeter, 1976b].) Streeter found that Kikuyu babies also discriminated the contrast not present in the adult language. In summary, cross-cultural studies of infant auditory perception confirm that certain discriminations are innate because they are not only present in young infants who have experience with the distinction but appear in infants without experience with adult production. Other distinctions seem to be learned quite early in life.

All human beings are endowed with roughly the same anatomy and physiology; it is reasonable to expect, therefore, that some perceptual systems or abilities are essentially universal. Even were these systems plastic, our physical and perceptual experiences are so common that they probably would render many perceptions nearly the same for everyone anyway. For example, children and adults from rural villages in New Guinea (Kennedy & Ross, 1975), Ethiopia (Deregowski, Muldrow, & Muldrow, 1972), and Ghana (Jahoda, Deregowski, Ampene, & Williams, 1977), where representational arts are unknown, seem to be able to identify or recognize immediately two-dimensional realistic representations of three-dimensional objects. Infant studies tend to support this nativist view (Dirks & Gibson, 1977), as do studies of the pictorially deprived Western child (Hochberg & Brooks, 1962).

How does selective experience influence perceptual ability and development? Follow-up research in speech perception helps to answer this question. Spanish infants perceive certain phoneme categories like American infants; Spanish adults, however, perceive the English boundary only very weakly. Experience with the Spanish language thus influences perception. Data from Spanish-speaking adults suggest, therefore, that discriminative abilities enjoyed in infancy but not used during ontogeny are attenuated but not lost. Likewise, adult Kikuyu discriminate an unused English voicing contrast, but not as well as one they use (Streeter, 1976b). The persistence of such perceptions, even in the absence of relevant experience, probably reflects their foundation in natural, resilient psychoacoustic properties of the auditory system. Pehaps general experience with the wide range of sounds produced in the natural environment is suffcient to maintain sensitivities that are native.

What of perceptual induction? What is the time frame for the acquisition of a new perception? Are new perceptions solely conditioned by context and environment? Are new perceptions limited other than by sensory discriminability? Do later specific experiences influence native distinctions which may be disused since infancy? In a study important both for its quality and uniqueness, Streeter and Landauer (1976) observed Kikuyu children learning English as a second language. Their youngest children (7½ years) who had no exposure to English could discriminate a voicing distinction common to Kikuyu as well as one found in English and other languages (Lisker & Abramson, 1964). Thus, the Kikuyu adult phoneme unavailable to infants was developed after 7½ years of specific experience. The oldest children (15 years) who had more exposure to English were much better at (English) voicing discriminations than were the younger children. These results suggest that specific experiences, too, sharpen discriminations that are naturally distinctive.

Together, psychological, anthropological, and developmental research make it possible to deduce the broad outlines of how language-processing begins. A limited set of phonemes along a perceptual (i.e., the voicing) continuum exists in different languages. Human infants distinguish the same ones in processing sounds long before they understand or produce speech. Such perceptions seem to have a pancultural validity, and their specialized processing serves to bias the newborn system in the direction of language analysis. During ontogeny linguistic processing is subject to modification, but under somewhat rigid constraints. These studies exemplify the benefits of combining psychological, developmental, and anthropological inquiry over a common subject; further, they illustrate the interaction of biological predisposition and selective experience in perceptual development. Similar arguments apply to the development of color perception (Bornstein, 1979; Jahoda and Marler et al., in this volume).

The topics in perceptual development to which psychologists have historically devoted their attention are those that have required answers to descriptive as well as theoretical questions. The degree to which similarities among humans are guided by biological or structural identities is difficult to specify, as is the degree to which differences among humans reflect anatomy or ecology or tuition. Nevertheless, developmental studies of perception show clear cross-cultural similarities as well as differences. Although perceptual studies often serve for this reason as models for other developmental and psychological processes—perceptionists, too, can define stimulus, response, and design with a high degree of accuracy—these studies have engaged only relatively modest experimental interest. In spite of clear warrant and advantage, there exists, in sum, a true paucity of data in cross-cultural perceptual development.

Cognition

Cognitive development has received an enormous degree of attention from cross-culturalists. Both similarities and cultural differences in thinking have been recognized, causing some controversy as to whether the processes underlying thought are culture-specific or universal and sometimes only superficially different. Childhood represents an ideal time to assay contributions of biology and experience to culturally varying modes of thought. As in the study of perception, contrasting theoretical views on nature and nurture have motivated much of the research in culture and cognition. Four lines of investigation have dominated the area. Witkin (1967) and Berry (1976) have scrutinized the roles that ecology and economy play in the differential development of "cognitive styles." Cole (e.g., Cole & Scribner, 1974) has emphasized the similarities that underlie diverse cultural expression. Psychometricians, usually interested in intelligence test scores, have concentrated on intercultural "deficiencies." Finally, Piagetians have trekked to the field in search of cognitive universals and confirmation of genetic epistemology. What are the contributions and implications of these four lines of inquiry? Let us look at each in turn.

Several psychological theories hold that development entails increasing differentiation of self, of perception, and of social function (e.g., Lewin, 1935; Werner, 1948). According to Witkin (1967), degree of differentiation or of articulation helps to determine cognitive style or "characteristic self-consistent modes of functioning found pervasively throughout an individual's cognitive, that is perceptual and intellectual activities [p. 234]." Cognitive style is measured by perceptual tests (e.g., rod and frame, embedded figures, etc.) toward which some individuals consistently behave in a more field-dependent manner, i.e., in need of information provided by the environment, whereas others act independent of field. Socialization patterns have been implicated in the determination of cognitive style, "strict" childrearing (i.e., overprotection, restriction, etc.) giving rise probabilistically to a dependent style and "permissive" patterns to a more independent style.

Cross-cultural studies submit this developmental relationship to a more comprehensive test because variation in socialization customs across cultures tends to be greater than within cultures. Thus, Berry (1966, 1976), Dawson (1967, 1973), and Witkin (1967; Witkin & Berry, 1975; Witkin et al., 1974) have studied differentiation globally. In a classic study, Berry (1966) compared Eskimo (Canada) and Temne (West Africa) for the antecedents and manifestations of cognitive style. The Eskimo are a migratory hunting people who rear children permissively; they proved to be field independent. The Temne are stationary and rarely wander from beaten bush paths. They rear children strictly and are more field dependent. Berry also found that Westernized subgroups within each culture were more field independent (a result that raises methodological problems of representativeness and validity). Thus, childrearing predicted cognitive style. But have childrearing practices themselves identifiable antecedents? Recently, Berry has added the "prime moving" influence of ecology, environment, and economy to the *socialization → cognitive style* formulation to yield a revised *ecology → culture → behavior* model, hypothesizing that cultural cognitive styles have adapted to cultural life styles. Eskimo and Temne data (among others) are marshalled to support his general view. This characterization does the true complexity of the Witkin-Berry formulation only little justice; Witkin and Berry (1975) and Berry (1976) have elsewhere provided more complete accounts.

Whereas psychological differentiation tracks intercultural *differences,* other views of cognition, such as the psychometric one, focus on relative *deficiencies* among people(s). The psychometric view holds that intelligence is stable, quantifiable, and inherited.

Binet's original tests of intelligence only date from the turn of this century (Binet & Simon, 1908/1916). However, it was not long afterward that their application in Western societies outside France began, for example, by Terman and others in the United States and by Burt in England. The application of intelligence tests in non-Western societies ensued not long after that. It is now well accepted that such tests are useless for purposes of assessing cultural differences or native abilities because they are culturally biased: Specifically, the selection, predictive purposes, and administration of questions in them fail to reconcile adequately for difference in the nature, background, and motives of the population on whom the questions were originally standardized and the populations on which they are later used. (Vernon [1969] and Cronbach and Drenth [1972] provide more complete reviews and criticisms of the literature.) These critiques notwithstanding, IQ tests predict academic performance, and culturally indigenous forms of such tests can serve special functions, as for within-culture assessment. Husén (1967) in this way has documented the positive change in Japanese mathematics scores with modernization, and Lloyd and Easton (1977), using a Yoruba (Nigeria) version of the Stanford-Binet, have confirmed cross-culturally the differential effects of social class on performance.

Two modified psychometric approaches have received some attention from cross-culturalists. Several attempts have been made to develop so-called "culture free" tests of intelligence. Typically they use universally familiar or unfamiliar materials (e.g., the Porteus Maze Test, the Goodenough Draw-a-Man Test, etc.). This development seems not to have been very successful despite its intensive history (Strodtbeck, 1964) because such tests tend inevitably to rely on talents and motivations differentially developed in different societies and to treat intelligence as a univariate trait. Failures of replication have also called the use of these instruments into question (cf. Porteus, 1931, with David, 1967). More recently, investigators have tried to assess similarities and divergences among patterns of abilities (for summaries, see Jahoda, in this volume; Lloyd, 1972; Vernon, 1969). However, formal elucidation of such patterns and proper modes of intercomparison are presently incomplete (e.g., Buss & Royce, 1975; Drenth, 1977).

If there are basic differences among human beings with regard to an "intelligence" that is both native and quantitative, the psychometricians have thus far failed to demonstrate them conclusively. The notion that universal processes may characterize thought is more palatable, and Cole (e.g., 1975) has concentrated on clarifying the ways in which different life experiences may modulate underlying common competences. Cole has argued that intelligence and differentiation are not entities of which different individuals have more or less. Further, he has suggested that it is inappropriate to consider mental functioning outside of its natural setting and linguistic context.

Cole arrived at these formulations from studies originally intended to explore why certain groups, for example the Kpelle (Liberia), experienced difficulty in learning mathematical concepts (Cole, Gay, Glick, & Sharp, 1971). He discovered that cultural socialization plays an important part in the child's familiarity, understanding, and accessibility to new cognitive tasks. Because cultural patterns differ, these precursors to learning differ concomitantly.

The implications of this line of reasoning for studies of cognition and its development in different cultures (or within the same "culture"—see Endnote 3) are manifold. First, when Western questions are asked with the aid of culturally familiar materials, cross-cultural "differences" frequently evaporate. For example, Cole (Cole et al., 1971) found that recall among unschooled Kpelle improved dramatically when target items were embedded in traditional folktales. Second, particular cultural contexts facilitate particularized learning. Kpelle estimate measures of rice, which they do habitually, quite accurately (and better than American college students); the behavior does not generalize to estimations of other quantities, however. Third, there exists a wide margin for cultural misunderstanding and methodological error that ought to give psychologists pause before concluding that cultural differences are not reducible to simple artifacts. On the basis of Luria's (1971) construct of "functional systems," Cole argues, fourth, for the universal nature of cognitive processes, thereby coming full circle to Lévy-Bruhl (1923/1966) on mentality and Brunswik (1958) on representative design. Based on these principles, Cole concluded that cross-cultural studies ought to be directed at how environment and experience mediate behavior. One substantive area in which Cole's approach has proved valuable is the study of memory (see Cole & Scribner, 1977; Meacham, 1975; Scribner, 1974; Wagner, 1978).

Cole's is one form of universalist-culturalist reconciliation. A second is Piaget's. His theory of cognitive development is founded in biology and therefore has clear universalist appeal; consequently, next to psychological differentiation, Piaget's "genetic epistemology" has generated the most research among cross-cultural developmental psychologists (see reviews in Dasen, 1972a, 1977a, 1977b; DeVos & Hipler, 1968; Furby, 1971; Greenfield, 1966; Lloyd, 1972; Modgil & Modgil, 1976; Werner, 1979).

Piaget's (e.g., 1952/1963, 1970) theory of cognitive growth posits an invariant and hierarchical stagelike progression from infant sensorimotor behavior through formal logic in adulthood. Originally grounded in Piaget's modest, informal, and parochial interviews with his own three young children, central aspects of the theory lend themselves to formal and catholic examination. Indeed, Piaget (1966/1974) himself recognized the suitability and desirability of cross-cultural studies.[4] Piaget supposed that if cognitive stages were rooted in biology and were invariant, children everywhere should necessarily proceed through an identical developmental sequence. He also opened to question how cultural experience (e.g., education or language) would modify the rate or endpoint of development. In short, Piaget proposed that cultural studies would test the validity of his theory and help to assess the relative contributions of biology and experience in development.

Both studies of description and verification began relatively early. One of the first was Margaret Mead's (1932) skeptical assessment of animism among Manus (Admirality Is.) children; not long afterward, Dennis (1943; Russell, 1940, 1942; Russell & Dennis, 1939, 1940) conducted systematic comparative examinations of animism among Hopi, Zuni, and American Caucasian children. The main conclusion from this extensive and continuing line of research is that children in most cultures across five continents can be arrayed into the cognitive-developmental stages that Piaget originally described (for summaries, see reviews cited above). There is therefore support both for stage progression with age and for an epigenetic view.

Factors that contribute to rates of development and their endpoints have been more complex to evaluate. In focusing on this question, Piaget's stage of "concrete operations" has received the most cross-cultural developmental scrutiny, and within it children's success on conservation tasks has been used to assess cognitive growth. Conservation, or understanding that physical properties of objects may remain invariant even over transformation, follows a known developmental course emerging between 5 and 7 years in Euramerican samples. Additionally, conservation takes many forms; successes are relatively obvious and modestly quantifiable; and tests of conservation are repeatable and tractable, even in the field. Thus, even short of full standardization (desperately needed in all cross-cultural work), measures of conservation have served to test nature and nurture in Piaget.

---

[4]Piaget's (1966/1974) article inaugurated the *International Journal of Psychology*.

Some environments seem to promote development of conservation; however, others, inhibit it. Consider studies that have demonstrated the influence of experience on cognitive development in the form of idiosyncratic training, cultural materialism, or language. Price-Williams, Gordon, and Ramirez (1969), for example, studied conservation abilities in village and town Mexican children. Some in each location were potters' children who would have had extensive experience with material transformations. Children of village potters excelled their peers on several measures of conservation, whereas children of town potters tended to conserve more frequently overall and only excelled their peers in conservation of substance. Special experience (with manipulation of clay) afforded a cognitive advantage to children in both village and town environments; however, in the experientially richer town situation variegated experience seems to have generally facilitated conservation (see the following). Tiv (Nigeria), too, conserve early with familiar materials (Price-Williams, 1961). Language, another category of special experience, seems also to facilitate development of conservation (Sevinç & Turner, 1976).

The effects of schooling or education on the acquisition of conservation are less clear cut. Some investigators have found retarded performance among unschooled children relative to those in school (e.g., Goodnow, 1969; Greenfield & Bruner, 1969). For example, half of uneducated Wolof (Senegal) children do not attain conservation of liquid by 12 years; their educated compatriots do so by 7 years of age, however (Bruner, Olver, & Greenfield, 1966). But, Chinese (Hong Kong) children with English schooling do not conserve (weight, volume, area) as consistently as do comparably schooled American children (Goodnow & Bethon, 1966), and schooled and unschooled Meru (Tanzania) children develop conservation of substance, weight, and volume at similar ages (Nyiti, 1976). Reviewing this literature, Dasen (1972a) found that four studies supported a positive influence of schooling on attainment of conservation, whereas six failed to support such a relation. (Lloyd's [1972] assessment shows a similar inconclusive balance.)

Urbanization, by contrast, may be a critical factor. Goodnow (1962) found that low SES urban Chinese (Hong Kong) children conserved as well as Western children; Poole (1968) found that a fully urban group of Hausa (Nigeria) children were more advanced on conservation tasks than matched suburban or rural groups; and Lloyd (1972) found that Yoruba (Nigeria) children from the city of Ibadan performed on a par with Western norms.

Perhaps, as Dasen (1972a) has suggested, contact with Western values is more directly relevant than schooling or urbanization to the development of conservation. For example, familial exposure to Western ideals was the only variable to bring Aboriginese (Australia) children to near Euramerican norms on conservation tasks, when level of education, urban exposure, and social class were held constant (Dasen, 1972b). But simply living in the West is no guarantee of higher cognitive attainment because fewer than 80% of rural Sardinian (Italy) adults conserve volume (Peluffo, 1967), whereas 100% of urban Euramericans conserve at about 15 years. Furby (1971) has concluded that schooling, urbanization, and Westernization are intrinsically linked in advancing cognitive skills; perhaps "modernization" is the appropriate overarching construct.

In summary, cross-cultural analyses have suggested that Piaget is largely justified in discussing a hierarchical, qualitative development of cognition in universalist terms. In the sense that all members of the human species seem to traverse the same developmental path, biological, maturationally dependent structures may be at work; it is still possible, however, that structurally shared, general experiences are sufficient to generate identical outcomes. Further, the rates of emergence and final resting levels of select Piagetian abilities seem to be modifiable through particular experiences. Although the exact composition is still in doubt, education, urbanization, and contact with Western modes of thought all seem to be influential in determining quantitative aspects of the theory. To what degree this is true because the tasks involved reflect essentially modern Western scientific thinking (originally tapped by Piaget) rather than alternative modes of thought valuable in other cultures cannot be determined.

Piagetian theory has influenced cross-cultural studies of development of a variety of other cognitive behaviors, including moral judgment (pp. 264–265), concept formation, classificatory propensity, and dream content. In each of these areas children everywhere seem to develop through similar stages; again, however, rate and endpoint vary.

Two areas of cognitive development have been particularly underemphasized in the cross-cultural literature. First, the effect of formal education on cognitive development and the interaction of Western styles of schooling with "traditional" culture have not been sufficiently examined (cf. Stevenson, Parker, Wilkinson, Bonnevaux, & Gonzalez, 1978). Greenfield (1966) first proposed that the correlation between age and experience in school, inevitable in the West, could be disentangled by testing cross-culturally. She did this in Senegal, and the technique has been used profitably since. Recently, Sharp, Cole, and Lave (1979), for example, showed that education among Indio and Mestizo (Mexico) children positively influenced mode of classification, hypothetical and abstraction capabilities, as well as performance on several school-related tasks, and through this contrast they found that amount of schooling did not affect performance on tasks requiring real-world knowledge (rather, age alone was influential). Second, cognitive growth in adults and cognitive change in the aged are still little explored in cross-cultural studies. Yet, adult gains in special knowledge, like Gladwin's (1970) report of learning Truk navigational techniques, fall into this category and may have much to say about the potential of cognition in all cultures.

Again in cognitive research, culture (as in cognitive style or IQ) or biology (as in Piaget) tends to be seen on balance as determinative. Clearly, Cole's approach and that of the Laboratory of Comparative Human Cognition (1979) will show the way to culture-sensitive studies of cognitive development in the future.

Language

Perhaps no two observations in the literature of child development are as beguiling as these: Young children everywhere have the potential to learn the intricate complexities of language with seemingly trivial facility, and at the same time they master whichever language they are exposed to. An increasing amount of cross-cultural research has been directed at elucidating these two crucial observations about language development. Some studies, for example, of syntactics, show that certain aspects of language are nearly universal; these findings help us to fathom the foregoing intriguing observations. Other studies, for example, of semantics, show that other aspects of language are highly idiosyncratic. Let us consider these first.

Our inability to communicate across cultures has presented ponderous difficulties since Babel, the main obstacle being semantic. However, philosophers, linguists, and anthropologists (including Humboldt, Boas, Sapir, and Whorf) have observed an additional important implication of differential language learning and use: The language we learn as children has consequences for the way we conceptualize the world and function in it. Luria (1974/1976), for example, has argued that "from the outset, the social forms of human life [language] begin to determine human mental development [p. 9]." Thus, Brown (1958) reported that the Hananòo (Philippines), for whom rice is a staple, distinguish verbally 92 kinds of "rice," and Munroe and Munroe (1975) reported that upcountry Swahili employs only a single word for "flying things." Not only are the Philippinos and Africans learning these forms as children, but in doing so the one group is succeeding in discerning, attending to, and using distinctions within an otherwise narrow category of objects in its world, whereas the other group is failing to distinguish among varieties of objects (e.g., birds and airplanes) or even between these two widely different classes of objects. Linguistic differentiations, which are clearly learned, affect cognitions in ways other than categorization and its special consequences. Two further examples show this. First, they may affect the child's physical conception of the world: For example, linguistic differentiations that exist in Thai facilitate the development of Thai children's conceptions of speed and duration relative to that of Japanese children in whose language such differentiations are lacking (Mori, 1976). Second, categorizations may affect the child's cognitive development: For example, languages that employ comparative forms (e.g., English or Greek) foster in children competency in solving equality versus difference relations (e.g., conservation) earlier than languages (e.g., Turkish) in which such forms are absent (Sevinç & Turner, 1976).

Semantics exemplify an extreme environmentalist view of language development and cultural consequence. Children naturally learn the language in whichever culture they are reared (flexibility), but their perceptual and thinking habits then follow the rules and inferences built into the language they learn (rigidity).

Other aspects of early language development appear to be less flexible and more rigid (and hence universal). The lawfulness with which the immature begin to make sounds (Jakobson, 1941/1969) is matched by the lawfulness with which the mature make sense (Chomsky, 1968). Indeed, the route between one linguistic stage and the next seems equally direct and sure everywhere in the world. Numerous studies of child language show in broad outline that development proceeds naturally, perhaps inevitably, through a fixed succession of stages. Crying at birth turns into babbling, then phonetic production, followed by one-word, two-word, and three-word utterances, and finally (when the child is about 4 years old) mature grammatical structures emerge. Each stage has been characterized by sets of rules.

Rheingold, Gewirtz, and Ross (1959) showed that infant vocalizations could be differentially reinforced, leading to the view that the frequency of particular sounds (and the origins of phonemes and words) might reflect the occurrence of natural social reinforcements. However, studies in widely varying language communities have shown that babbling sounds are similar everywhere in the first year (McNeill, 1970). Nakazima (1975), for example, observed that the quality and range of sounds in prelinguistic babbling does not differ between American and Japanese infants.

The curiously restricted array of sounds that characterize infantile phonetic production provides additional support for universalist notions of language development. Phonemes (the meaningful units of speech) are constructed of subelements (distinctive features). Jakobson (1941/1969) has observed that the order or appearance of these distinctive features is relatively fixed. (The ontogenetic order also correlates with the frequency with which those sounds are found in languages around the world.) After babbling, children first tend to produce front oral-cavity consonants (e.g., /p/, /b/, /t/, /d/, /m/, and /n/) and mid- to back-vowels (e.g., /a/, /ə/, /o/, and /u/). Jakobson (1941/1969) observed that this development occurs in a wide variety of languages, including English, Swedish, and Japanese. Jakobson further found that consonant-vowel combinations of these pairs were frequently the earliest to appear (e.g., /pa/), and he proposed that this nearly universal propensity reflected children's maximizing sound contrasts, that is, /p/ is unvoiced, soft, and produced at the front whereas /a/ is voiced, loud, and produced at the back.

A well-known but still intriguing fact to American parents related to this distribution is that two of these early-appearing pairs, viz. /pa/ and /ma/, tend to be used more frequently and to acquire particular meaning quite early in life. But if Jakobson is correct and the phenomenon is based on children's maximization of speech contrasts, then the American observation should be a more universal one. Murdock (1959) tested this hypothesis by tallying the use of front-consonant/back-vowel phonemes as familial descriptors in 1,072 languages and comparing this frequency with other combinations, (e.g., front-consonant/front-vowel, back-consonant/back-vowel, etc.) Fifty-seven percent of languages use the front-consonant/back-vowel class for initial parental kin terms. Thus, a strong universal propensity to produce certain sounds—one that is probably tied evolutionally to articulatory abilities and perceptual capabilities—is connected with an equally strong propensity to use those sounds in a nearly universally meaningful way—one that is probably tied experientially to the close and frequent association of sound and object.

Single words are first used by children everywhere in naming or in reference to operations. Further, all children employ intonations in combination with rudimentary semantics to increase the range of their otherwise limited communication at the one-word stage (Menyuk & Bernholz, 1969).

Before they are 2, American children begin to concatenate single words to form two-word "sentences." These strings actually represent the first possibility for truly grammatical expression. Studies of the two-word language stage show that the child's use of word pairs is essentially lawful in that these pairs with few mystifying exceptions serve specific fixed functions. Children around the world seem to adhere to a common set of restrictive rules related to concrete references the child might wish to convey or to relations between things the child sees as central. Slobin (1970, 1972, 1974), who studied two-word grammars on an international scale, has found that children nearly everywhere begin using word pairs as "operations of reference" or as "relations." Operations of reference denote the presence, recurrence, or nonexistence of objects in the child's world; relations denote actions taken on objects. Slobin (1972) found that this classification system and its subtypes are common not only among English but among beginning German, Russian, Finnish, Turkish, Samoan, and Luo (Kenya) speakers. "Indeed, if you ignore word order and read through transcriptions of two-word utterances in the various languages..., the utterances read like direct translations of one another [Slobin, 1970, p. 177]."

Bowerman (1975) has culled from the literature further examples of universals in linguistic development. Looking at children learning Samoan, Finnish, English, and Luo, she found extensive cross-linguistic similarities among two- and three-term constructions meant to express relational concepts. She also found that higher-level syntactic patterns emerge in a uniform developmental order.

Other examples of rule-bound epigenetic language behavior appear in children's erroneous application of grammatical rules. In English, it is common for children who have mastered a regular form, like tensing or pluralization, to misapply the regular rule to irregular cases. "He goed" is known to child linguists as "overgeneralization" of a rule. However, overgeneralization seems to be a rule itself because, as Slobin (1973) reports, children learning languages as diverse as Russian and Arabic likewise overgeneralize.

Regularity in development has a tendency to evoke maturation by way of explanation, yet the child's arrival at the two-word stage is not wholly dependent on maturation. Studies in the West show that American (Braine, 1963), French (Guillaume, 1927/1973), and Russian (El'Konin, 1958/1973) children reach the two-word stage at 1½ years. By contrast, non-Western children do not reach the same stage for another half-year at minimum (Slobin, 1972). Slobin (1972) hypothesizes that cultures vary in the density of language addressed to children and that this factor is responsible for developmental differences. (This view may have some merit because later-born and institutionalized children both have less speech directed toward them and both typically develop speech late.)

Language universals promote a belief in the existence of rules underlying development, though the rules may not be equally obvious in all languages. Natural experiments help to expose them to study. Thus, Slobin (1973) hypothesized that children come to language acquisition endowed with a set of organizational proclivities, for example, that they operate on a recency rule, which reads: "attend to the ends of words when scanning linguistic input in a search for cues to meaning [p. 191]." Though Slobin's hypothesis is unfortunately not testable in all language communities, French provides a natural test and an interesting confirmation. Slobin found that French children tend to learn the second half of the divided French negative, *ne...pas,* before the first half.

Cross-cultural developmental study has revealed that language acquisition is characterized by a surprising number of universal phenomena and processes. On reflection, this state of affairs is not entirely surprising. Structurally, after all, the task of human infants everywhere is to learn the common properties of language (semanticity, productivity, and displacement, according to Brown [1973]), and along the way they get similar sorts of aid. Ferguson (1964, 1978), for example, found that parents in a widely diverse group of cultures conventionally address young children in *motherese,* a language characterized by simplified syntax, abbreviated utterances, long pauses, baby talk, etc. Therefore, regularities in development need not necessarily imply maturational universals but could implicate structural ones.

*   *   *

The cross-cultural developmental study of language has never directly addressed the experimental question King James posed regarding the "natural" language of man since society would never suffer such an experimental manipulation of children. However, we have a "natural experiment" that approximates James's ideal. The children involved were congenital deaf-mutes, 1½ to 4 years of age, and not exposed to any formal language, even AMESLAN, standard American Sign Language. Nevertheless, these children, living in a closed society, spontaneously signed. Thus, the children are akin to the infants James thought to sequester from society, and as he suspected they naturally developed a language, only it was silent. Goldin-Meadow and Feldman (1977) constructed descriptive categories of their "natural signs" and found, among other linguistic phenomena, ordered pairs of signs in phrases that, like the two-word grammars universal among children who speak, marked object and action reference. This cross-"cultural" study answers James's question only indirectly; yet it shows that linguistically isolated human beings are motivated to communicate and will develop language that is structured in apparently universal ways.

Social Behavior

The meaning and origins of personality, or social behaviors generally, are hotly debated issues in contemporary psychology. Some argue that social behaviors reflect situational demands (e.g., Mischel, 1968), whereas others argue that personality characteristics are dispositional and stable from infancy (e.g., Thomas, Chess, & Birch, 1970). The submission of social behaviors to cross-cultural developmental analysis helps us to assess the degree to which they may be innate or the product of cultural experience. Whereas, for example, some cross-cultural studies claim to have uncovered the possible existence of select primary personality traits (Cattell, Schmidt, & Pawlik, 1973), even among newborns (Freedman, 1974, 1976), it is clear that the configuration of the child's "social network matrix" changes from culture to culture thereby markedly altering potential socialization patterns (Lewis & Feiring, 1979).

The oldest points of contact between anthropology and child studies centered around culture and personality. Several reasons can be discerned for this connection. Some had to do with analyzing the influence of culture over the individual. When Margaret Mead first went into the field, she went to determine the degree to which personality and social behaviors were plastic. *Coming of Age in Samoa* (1928) analyzed alternative ways and consequences of bringing children into adulthood. Other reasons have had to do with testing psychological or anthropological theories. To a certain degree psychological anthropology (Bornstein, 1978) was originally impelled by the universalist claims of Freudianism (Malinowski, 1927/1966) and psychodynamic beliefs in the influence of childrearing practices on patterns of adult personality. Historically, anthropologists have been interested in description per se, and so they have focused on social behavior and child behavior as subjects simply worthy of description. Finally, anthropologists believe that studies that cross cultures help to illuminate the origins and meaning of behavior at home.

What are some prominent social behaviors thus far submitted to cross-cultural developmental study? What have such studies revealed about the origins and development of social behavior?

Our understanding of gender identity best exemplifies the profitable association between psychological and anthropological studies of human social development. Men and women in Western cultures adhere more or less strictly to conventional modes of behavior, called "sex roles" in the jargon of contemporary psychology. Despite growing social acceptance in the West of wider latitude in the definition of sex roles, we readily acknowledge an understanding of "masculine" versus "feminine" patterns of behavior. In fact, these patterns are so self-expressive, independent, common, homogeneous, and unusually stable that we have come to think of them to a large degree as being biologically determined. They are in lower organisms, and the relevance of primary sexual characteristics to gender identification in humans is manifest in hormones, anatomy, and the course of maturation. Moreover, select differences in secondary sexual characteristics between boys and girls emerge quite early. Of course, the fact that male and female sex roles are expressive, independent, common, homogeneous, and stable in no way guarantees them a basis in biology or (even) a universal character. Like many other aspects of personality, gender identity is complex and may have many causes. It expresses itself in a myriad of ways, including demeanor, gesture, dress, and sexual preferences, all of which are susceptible to cultural influence. Thus, patterns of masculinity and femininity have been shown to vary with social class, ethnic group, or male presence in the household. This variation notwithstanding, there exists an identifiable, common, and coherent pattern to gender identity across a wide variety of cultures. That sex roles can be so similar worldwide and be learned is not self-contradictory when one considers that similar socialization pressures may operate or capitalize on biological predispositions. In an extensive cross-cultural survey, Barry et al. (1957; see p. 242, above) found nearly universal promotion of independence and achievement in boys and of reliability, nurturance, and obedience in girls. Such patterns of child rearing, they argued, carry a survival utility that matches the requirements of the preindustrial economies which they characterize.

The most conclusive way to assess the degree to which sex roles are a product of biology or culture would simply be to look for cultural exceptions.

This is the strategy adopted by anthropologists who first promoted the idea that culture determines personality. Specifically, one would want to describe three cells of a 2 × 2 table, cells that complement boys and girls being reared to conform to the Western and nearly universal tradition of masculine and feminine behavior. It was Margaret Mead's good fortune to find three societies that provided data filling these empty cells. Between 1931 and 1933 she lived in New Guinea among the Arapesh, the Mundugumor, and the Tchambuli. Among the Arapesh, both men and women displayed a personality that "we would call maternal in its parental aspects, and feminine in its sexual aspects." According to Mead, men and women both were sensitive, cooperative, and nonaggressive. Among the Mundugumor, men and women both possessed personalities "that we in our culture would find only in an undisciplined and very violent male." Together, these two societies show that one pattern of secondary sexual characteristics widely conceived in the West to be male and another widely conceived to be female may describe either sex whose socialization experiences have promoted, respectively, "masculinity" or "femininity." Finally, Mead described Tchambuli women as dominant aggressors, and Tchambuli men as sensitive, emotional, subservient, dependent, and insecure. In other words, the Tchambuli pattern approximately reversed the pattern of male-displayed masculine behaviors and female-displayed feminine behaviors known in the West and once thought to be both universal and natural. Although hindsight and additional study tell us that Mead's report may have been exaggerated or simplistic and her conclusions too emphatic, nonetheless Mead's (1935) *Sex and Temperament in Three Primitive Societies* irrevocably demonstrated that secondary sexual characteristics, once thought to be rigid and sex-linked, were as plastic and conditioned by socialization and cultural expectations as are a variety of other adaptive social behaviors. Mead (1935) wrote:

> We are forced to conclude that human nature is almost unbelieveably malleable, responding accurately and contrastingly to contrasting cultural conditions. ... Standardized personality differences between the sexes are of this order, cultural creations to which each generation, male and female, is trained to conform [p. 281].

At the time Mead wrote, anthropologists were more limited than today both in field travel and in theory. Mead was the exponent of a view that personality is an extension of culture, but did not, at that time, discuss why different cultures produced different results. We know from theorizing in perception (Berry) and in cognition (Cole) that many cultural behaviors have material antecedents. Thus, further study among the Arapesh has shown that their deference and gently tempered disposition are probably conditioned by economics and are functionally adaptive; the Arapesh whom Mead studied produced little or nothing themselves but only mediate in trade among other groups. Our understanding of these determinants does not detract from the importance or impact of Mead's original descriptions; rather, it serves to place the origins of the behavior patterns she described in a more realistic, understandable, and comprehensive context.

Mead's investigation, as many of those that followed, attempted to examine direct links between child training and personality. Years before, Freud had suggested that family structure fosters specific social and personality dynamics, and his ideas impelled a seminal series of cross-cultural studies of personality (see Kline, 1977; Malinowski, 1927/1966; Stephens, 1962). Much of this line of work followed Freudian methods and invested in detailed case studies (e.g., DuBois, 1944; see Barnouw, 1963, for a summary). One rather unique source of data about antecedents of personality in family structure derived from research on the Israeli kibbutz. In most communities around the world, at least one of the child's biological parents acts as a primary caregiver. On early Israeli kibbutzim, however, parents did not rear their own children; rather, there was multiple caregiving, a situation that attracted social and developmental psychologists interested in the effects on personality of typical and atypical parent-child relations (Beit-Hallahmi & Rabin, 1977; Spiro, 1958). This literature showed, in summary, that kibbutz children are normal on a host of personality factors, such as frequency of pathology and personal effectiveness. They are only moderately attached to others, however, and they show reduced levels of interpersonal rivalry and ambivalence.

Further studies of culture and personality transcended idiographic analysis to seek general relations between culture and social developments. In *Child Training and Personality,* Whiting and Child (1953) studied social behavior on a global level. They used the hologeistic method (previously described) and extended the relationship between socialization and personality both forward and backward in time. They hypothesized that specific configurations of personality should be linked to specific early experiences, as is aggressiveness to punitiveness or guilt. This analysis relied on a mixture of learning theory and psychoanalysis (Miller & Dollard, 1941). Reviews and extensions of this correlational research have lent it credibility (Harrington & Whiting, 1972; Whiting, 1961, 1968), and B. Whiting's (1963) *Six Cultures* study refined the original cross-cultural survey method by combining ethnographies with interviews and actual child observations on an international scale (see Jahoda, in this volume).

Among the most thoroughly investigated aspects of personality development in modern cross-cultural research is achievement motivation, defined variously as an individual's desire for challenge and responsibility, to compete, and to match an internally structured standard of excellence.

McClelland and his associates (Atkinson, 1958; McClelland, Atkinson, Clark, & Lowell, 1953) first sought the origin of individual differences in need for achievement in child-rearing experiences. In general, they found that benign paternal neglect combined with early maternal independence training correlated with a high achievement motive in boys; but boys of authoritarian fathers scored low (Rosen & D'Andrade, 1959). Because strong ethnic differences emerged in his original studies, McClelland (1961; McClelland & Friedman, 1952) further sought to corroborate the existence of national differences by correlating child-training practices with need achievement.

Numerous investigators have followed this line of thought. Brazilian, German, Polish, Italian, Indian, Turkish, and Japanese, among others, have been studied, and Brislin, Lonner, and Thorndike (1973) have summarized the rather extensive international literature that has grown up around need for achievement. LeVine (1966), for example, found that the entrepreneurial Ibo (Nigeria) evoked greater need for achievement in children than their less progressive Hausa or Yoruba neighbors; and Olsen (1971) found that high levels of need achievement among Chinese were related to patterns of child rearing. Authoritarian families typically generate lower need levels cross-culturally, as shown in Brazil (Rosen, 1962) and in Turkey (Bradburn, 1963), for example.

Cross-cultural developmental studies of gender and need for achievement strongly suggest that differential experiences during the formative years of development mold diverse aspects of social behavior. For example, Mead's descriptive analysis underscores the critical role that culture can play in sex-role behavior. However, anthropologists and psychologists who followed her, but into other fields, have since found that, despite culture's strong if not pervasive influence, residual male-female distinctions sometimes remain, especially in traditional societies. Such differences—and the set of social and cognitive concomitants that flow from them—may simply reflect structural distinctions between men and women. For example, hunting may play on strength and good spatial relations, whereas childrearing could be seen to follow quite naturally from childbearing. Likewise, other male-female distinctions defy the laws of chance in their consistency: For example, around the world polygyny is common, but polyandry is virtually unknown, and males are almost always more aggressive than females, even as children.

Some social behaviors are therefore likely to be biologically rooted, suggesting that socialization processes only influence human nature in parts and to degrees. Of course, more universal patterns of socialization (as in Barry et al., 1957), too, will tend to promote equally universal patterns of social behavior. One such behavior for which a mixed maturational-social foundation has been hypothesized is moral judgment. Although moral judgments have previously been thought to be learned and, hence, to be culturally arbitrary, cross-cultural developmental studies in the last decade have provided a surprising amount of support for a more universalist claim to their expression.

Following Piaget's (1932/1962) seminal studies of moral judgment in young children, Kohlberg (1969) developed a refined system to describe the child's developing moral values. Like other Piagetian stage-like progressions, Kohlberg's scheme organizes stages into a hierarchy through which children progress in an invariant manner loosely tied to maturation and social demand. Kohlberg found that judgments change from an orientation toward physical effects (punishment or reward) through an orientation toward convention and expectancy (duty) to an orientation of shared standards or rights (contract or conscience). To determine the universality of such a sequence, Kohlberg (1966; Kohlberg & Kramer, 1969) compared moral judgments among American, Canadian, English, Mexican, and Taiwanese children; Turiel (1969) compared American, Turkish, and Mexican children; White (1975; White, Bushnell, & Regnemer, 1978) studied Bahamian children; and Saraswathi, Saxena, and Sundaresan (1977) studied Indian childen. Although the development of moral thinking, like other developmental functions, is related to organismic factors *and* general social climate, "the ways in which the growing child interprets and integrates his social environment should not differ from culture to culture [Turiel, 1969, p. 122]." Kohlberg (1966) found invariance in the sequence of stages through which children in different cultures pass although those from traditional societies or less urban locations tended to lag behind their industrialized or urban age peers in his schedule of moral development. Turiel, White, and others have also found Kohlberg's prescribed ordering, though these studies, like other cognitive-developmental ones in the Piagetian mold, tend to show variable rates and endpoints of moral judgment across cultures.

Moral judgment, need for achievement, personality, and gender identity represent social behaviors whose origins and expressions are more comprehensively described and better understood because of their submission to cross-cultural developmental study. Social behaviors particularly are organized and nurtured to meet the needs of the society. For example, Roberts, Sutton-Smith, and Kendon (1963) have shown that games that differ from society to society prepare children for adult modes of competition which vary inter-societally in parallel ways. Likewise, LeVine (1960) has shown through cross-cultural example how adult patterns of social behavior become inculcated: Adult Nuer (Sudan), who settle disputes by feuds, encourage their children to fight for themselves; in contrast, adult Gusii

(Kenya), who adhere to rules of law, train their children to report interpersonal conflicts to adults.

It is impossible in so short a space even to mention numerous other subjects to which those studying socialization processes in the context of culture have addressed themselves. Again, some efforts uncover social universals: Brazilians, Chinese, Rhodesians, and Lebanese grow to be as sensitive to small-group social pressure as Americans (Asch, 1955; Whittaker & Meade, 1967). Other studies show cultural divergence: Australian students place independence and self-respect above obedience and social recognition, whereas Papuan (New Guinea) students rank these pairs oppositely (Feather & Hutton, 1974). Still other studies have served to test standing hypotheses: Bowlby (1969) hypothesized that separation protest indexes infant social attachment which itself he thought reflected continuity of mother-infant interaction; but Kagan's (1976) comparisons of children in minimal contact with mothers (Israel), in moderate contact (U.S.), or in constant contact (Botswana) have shown similar protest patterns across settings. In short, cross-cultural developmental studies of social values and behaviors serve to increase our understanding of the complex developmental relation between character and culture in unique and unparalled ways.

Summary

Cross-cultural developmental research describes behavior, tests hypotheses that originate in more limited domains (such as the laboratory), and alerts us to possibilities about behavior that otherwise might escape notice. The second half of this chapter has reviewed select aspects of this literature. The results of this review are enlightening. Early motor behavior which had long been considered to follow a ballistic, genetically programmed course has proven to be subject to experiential conditioning. Studies of speech perception have shown that infants in different cultures are innately predisposed to perceive a set of sounds which are eventually important in language understanding, a counterintuitive finding given wide cultural variation in language production. Aspects of cognitive-developmental theory are to an impressive (if predicted) degree substantiated by cross-cultural research. Cross-cultural similarities in the nature and structure of childrens' language production have evidenced development that would otherwise not be expected to follow a uniform course. Finally, cultural conditioning has been found to exert a surprisingly strong influence over sex-role behaviors once dogmatically thought to be biologically determined. Cross-cultural developmental comparison has caused us to rethink the origins and developmental course of behavior. Without it, our conclusions about some of the basics of human nature, as exemplified in motor development, perception, cognition, language acquisition, and social behavior, are at best shortsighted, ethnocentric, and suspect. In the absence of cross-cultural developmental research, our psychology would be incorrect.

CONCLUSION

Humans, who are uniquely but commonly endowed, experience widely varying conditions in growing up. The global purposes of psychology are to describe accurately and to explain completely the contributions and consequences of endowment and experience to the nature of human behavior over the life span. One concern of cross-cultural developmental psychology is description and inventory; without its approach the true variation and expanse of human behavior would not be known. A further concern is elucidation of the contributions of heredity and environment to man's propensities to perceive, think, speak, feel, and act in the ways he does. Among the many perspectives available to psychologists to account for the twin charges of description and explanation, the cross-cultural developmental method of comparison occupies an optimal position because it ipso facto encompasses the entire range of behavior of the human species across its worldwide context and over its life-span ontogeny.

The potential of cross-cultural developmental comparison is only slowly being fulfilled. A summary account of the lessons learned from its past and of those to be considered in its future will help us to evaluate its progress and prospects.

Cross-cultural developmental research began (and continues) basically as single-experiment studies; these have proved less than satisfactory, and the occasion to mount a more substantial effort has come to represent an investigator's career rather than a single experiment. Moreover, the method has grown increasingly sophisticated along the way, and frankly it has become somewhat difficult for cross-cultural developmental psychologists to meet the rigorous criteria and standards they have established for themselves.

Nevertheless, what psychologists learn from cross-cultural developmental comparison, what implications they draw from it, and what actions they take because of it will be all the more sound and conclusive. For example, the knowledge gained from cross-cultural developmental study has begun to alter our beliefs as ethnocentric parents about the nature of children and our beliefs as ethnocentric psychologists about the nature of human development. Among its lessons are included an increased awareness of similarities and differences among humans, a greater accounting of the variability that characterizes cultural and individual behavior, and a deeper reflection into one's own culture. For these reasons, academic psychology, which is by and large a Western adventure, is considerably advanced. Equally important, cross-cultural developmental study has both practical and applied potential.

Because of it, we are in possession of a better understanding of the normal and abnormal as well as the common and uncommon in behavior.

Past study of cross-cultural developmental psychology may be turned on itself, just as feedback helps to keep any system on a productive, steady course. What implications has this review of cross-cultural developmental study for its future?

The immediate lessons lay in three areas. To the extent that the method endeavors to be *cross-cultural*, greater involvement of non-Western societies, the construction and widespread acceptance of reliable and valid tasks and instruments, and a closer familiarity and greater consultation on the part of psychologists with pertinent ethnographic or anthropological materials will be required. To the extent that the method endeavors to be *developmental*, its progress will, at minimum, depend on increasing utilization of cross-sectional and (optimally) longitudinal designs and a fuller representation of the life span. Childhood has heretofore predominated in cross-cultural developmental study, and although infancy has attracted increasing attention recently (e.g., Ainsworth, 1967; Freedman, 1974, 1976; Leiderman, Tulkin, & Rosenfeld, 1977), aging and death continue to be neglected (cf. Erikson, 1950; Steele, 1977). Finally, to the extent that the method endeavors to represent *psychology*, it must include all areas of psychological inquiry. Though there exist by no means sufficient data to accommodate a general theory of human psychology, cross-cultural developmental study holds out the greatest promise to psychology. As these correctives become commonplace, psychologists will accumulate comparable descriptive and explanatory data on many facets of psychological life from diverse societies.

Contemporary cross-cultural developmental psychology needs to accelerate its efforts if it intends to address these goals. The twentieth century has witnessed an increasing social homogenization: Urbanization, Westernization, and modernization conspire to unify culture, style, education, and the general flow of information. Few societies are any longer self-contained or uninfluenced by life elsewhere. If determinants are correct, the forces of modernization will bring about globally a structural similarity of ecology, economy, and demography that will, in turn, doubtless mean the end of gross cultural diversity barely a century after anthropological study of man formally began (Tylor, 1871). Thus as children's learning has moved from haphazard observation and imitation characteristic of traditional societies to uniform curriculum and explicit instruction characteristic of modern school rooms, practical problems associated with indigenous modes of thought have tended to disappear. The theoretical possibility of assessing the nature and growth of traditional thinking is vanishing simultaneously.

I have endeavored in these pages to discuss the history and philosophy of cross-cultural developmental comparison, the ways in which it is conducted, the issues on which it focuses, and its value as I see it. The cross-cultural developmental method contributes uniquely to the goals of psychology: description, explanation, and prediction of behavior. The method is increasingly prominent and necessary in contemporary psychology and will, I believe, provide a major focus of future psychological investigation.

ENDNOTE 1: CHILD AND "PRIMITIVE"

In this chapter, culture and development are associated in a fashion that emphasizes the theoretical and practical rewards of cross-cultural studies of human psychological development. Yet the child and the "primitive" have been linked before in the evolution of social scientific thought; vestiges of that association continue today.

An analogy of child with "primitive" pervaded early philosophy, anthropology, and psychology. In philosophy, the idea that the modern mind evolved from a traditional or primitive one appeared as early as the eighteenth century in Condorcet and reappeared in the early nineteenth century in Compte. Given the overt penchant for evolutionary order that was the *Zeitgeist* of nineteenth-century thinking, the leap from Haekel's anatomical-morphological dictum "ontogeny recapitulates phylogeny" to a social Darwinist parallelism between the child and "primitive" (Gould, 1977) was apparently inevitable. Individuals *and* races were thought to recapitulate the development of the human race in toto. Thus, in *The Child: A Study in the Evolution of Man,* Chamberlain (1901) portrayed child development as a prototype of human evolution, while Frobenius (1909/1960) blatantly entitled his popular account of the lives, customs, and thoughts of "primitive" races *The Childhood of Man.*

Most substantive points of parallel were drawn from cognition or from emotion. A few examples will suffice to illustrate this climate of thought which has continued since the turn of the century. Edward Tylor's (1871) *Primitive Culture* suggested that myth and animism characterize a child-like state of the primitive belief that invariably preceded more civilized stages. Herbert Spencer's (1896) *The Principles of Sociology* illustrated the evolution of human emotions, including impulsiveness, indifference, and justice, by suggesting a parallel with social development in children. G. Stanley Hall (1905, 1908), too, was prone to discuss nonwhites as children of the human race: He claimed, for example, that Africans had developed psychosexually only to a stage analogous to the Caucasian adolescent and that American Indians had not progressed in linguistic complexity beyond the level of a child. The classification of child and "primitive" together has persisted in developmental theories of mentality. Lévy-Bruhl (1923/1966) placed prelogical thought of "primitives" and children below that of civilized adults, and Piaget (1970), whose roots can be traced back to Lévy-Bruhl, has argued that individual cognitive development follows a stage-like progression similar to that followed in cultural development. Piaget's genetic epistemology is matched by H. Werner's (1948) orthogenetic theory of individual and historical parallels in social and personality development. Finally, in the psychoanalytic view, "primitive" and childlike thought are grouped together as predominantly "primary process."

The implications of this view for social and political action have been extraordinary. The child-primitive equation seems to have been more than metaphor in helping to rationalize racism and imperialism, to tailor education, and to foster paternalism since the nineteenth century. For twentieth-century psychology, child and "primitive" represent similar, early, or unusual stages in development, a classification that has often permitted synchronic analysis of diachronic development. In this way, cross-cultural universals have frequently served to goad developmental studies. For example, on the basis of Ekman's (1973) finding that certain facial expressions are universal, Young-Browne, Rosenfeld, and Horowitz (1977) assessed the infant's discrimination of those same expressions.

ENDNOTE 2: CULTURE AND CONCEPTS OF DEVELOPMENT

Chronological age is an obvious and consequential marker of human development. In our own culture, age determines when the child begins formal education, assumes legal responsibility for actions, etc., just as age restricts the adult's qualification to hold public office, to retain employment, etc. In the West, developmental status is also recognized so that we are acutely aware, too, of the more sophisticated concept of stage: Both psychosocial development (Freud) and cognitive development (Piaget) are widely conceptualized to progress through stages.

Anthropological study shows quite clearly that the West is not unique in either regard and that human cultures universally acknowledge that growth, change, and psychological development proceed by age as well as by stage. Ethnographic reports concur that even the most disparate societies punctuate the life cycle with transitions that reflect the natural passage of time, indexes of physical maturation, or artificial social events. For example, simple age-group systems are widespread (Stewart, 1977). Birth, walking, speech, puberty, pregnancy, and senility are all used to partition the life span into biological divisions; and, weaning, the birth of a successive child, naming, circumcision, changes in child dress or parental sleeping arrangements, and marriage all represent social-developmental transitions.

Some societies acknowledge many life transitions (Ainu of Japan), others few (Cree Indians of America). Certain transitions are nevertheless nearly universal, as from infant to child and from child to adult. In marking transitions, some cultures rely more on chronological or maturational determinants, others on social determinants. Thus markers for the same developmental phenomenon vary across cultures; according to Whiting and Whiting (1960), nearly twice as many societies determine weaning by social events as by physical ones, for example. Moreover, societies nearly always mark transitions with nominal differentiation. On Okinawa, for example, children younger than 5 years are called "senseless" and thought to be incapable of learning right from wrong; after 5, children are increasingly responsible for their actions and are no longer excused (Munroe & Munroe, 1975). In Mexico, the "juventud" is prized (H. Wagner, 1977), but under the law in the United States "minors" are treated as a special class.

An inevitable consequence of transitions from one stage of life to another is the alteration of social rites and responsibilities carried by the individual's new-found status. Formal "rites of passage" (Van Gennep, 1960) typically denote the changing status of the individual vis-à-vis society.

ENDNOTE 3: INTRA-CULTURAL
DEVELOPMENTAL PSYCHOLOGY

Cross-cultural studies carry significant implications for intra-cultural ones.[5] First, the modern world is characterized by immigration and human mobility to a greater degree than ever before in its history. As a consequence, cultures mix today with increasing frequency and permanency. Surveys in 1978 showed, for example, that children attending the primary schools of greater London speak more than 50 languages; in addition to language differences, immigrant children perpetuate aspects of their home culture that for (at least) the first generation tend to maintain a strong socializing influence (e.g., Caudill & Frost, 1975; Knight & Kagan, 1977). Considerable theoretical and applied understanding of the diversity of cultures within a single locale might accrue from the practice of cross-cultural study, therefore.

Second, cross-cultural phenomena provide models for intra-cultural ones. For example, Stein et al. (1975), who were interested in the effects of malnutrition on cognitive development in New York City ghettos, initially studied long-term effects of the Dutch famine of 1944-1945 (see p. 240 above). Likewise, Steele (1977) suggests that moderns in the Western societies might benefit substantially from understanding how ancient civilizations, like the Maya Indians of Mesoamerica, adjusted so effectively to dying, death, and bereavement.

Third, the philosophy of cross-cultural study has additional conceptual impact on intra-cultural study because sub-cultural customs, beliefs, attitudes, behaviors, and experiences are often as divergent from those of the dominant or "prestige" culture as are cross-cultural differences in strength, degree, and pervasiveness. For example, different classes (or other intra-cultural strata) effectively assume socializing roles analogous to different cultures. In support of this view, many psychological measures show fundamental class or ethnic differences revolving around traditionally cultural variables, such as language, social environment, or child training (e.g., Bernstein, 1971; Kagan & Klein, 1973; Labov, 1970; Scarr & Weinberg, 1976). In this light, cross-cultural psychology's "deficit versus difference" distinction vis-à-vis logic, intelligence, etc. could be applied to intra-cultural comparisons; appropriately new modes of expectation and education might follow from the difference approach (see Cole & Bruner, 1971).

ACKNOWLEDGMENTS

Preparation of this chapter was partially supported by the Spencer Foundation. I wish to thank Helen G. Bornstein, Kay Ferdinandsen, and Joan Stiles-Davis for comments.

---

[5]*Culture* is a complex and an amorphous concept in theory and in practice. I have used the term to imply one political system within the same national boundaries. One need not argue over definitions to accept that a cross-cultural study is one that compares children living in Des Moines, Iowa, USA with children living in Guadalajara, Mexico, whereas an intra-cultural study is one that compares white Anglo-Saxon children living in San Diego's suburbs with Spanish-surnamed second-generation Mexican children living in San Diego's barrio.

REFERENCES

Abramson, A. S., & Lisker, L. Voice-timing perception in Spanish word-initial stops. *Journal of Phonetics*, 1973, *1*, 1–8.

Ainsworth, M. *Infancy in Uganda*. Baltimore: Johns Hopkins University Press, 1967.

Allport, G. W., & Pettigrew, T. F. Cultural influences on the perception of movement: The trapezoidal illusion among Zulus. *Journal of Abnormal and Social Psychology*, 1957, *55*, 104–113.

Anonymous. Visiting anthropologist shows drawing due to form of culture. *Rockefeller Institute Quarterly*, 1961, *5*, 7.

Asch, S. E. Opinions and social pressure. *Scientific American*, 1955, *192*, 31–35.

Atkinson, J. W. (Ed.). *Motives in fantasy, action and society*. Princeton, NJ: Van Nostrand, 1958.

Ball, R. S. The Gesell developmental schedules: Arnold Gesell (1880-1961). *Journal of Abnormal Child Psychology*, 1977, *5*, 233–239.

Barnouw, V. *Culture and personality*. Homewood, IL: Dorsey Press, 1963.

Barry, H., Bacon, M. K., & Child, I. L. A cross-cultural survey of some sex differences in socialization. *Journal of Abnormal and Social Psychology*, 1957, *55*, 327–332.

Bayley, N. Comparisons of mental and motor test scores for ages 1-15 months by sex, birth order, race, geographical location, and education of parents. *Child Development*, 1965, *36*, 379–412.

Bayley, N. *Bayley scales of infant development*. New York: Psychological Corporation, 1969.

Bayley, N. Development of mental abilities. In P. Mussen (Ed.), *Carmichael's manual of child psychology* (Vol. 1). New York: Wiley, 1970.

Beit-Hallahmi, B., & Rabin, A. I. The kibbutz as a social experiment and as a child-rearing laboratory. *American Pychologist*, 1977, *32*, 532–541.

Benedict, R. Continuities and discontinuities in cultural conditioning. *Psychiatry*, 1938, *1*, 161–167.

Bernstein, B. *Class, codes and control*. Bungay, England: Routledge & Kegan Paul, 1971.

Berry, J. W. Temne and Eskimo perceptual skills. *International Journal of Psychology*, 1966, *1*, 207–229.

Berry, J. W. Ecological and cultural factors in spatial perceptual development. *Canadian Journal of Behavioural Science*, 1971, *3*, 324–336.

Berry, J. W. *Human ecology and cognitive style*. New York: Wiley, 1976.

Binet, A., & Simon, T. [The development of intelligence in the child] (E. S. Kiffe, trans.). In H. H. Goddard (Ed.), *The development of intelligence in children*. Baltimore: Williams & Wilkins, 1916. (Originally published, 1908.)

Boas, F. *The mind of primitive man*. New York: Macmillan, 1911.

Bornstein, M. H. The psychophysiological component of cultural difference in color naming and illusion susceptibility. *Behavior Science Notes*, 1973, *8*, 41–101.

Bornstein, M. H. Psychology and anthropology: Cross-cultural studies in thinking and intelligence. *Intelligence*, 1978, *2*, 393–403.

Bornstein, M. H. Perceptual development: Stability and change in feature perception. In M. H. Bornstein & W. Kessen (Eds.), *Psychological development from infancy*. Hillsdale, NJ: Lawrence Erlbaum Associates, 1979.

Bovet, M. C., Dasen, P. R., & Inhelder, B. Etapes de l'intelligence sensori-mortice chez l'enfant Baoulé. *Archives de Psychologie*, 1974, *41*, 363–386.

Bowerman, M. F. Cross-linguistic similarities at two stages of syntactic development. In E. H. Lenneberg & E. Lennenberg (Eds.), *Foundations of language development: A multidisciplinary approach* (Vol. 1). New York: Academic Press, 1975.

Bowlby, J. *Attachment and loss* (Vol. 1). New York: Basic Books, 1969.

Bradburn, N. M. Achievement and father dominance in Turkey. *Journal of Abnormal and Social Psychology*, 1963, *67*, 464–468.

Braine, M. D. S. The ontogeny of English phrase structure: The first phase. *Language*, 1963, *39*, 1–13.

Brislin, R. W., & Baumgardner, S. Nonrandom sampling of individuals in cross-cultural research. *Journal of Cross-Cultural Psychology*, 1971, *2*, 397–400.

Brislin, R. W., Lonner, W. J., & Thorndike, R. *Cross-cultural research methods*. New York: Wiley, 1973.

Bronfenbrenner, U. *Two worlds of childhood: U.S. and U.S.S.R.* New York: Simon & Schuster, 1970.

Brown, R. *Words and things*. Glencoe, IL: Free Press, 1958.

Brown, R. *A first language: The early stages*. Cambridge, MA: Harvard University Press, 1973.

Bruner, J. S., Olver, R., & Greenfield, P. *Studies in cognitive growth*. New York: Wiley, 1966.

Brunswik, E. *Representative design in the planning of psychological research*. Berkeley: University of California Press, 1958.

Bullen, A. K. A cross-cultural approach to the problem of stuttering. *Child Development*, 1945, *16*, 1–88.

Buss, A. R., & Royce, J. R. Detecting cross-cultural commonalities and differences: Intergroup factor analysis. *Psychological Bulletin*, 1975, *82*, 128–136.

Campbell, D. T. The mutual methodological relevance of anthropology and psychology. In F. L. K. Hsu (Ed.), *Psychological anthropology*. Homewood, IL: Dorsey Press, 1961.

Campbell, D. T. Distinguishing differences of perception from failures of communication in cross-cultural studies. In F. C. S. Northrop & H. H. Livingston (Eds.), *Cross-cultural understanding: Epistemology in anthropology*. New York: Harper & Row, 1964.

Campbell, D. T., & Stanley, J. C. *Experimental and quasi-experimental designs for research*. Chicago, IL: Rand McNally, 1963.

Cattell, R. B., Schmidt, L. R., & Pawlik, K. Cross-cultural comparison (U.S.A., Japan, Austria) of the personality factor structures of 10 to 14 year olds in objective tests. *Social Behavior and Personality*, 1973, *1*, 182–211.

Caudill, W. C., & Frost, L. A comparison of maternal care and infant behavior in Japanese-American, American, and Japanese families. In U. Bronfenbrenner & M. A. Mahoney (Eds.), *Influences on human development*. Hinsdale, IL: Dryden Press, 1975.

Chamberlain, A. F. *The child: A study in the evolution of man*. London: Walter Scott, 1901.

Chomsky, N. A. *Language and mind*. New York: Harcourt, Brace & Jovanovich, 1968.

Cole, M. An ethnographic psychology of cognition. In R. W. Brislin, S. Bochner, & W. J. Lonner (Eds.), *Cross-cultural perspectives on learning*. New York: Wiley, 1975.

Cole, M., & Bruner, J. S. Cultural differences and inferences about psychological processes. *American Psychologist*, 1971, *26*, 867–876.

Cole, M., Gay, J., Glick, J., & Sharp, D. W. *The cultural context of learning and thinking*. New York: Basic Books, 1971.

Cole, M., & Scribner, S. *Culture and thought: A psychological introduction*. New York: Wiley, 1974.

Cole, M., & Scribner, S. Cross-cultural studies of memory and cognition. In R. V. Kail & J. W. Hagen (Eds.), *Perspectives on the development of memory and cognition*. Hillsdale, NJ: Lawrence Erlbaum Associates, 1977.

Coren, S., & Girgus, J. S. *Seeing is deceiving: The psychology of visual illusions*. Hillsdale, NJ: Lawrence Erlbaum Associates, 1978.

Cronbach, L. J., & Drenth, P. *Mental tests and cultural adaptation*. Hague: Mouton, 1972.

Dasen, P. R. Cross-cultural Piagetian research: A summary. *Journal of Cross-Cultural Psychology*, 1972, *3*, 23–39. (a)

Dasen, P. R. The development of conservation in Aboriginal children: A replication study. *International Journal of Psychology*, 1972, *7*, 85–95. (b)

Dasen, P. R. (Ed.). *Piagetian psychology: Cross-cultural contributions.* New York: Gardner Press, 1977. (a)

Dasen, P. R. Are cognitive processes universal? A contribution to cross-cultural Piagetian psychology. In N. Warren (Ed.), *Studies in cross-cultural psychology* (Vol. 1). New York: Academic Press, 1977. (b)

David, K. H. Effect of verbal reinforcement on Porteus Maze scores among Australian Aborigine children. *Perceptual and Motor Skills,* 1967, *24,* 986.

Dawson, J. L. M. Cultural and physiological influences upon spatial-perceptual processes in West Africa (Parts I and II). *International Journal of Psychology,* 1967, *2,* 115–128; 171–185.

Dawson, J. L. M. *Culture and perception.* New York: Wiley, 1973.

DéCarie, T. C. A study of the mental and emotional development of the thalidomide child. In B. M. Foss (Ed.), *Determinants of infant behavior* (Vol. 4). London: Methuen, 1969.

Dennis, W. Infant reaction to restraint. *Transactions of the New York Academy of Science,* 1940, *2,* 211–212.

Dennis, W. Animism and related tendencies in Hopi children. *Journal of Abnormal and Social Psychology,* 1943, *38,* 21–36.

Dennis, W., & Dennis, M. G. The effect of cradling practices upon the onset of walking in Hopi children. *Journal of Genetic Psychology,* 1940, *56,* 77–86.

Deregowski, J. B. An aspect of perceptual organization: Some cross-cultural studies. In H. McGurk (Ed.), *Ecological factors in human development.* Amsterdam: North-Holland, 1977.

Deregowski, J. B., Muldrow, E. S., & Muldrow, W. F. Pictorial recognition in a remote Ethiopian population. *Perception,* 1972, *1,* 417–425.

DeVos, G. A., & Hippler, A. A. Cultural psychology: Comparative studies of human behavior. In G. Lindzey & E. Aronson (Eds.), *The handbook of social psychology* (Vol. 4). Reading, MA: Addison-Wesley, 1968.

Dirks, J., & Gibson, E. Infants' perception of similarity between live people and their photographs. *Child Development,* 1977, *48,* 124–130.

Drenth, P. J. D. The uses of intelligence tests in developing countries. In Y. H. Poortinga (Ed.), *Basic problems in cross-cultural psychology.* Amsterdam: Swets & Zeitlinger, 1977.

Dubois, C. *The people of Alor: A social-psychological study of an East Indian island.* Minneapolis: University of Minnesota Press, 1944.

Eimas, P. D. Speech perception in early infancy. In L. B. Cohen & P. Salapatek (Eds.), *Infant perception: From sensation to cognition* (Vol. 2). New York: Academic Press, 1975.

Eimas, P. D., Siqueland, E. R., Jusczyk, P., & Vigorito, J. Speech perception in infants. *Science,* 1971, *171,* 303–306.

Ekman, P. Cross-cultural studies of facial expression. In P. Ekman (Ed.), *Darwin and facial expression: A century of research in review.* New York: Academic Press, 1973.

El'Konin, D. B. [General course of development in the child of the grammatical structure of the Russian language (according to A. N. Gvozdev)] (D. Slobin, trans.). In C. A. Ferguson & D. I. Slobin (Eds.), *Studies of child language development.* New York: Holt, Rinehart & Winston, 1973. (Originally published, 1958.)

Erikson, E. H. *Childhood and society.* New York: Norton, 1950.

Feather, N. T., & Hutton, M. A. Value systems of students in Papua New Guinea and Australia. *International Journal of Psychology,* 1974, *9,* 91–104.

Ferguson, C. A. Baby talk in six languages. *American Anthropologist,* 1964, *66,* 103–114.

Ferguson, C. A. Talking to children: A search for universals. In J. H. Greenberg (Ed.), *Universals of human language* (Vol. 1). Stanford, CA: Stanford University Press, 1978.

Firkowska, A., Ostrowska, A., Sokolowska, M., Stein, Z., Susser, M., & Wald, I. Cognitive development and social policy. *Science,* 1978, *200,* 1357–1362.

Freedman, D. G. *Human infancy: An evolutionary perspective.* Hillsdale, NJ: Lawrence Erlbaum Associates, 1974.

Freedman, D. G. Infancy, biology, and culture. In L. P. Lipsitt (Ed.), *Developmental psychobiology: The significance of infancy.* Hillsdale, NJ: Lawrence Erlbaum Associates, 1976.

Frijda, N., & Jahoda, G. On the scope and methods of cross-cultural research. *International Journal of Psychology,* 1966, *1,* 109–127.

Frobenius, L. [*The childhood of man*] (A. H. Keane, trans.). New York: Meridian, 1960. (Originally published, 1909.)

Furby, L. A theoretical analysis of cross-cultural research in cognitive development: Piaget's conservation task. *Journal of Cross-Cultural Psychology,* 1971, *2,* 241–255.

Geber, M. Developpement psychomoteur de l'enfant africain. *Courrier,* 1956, *6,* 17–28.

Geber, M. The psycho-motor development of African children in the first year, and the influence of maternal behavior. *Journal of Social Psychology,* 1958, *47,* 185–195.

Geber, M., & Dean, R. F. A. Gesell tests on African children. *Pediatrics,* 1957, *20,* 1055–1065. (a)

Geber, M., & Dean, R. F. A. The state of development of newborn African children. *Lancet,* 1957, *272,* 1216–1219. (b)

Gesell, A. L. The ontogenesis of infant behavior. In L. Carmichael (Ed.), *Manual of child psychology.* New York: Wiley, 1946.

Gesell, A. L., & Amatruda, C. S. *The embryology of behavior: The beginnings of the human mind.* New York: Harper, 1945.

Gladwin, T. *East is a big bird.* Cambridge, MA: Harvard University Press, 1970.

Goldin-Meadow, S., & Feldman, H. The development of language-like communication without a language model. *Science,* 1977, *197,* 401–403.

Goodnow, J. J. A test for milieu effects with some of Piaget's tasks. *Psychological Monographs,* 1962, *76* (No. 555).

Goodnow, J. J. Problems in research on culture and thought. In D. Elkind & J. H. Flavell (Eds.), *Studies in cognitive development: Essays in honor of Jean Piaget.* New York: Oxford University Press, 1969.

Goodnow, J. J., & Bethon, G. Piaget's tasks: The effects of schooling and intelligence. *Child Development,* 1966, *37,* 573–582.

Gould, S. J. *Ontogeny and phylogeny.* Cambridge, MA: Harvard University Press, 1977.

Greenfield, P. M. On culture and conservation. In J. S. Bruner, R. R. Olver, & P. M. Greenfield (Eds.), *Studies in cognitive growth.* New York: Wiley, 1966.

Greenfield, P. M., & Bruner, J. S. Culture and cognitive growth. In D. A. Goslin (Ed.), *Handbook of socialization theory and research.* Chicago: Rand McNally, 1969.

Griffiths, R. *The abilities of babies: A study in mental measurement.* New York: McGraw-Hill, 1954.

Guillaume, P. The development of formal elements in the child's speech. In C. A. Ferguson & D. I. Slobin (Eds.), *Studies of child language development.* New York: Holt, Rinehart & Winston, 1973. (Originally published, 1927.)

Hall, G. S. The Negro in Africa and America. *Pedagogical Seminary,* 1905, *12,* 350–368.

Hall, G. S. How far are the principles of education along indigenous lines applicable to American Indians? *Pedagogical Seminary,* 1908, *15,* 365–369.

Harrington, C., & Whiting, J. W. M. Socialization process and personality. In F. L. K. Hsu (Ed.), *Psychological anthropology.* Cambridge, MA: Schenkman, 1972.

Hochberg, J., & Brooks, V. Pictorial recognition as an unlearned ability: A study of one child's performance. *American Journal of Psychology,* 1962, *75,* 624–628.

Husén, T. *International study of achievement in mathematics: A comparison of twelve countries* (Vol. 1). New York: Basic Books, 1967.

Jahoda, G. Retinal pigmentation, illusion susceptibility and space perception. *International Journal of Psychology,* 1971, *6,* 199–208.

Jahoda, G., Deregowski, J. B., Ampene, E., & Williams, N. Pictorial recognition as an unlearned ability: A replication with children from pictorially deprived environments. In G. Butterworth (Ed.), *The child's representation of the world*. New York: Plenum Press, 1977.

Jahoda, G., & McGurk, H. Development of pictorial depth perception: Cross-cultural replications. *Child Development*, 1974, *45*, 1042–1047.

Jakobson, R. *Child language, aphasia and phonological universals*. New York: Humanities Press, 1969. (Originally published, 1941.)

Kagan, J. Emergent themes in human development. *American Scientist*, 1976, *64*, 186–196.

Kagan, J., & Klein, R. E. Cross-cultural perspectives on early development. *American Psychologist*, 1973, *28*, 941–961.

Kagan, J., Klein, R. E., Finley, G. E., Rogoff, B., & Nolan, E. A cross-cultural study of cognitive development. *Monographs of the Society for Research in Child Development*, 1979, *44*(5, Serial No. 180).

Kennedy, J. M., & Ross, A. S. Outline picture perception by the Songe of Papua. *Perception*, 1975, *4*, 391–406.

Kessen, W. (Ed.). *Childhood in China*. New Haven, CT: Yale University Press, 1975.

Kidd, D. *Savage childhood: A study of Kafir childhood*. London: Black, 1906.

King, E. J. *Other schools and ours: Comparative studies for today*. London: Holt, Rinehart & Winston, 1973.

Kline, P. Cross-cultural studies and Freudian theory. In N. Warren (Ed.), *Studies in cross-cultural psychology* (Vol. 1). New York: Academic Press, 1977.

Knight, G. P., & Kagan, S. Acculturation of prosocial and competitive behaviors among second- and third-generation Mexican American children. *Journal of Cross-Cultural Psychology*, 1977, *8*, 273–284.

Kohlberg, L. Moral education in the schools: A developmental view. *School Review*, 1966, *74*, 1–30.

Kohlberg, L. Stage and sequence: The cognitive developmental approach to socialization. In D. Goslin (Ed.), *Handbook of socialization theory and research*. Chicago: Rand McNally, 1969.

Kohlberg, L., & Kramer, R. Continuities and discontinuities in childhood and adult moral development. *Human Development*, 1969, *12*, 93–120.

Kroeber, A. L. *Anthropology*. New York: Harcourt Brace, 1948.

Laboratory of Comparative Human Cognition. What's cultural about cross-cultural cognitive psychology? *Annual Review of Psychology*, 1979, *30*, 145–172.

Labov, W. The logic of nonstandard English. In F. William (Ed.), *Language and poverty: Perspectives on a theme*. Chicago: Markham, 1970.

Landauer, T. K., & Whiting, J. W. M. Infantile stimulation and adult stature of human males. *American Anthropologist*, 1964, *66*, 1007–1028.

Lasky, R. E., Syrdal-Lasky, A., & Klein, R. E. VOT discrimination by four to six and a half month old infants from Spanish environments. *Journal of Experimental Child Psychology*, 1975, *20*, 215–225.

Leiderman, P. H., Tulkin, S. R., & Rosenfeld, A. (Eds.). *Culture and infancy: Variations in the human experience*. New York: Academic Press, 1977.

LeVine, R. A. The internalization of political values in stateless societies. *Human Organization*, 1960, *19*, 51–58.

LeVine, R. A. *Dreams and deeds*. Chicago: University of Chicago Press, 1966.

LeVine, R. A. Cross-cultural study in child psychology. In P. H. Mussen (Ed.), *Carmichael's manual of child psychology* (Vol. 2). New York: Wiley, 1970.

Lévi-Strauss, C. *The savage mind*. Chicago: University of Chicago Press, 1966.

Lévy-Bruhl, L. [*Primitive mentality*] (L. Clare, trans.). London: Allen & Unwin, 1966. (Originally published, 1923.)

Lewin, K. A. *A dynamic theory of personality.* New York: McGraw-Hill, 1935.

Lewis, M., & Feiring, C. The child's social network: Social object, social functions, and their relationship. In M. Lewis & L. A. Rosenblum (Eds.), *The genesis of behavior* (Vol. 2). New York: Plenum, 1979.

Liberman, A. M., Cooper, F. S., Shankweiler, D. P., & Studdert-Kennedy, M. Perception of the speech code. *Psychological Review,* 1967, *74,* 431–461.

Lisker, L., & Abramson, A. S. A cross-language study of voicing in initial stops: Acoustical measurements. *Word,* 1964, *20,* 384–422.

Lloyd, B. B. *Perception and cognition: A cross-cultural perspective.* Harmondsworth: Penguin Books, 1972.

Lloyd, B. B., & Easton, B. The intellectual development of Yoruba children. *Journal of Cross-Cultural Psychology,* 1977, *8,* 3–16.

Luria, A. R. [A child's speech responses and the social environment] (M. Vale, trans.). In M. Cole (Ed.), *The selected writings of A. R. Luria.* New York: M. E. Sharpe, 1978. (Originally published, 1930.)

Luria, A. R. Towards the problem of the historical nature of psychological processes. *International Journal of Psychology,* 1971, *6,* 259–272.

Luria, A. R. [*Cognitive development: Its cultural and social foundations*] (M. Lopez-Morillas & L. Solotaroff, trans.). Cambridge, MA: Harvard University Press, 1976. (Originally published, 1974.)

Lusk, D., & Lewis, M. Mother-infant interaction and infant development among the Wolof of Senegal. *Human Development,* 1972, *15,* 58–69.

Malinowski, B. *Sex and repression in savage society.* Cleveland, OH: World, 1966. (Originally published, 1927.)

McClelland, D. C. *The achieving society.* New York: Free Press, 1961.

McClelland, D. C., Atkinson, J. W., Clark, R. A., & Lowell, E. L. *The achievement motive.* New York: Appleton-Century-Crofts, 1953.

McClelland, D. C., & Friedman, G. A. A cross-cultural study of the relationship between child-training practices and achievement motivation appearing in folk tales. In G. E. Swanson, T. M. Newcomb, & E. L. Hartley (Eds.), *Readings in social psychology.* New York: Holt, 1951.

McNeill, D. *The acquisition of language: The study of developmental psycholinguistics.* New York: Harper & Row, 1970.

Meacham, J. A. Patterns of memory abilities in two cultures. *Developmental Psychology,* 1975, *11,* 50–53.

Mead, M. *Coming of age in Samoa: A psychological study of primitive youth for Western civilization.* New York: Morrow, 1928.

Mead, M. An investigation of the thought of primitive children, with special reference to animism. *Journal of the Royal Anthropological Institute,* 1932, *62,* 173–190.

Mead, M. *Sex and temperament in three primitive societies.* New York: Morrow, 1935.

Mead, M., & MacGregor, F. C. *Growth and culture.* New York: Putnam's Sons, 1951.

Menyuk, P., & Bernholz, N. Prosodic features and children's language productions. *Quarterly Progress Report, No. 93.* Cambridge, MA: M.I.T. Research Laboratory of Electronics, 1969, 216–219.

Meredith, H. V. *Human body growth in the first ten years of life.* Columbia, SC: State Printing, 1978.

Miller, N. E., & Dollard, J. *Social learning and imitation.* New Haven, CT: Yale University Press, 1941.

Miller, R. J. Cross-cultural research in the perception of pictorial materials. *Psychological Bulletin,* 1973, *80,* 135–150.

Mischel, W. *Personality and assessment.* New York: Wiley, 1968.

Modgil, S., & Modgil, C. *Piagetian research: Compilation and commentary* (Vol. 8). Windsor, England: NFER, 1976.

Montagu, A. (Ed.). *Culture and human development: Insights into growing human.* Englewood Cliffs, NJ: Prentice-Hall, 1974.

Mori, I. A cross-cultural study on children's conception of speed and duration: A comparison between Japanese and Thai children. *Japanese Psychological Research,* 1976, *18,* 105–112.

Munroe, R. L., & Munroe, R. H. *Cross-cultural human development.* Monterey, CA: Brooks/Cole, 1975.

Murdock, G. P. Cross-language parallels in parental kin terms. *Anthropological Linguistics,* 1959, *1,* 1–5.

Nakazima, S. Phonemicization and symbolization in language development. In E. H. Lenneberg & E. Lenneberg (Eds.), *Foundations of language development: A multidisciplinary approach* (Vol. 1). New York: Academic Press, 1975.

Naroll, R., & Cohen, R. (Eds.). *A handbook of method in cultural anthropology.* New York: Natural History Press, 1970.

Nyiti, R. M. The development of conservation in the Meru children of Tanzania. *Child Development,* 1976, *47,* 1122–1129.

Olsen, N. J. Sex differences in child training antecedents of achievement motivation among Chinese children. *Journal of Social Psychology,* 1971, *83,* 303–304.

Peluffo, N. Culture and cognitive problems. *International Journal of Psychology,* 1967, *2,* 187–198.

Piaget, J. [*The moral judgment of the child*] (M. Gabain, trans.). New York: Collier, 1962. (Originally published, 1932.)

Piaget, J. [*The origins of intelligence in children*] (M. Cook, trans.). New York: Norton, 1963. (Originally published, 1952.)

Piaget, J. Piaget's theory. In P. Mussen (Ed.), *Carmichael's manual of child psychology* (Vol. 1). New York: Wiley, 1970.

Piaget, J. [Need and significance of cross-cultural studies in genetic psychology] (C. Dasen, trans.). In J. W. Berry & P. R. Dasen (Eds.), *Culture and cognition.* London: Methuen, 1974. (Originally published, 1966.)

Pick, H. L., Jr., & Pick, A. D. Sensory and perceptual development. In P. Mussen (Ed.), *Carmichael's manual of child psychology* (Vol. 1). New York: Wiley, 1970.

Poole, H. E. The effect of urbanization upon scientific concept attainment among Hausa children of northern Nigeria. *British Journal of Educational Psychology,* 1968, *38,* 57–63.

Popper, K. *Conjectures and refutations: The growth of scientific knowledge.* New York: Basic Books, 1962.

Porteus, S. D. *The psychology of a primitive people.* London: Edward Arnold, 1931.

Price-Williams, D. R. A study concerning concepts of conservation of quantities among primitive children. *Acta Psychologica,* 1961, *18,* 297–305.

Price-Williams, D. R. *Cross-cultural studies.* Harmondsworth: Penguin Books, 1969.

Price-Williams, D. R., Gordon, W., & Ramirez, M., III. Skill and conservation: A study of pottery-making children. *Developmental Psychology,* 1969, *1,* 769.

Rebelsky, F. G. Infancy in two cultures. *Nederlands Tijdschrift voor de Psychologie,* 1967, *22,* 379–385.

Rebelsky, F. G. First discussant's comments: Cross-cultural studies of mother-infant interaction. *Human Development,* 1972, *15,* 128–130.

Rheingold, H. L., Gewirtz, J. L., & Ross, H. W. Social conditioning of vocalizations in the infant. *Journal of Comparative and Physiological Psychology,* 1959, *52,* 68–73.

Rivers, W. H. R. Introduction and vision. In A. C. Haddon (Ed.), *Report of the Cambridge anthropological expedition to the Torres Straits* (Vol. 2). Cambridge: Cambridge University Press, 1901.

Roberts, J. M., Sutton-Smith, B., & Kendon, A. Strategy in games and folktales. *Journal of Social Psychology,* 1963, *61,* 185–199.

Roche, A. (Ed.). Secular trends in human growth, maturation, and development. *Monographs of the Society for Research in Child Development,* 1979, *44*(3–4, Serial No. 179).

Rohner, R. P. *They love me, they love me not.* New Haven, CT: HRAF Press, 1978.

Rosen, B. C. Socialization and achievement motivation in Brazil. *American Sociological Review,* 1962, *27,* 612–624.

Rosen, B. C., & D'Andrade, R. The psychosocial origins of achievement motivation. *Sociometry,* 1959, *22,* 185–218.

Rudel, R. G., & Teuber, H.-L. Discrimination of direction of line in children. *Journal of Comparative and Physiological Psychology,* 1963, *56,* 892–898.

Russell, R. W. Studies in animism: II. The development of animism. *Journal of Genetic Psychology,* 1940, *56,* 353–366.

Russell, R. W. Studies in animism: V. Animism in older children. *Journal of Genetic Psychology,* 1942, *60,* 329–335.

Russell, R. W., & Dennis, W. Studies in animism: I. A standardized procedure for the investigation of animism. *Journal of Genetic Psychology,* 1939, *55,* 389–400.

Russell, R. W., & Dennis, W. Piaget's questions applied to Zuni children. *Child Development,* 1940, *2,* 181–187.

Saraswathi, T. S., Saxena, K., & Sundaresen, J. Development of moral judgment of Indian children between ages eight to twelve years. In Y. H. Poortinga (Ed.), *Basic problems in cross-cultural psychology.* Amsterdam: Swets & Zeitlinger, 1977.

Scarr, S., & Weinberg, R. A. IQ test performance by black children adopted by white families. *American Psychologist,* 1976, *31,* 726–739.

Scribner, S. Developmental aspects of categorized recall in a West African society. *Cognitive Psychology,* 1974, *6,* 475–494.

Segall, M. H., Campbell, D. T., & Herskovits, M. J. *The influence of culture on visual perception.* Indianapolis: Bobbs-Merrill, 1966.

Serpell, R. *Culture's influence on behaviour.* London: Methuen, 1976.

Sevinç, M., & Turner, C. Language and the latent structure of cognitive development. *International Journal of Psychology,* 1976, *11,* 231–250.

Shapiro, M. B. The rotation of drawings by illiterate Africans. *Journal of Social Psychology,* 1960, *52,* 17–30.

Sharp, D., Cole, M., & Lave, C. Education and cognitive development: The evidence from experimental research. *Monographs of the Society for Research in Child Development,* 1979, *44*(1–2, Serial No. 178).

Slobin, D. I. Universals of grammatical development in children. In G. B. Flores d'Arcais & W. J. M. Levelt (Eds.), *Advances in psycholinguistics.* New York: Elsevier, 1970.

Slobin, D. I. Children and language: They learn the same way all around the world. *Psychology Today,* 1972, *6,* 71–74; 82.

Slobin, D. I. Cognitive prerequisites for the development of grammar. In C. A. Ferguson & D. I. Slobin (Eds.), *Studies of child language development.* New York: Holt, Rinehart & Winston, 1973.

Slobin, D. I. *Psycholinguistics.* Glenview, IL: Scott, Foresman, 1974.

Smith, H. *The Russians.* New York: Ballantine, 1977.

Spencer, H. *The principles of sociology.* New York: Appleton, 1896.

Spiro, M. E. *Children of the kibbutz.* Cambridge, MA: Harvard University Press, 1958.

Steele, R. L. Dying, death, and bereavement among the Maya Indians of Mesoamerica. *American Psychologist,* 1977, *32,* 1060–1068.

Stein, Z., Susser, M., Saenger, G., & Marolla, F. *Famine and human development: The Dutch hunger winter of 1944–1945.* New York: Oxford University Press, 1975.

Stephens, W. N. *The Oedipus complex hypothesis: Cross-cultural evidence.* Glencoe, IL: Free Press, 1962.

Stevenson, H. W., Parker, T., Wilkinson, A., Bonnevaux, B., & Gonzalez, M. Schooling, environment, and cognitive development: A cross-cultural study. *Monographs of the Society for Research in Child Development,* 1978, *43* (3, Serial No. 175).

Stewart, F. H. *Fundamentals of age-group systems.* New York: Academic Press, 1977.

Streeter, L. A. Language perception of 2-month-old infants shows effects of both innate mechanisms and experience. *Nature,* 1976, *259,* 39–41. (a)

Streeter, L. A. Kikuyu labial and apical stop discrimination. *Journal of Phonetics,* 1976, *4,* 43–49. (b)

Streeter, L. A., & Landauer, T. K. Effects of learning English as a second language on the acquisition of a new phonemic contrast. *Journal of the Acoustical Society of America,* 1976, *59,* 448–451.

Strodtbeck, F. L. Considerations of metamethod in cross-cultural studies. In A. K. Romney & R. G. D'Andrade (Eds.), Transcultural studies in cognition. *American Anthropologist,* 1964, *66,* 223–229.

Super, C. M. Environmental effects on motor development: The case of "African infant precocity." *Developmental Medicine and Child Neurology,* 1976, *18,* 561–567.

Tanner, J. M. Physical growth. In P. Mussen (Ed.), *Carmichael's manual of child psychology* (Vol. 1). New York: Wiley, 1970.

Tanner, J. M. *Foetus into man: Physical growth from conception to maturity.* London: Open Books, 1978.

Thomas, A., Chess, S., & Birch, H. The origins of personality. *Scientific American,* 1970, *223,* 102–109.

Thut, I. N., & Adams, D. *Educational patterns in contemporary societies.* New York: McGraw-Hill, 1964.

Turiel, E. Developmental processes in the child's moral thinking. In P. Mussen, J. Langer, & M. Covington (Eds.), *Trends and issues in developmental psychology.* New York: Holt, Rinehart & Winston, 1969.

Tylor, E. B. *Primitive culture.* London: Murray, 1871.

Van Gennep, A. T. [*The rites of passage*] (M. Vizedom & G. Caffee, trans.). Chicago: University of Chicago Press, 1960.

Vernon, P. E. *Intelligence and cultural environment.* London: Methuen, 1969.

Wagner, D. A. Ontogeny of the Ponzo illusion: Effects of age, schooling, and environment. *International Journal of Psychology,* 1977, *12,* 161–176.

Wagner, D. A. Memories of Morocco: The influence of age, schooling and environment on memory. *Cognitive Psychology,* 1978, *10,* 1–28.

Wagner, H. A comparison of selected differences in adolescence in Mexico and the United States of America. *Adolescence,* 1977, *12,* 381–384.

Warren, N. African infant precocity. *Psychological Bulletin,* 1972, *78,* 353–367.

Werner, E. E. Infants around the world: Cross-cultural studies of psychomotor development from birth to two years. *Journal of Cross-Cultural Psychology,* 1972, *3,* 111–134.

Werner, E. E. *Cross-cultural human development.* Monterey, CA: Brooks/Cole, 1979.

Werner, H. *Comparative psychology of mental development.* New York: Follett, 1948.

White, C. B. Moral development in Bahamian school children: A cross-cultural examination of Kohlberg's stages of moral reasoning. *Developmental Psychology,* 1975, *11,* 535–536.

White, C. B., Bushnell, N., & Regnemer, J. L. Moral development in Bahamian school children: A 3-year examination of Kohlberg's stages of moral development. *Developmental Psychology,* 1978, *14,* 58–65.

Whiting, B. B. (Ed.). *Six cultures: Studies of child rearing.* New York: Wiley, 1963.

Whiting, J. W. M. Socialization process and personality. In F. L. K. Hsu (Ed.), *Psychological anthropology.* Homewood, IL: Dorsey Press, 1961.

Whiting, J. W. M. Methods and problems in cross-cultural research. In G. Lindzey & E. Aronson (Eds.), *Handbook of social psychology* (Vol. 2). Reading, MA: Addison-Wesley, 1968.

Whiting, J. W. M., & Child, I. L. *Child training and personality: A cross-cultural study.* New Haven, CT: Yale University Press, 1953.

Whiting, J. W. M., & Whiting, B. B. Contributions of anthropology to the methods of studying child rearing. In P. Mussen (Ed.), *Handbook of research methods in child development.* New York: Wiley, 1960.

Whittaker, J. O., & Meade, R. D. Social pressure in the modification and distortion of judgment: A cross-cultural study. *International Journal of Psychology,* 1967, *2,* 109–113.

Williams, J. R., & Scott, R. B. Growth and development of Negro infants: IV. Motor development and its relationship to child rearing practices in two groups of Negro infants. *Child Development,* 1953, *24,* 103–121.

Witkin, H. A. A cognitive-style approach to cross-cultural research. *International Journal of Psychology,* 1967, *2,* 223–250.

Witkin, H. A., & Berry, J. W. Psychological differentiation in cross-cultural perspective. *Journal of Cross-Cultural Psychology,* 1975, *6,* 4–87.

Witkin, H. A., Price-Williams, D., Bertini, M., Christiansen, B., Oltman, P. K., Ramirez, M., & Van Meel, J. Social conformity and psychological differentiation. *International Journal of Psychology,* 1974, *9,* 11–29.

Wundt, W. *Elements of folk psychology.* London: Allen & Unwin, 1916.

Young-Browne, G., Rosenfeld, H. M., & Horowitz, F. D. Infant discrimination of facial expressions. *Child Development,* 1977, *48,* 555–562.

Zelazo, P. R., Zelazo, N. A., & Kolb, S. "Walking" in the newborn. *Science,* 1972, *176,* 314–315.

Biographical Notes

THOMAS M. ACHENBACH is a Research Psychologist at the NIMH Laboratory of Developmental Psychology. He received his B.A. from Yale University and Ph.D. from the University of Minnesota. Achenbach worked with Jean Piaget as a Social Science Research Council Faculty Fellow and was Associate Professor at Yale in the Department of Psychology and the Child Study Center. His current interests focus on psychopathology in children, cognitive development, and relations between cognition and psychopathology. He is editorial and research consultant for numerous journals and organizations and is the author of *Developmental Psychopathology* and *Research in Developmental Psychology: Concepts, Strategies, Methods.*

ALFRED L. BALDWIN, Professor of Psychology and Psychiatry at the University of Rochester, holds A.B. and M.A. degrees from the University of Kansas and a Ph.D. from Harvard University. He was formerly at the Fels Research Institute for Human Development and Professor at the University of Kansas, Cornell University, and New York University. Baldwin has devoted his professional career primarily to the study of parent-child relations and the interactions of the members of the family. He has published two books, *Behavior and Development in Childhood* and *Theories of Child Development.*

COLIN G. BEER took a B.Sc. and M.Sc. at Otago University in Zoology and a D.Phil. at Oxford University. Beer has studied with B. J. Marples, N. Tinbergen, and D. S. Lehrman and has taught at Otago University, Rutgers University, and Oxford University. He is currently a member of the Institute of Animal Behavior at Rutgers University. Beer's main research interests are in reproductive and social behavior of birds. He has contributed numerous articles to scientific journals and books, is joint editor of *Function and Evolution in Behaviour–Essays in Honour of Professor Niko Tinbergen,* and is associate editor of the *Advances in the Study of Behavior.*

MARC H. BORNSTEIN is Assistant Professor of Psychology at Princeton University. A Columbia College B.A. and Yale University Ph.D., Bornstein spent one postdoctoral year at the Max Planck Institute for Psychiatry in Munich and a second at Yale. Bornstein has received the C. S. Ford Cross-Cultural Research Award and the B. R. McCandless Young Scientist Award. He is editor of *The Crosscurrents in Contemporary Psychology Series* and a member of societies in child development, anthropology, and visual science. Bornstein has published studies in human experimental, methodological, comparative, developmental, and cross-cultural psychology.

ROBERT J. DOOLING is an Assistant Professor in Behavioral Sciences at Rockefeller University. His B.S. (biology) is from Creighton University and his Ph.D. (psychology) is from St. Louis University. Dooling spent several postdoctoral years at the Laboratory of Comparative Psychoacoustics at the Central Institute for the Deaf in St. Louis, and his interests are in auditory perception and communication in animals. He is a member of the Acoustical Society of America, the Psychonomic Society, and the Society of Sigma Xi. He has published several studies in perception.

GUSTAV JAHODA is Professor of Psychology at the University of Strathclyde, Glasgow. Holding B.Sc., M.Sc., and Ph.D. degrees of the University of London, he has previously held posts at Oxford, Manchester, and in Ghana. Former president of the International Association of Cross-Cultural Psychology, he has conducted research mainly in West Africa, but also in Malawi, India, and Hong Kong. Author of *White Man* and *The Psychology of Superstition,* Jahoda has published extensively on cross-cultural topics.

PETER R. MARLER is Professor of Zoology at the Rockefeller University and Director of the University Field Research Center for Ethology and Ecology. Marler took a B.Sc. from University College, London and two Ph.D. degrees, one from University College (botany) and one from Cambridge (zoology). He is a past Guggenheim Fellow, a member of the National Academy of Science and of professional societies in behavior, biology, ornithology, psychology, and zoology, and on the editorial boards of journals in biology, psychology, and zoology. Marler has contributed numerous ethological studies—his research interests focus on behavioral development of animals—and is the coauthor of *Mechanisms of Animal Behavior* and volume three of the *Handbook of Neurobiology*.

VICTORIA SEITZ is Assistant Professor of Psychology at the Yale University Child Study Center. Her B.A. and M.A. were earned at the University of Denver; her Ph.D. in experimental psychology with a minor in mathematical statistics is from the University of Illinois at Champaign-Urbana. She is a member of the Convention Board of the American Psychological Association, the author of numerous research publications, and coauthor of the books, *Imitation: A Developmental Perspective* and *Intellectual and Personality Characteristics of Children: Social Class and Ethnic Group Differences*.

STEPHEN ZOLOTH received a B.A. from the University of California, Santa Cruz and a Ph.D. from the University of Pennsylvania. Zoloth was a Research Fellow at the Rockefeller University and is a past member of professional associations in psychology and animal behavior. He is currently taking an M.A. in Public Health at the University of California, Berkeley.

Author Index

Subject Index